SECOND EDITION

THE CHRISTIAN APOLOGIST

Always Being Prepared to Make a Defense

Andrews provides an excellent apologetic tool for Christians seeking to better understand & defend the Word of God."—Christian Publishing House

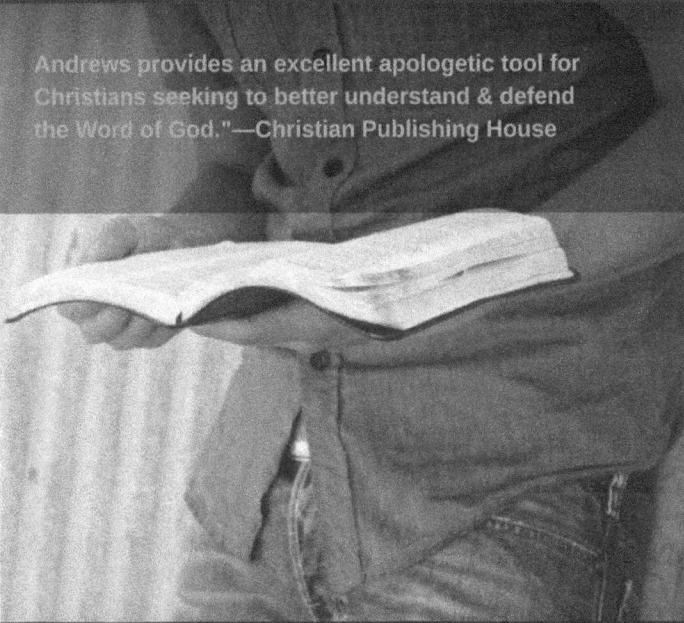

EDWARD D. ANDREWS

i

THE CHRISTIAN APOLOGIST

Always Being Prepared to Make a Defense

Edward D. Andrews

Christian Publishing House
Cambridge, Ohio

CHRISTIAN
PUBLISHING
HOUSE

FOUNDED 2005

THE CHRISTIAN APOLOGIST: Always Being Prepared to Make a Defense by Edward D. Andrews

ISBN-13: 978-1-945757-27-3

ISBN-10: 1-945757-27-2

APOLOGETICS
DEFENDING THE FAITH

PREFACE

THE CHRISTIAN APOLOGIST is designed so that any Christian can study through it as a personal book study. However, it also can be used in a home or church Bible study group setting. In addition, it can be used in a seminary course on apologetics or evangelism. It covers deep subject material; however, Andrews makes it very easy to understand.

Evangelism is the work of a Christian evangelist. All true Christians are obligated to partake to some extent, which seeks to persuade other people to become Christian, especially by sharing the basics of the Gospel and the deeper message of biblical truths. Today the Gospel is almost an unknown, so what does the Christian evangelist do? **Preevangelism** is laying a foundation for those who do not know the Gospel, giving them background information so that they are able to grasp what they are hearing. The Christian evangelist is preparing their listener's minds and hearts so that they will be receptive to the biblical truths. In many ways, this is known as apologetics.

Christian apologetics [Greek: *apologia,* "verbal defense, speech in defense"] is a field of **Christian theology** that endeavors to offer a reasonable and sensible basis for the **Christian faith,** defending the faith against objections. It is reasoning from the Scriptures, explaining and proving, as one instructs in sound doctrine, many times having to overturn false reasoning before he can plant the seeds of truth. It can also be earnestly contending for the faith and saving one from losing their faith as they have begun to doubt. Moreover, it can involve rebuking those who contradict the truth. It is being prepared to make a defense to anyone who asks the Christian evangelist for a reason for the hope that is in him or her. (Jude 1.3, 21-23; 1 Peter 3.15; Acts 17:2-3; Titus 1:9)

What do we mean by **obligated** and what we mean by **evangelism** are the significant part and are indeed related to each other?

EVANGELISM: An evangelist is a proclaimer of the gospel or good news and all biblical truths. There are levels of evangelism which is pictured in first-century Christianity. All Christians evangelized in the first century, but a select few fit the role of a full-time evangelist (Eph. 4:8, 11-12), like Philip and Timothy.

Both Philip and Timothy are specifically mentioned as evangelizers. (Ac 21:8; 2 Tim. 4:5) Philip was a full-time evangelist after Pentecost, who was sent to the city of Samaria, having great success. An angel even directed Philip to an Ethiopian Eunuch to share the good news about Christ with him. Because of the Eunuch's already knowing God by way of the Old Testament, Philip was able to help him understand that the Hebrew Scriptures pointed to Christ as the long-awaited Messiah. In the end, Philip baptized the Eunuch. Thereafter, the Spirit again sent Philip on a mission to Azotus and all the cities on the way to Caesarea. (Ac 8:5, 12, 14, 26-40) Paul evangelized in many lands, setting up one congregation after another. (2 Cor. 10:13-16) Timothy was an evangelizer or missionary, and Paul placed distinct importance on evangelizing when he gave his parting encouragement to Timothy. (2 Timothy 4:5; 1 Timothy 1:3)

The office of apostle and evangelist seems to overlap in some areas, but could be distinguished in that apostles traveled and set up congregations, which took evangelizing skills and developed the congregations after they were established. The evangelists were more of a missionary, being stationed in certain areas to grow and develop congregations. In addition, if we look at all of the apostles and the evangelists, plus Paul's more than one hundred traveling companions, it seems very unlikely that they could have had Christianity at over one million by the 150 C.E. This was accomplished because all Christians were obligated to carry out some level of evangelism.

OBLIGATED: In the broadest sense of the term for evangelizer, all Christians are obligated to play some role as an evangelist.

• *Basic Evangelism* is planting seeds of truth and watering any seeds that have been planted. [In the basic sense of this word (*euaggelistes*), this would involve all Christians.] In some cases, it may be that one Christian planted the seed, which was initially rejected, so he was left in a good way because the planter did not try to force the truth down his throat. However, later he faces something in life that moves him to reconsider those seeds, and other Christians then water what the first Christian had already planted. This evangelism can be carried out in all available methods: informal, house-to-house, street, phone, internet, and the like. The amount of time invested in the evangelism work is up to each Christian to decide for themselves.

• *Making Disciples* is having any role in the process of getting an unbeliever from his unbelief state to the point of accepting Christ as his Savior and being baptized. Once the unbeliever has become a believer, he is still developed until he has become strong. Any Christian could potentially carry this one person through all of the developmental stages. On the other hand, it may be that several have some parts. It is like a person specializing in a certain aspect of a job, but all are aware of the other elements, if they are called on to carry out that phase. Again, each Christian must decide for themselves what role they are to have and how much of a part, but they should be prepared to fill any role if needed.

• *Part-Time or Full-Time Evangelist* is one who sees this as their calling and chooses to be very involved as an evangelist in their local church and community. They may work part-time to supplement their work as an evangelist. They may be married with children, but they realize their gift is in the field of evangelism. If it were the wife, the husband would work toward supporting her work as an evangelist and vice-versa. If it were a single person, they would supplement their work by being employed part-time, but also the church would help as well. This person is well trained in every aspect of bringing one to Christ.

• *Congregation Evangelists* should be very involved in evangelizing their communities and helping the church members play their role at the basic levels of evangelism. There is nothing to say that one church could not have many within who take on part-time or full-time evangelism within the congregation, which would and should be cultivated and supported by congregation evangelists.

INTRODUCTION The Work of an Evangelist

Why do Christians desire to talk about their beliefs? Jesus said, "And this gospel of the kingdom will be proclaimed in the whole inhabited earth for a testimony to all the nations, and then the end will come." (Matt. 24:14) This is the assignment that all Christians are obligated to be a part of, based on their gifts and talents to the best of their abilities. Jesus also said, "You shall love your neighbor as yourself." (Matt. 22:39) Jesus commanded that we "go therefore and make disciples of all nations, baptizing them" and "teaching them to observe all that I have commanded you." (Matt. 28:19-20) All true Christians[1] have a determination to imitate God, which moves us to persist in reflecting his glory through our sharing of the Good News with others.

Within the heart of each true Christian is the desire that he 'loves the Lord his God with all his heart and with all his soul and with all his mind.' (Matt. 22:37) If this is the case, we to would be patient, not wishing that any should perish, but that all should reach repentance.' (2 Pet 3:9) For the true Christian, "for out of the abundance of the heart his mouth speaks." (Luke 6:45) The apostle Paul helps see the importance of the work that lies ahead,

---

[1] As of the early 21ˢᵗ century, Christianity has around 2.2 billion adherents, out of about 7 billion people. Of these 2.2 billion, there are true Christians and there are false Christians. We are going to use one doctrine herein (inerrancy of Scripture), in establishing who is a true Christian, as opposed to who is a false Christian. You are **not** a true Christian if you do not accept **full inerrancy** of Scripture. This means that a true Christian would agree with the entire short statement below.

1. God, who is Himself Truth and speaks truth only, has inspired Holy Scripture in order thereby to reveal Himself to lost mankind through Jesus Christ as Creator and Lord, Redeemer and Judge. Holy Scripture is God's witness to Himself.

2. Holy Scripture, being God's own Word, written by men prepared and superintended by His Spirit, **is of infallible divine authority in all matters upon which it touches**: it is to be believed, as God's instruction, in all that it affirms, obeyed, as God's command, in all that it requires; embraced, as God's pledge, in all that it promises.

3. The Holy Spirit, Scripture's divine Author, both authenticates it to us by His inward witness and opens our minds to understand its meaning.

4. Being wholly and verbally God-given, **Scripture is without error or fault in all its teaching**, no less in what it states about God's acts in creation, about the events of world history, and about its own literary origins under God, than in its witness to God's saving grace in individual lives.

5. The authority of Scripture is inescapably impaired if this total divine inerrancy is in any way limited or disregarded, or made relative to a view of truth contrary to the Bible's own; and such lapses bring serious loss to both the individual and the Church.—http://bible-translation.net/page/chicago-statement-on-biblical-inerrancy-icbi

Romans 10:14-15 Updated American Standard Version (UASV)

¹⁴ How then will they call on him in whom they have not believed? And how are they to believe in him of whom they have never heard? And how will they hear without someone to preach? ¹⁵ And how are they to preach unless they are sent? As it is written, "How beautiful are the feet of those who declare good news of good things!"²

Many have used these two verses as the foundational texts for sending missionaries around the world for centuries. However, as was explained in the preface, these verses and others are just as important to the evangelism work that needs to be carried out by every Christian in their local community. This author believes that we should dial back on sending missionaries around the world and focus on evangelizing our own communities.

10:14a. Calling requires faith. **How ... can they call on the one they have not believed in?** In the Old Testament, calling on the name of the Lord was a metaphor for worship and prayer (Gen. 4:26; 12:8; Ps. 116:4). No one can call out to God who has not believed in him.

10:14b. Faith requires hearing. **And how can they believe in the one of whom they have not heard?** More than anything else, this question is the crux of all missiological activity since the first century. God has ordained that people have to hear (or read, or otherwise understand the content of) the word of God in order to be saved. One who knows the gospel must communicate it to one who does not know it.

10:14c. Hearing requires preaching. **And how can they hear without someone preaching to them?** Since no other media except the human voice was of practical value in spreading the gospel in the first century, **preaching** is Paul's method of choice. And yet, in the media-rich day in which we minister, has anything replaced preaching as the most effective way to communicate the gospel? We thank God for the printed page, and even for cutting-edge presentations of the gospel circling the globe on the internet. But it is still the human voice that cracks with passion, the human eye that wells with tears of gratitude, and the human frame that shuffles to the podium, bent from a lifetime of Service to the gospel, that reaches the needy human heart most readily. Hearing may not *require* **preaching** in person today, but it always benefits from it.

---

² Quotation from Isa 52:7; Nah 1:15

10:15. Preaching requires sending. **And how can they preach unless they are sent?** Even when his servants were unwilling (e.g., Jonah), God has been sending the message of salvation to the ends of the earth from the beginning. Paul, a "sent one" (apostle, *apostolos*), was sent to the Gentiles, and he needed the church at Rome to help him. But he also wanted them to be available for God to send them. There were many, many Jews in Rome who were still stumbling over the stone in the path of salvation. How would they ever call on the name of the Lord unless someone is sent? Paul wants the church at Rome to get in step with those who have borne good news to Israel before, most specifically those who brought the good news of their deliverance from captivity in Assyria:

Original Context	Isaiah 52:7	Romans 10:15	Paul's Application
"Good news" in its earliest contexts was that of victory in battle. In Isaiah it is deliverance from captivity in Assyria (cf. Isa. 52:4, 11–12), a type of the coming deliverance from sin.	How beautiful on the mountains are the feet of those who bring good news, who proclaim peace, who bring good tidings, who proclaim salvation, who say to Zion, "Your God reigns!"	And how can they preach unless they are sent? As it is written, "How beautiful are the feet of those who bring good news!"	Just as the "good news" was delivered to Israel in the Old Testament, so it still must be delivered in Paul's day. It is a different gospel—a better one—of permanent deliverance from captivity to sin.

Six key terms, taken in reverse order, summarize God's plan for taking the good news of the gospel to those in need: send, preach, hear, believe, call, saved.[3]

Every Christian should realize that effective communication would be one of the determining factors in whether the unbeliever will accept the truth. Some may feel that the message will get through to the unbeliever if he is receptive to the Good News regardless of communication skills. While that may be true on occasion, it is not the rule it is the exception. Moreover, it needs to be realized that our communicating skills are to be used to affect the hearts and minds of both the receptive and unreceptive. With the **unreceptive**, our skills must be stronger, as we are reasoning from the Scriptures, to overturn whatever has made this one unreceptive to the truth. It might be best if I were to put it this way, effective communication skills

---

[3] Kenneth Boa and William Kruidenier, *Romans*, vol. 6, Holman New Testament Commentary (Nashville, TN: Broadman & Holman Publishers, 2000), 314–315.

do not guarantee that one will accept the truth of God's Word, but a lack of communication skills means that it is far less likely that they will accept the truth of God's word.

Like a firefighter and a police officer, a Christian evangelist is on the job 24/7, as the opportunity to share a biblical message may occur at any time. Moreover, our conduct is always on display, and it is a form of witnessing to others. (1 Pet. 2:12) Whether we realize it or not, we are always sending and receiving messages consciously and subconsciously with others by our tone, demeanor, body language, etc. Again, our ability to communicate with clearness and precision, resolution, and assurance is usually the difference between being successful and unsuccessful in our efforts to reach the hearts and minds of prospective (i.e., future) Christian disciples.

All Christians are Expected to Carry Out the Work of An Evangelist

Before delving into our book on Evangelism, let us take a moment to listen to one of the world's leading authorities on Spiritual disciplines for our Christian life by Donald S. Whitney, who covers our obligation to evangelize very well,

> Most of those reading this book will not need convincing that evangelism is expected of every Christian. All Christians are not expected to use the same methods of evangelism, but all Christians are expected to evangelize.
>
> Before we go further, let's define our terms. What is evangelism? If we want to define it thoroughly, we could say that evangelism is to present Jesus Christ in the power of the Holy Spirit to sinful people, in order that they may come to put their trust in God through Him, to receive Him as their Savior, and serve Him as their King in the fellowship of His Church.[4] If we want to define it simply, we could say that New Testament evangelism is communicating the gospel. Anyone who faithfully relates the essential elements of God's salvation through Jesus Christ is evangelizing. This is true whether your words are spoken, written, or recorded, and whether they are delivered to one person or to a crowd.

---

[4] See J. I. Packer, Evangelism and the Sovereignty of God (Downers Grove, IL: InterVarsity Press, 1979), pages 37-57.

Why is evangelism expected of us? The Lord Jesus Christ Himself has commanded us to witness. Consider His authority in the following:

"Therefore go and make disciples of all nations, baptizing them in the name of the Father and of the Son and of the Holy Spirit, and teaching them to obey everything I have commanded you. And surely I will be with you always, to the very end of the age" (Matt. 28: 19-20).

"He said to them, 'Go into all the world and preach the good news to all creation'" (Mark 16: 15).

"And repentance and forgiveness of sins will be preached in his name to all nations, beginning at Jerusalem" (Luke 24: 47).

"Again Jesus said, 'Peace be with you! As the Father has sent me, I am sending you'" (John 20: 21).

"But you will receive power when the Holy Spirit comes on you; and you will be my witnesses in Jerusalem, and in all Judea and Samaria, and to the ends of the earth" (Acts 1: 8).

These commands weren't given to the apostles only. For example, the apostles never came to this nation. For the command of Jesus to be fulfilled and for America to hear about Christ, the gospel had to come here by other Christians. And the apostles will never come to your home, your neighborhood, or to the place where you work. For the Great Commission to be fulfilled there, for Christ to have a witness in that "remote part" of the earth, a Christian like you must discipline yourself to do it.

Some Christians believe that evangelism is a gift and the responsibility of only those with that gift. They appeal to Ephesians 4:11 for support: "It was he who gave some to be apostles, some to be prophets, some to be evangelists, and some to be pastors and teachers." While it is true that God gifts some for ministry as evangelists, He calls all believers to be His witnesses and provides them with both the power to witness and a powerful message. Every evangelist is called to be a witness, but only a few witnesses are called to the vocational ministry of an evangelist. Just as each Christian, regardless of spiritual gift or ministry, is to love others, so each believer is to evangelize whether or not his or her gift is that of an evangelist.

Think of our responsibility for personal evangelism from the perspective of 1 Peter 2:9: "But you are a chosen people, a royal priesthood, a holy nation, a people belonging to God." Many Christians who are

8

familiar with this part of the verse don't have a clue how the rest of it goes. It goes on to say that these privileges are yours, Christian, "that you may declare the praises of him who called you out of darkness into his wonderful light." We normally think of this verse as establishing the doctrine of the priesthood of all believers. But it is equally appropriate to say that it also exhorts us to a kind of prophet hood of all believers. God expects each of us to "declare the praises" of Jesus Christ.[5]

While this author agrees with Whitney's every word in the above, I would emphasize that we are to evangelize, so as to make disciples, which is more involved that simply sharing the Gospel. Paul summarizes the most basic elements of the gospel message, that is, the death, burial, resurrection, and appearances of the resurrected Christ. (1 Cor. 18:1-8) Therefore, the Gospel explained in detail or simply stated as Paul has put it, will not be enough to convert many unbelievers to the faith. Therefore, it is best to understand our responsibility as evangelist, in the sense of being able to proclaim or explain our Christian teachings both offensively and defensively: to **(1)** defend God's Word, **(2)** defend the faith, **(3)** pull some who doubt back from the fire, and **(4)** most importantly, to help the lost find salvation.

All Christians are to be Evangelizers

Today, we live in a world where Genesis 6:5 and 8:21 is magnified a thousandfold. Certainly, most normal humans, who do not suffer from mental distress, want to do good to others and live a peaceful life. Why then has there been so much evil in human history, and why is there so much evil today? We will have to turn to the words of our Creator for the answers.

Mentally Bent Toward Evil

Psalm 51:5 Updated American Standard Version (UASV)

[5] Behold, I was brought forth in iniquity,[6]
and in sin did my mother conceive me.

---

[5] Whitney, Donald S. (2012-01-05). Spiritual Disciplines for the Christian Life with Bonus Content (Pilgrimage Growth Guide) (p. 100-101). Navpress.

[6] Iniquity "signifies an offense, intentional or not, against God's law." (VCEDONTW, Volume 1, Page 122) Really, anything not in harmony with God's personality, standards, ways, and will, which mars one's relationship with God.

King David had his adultery with Bathsheba and the subsequent murder of her husband exposed, for which he accepted full responsibility. His words about the human condition give us one reason for the evil of man. He says, "I was brought forth in iniquity." What is iniquity? The Hebrew word *awon* essentially relates to erring, acting illegally, or wrongly.

David stated that his problem was a corrupt heart, saying; **surely, I was sinful at birth**. He entered this world a sinner in nature long before he became a sinner in actions. In fact, this internal corruption predated his **birth**, actually beginning nine months earlier when he was **conceived** in the womb. It was at conception that the Adamic sin nature was transmitted to him. The problem of what he did, sin, arose from what he was, a sinner.[7]

David is not here casting the blame onto his mother, as God never intended mothers to conceive and give birth to children who would sin. Nevertheless, when Adam and Eve rebelled, and were expelled from the Garden of Eden, they lost their ability to pass on perfection. Therefore, every child was born missing the mark of perfection. The Hebrew term translated as "sin" is *chattath;* in Greek, the word is *hamartia*. Both carry the meaning of missing the mark of perfection.

The verbal forms occur in enough secular contexts to provide a basic picture of the word's meaning. In Judges 20:16 the left-handed slingers of Benjamin are said to have the skill to throw stones at targets and "not miss." In a different context, Pro. 19:2 speaks of a man in a hurry who "misses his way" (RSV, NEB, KJV has "sinneth"). A similar idea of not finding a goal appears in Pro. 8:36; the concept of failure is implied.[8]

Genesis 6:5 The American Translation (AT)	**Genesis 8:21** The American Translation (AT)
[5] When the LORD saw that the wickedness of man on the earth was great, and that the **whole bent of his thinking was** never anything but **evil**, the LORD regretted that he had ever made man on the earth.	[21] I will never again curse the soil, though the **bent of man's mind** may be **evil from his very youth**; nor ever again will I ever again destroy all life creature as I have just done.

---

[7] Anders, Max; Lawson, Steven (2004-01-01). Holman Old Testament Commentary - Psalms: 11 (p. 266). B&H Publishing. Kindle Edition.

[8] G. Herbert Livingston, "638 חטא," ed. R. Laird Harris, Gleason L. Archer Jr., and Bruce K. Waltke, *Theological Wordbook of the Old Testament* (Chicago: Moody Press, 1999), 277.

All of us have inherited a sinful nature, meaning that we are currently unable to live up to the mark of perfection in which we were created. In fact, Genesis 6:5 says we all suffer from, 'our whole bent of thinking, which is nothing but evil." Genesis 8:21 says that 'our mind is evil from our very youth.' Jeremiah 17:9 says that our hearts are treacherous and desperately sick." What does all of this mean? It means that before the fall, our natural inclination; our natural leaning was toward good. However, our natural inclination, our natural leaning, was toward bad, wicked, and evil after the fall.

We should never lose sight of the fact that unrighteous desires of the flesh are not to be taken lightly. (Rom. 7:19, 20) Nevertheless, if it is our desire to have a righteous relationship before God, it will be the stronger desire. Psalm 119:165 says, "Abundant peace belongs to those who love Your instruction; nothing makes them stumble." We need to cultivate our love for doing right, which will strengthen our conscience, the sense of what is right and wrong that governs somebody's thoughts and actions, urging us to do right rather than wrong. It is only through studying the Bible that we can train the conscience. Once it is trained, it will prick us like a needle in the arm when we are thinking of doing something wrong. It will feel like a pain in our heart, a sadness, and nervousness, which is the voice saying, 'do not do this.' Moreover, if we ignore our voice, it will grow silent over time and will stop telling us what is wrong. (Romans 2:14-15)

James 1:14-15 Updated American Standard Version (UASV)

14 But each one is tempted when he is carried away and enticed by his own desire.9 15 Then the desire when it has conceived gives birth to sin, and sin when it is fully grown brings forth death.

We have a natural desire for wrongdoing, and Satan is the god of this world (2 Cor. 4:3-4), and he caters to the fallen flesh. James also tells us, "each person is tempted when he is lured and enticed by his own desire. Then desire when it has conceived gives birth to sin, and sin, when it is fully grown, brings forth death." (James 1:14-15) We resist the devil by immediately dismissing any thought that is contrary to God's values found in his Word, which enters our mind; we do not entertain it for a moment, nor do we cultivate it, causing it to grow. We then offer rational prayers in our head, or better yet, aloud so we can defeat fleshly irrational thinking with rational biblical thinking. The Apostle Peter, referring to the Devil

---

9 Or "own *lust*"

wrote, "Resist him, firm in your faith, knowing that your brotherhood is experiencing the same kinds of suffering throughout the world." (1 Peter 5:9)

Matthew 24:14 Updated American Standard Version (UASV)

[14] And this gospel of the kingdom will be proclaimed in all the inhabited earth[10] as a testimony to all the nations, and then the end will come.

With much of what people see today, one wonders what the Goods News could be.

Isaiah 52:7-8 Updated American Standard Version (UASV)

[7] How beautiful upon the mountains
  are the feet of him who brings good news,
who publishes peace, who brings good news of happiness,
  who proclaims salvation,
  who says to Zion, "Your God has become king!"[11]
[8] Listen! your watchmen lift up their voices;
  together they sing for joy;
for eye to eye they see
  when Jehovah returns to Zion.

In the days of Isaiah, no individual was identified as "him who brings good news." However, we know, that in the first century C.E., Jesus was identified as the bearer of good news, the prince of peace, and the king of God's Kingdom. During Jesus' three and a half year ministry, he proclaimed the good news about his giving "his soul as a ransom for many" (Matt. 20:28), **releasing** any who has faith in him from all the effects of inherited sin from Adam, including sickness and death. (Matt. 9:35) Jesus gave us a perfect zealous example of proclaiming the good news at every opportunity, to teach about the kingdom of God, so as to make disciples. (Matt. 5:1-2; Mark 6:34; Luke 19:1-10; John 4:5-26) Thereafter, his disciples would follow his example, and in a greater sense (John 14:12-14), they

---

[10] Or *in the whole world*

[11] Or *"Your God Reigns!"*

would 'bring good news' "in all the inhabited earth[12] as a testimony to all the nation." (Matthew 24:14)

In his letter to the congregation in Rome, the apostle Paul quotes Isaiah 52:7, which served to emphasize the important work of proclaiming the good news. Beginning in verse 14, Paul asks several important questions, "How then will they call on him in whom they have not believed? And how are they to believe in him of whom they have never heard? And how will they hear without someone to preach? And how are they to preach unless they are sent?" (Rom. 10.14-15) We should note that Paul, under inspiration, expanded upon Isaiah's words, going from **a singular "him" or "one"** who brings good news, to a plural "**those** who declare good news of good things!" Emulating Jesus Christ, all Christians today are proclaimers of the good news of the kingdom. What is meant by the words "how beautiful are the feet"? Isaiah was speaking as though the proclaimer of good news was approaching Jerusalem from the neighboring mountains of Judah. Thus, literally, it would have been impossible to see the feet of the messenger. Rather, the focus is on the one bringing the good news, the feet that bring him are pictorial of the messenger himself. In the oppressive years of the early first-century, we can only picture the beautiful sight of Jesus and his disciples as they traveled throughout Palestine. The same is true today as Christian proclaimers bring million the good news of the kingdom throughout the world.

Nahum 1:15 Updated American Standard Version (UASV)

15 Behold, upon the mountains, the feet of him
   who brings good news,
   who publishes peace!
Keep your feasts, O Judah;
   fulfill your vows,
for never again shall the worthless[13] pass through you;
   he is cut off completely.

Judah had thus long suffered under the heavy hand of Assyria. Therefore, Nahum's prophecy regarding Nineveh's looming destruction was indeed good news. Assyria would never again interfere in the lives of God's people. Nothing would get in the way of the Judeans from carrying

---

12 Or *in the whole world*

13 Or *wicked*

out pure worship and celebrating the festivals. This liberation from the Assyrian persecutor would be complete. (Nah. 1:9) Some 688 years later, the apostle Paul at Romans 10:15 apply the expression from Isaiah 52:7 and Nahum 1:15 to those whom the Father sends forth as Christian proclaimers of the good news. These ones are to proclaim the "good news of the kingdom." (Matthew 24:14)

Romans 10:15 Updated American Standard Version (UASV)

[15] And how are they to preach unless they are sent? As it is written, "How beautiful are the feet of those who declare good news of good things!"[14]

Christianity today has sadly fallen away from the evangelism that they had been assigned, the preaching and teaching of the good news, and the making of disciples. (Matt. 24:14; 28:19-20; Ac 1:8) The first-century Christians were very zealous when it came to sharing the good news and biblical truths with others. In fact, the new believers were taught the basics of the faith before they were baptized. Once they were baptized, they were immediately involved in spreading these same biblical truths to others. This is why just seventy years after the sacrificial death of Jesus Christ, there were more than a million Christians spread all throughout the then known world of the Roman Empire. Christians today should have this same zeal because Jesus gave only one command that was to be carried out after his departure, the making of disciples.

The good news is that this current evil age that we live in is not all that we have to look forward to, as all have the opportunity of gaining eternal life. Yes, the path of salvation is open to all. Therefore, Christians today should be in the work of being used by God to help as many as possible to find the path of salvation, before Christ's second coming.

John 3:16 Updated American Standard Version (UASV)	**John 3:36** Updated American Standard Version (UASV)
[16] For God so loved the world that he gave his only-begotten Son, in order that everyone **trusting in** him will not be destroyed but have eternal life.	[36] The one **trusting in** the Son has eternal life, but the one who disobeys the Son will not see life, but the wrath of God remains on him.

---

[14] Quotation from Isa 52:7; Nah 1:15

A Grammar of New Testament Greek series, by James Moulton, says, "The importance of the difference between mere belief … and personal trust."[15] Both these senses can be conveyed using the Greek word *pisteuo*. The context helps us to identify the different senses of the meaning of *pisteuo*. Then again, we also have the different grammatical constructions that also convey what the Bible author had meant by his use of the word. When *pisteuo* is simply followed by a noun in the dative case, it is merely rendered as "believe," such as the chief priest and elders response to Jesus at Matthew 21:25, "If we say, 'From heaven,' he will say to us, 'Why then did you not **believe him**?' However, in Romans 4:3, we have *pisteuo* follow by a noun in the dative in the Updated American Standard Version, yet it is rendered "For what does the Scripture say? "Abraham **put faith in** God, and it was credited to him as righteousness." (The ASV, RSV, ESV, NASB and others have "Abraham **believed** God")

If *pisteuo* is followed by the Greek preposition *epi*, "on," it can be rendered "believe in" or believe on." At Matthew 27:42, it reads, "we will **believe in** him [i.e., Jesus]." At Acts 16:31, it reads, "And they said, **Believe on** the Lord Jesus Christ, and thou shalt be saved …" (KJV, UASV similarly) What is the difference between "**believing in** Jesus" and "**believing on** Jesus"? **Believing in** Jesus is merely acknowledging that he exists while **believing on** Jesus is to accept absolutely, have no doubt or uncertainty, trust in, put faith in or trust in, and exercise faith in the Lord Jesus Christ.

If *pisteuo* is followed by the Greek preposition *eis*, ("into, in, among," accusative case), it is generally rendered "trusting in" or "trust in." (John 3:16, 36; 12:36; 14:1) The grammatical construction of the Greek verb *pisteuo* "believe" followed by the Greek preposition *eis* "into" in the accusative gives us the sense of having faith into Jesus, putting faith in, trusting in Jesus.

Revelation 21:3-4 Updated American Standard Version (UASV)

3 And I heard a loud voice from the throne, saying, "Behold, the tabernacle of God is among men, and he will dwell[16] among them, and they shall be his people,[17] and God himself will be among them,[18] 4 and he will

---

[15] James Moulton, A Grammar of New Testament Greek, Vol. 1: Prolegomena (London, England: T & T Clark International, 2006), 68.

[16] Lit *he will tabernacle*

[17] Some mss *peoples*

wipe away every tear from their eyes, and death shall be no more, neither shall there be mourning, nor crying, nor pain anymore, for the former things have passed away."

In the O[ld] T[estament] the kingdom of God is usually described in terms of a redeemed earth; this is especially clear in the book of Isaiah, where the final state of the universe is already called new heavens and a new earth (65:17; 66:22) The nature of this renewal was perceived only very dimly by OT authors, but they did express the belief that a humans ultimate destiny is an earthly one.[19] This vision is clarified in the N[ew] T[estament]. Jesus speaks of the "renewal" of the world (Matt 19:28), Peter of the restoration of all things (Acts 3:21). Paul writes that the universe will be redeemed by God from its current state of bondage (Rom. 8:18-21). This is confirmed by Peter, who describes the new heavens and the new earth as the Christian's hope (2 Pet. 3:13). Finally, the book of Revelation includes a glorious vision of the end of the present universe and the creation of a new universe, full of righteousness and the presence of God. The vision is confirmed by God in the awesome declaration: "I am making everything new!" (Rev. 21:1-8)

The new heavens and the new earth will be the renewed creation that will fulfill the purpose for which God created the universe. It will be characterized by the complete rule of God and by the full realization of the final goal of redemption: "Now the dwelling of God is with men" (Rev. 21:3).

The fact that the universe will be created anew[20] shows that God's goals for humans is not an ethereal and disembodied existence, but a bodily existence on a perfected earth. The scene of the beatific vision is the new earth. The spiritual does not exclude the created order and will be fully realized only within a perfected creation. (Elwell 2001, 828-29)

---

[18] One early ms and be *their God*

[19] It is unwise to speak of the written Word of God as if it were of human origin, saying 'OT authors express the belief,' when what was written is the meaning and message of what God wanted to convey by means of the human author.

[20] Create anew does not mean a complete destruction followed by a re-creation, but instead a renewal of the present universe.

Jesus Set the Example As to Proclaiming the Kingdom Good News

Christians today should be seeking to walk in the steps of their exemplar, Jesus Christ. Yes, we have been called so that we might follow in Jesus' steps.

1 Peter 2:21 Updated American Standard Version (UASV)

21 For to this you were called, because Christ also suffered for you, leaving you an example, so that you should follow in his footsteps,

In imitation of Jesus Christ, we should be willing to suffer the greatest difficulties if need be, even to the point of death, in order to uphold the sovereignty of God as we take every opportunity proclaim good news.

Luke 4:16-21 Updated American Standard Version (UASV)

16 And he came to Nazareth, where he had been brought up; and as was his custom, he went to the synagogue on the Sabbath day, and he stood up to read. 17 And the scroll21 of the prophet Isaiah was given to him. And he unrolled the scroll22 and found the place where it was written,

18 "The Spirit of the Lord is upon me,
  because he has anointed me
  to proclaim good news23 to the poor.
He has sent me to proclaim release to the captives
  and recovering of sight to the blind,
  to set free those who are oppressed,
19 to proclaim the favorable year of the Lord."

20 And he rolled up the scroll24 and gave it back to the attendant and sat down; and the eyes of all in the synagogue were fixed on him. 21 And he began to say to them, "Today this Scripture has been fulfilled in your hearing."

A survey of the Gospels indicates that Jesus' publishing program—via his traveling throughout Galilee and Judea and proclaiming the good news of the kingdom—was extensive and effective. Thousands and thousands of

21 Or a *roll*

22 Or *roll*

23 Or *the gospel*

24 Or *roll*

people heard the word from Jesus himself. In ancient times, the method of oral publication was far more effective than written publication. Books were expensive to make, and many people did not read. Most relied on oral proclamation and aural reception to receive messages. Indeed, most education was based upon oral delivery and aural reception/memorization to transmit texts. Thus, Jesus taught his disciples orally, and they committed his teachings to memory. When it came time, several years later, for the disciples to put these teachings into writing, they were aided by the Holy Spirit, who would remind the disciples of all that Jesus had taught them (John 14:26). Jesus' disciples, commissioned by him, continued the same publishing work after Jesus' death and resurrection. This publishing is known as the *kerygma* (Greek for "proclamation"). The word *kerygma* is taken straight from a well-known practice in ancient times. A king publicized his decrees throughout his empire by means of a *kerux* (a town crier or herald). This person, who often served as a close confidant of the king, would travel throughout the realm, announcing to the people whatever the king wished to make known. In English, we known him as a herald. Each New Testament disciple considered himself or herself to be like the *kerux*—a herald and publisher of the Good News.[25]

Yes, Jesus was an evangelizer, and he trained hundreds of evangelizers throughout his three and half years of ministry. "He went throughout all Galilee, teaching in their synagogues and proclaiming the gospel of the kingdom." (Matthew 4:23) Then he said to his disciples, "The harvest is plentiful, but the laborers are few; 38, therefore, pray earnestly to the Lord of the harvest to send out laborers into his harvest." (Matt. 9:37-38). The apostles set up Christian congregations, with every Christian following the footsteps of Christ, to be an evangelizer.

While there is nothing wrong with helping our neighbor deal with the world's social ills or taking some time to support a political candidate that we hope will implement laws that will allow for the greater work of evangelizing. Yes, Christianity has become a social institution, working night and day to save the world of humankind that is alienated from God, which has diverted them from the lifesaving work of being an evangelist. In the days of the Cold War between the United States and the former Soviet Union, a citizen of the United States would consider it treason if another citizen spent time promoting communism from the former Soviet Bloc.

---

[25] Philip Comfort, *Encountering the Manuscripts: An Introduction to New Testament Paleography & Textual Criticism* (Nashville, TN: Broadman & Holman, 2005), 2.

While we are citizens of this world, and of the country that we live in, our true Kingdom is the Kingdom of God in the person of Jesus Christ. Below we will quote the *Holman Illustrate Bible Dictionary* at length, to understand and appreciate what the Kingdom of God is.

The Kingdom of God

In the NT the fullest revelation of God's divine rule is in the person of Jesus Christ. His birth was heralded as the birth of a king (Luke 1:32–33). The ministry of John the Baptist prepared for the coming of God's kingdom (Matt. 3:2). The crucifixion was perceived as the death of a king (Mark 15:26–32).

Jesus preached that God's kingdom was at hand (Matt. 11:12). His miracles, preaching, forgiving sins, and resurrection are an in-breaking of God's sovereign rule in this dark, evil age.

God's kingdom was manifested in the church. Jesus commissioned the making of disciples on the basis of His kingly authority (Matt. 28:18–20). Peter's sermon at Pentecost underscored that a descendent of David would occupy David's throne forever, a promise fulfilled in the resurrection of Christ (Acts 2:30–32). Believers are transferred from the dominion of darkness into the kingdom of the Son of God (Col. 1:13).

God's kingdom may be understood in terms of "reign" or "realm." Reign conveys the fact that God exerts His divine authority over His subjects/kingdom. Realm suggests location, and God's realm is universal. God's reign extends over all things. He is universally sovereign over the nations, humankind, the angels, the dominion of darkness and its inhabitants, and even the cosmos, individual believers, and the church.

In the OT the kingdom of God encompasses the past, present, and future. The kingdom of God had implications in the theocratic state. The kingdom of God is "already" present but "not yet" fully completed, both a present and future reality. The kingdom was inaugurated in the incarnation, life, ministry, death, and resurrection of Jesus. God's kingdom blessings are in some measure possessed now. People presently find and enter God's kingdom. God is now manifesting His authoritative rule in the lives of His people. God's kingdom, however, awaits its complete realization. His people still endure sufferings and tribulations. When fully consummated, hardships will cease. Kingdom citizens currently dwell alongside inhabitants of the kingdom of darkness. God will eventually dispel all darkness. The final inheritance of the citizens of God's kingdom is yet to be fully realized. The resurrection body for life in the eschatological kingdom is a blessing awaiting culmination.

God's kingdom is soteriological in nature, expressed in the redemption of fallen persons. The reign of Christ instituted the destruction of all evil powers hostile to the will of God. Satan, the "god of this age," along with his demonic horde, seeks to hold the hearts of people captive in darkness. Christ has defeated Satan and the powers of darkness and delivers believers. Although Satan still is active in this present darkness, his ultimate conquest and destruction are assured through Christ's sacrificial death and resurrection. Sinners enter Christ's kingdom through regeneration.

Many of Jesus' parables emphasize the mysterious nature of God's kingdom. For example, an insignificant mustard seed will grow a tree, as God's kingdom will grow far beyond its inception (Matt. 13:31–32). The kingdom of God is like seed scattered on the ground. Some seed will fall on good soil, take root, and grow. Other seed, however, will fall on hard, rocky ground and will not grow. Likewise, the kingdom will take root in the hearts of some but will be rejected and unfruitful in others (Matt. 13:3–8). As wheat and tares grow side by side, indistinguishable from each other, so also the sons of the kingdom of God and the sons of the kingdom of darkness grow together in the world until ultimately separated by God (Matt. 13:24–30, 36–43).

Although closely related, the kingdom and the church are distinct. George Eldon Ladd identified four elements in the relationship of the kingdom of God to the church. The kingdom of God creates the church. God's redemptive rule is manifested over and through the church. The church is a "custodian" of the kingdom. The church also witnesses to God's divine rule.

The kingdom of God is the work of God, not produced by human ingenuity. God brought it into the world through Jesus Christ, and it presently works through the church. The church preaches the kingdom of God and anticipates the eventual consummation.[26]

The last sentence of our quote says in part, "the church preaches the kingdom of God." This has not been the case for almost 2,000 years.

---

[26] Stan Norman with Gentry Peter, "Kingdom of God," ed. Chad Brand, *Holman Illustrated Bible Dictionary* (Nashville, TN: Holman Bible Publishers, 2003), 988–989.

Today, the church preaches from the pulpit to those who are already Christian and those who happen into the church. Let us take another look at our key verses,

Romans 10:13-17 Updated American Standard Version (UASV)

13 For "everyone who calls on [through worship and prayer] the name of the Lord[27] will be saved.""

14 How then will they call on him in whom they have not believed? And how are they to believe in him of whom they have never heard? And how will they hear without someone to preach? 15 And how are they to preach unless they are sent? As it is written, "How beautiful are the feet of those who declare good news of good things!"[28]

16 But they have not all obeyed the gospel. For Isaiah says, "Lord,[29] who has believed what he has heard from us?" 17 So faith comes from hearing, and hearing through the word of Christ.

14. Paul now launches into a series of rhetorical questions. The first is *How, then, can they call*[54] *on the one they have not believed in?* Paul does not define his *they*. Obviously this is a term with wide application and may be seen as equivalent to "all people". But the apostle may have the Jews especially in view. Throughout these chapters he is discussing the plight of his own nation, and they will be prominently in mind, whatever other application we may fairly discern. Paul advances to *And how can they believe in the one of whom they have not heard?* It is possible to cavil at NIV's rendering *of whom* they have not heard, a rendering shared by several recent translations. But NASB has it right with "How shall they believe in Him whom they have not heard?" The point is that Christ is present in the preachers; to hear them is to hear him (cf. Luke 10:16), and people ought to believe when they hear him. Paul's third question is *And how can they hear without* someone preaching to them? It is important to see the impossibility of hearing without someone preaching. "Hearing" is a reflection of first-century life. Paul does not raise the possibility of the message being read. While there were people who could read, the ordinary first-century citizen depended rather on being able

---

27 Quotation from Joel 2:32, which reads, "everyone who calls on the name of Jehovah shall be saved." In other words, Paul was referring to the Father not the Son.

28 Quotation from Isa 52:7; Nah 1:15

29 Quotation from Isaiah 53:1, which reads, "Who has believed our message? And to whom has the arm of Jehovah been revealed?"

> to hear something. If the message of God was going to be effective in biblical times, it had to be heard. And for this a preacher was needed.[30]

Again, missionaries have been sent out throughout the last few centuries, but this is not the first-century way, it is the way of the last few centuries. However, over the last few decades, many trained in missions have come to realize the error of their ways. They have tried to grow the church by going outside of their community, to grow it back to their community. This was mistake number one. The other alternative was to grow from your community out to the rest of the world. Their second mistake was to use just a select few (missionaries), believing they were going to get the Great Commission accomplished. Of late, we hear much about having missionary churches that evangelize their own community with their own members. While this belief is best and correct, I am unaware of any who are doing it as it should be done, and most are not doing it.

While modern technology is great, there is but one way to reach "the whole world as a testimony to all nations" (Matt. 24:14). Yes, it is the human voice, but not as the Holman Commentary suggests with one man walking to a podium to preach, but for hundreds of millions to take to their communities, trained to preach (herald, proclaim) the message, and to teach what they had been taught "to one who does not know it."

First-Century Christians Evangelized

> [Jesus] reminded them in John 20:20 of his crucifixion: "He showed them his hands and side. The disciples were overjoyed when they saw the Lord." Then he reminded them again about his peace in verse 21. Jesus said, "Peace be with you!" Jesus proclaimed peace, reminded them of his crucifixion, pronounced peace again, and then told them, "As the Father has sent me, I am sending you" (John 20: 21). With that one command, Jesus announced two thousand years of direction for the church, still in effect for the churches of today, even your church. He proclaimed that we are sent. The church is, and you are individually, God's missionary to the world. Your church is God's instrument to reach the world, and it includes reaching your community. We are sent on mission by God. We are to be a missions-centered church by calling, nature, and choice. We are called to be

---

[30] Leon Morris, *The Epistle to the Romans*, The Pillar New Testament Commentary (Grand Rapids, MI; Leicester, England: W.B. Eerdmans; Inter-Varsity Press, 1988), 389–390.

on mission in our community. We have been sent to be on mission in our context, and we must accept that call, that directive to be on mission where God has placed us, not five, not fifty, not five hundred years ago and not thirty miles away, not three hundred miles away, not three thousand miles away. We are exhorted to be on mission where God has placed us now, and our job is to [evangelize] wherever we are.[31]

Yes, the Great Commission was an assignment given to all Christians, which starts right in your own backyard. You can effectively evangelize the world, if you do it one community at a time, starting with your community.

Matthew 28:19-20 Updated American Standard Version (UASV)

[19] Go therefore and make disciples of **all nations**, ... teaching them ... I am with you always, to the end of the age."

In the Greek, the words for "all nations" are *panta ta ethnē*. We get our English word ethnic from the Greek word *ethnē*. When we hear (or read) Jesus' command to "go to all nations," we think countries. But when Jesus spoke those words, there were no countries as we understand them today. The nation-state is an invention of the modern era. In Jesus' day there were groups of people, and there were empires. Jesus' instructions mean that we must go to all the people groups in the world. The Jewish disciples of that day knew that Jesus was speaking about the Gentiles. The gospel was to go beyond the Jewish nation. But they also thought of Phoenicians, Macedonians, Greeks, Romans, and others Jesus did not use the word for empires like the Roman Empire, the Persian, or the Greek. Jesus used the word for peoples, and the Jews knew this meant all the different kinds of Gentiles. It meant to go to all the different kinds of people that existed. This is still God's plan today. In today's world, we have to remember that we are still sent ... to all different kinds of peoples. The word peoples represents every ethno-linguistic people group around the world, all the different ethnicities present in our cities, and even the different generations that live in our communities.[32]

---

[31] Putman, David; Ed Stetzer (2006-05-01). Breaking the Missional Code: Your Church Can Become a Missionary in Your Community (pp. 30-31). B&H Publishing. Kindle Edition.

[32] Putman, David; Ed Stetzer (2006-05-01). Breaking the Missional Code: Your Church Can Become a Missionary in Your Community (p. 34). B&H Publishing. Kindle Edition

Who all were involved in the evangelism work of the first-century? The evidence is all too clear that all Christians were evangelizing their communities, with a select few, taking the message everywhere.

Acts 1:14 Updated American Standard Version (UASV)

[14] All these with one mind were continually devoting themselves to prayer, together with the women and Mary the mother of Jesus, and his brothers.

Acts 2:1, 4 Updated American Standard Version (UASV)

2 When the day of Pentecost was being fulfilled, they were all together in one place. [4] And they were all [men and women] filled with the Holy Spirit and began to speak with other tongues,[33] as the Spirit was giving them utterance.[34]

2:4. A third physical phenomenon experienced on the Day of Pentecost was the use of different languages. Throughout Acts, Luke uses different verbs to describe the coming of the Spirit upon new believers. This first time was a unique event, never again repeated in exactly the same way. When we look at the entire New Testament teaching on the Holy Spirit, we see the word *baptism* associated with initial conversion and the word *filling* with ministry. The first seems to happen once without repetition; the second occurs with frequency as believers allow God's Spirit to produce powerful work through them.

Most evangelical scholars believe the **tongues** of Pentecost were genuine languages, not the ecstatic sounds Paul dealt with at Corinth (1 Cor. 14:1–12). Two arguments rise strongly to emphasize that these tongues represented languages not previously learned. First, the use of the word *dialektos* in verses 6 and 8 can only refer to a language or dialect. Second, the paragraph that follows (vv. 5–12) specifically emphasizes the fact that people of different languages understood the message of the Christians in their own language.

Some argue for a miracle of hearing as well as speaking in this chapter. The text does not really justify that. On the other hand, when people filled with the Holy Spirit proclaim the gospel, a supernatural ministry always

---

[33] Or *languages*

[34] Or *enable them to speak*

24

takes place. When the hearers respond, a miracle of understanding certainly follows.[35]

Acts 2:17 Updated American Standard Version (UASV)

[17] "'And it shall be in the last days, God says,
that I will pour out my Spirit on all flesh,
and your sons and your daughters shall prophesy,*
  and your young men shall see visions,
  and your old men shall dream dreams; (See Joel 2:28-29)

> * The Greek behind the word "prophecy" here does not carry the meaning of "prediction," or "foretelling," (Gr., *propheteuo*), but literally means "a speaker out [Gr., pro, "before" or "in front of," and *phemi*, "say"]" and thus describes a proclaimer, one who proclaims messages of God. That is, namely **"to proclaim an inspired revelation, *prophesy* ... Acts 2:17f; John 3:1; 19:6; 21:9; 1 Cor, 11:4f ...; 13:9; 14:1, 3–5, 24, 31, 39; Rev. 11:3 ...**[36]

Matthew 24:14 Updated American Standard Version (UASV)

[14] And this gospel of the kingdom will be **proclaimed in all the inhabited earth**[37] as a testimony to all the nations, and then the end will come.

Acts 1:8 Updated American Standard Version (UASV)

[8] But you will receive power when the Holy Spirit has come upon you; and you will be my witnesses **in both Jerusalem** and in **all Judea and Samaria**, and to **the extremity of the earth**."

The prophecy of Jesus that the Good News would be "**proclaimed throughout the [then known] whole world** to all the nations [peoples], and then the end will come," was applicable to them, and was carried out. The "nations" (Gr., *ethnē*), means the same as it does at Matthew 28:19, where we are commanded to "make disciples of **all nations**." The first-

---

[35] Kenneth O. Gangel, *Acts*, vol. 5, Holman New Testament Commentary (Nashville, TN: Broadman & Holman Publishers, 1998), 25–26.

[36] William Arndt, Frederick W. Danker, and Walter Bauer, *A Greek-English Lexicon of the New Testament and Other Early Christian Literature* (Chicago: University of Chicago Press, 2000), 890.

[37] Or *in the whole world*

century Christians made disciples of **all nations** (the peoples), in all of **the then known world,**[38] before **the end came** for the natural nation of Israel, as the Romans destroyed Jerusalem in 70 C.E.,[39] killing over a million Jews, and taking hundreds of thousands captive. The apostle Paul wrote the Christians in Colossae about ten years earlier, 60 C.E, commenting on the spread of Christianity

Colossians 1:23 Updated American Standard Version (UASV)

[23] if indeed you continue in the faith firmly established and steadfast, and not moved away from the hope of the gospel that you have heard, which was **proclaimed in all creation under heaven**, and of which I, Paul, became a minister.

About 60-61 C.E., the apostle Paul wrote that the good news was **"proclaimed in all creation under heaven."** (Col. 1:23) Did Paul mean that the good news had already reached faraway places like India, the Far East, Africa, Spain, Gaul, Britain, the Baltics, and Thule? While this does not seem likely, we should not speculate one way or the other. Paul was making the point that the good news had been spread through the then known world as far as the readers knew, and regardless of the exact specifics, we know it was extensive. The good news had been spread as far as Parthia, Elam, Media, Mesopotamia, Arabia, Asia Minor, the parts of Libya toward Cyrene, and Rome.

First-Century Christian Worship and the Truth

The early Christians met in congregations, which for many of them, were private homes to take in the truth. (Rom. 16:3-5) The book of Hebrews tells us some of what took place at these meetings. They were there, in part, to "consider how to stir up one another to love and good works, not neglecting to meet together, as is the habit of some, but encouraging one another, and all the more as you see the Day drawing near." (Heb. 10:24-25) Tertullian of the late second, early third century (c.155–after 220 C.E.), wrote, "We meet to read the books of God … In any case, with those holy words we feed our faith, we lift up our hope, we

---

[38] Christianity had spread from Jerusalem to Rome, Macedonia, Greece, Asia, Bithynia, Pontus, Galatia, Cappadocia, Pamphylia, Syria, Cyprus, Crete, Babylon, Persian Gulf, Spain, Italy, Malta, Illyricum, Media, Parthia, Elam Arabia, Cyrene, Libya, Egypt, and Ethiopia.

[39] Dates of events before the Common Era (Also known as AD) are marked by the abbreviation B.C.E. Dates of events during the Common Era are marked by the abbreviation C.E.

confirm our confidence."[40] In order to become a Christian, certain requirements had to be met, as we can see from the *Zondervan Handbook to the History of Christianity*,

> As before, people who converted to Christianity were baptized. First, however, the new believer would be properly instructed in the beliefs and practices of Christianity. These 'beginner' Christians were the 'catechumens' (from the Greek meaning 'oral handing down', that is, teaching by word of mouth) and the way in which they were instructed developed as time went on. In the First apology, published in the middle of the second century, the Christian writer Justin Martyr (c. 100-165) gives us a valuable insight into how people were admitted into the church in Rome:[41]
>
> As many as are persuaded and believe that what we teach and say is true, and undertake to be able to live accordingly, are instructed to pray and to entreat God with fasting, for the remission of their sins that are past, we praying and fasting with them. Then they are brought by us where there is water, and are regenerated in the same manner in which we were ourselves regenerated. For, in the name of God, the Father and Lord of the universe, and of our Saviour Jesus Christ, and of the Holy Spirit, they then receive the washing with water.[42]

Thus, there were clear requirements before someone could be baptized: the education of basic doctrinal beliefs, praying, fasting, and a commitment to live a moral life and an understanding of Christian beliefs. These new believers were discovered by taking the message into the community. Then, they were taught to become a disciple of Jesus Christ. They were then organized into Christian congregations. These same disciples (learners) were trained to make more disciples, in the same way, preaching the Good News, and sharing the basic doctrinal beliefs.

Acts 5:42 Updated American Standard Version (UASV)

[41] So they went out from before the Sanhedrin, rejoicing that they were counted worthy to suffer dishonor for the name. [42] And every day in the

---

[40] Thomas C. Oden, Ministry Through Word and Sacrament, Classic Pastoral Care, 59 (New York: Crossroad, 1989).

[41] Jonathan Hill, *Zondervan Handbook to the History of Christianity*, 46 (Grand Rapids: Zondervan, 2006).

[42] Justin Martyr, "The First Apology of Justin", in The Ante-Nicene Fathers, Volume I: The Apostolic Fathers With Justin Martyr and Irenaeus, ed. Alexander Roberts, James Donaldson and A. Cleveland Coxe, 183 (Buffalo, NY: Christian Literature Company, 1885).

temple and from house to house they kept right on teaching and proclaiming the good news that the Christ was Jesus.

5:41–42 The apostles were not persuaded. They would continue to obey God rather than men. In fact, they rejoiced at having suffered for the name, very much in accord with the beatitude of their Lord (Luke 6:22f.). And the witness to the name continued—publicly in the temple and privately in the homes of the Christians. Luke seems to have used a common Greek rhetorical construction in v. 42 called a chiasm, which is most easily pictured as an A-B-B-A pattern. In the temple (A) and in homes (B), the apostles taught (B) and preached the gospel (A). Teaching was the task within the Christian fellowship, preaching the public task in the temple grounds. If there is any significance to his using such a device, it would be to give emphasis to the beginning and concluding elements. Their witness, their preaching of the gospel, was their primary task and occupation.[43]

Acts 14:21-23 Updated American Standard Version (UASV)

[21] After they had preached the gospel to that city and had made many disciples, they returned to Lystra and to Iconium and to Antioch, [22] strengthening the souls of the disciples, encouraging them to remain in the faith, and saying, "Through many tribulations we must enter the kingdom of God." [23] And when they had appointed elders for them in every congregation,[44] with prayer and fasting they committed them to the Lord in whom they had believed.

14:21a. Journeying sixty miles southeast, Paul and Barnabas reached Derbe, preached the gospel there, and **won a large number of disciples.** Wait a minute! Were there no believers left behind at Lystra? Not yet. That awaits a future visit. Why would Luke so hurriedly mention ministry in a town where the results were so obviously significant? Probably because he knows he will revisit this town in his accounts of the second and third journeys and give it more press at that time.

---

[43] John B. Polhill, *Acts*, vol. 26, The New American Commentary (Nashville: Broadman & Holman Publishers, 1992), 174.

[44] **Congregation:** (Heb. *qahal*; Gr. *ekklesia*) A congregation of Christians. A group of Christians, who gather for a Christian meeting, implying an interacting membership. In the Hebrew Scriptures, it usually refers to the nation of Israel, i.e., "the assembly of Israel" or "the congregation of Israel." In the Greek New Testament, it refers to congregations of Christians, as well as the Christian congregation as a whole.–Nu 20:8; De 4:10; 1 Ki 8:22; Ac 9:31; Rom. 16:5; 1 Cor. 14:4.

Longenecker suggests Luke is simply a man of his times, more interested in the larger cities, the central target of most of the missionary activity in Acts. He does offer a suggestion of importance for Lystra and Derbe, however, and an applicational note worth reproducing here:

> Probably the larger and more influential churches were in Antioch and Iconium as well, though the congregations in the smaller and more rural towns seem to have contributed more young men as candidates for the missionary endeavor (e.g., Timothy from Lystra—16:1–3; Gaius from Derbe 20:4)—a pattern not all together different from today, where the larger churches often capture the headlines and the smaller congregations provide much of the personnel (Longenecker, 438).

14:21b–22. In Derbe the missionaries could very well have headed southeast 150 miles to Tarsus and then easily returned to Syrian Antioch, but it was not yet time to go home. The churches of southern Galatia needed encouragement in their time of suffering, so they returned to the cities where they knew opposition awaited in order to tell the Christians, **We must go through many hardships to enter the kingdom of God.** These churches of southern Galatia were the likely recipients of the epistle to the Galatians written between the end of the first journey and the Jerusalem Council. When we read Galatians, therefore, we might think about these believers and remember how they came to Christ, enduring opposition from both Jews and Gentiles in the earliest days of their faith.

We wonder why Luke doesn't tell us about renewed opposition in these three cities which had treated the missionaries so badly. Perhaps we should conclude that on the return trip they confined their ministry exclusively to small groups of believers and therefore did not offend synagogue leaders or influential people in either Gentile or Jewish communities of those cities.

Let's not try to find a theology of suffering in the latter part of verse 22. Some popular religions today argue that people must find salvation through suffering. I have watched faithful followers of Catholicism plod forward on bleeding knees at the shrine of Lourdes in Portugal. I have seen flagalantes beat their backs bloody in the Philippines to earn favor with God. No, salvation does not come through suffering, nor were the missionaries talking here about salvation since their encouragement came to people already in the family of God. Rather, they reflected the word of the

Lord Jesus about sharing his sufferings along the way to heaven (Rom. 8:17; Phil. 3:10–11; Col. 1:24).

14:23. The appointing of elders to new congregations affords sufficient consequence to give further space to it in "Deeper Discoveries." Here we notice only that a different word appears, *cheirotonesantes*, rather than the usual *presbyteroi* or *episkopoi*, the latter two used interchangeably in the New Testament. The niv offers two marginal notes as options to the main text: "Barnabas ordained elders," or "Barnabas had elders elected." We should recognize the nature of these fledging churches. The manner of selecting leadership in established congregations like Jerusalem (Acts 6) would of necessity have been a very different process than that used with church planting efforts in the Gentile world of Asia Minor.[45]

Acts 20:20 Updated American Standard Version (UASV)

[20] how I did not shrink from declaring to you anything that was profitable, and teaching you in public and from house to house,

20:20 A second characteristic of Paul's ministry was the openness of his proclamation (v. 20). He kept no secrets, held nothing back. Whatever was true to the gospel and helpful to the faithful, he preached both publicly and from house to house. Mention of public proclamation recalls Paul's days in the synagogue of Ephesus and the lecture hall of Tyrannus (19:8f.). The reference to houses most likely is to the house-church meetings of the Ephesian Christians. In contrast, some were not so open in their witness, i.e., false teachers who advocated hidden and secret doctrines. Paul warned the Ephesian leaders later in his speech that such would arise to plague their own church (v. 29f.). He reminded them of the honesty and openness of his own preaching. When one was faithful to the truth, there was nothing to hide.[46]

---

[45] Kenneth O. Gangel, *Acts*, vol. 5, Holman New Testament Commentary (Nashville, TN: Broadman & Holman Publishers, 1998), 235–236.

[46] John B. Polhill, *Acts*, vol. 26, The New American Commentary (Nashville: Broadman & Holman Publishers, 1992), 424.

Review Questions

(1) Why do Christians desire to talk about their beliefs?

(2) Every Christian should realize what about effective communication."

(3) What similarity is there between the police/firefighters and Christian evangelists?

(4) In short, explain why all Christians are obligated to evangelize.

(5) What is the kingdom of God?

(6) Who has carried the bulk of the evangelizing work for centuries, and why is it necessary to refocus our attention on churches and communities?

(7) Please explain how the first-century Christians evangelized and what they accomplished.

(8) In the early church, what was a prospective disciple to go through before they could be a baptized member?

CHAPTER 1 Pay Much Closer Attention

Hebrews 2:1 Updated American Standard Version (UASV)

2 For this reason we must **pay much closer attention**[47] to the things that have been heard, so that we do not drift away[48] from it.

In the United States in 2010, traffic accidents were 12 per 100,000. Many of these deaths could have been avoided. How? Most occur because of distractions, **not paying much closer attention**, and **drifting away** into an object or head-on traffic. The driver is looking around, reading signs, changing the radio station, eating food, talking, or especially texting on a cell phone, instead of paying much closer attention to the road. These drivers refuse to accept that the tragedies they see on the internet or on television can really happen to them. Immature ones can watch, even drive by the scene where four teens are horrifically killed in a head-on collision because of texting and then texting while driving the next day.

Go back 2,000 years to the first-century, and the author of Hebrews is speaking of another type of distraction, which was contributing to the loss of eternal life among the Hebrew Christians. The author was making a point of Jesus' superior position over the angels, the Aaronic priesthood, and the like when he penned, "We must **pay much closer attention** to what we have heard, **lest we drift away** from it." Why were these Hebrew Christians being exhorted to pay much closer attention to avoid drifting away? The author penned Hebrews about 61 C.E., while Jesus ascended back to heaven in 33 C.E., some 28-years earlier. The expectation of Jesus' return was very high, so much time was elapsing, and some of the Hebrew Christians were starting to drift away from the faith.

2:1. This verse introduces us to the plight of the readers. They had heard the gospel. They appeared ready to desert Jesus for some trifling

---

[47] **Pay Attention:** (Gr. *prosechō*) The sense of *prosechō* is to give heed or the need to pay attention. One must hold more firmly to what they believe, or what they have known to be true. Paul is telling these Hebrew Christians, who no longer have the visual aids like the temple, or the Jewish high priest, you need to hold more firmly to the things that you have heard.

[48] **Drift Away:** (Gr. *pararreō*) The sense of *pararreō* is to disbelieve or drift away gradually or slowly from what one had formerly known to be true. It is like being carried away by water current. These Hebrew Christians because of their daily harassment from the Jews in and around Jerusalem, living in the place where they can see what we now call the eighth wonder of the world, the Jewish temple, were gradually giving up their belief in the truth.–Heb. 2:1.

replacement. The writer of Hebrews was horrified at this prospect!

Therefore reminded the people of the importance of the message about Jesus. The readers needed to listen because the truths of the gospel were too important to push aside. Issues of spiritual life and death were at stake. Whatever they did, the readers must hold fast to Jesus.

The idea of **drifting away** compared the audience to a boat sailing past warning signs to meet destruction and ruin on a rocky shore or in a raging rapid. The Hebrews needed to do something. They were listless while their situation demanded positive action. "Pay attention to your plight," said our writer, "lest you carelessly fall into ruin."[49]

Hebrew Christians Needed to Pay Much Closer Attention

Judaism is mostly identified with the religion of the Jews in the first century B.C.E. and the first and second centuries C.E. It should not be confused with the Israelite religion of the Old Testament from Abraham, the first Hebrew, to Moses and the Exodus (opening of OT), to the penning of Ezra, Nehemiah, and Malachi (closing of OT). Judaism twisted the Old Testament 39 books, coming up with oral laws that would make up the Mishnah[50] (c. 200 C.E.) and the Talmud (c. 500 C.E.) Why would those Jewish Christians want to return to Judaism? When we think of the things carried out under the Law, it was made up of things that the eye could see. People were able to see the priest going about their business, and they could smell the burnt sacrifices. They could see the temple compound, the eighth wonder of the world. On the other hand, Christianity was not based on the things seen but rather on things unseen. Those Jewish Christians had a high priest in Jesus Christ, but many had never seen him, as he had ascended back to heaven prior to them becoming a Christian. (Heb. 4:14) The Jewish Christians had a temple, but it was in heaven itself. (Heb. 9:24) Jews of Judaism were proud of their physical circumcision, while with the Jewish Christians, "circumcision is a matter of the heart, by the Spirit." (Rom. 2:29) Thus, we can see that the Hebrew Christian's faith was previously, under

---

[49] Thomas D. Lea, *Hebrews, James*, vol. 10, Holman New Testament Commentary (Nashville, TN: Broadman & Holman Publishers, 1999), 24.

[50] The Mishnah is the Jewish law from the oral tradition, as distinguished from law derived from the scriptures, but more like read into the Scriptures. The Talmud is a book of Jewish law, i.e., the collection of ancient Jewish writings that forms the basis of Jewish religious law, consisting of the early scriptural interpretations Mishnah and the later commentaries on them Gemara (literally, "study").

Judaism, was based on touchable, perceptible, concrete, and physical things, which had become a matter of faith after their conversion.

Those Jewish Christians were actually missing things that were seen because it had been a part of their lives since birth. Thus, the author of Hebrews, which this author accepts as being Paul,[51] felt the need to help them see that they actually had something far superior. While it was based primarily on faith as opposed to sight, it was superior to anything they had under the Mosaic Law. Making this point, Paul writes, "For if the blood of goats and bulls, and the sprinkling of defiled persons with the ashes of a heifer, sanctify for the purification of the flesh, how much more will the blood of Christ, who through the eternal Spirit offered himself without blemish to God, purify our conscience from dead works to serve the living God." (Heb. 9:13-14) Earlier in the letter, Paul penned,

Hebrews 7:26-28 Updated American Standard Version (UASV)

[26] For it is fitting for us to have such a high priest who is loyal, innocent, undefiled, separated from the sinners, and exalted above the heavens. [27] He has no need, like those high priests, to offer sacrifices daily, first for his own sins and then for those of the people, since he did this once for all when he offered up himself. [28] For the law appoints men as high priests who have weakness, but the statement of the oath, after the law, appoints a Son, who is made perfect forever.

While the above things about Jesus are the most important reasons for penning the book of Hebrews, Jesus himself offered another reason why those Jewish Christians and all other Christians need "must **pay much closer attention** to what we have heard, **lest we drift away** from it." They lived in Jerusalem; it was 61 C.E., many years since Jesus' ascension, but very close to when some of his words were going to find fulfillment. He had foretold the destruction of Jerusalem. He said,

Luke 19:43-44 Updated American Standard Version (UASV)

[43] For the days will come upon you, when your enemies will set up a barricade of pointed stakes[52] around you and surround you and hem you in

---

[51] Who Authored the Book of Hebrews: A Defense for Pauline Authorship
https://christianpublishinghouse.co/2016/11/02/who-authored-the-book-of-hebrews-a-defense-for-pauline-authorship/

[52] **Barricade**: (Gr. *Charax*) The Greek noun means pointed stakes, poles, used as a tall fence or enclosure driven into the ground side by side to keep out enemies or intruders. However, it can be used

on every side [44] and tear you down to the ground, you and your children within you. And they will not leave one stone upon another in you, because you did not know the time of your visitation."

Was Jerusalem ever surrounded by pointed stakes, as Jesus foretold would happen? If so, when would this take place? Just how close were they? Jesus foretells the destruction of Jerusalem, his words coming true in the year 70 C.E. when the Romans, under General Titus, erected pointed stakes, poles, used as a tall wall or enclosure driven into the ground side by side to keep the Jewish people trapped within their fortified city. He gave the following instructions,

Luke 21:20-21 Updated American Standard Version (UASV)

[20] "But when you see Jerusalem surrounded by armies, then know[53] that its desolation has come near. [21] Then let those who are in Judea flee to the mountains, and let those who are in the midst of the city depart, and let not those who are out in the country enter it;

Excursion The Great Tribulation

Matthew 24:15 Update American Standard Version (UASV)

The Abomination of Desolation

[15] "Therefore when you see the abomination of desolation, which was spoken of through Daniel the prophet, standing in the holy place (let the reader understand),

Matthew 24:13 reads, "But **the one who endures to the end** will be saved." Matthew 24:14 said, "this gospel of the kingdom will be proclaimed throughout the whole world as a testimony to all nations, **and then the end will come**." Matthew 24:15 begins with the Greek word *hotan* "whenever" followed by *oun* "therefore, which reads in English, "Therefore when," which connects what preceded, **"the end,"** and leads into what follows. Let us take a moment to investigate verse 15.

---

to keep enemies within an ancient fortified city. In 70 C.E., the Roman general, Titus, surrounded Jerusalem with a barricade.–Luke 19:43

[53] Or *then recognize*

In verse 3-14, Jesus outlined the signs of "the end of the age." Here in Mathew, Jesus begins with **"Therefore when** you see the abomination of desolation, which was spoken of through Daniel the prophet, standing in the holy place (let the reader understand)." If we look at the corresponding accounts in Mark and Luke, they offer us additional insights. Mark 13:14 says, "standing where it ought not to be." Luke 21:20 adds Jesus' words, "But when you see Jerusalem surrounded by armies, then know[54] that its desolation has come near." The complete picture is an "abomination" "standing in the holy place," i.e., "where it ought not be," namely, "Jerusalem surrounded by armies,"

This is a reference to the Roman army, which assaulted Jerusalem and its temple starting in 66 C.E., under General Cestus Gallus. The temple was the "holy place," and the abomination was the Roman army "standing where it ought not to be." As for the "desolation" it came in 70 C.E. when General Titus of the Roman army completely desolated Jerusalem and its temple. Specifically, what was this "abomination"? Moreover, in what sense was it "standing in the holy place"?

When Jesus urged the readers to *understand*, what were they to *understand*? They were to *understand* that "which was spoken of through Daniel the prophet," i.e. Daniel 9:27. Part "b" of verse 27 reads, "And upon the wing of abominations shall come the one causing desolation, even until a complete destruction, one that is decreed, is poured out on the one causing desolation."—Daniel 9:26-27; see also Daniel 11:31; 12:11.

> The *abomination of desolation* is an expression that recurs in Daniel with some variation in wording (Daniel 8:13; 9:27; 11:31; 12:11), where most scholars agree that there is a reference to the desecration perpetrated by Antiochus Epiphanes when he built an altar to Zeus in the temple and offered swine and other unclean animals on it as sacrifices (cf. 1 Macc. 1:41–61).[55]

We can have it but one of two ways, as Jesus' words is a clear reference to the Roman armies of 66 – 70 C.E. It may very well be that Daniel's prophecy points to Antiochus Epiphanes "who in 167 [B.C.E., 200-years before Jesus uttered his prophecy] plundered the temple, ordered the sacrificial system to cease, and polluted the altar of the Lord by turning

---

[54] Or *then recognize*

[55] Leon Morris, *The Gospel According to Matthew*, The Pillar New Testament Commentary (Grand Rapids, MI; Leicester, England: W.B. Eerdmans; Inter-Varsity Press, 1992), 603.

it into a pagan altar, where unclean sacrifices were offered to pagan deities."[56] This would be no different from Matthew referring to Hosea 11:1 (When Israel was a child ... and out of Egypt I called my son). In that case, Matthew did not use Hosea's intended meaning but carried out an *Inspired Sensus Plenior Application*, by having a whole other meaning, a completely different meaning for those words, making them applicable to Jesus being called back out of Egypt. It could be that Jesus used Daniel's prophecy about Antiochus Epiphanes and gave it an *Inspired Sensus Plenior Application*, by having a whole other meaning, a completely different meaning for those words, making them applicable to the Roman armies desolating Jerusalem between 66 and 70 C.E. Then, again, it could be that was what Daniel was pointing to all along, and Jesus used Daniel's words in a grammatical-historical application. Either way, it still comes out the same.

During the days of the Maccabees this expression was used to describe the sacrilege of Antiochus IV Epiphanes, the Seleucid king who decreed that an altar to Olympian Zeus and perhaps a statue of himself were to be erected in the temple on 15 Chislev, 167 b.c.: "They erected a desolating sacrilege on the altar of burnt offering. They also built altars in the surrounding towns of Judah." Antiochus further decreed that the Sabbath and other festal observances were to be profaned, that circumcision was to be abolished, and that swine and other unclean animals were to be sacrificed in the temple (cf. 1 Macc. 1:41–50). This was one of the lowest points of Jewish history and was considered by many the primary focus of Daniel's prophecy. Jesus now quotes Daniel directly to clarify that the fulfillment of the "abomination that causes desolation" is yet future.[57]

IMAGE: STANDARD OF THE 10TH ROMAN LEGION This legion

---

[56] Larry Chouinard, *Matthew*, The College Press NIV Commentary (Joplin, MO: College Press, 1997), Mt 24:15.

[57] Clinton E. Arnold, *Zondervan Illustrated Bible Backgrounds Commentary: Matthew, Mark, Luke*, vol. 1 (Grand Rapids, MI: Zondervan, 2002), 148.

attacked and destroyed Jerusalem in the Jewish War (A.D. 70).

When Jesus uttered those words in verse 15, the abomination of desolation was yet to appear. Jesus was clearly pointing to the Roman army of 66 C.E., with its distinctive standards, which were idols to the Romans and the empire, but an abomination to the Jews.

> Judæa was under the charge of a Roman official, a subordinate of the governor of the Roman province of Syria, who held a relation to that functionary similar to that which the Governor of Bombay holds to the Governor-General at Calcutta. Roman soldiers paraded the streets of Jerusalem; **Roman standards** waved over the fastnesses of the country; Roman tax-gatherers sat at the gate of every town. To the Sanhedrin, the supreme Jewish organ of government, only a shadow of power was still conceded, its presidents, the high priests, being mere puppets of Rome, set up and put down with the utmost caprice. So low had the proud nation fallen whose ideal it had ever been to rule the world, and whose patriotism was a religious and national passion as intense and unquenchable as ever burned in any country.[58]

Matthew 24:16 (UASV)	Mark 3:14b (UASV)	Luke 21:21 (UASV)
[16] then let those who are in Judea flee to the mountains.	[14] "… then let those who are in Judea flee to the mountains.	[21] Then let those who are in Judea flee to the mountains, and let those who are in the midst of the city depart, and let not those who are out in the country enter it;

Looking at verse 20 of Luke 21, we know that it fits the fact that General Cestius Gallus had "the holy city" Jerusalem (Matt. 4:5) surrounded, which had become the center of the Jewish revolt against Rome. Thirty-three years had passed since Jesus uttered his prophecy, but now the "abomination of desolation" of Rome was near. Gallus and his armies were responding to the Jewish revolt, at the time of the celebration of the festival of booths (tabernacles), October 19-25. On about November 3-4, the Roman army entered the city of Jerusalem, where they attacked the

---

[58] James Stalker, *The Life of Jesus Christ* (Chicago: Henry A. Sumner and Company, 1882), 30–31.

temple wall for five days, weakening it on the sixth day. However, for some unforsaken reason, he pulls away. On this attack of Cestius Gallus, Josephus' *Wars of the Jews 2.539*, says that "had he but continued the siege a little longer, had certainly taken the city; but it was, I suppose, owing to the aversion God had already at the city and the sanctuary, that he was hindered from putting an end to the war that very day." A footnote in Flavius Josephus and William Whiston reads,

> There may another very important, and very providential, reason be here assigned for this strange and foolish retreat of Cestius; which, if Josephus had been now a Christian, he might probably have taken notice of also; and that is, the affording the Jewish Christians in the city an opportunity of calling to mind the prediction and caution given them by Christ about thirty-three years and a half before, that "when they should see the abomination of desolation" [the idolatrous Roman armies, with the images of their idols in their ensigns, ready to lay Jerusalem desolate,] "stand where it ought not;" or, "in the holy place;" or, "when they should see Jerusalem encompassed with armies," they should then "flee to the mountains." By complying with which those Jewish Christians fled to the mountains of Perea, and escaped this destruction. See Lit. Accompl. of Proph. pp. 69–70. Nor was there, perhaps, any one instance of a more unpolitic, but more providential conduct than this retreat of Cestius, visible during this whole siege of Jerusalem; which yet was providentially such a "great tribulation, as had not been from the beginning of the world to that time; no, nor ever should be."—Ibid., pp. 70–71.[59]

Matthew 24:17-18 (UASV)	Mark 13:15-16 (UASV)
[17] Let the man who is on the housetop not go down to take what is in his house, [18] and let the man who is in the field not turn back to take his cloak.	[15] let the man who is on the housetop not go down, nor enter his house, to take anything out; [16] and let the man who is in the field not turn back to take his cloak.

---

[59] Flavius Josephus and William Whiston, *The Works of Josephus: Complete and Unabridged* (Peabody: Hendrickson, 1987).

When General Gallus suddenly withdrew his armies for no seemingly good reason, they suffered substantial fatalities at the hands of the Jews, who were pursuing them. This would wake the Jewish and Gentile Christians to Jesus' words and that a great tribulation would soon be upon them. (Matt. 24:21) This allowed them to flee and for no Christian, to return until the tribulation had passed. Eusebius of Caesarea (260/265 – 339/340 C.E.), a Christian, who was a Roman historian, writes,

> But the people of the church in Jerusalem had been commanded by a revelation, vouchsafed to approved men there before the war, to leave the city and to dwell in a certain town of Perea called Pella.[60] And when those that believed in Christ had come thither from Jerusalem, then, as if the royal city of the Jews and the whole land of Judea were entirely destitute of holy men, the judgment of God at length overtook those who had committed such outrages against Christ and his apostles, and totally destroyed that generation of impious men. (Eusebius, Ecclesiastical History 3.5.3)

Josephus, first-century Jewish historian (33- 100 C.E.), tells us that the Jews waited for God's help, not realizing this was the day of the Lord, a judgment day upon them,

> A false prophet[61] was the occasion of these people's destruction, who had made a public proclamation in the city that very day, that God commanded them to get up upon the temple, and that there they should receive miraculous signs of their deliverance. Now, there was then a great number of false prophets suborned by the tyrants to impose upon the people, who denounced this to them, that they should wait for deliverance from God: and this was in order to keep them from deserting, and that they might be buoyed up above fear and care by such hopes. Now, a man that is in adversity does easily comply with such promises; for when a such a seducer makes him believe that he shall be delivered from those miseries which oppress him, then it is that the patient is full of hopes of such deliverance. (Josephus, Wars of the Jews 6.285–87)

---

[60] Pella was a town situated beyond the Jordan, in the north of Perea, within the dominions of Herod Agrippa II. The surrounding population was chiefly Gentile. See Pliny V. 18, and Josephus, B. J. III. 3. 3, and I. 4. 8. Epiphanius (De pond. et mens. 15) also records this flight of the Christians to Pella.

[61] Reland here justly takes notice that these Jews who had despised the true Prophet, were deservedly abused and deluded by these false ones.

Dio Chrysostom expresses wonder at the level of Jewish fight that they possessed to the very end of the revolt,

> The Jews resisted [Titus] with more ardor than ever, as if it were a kind of windfall [an unexpected piece of luck] to fall fighting against a foe far outnumbering them; they were not overcome until a part of the Temple had caught fire. Then some impaled themselves voluntarily on the swords of the Romans, others slew each other, others did away with themselves or leaped into the flames. They all believed, especially the last, that it was not a disaster but victory, salvation, and happiness to perish together with the Temple. (Dio Chrysostom, Orations 66.6–2–3.)

Zondervan's Illustrated Bible Background Commentary on Matthew 24:17 tell us, "Likewise, there will not be time to gather provisions in the home. The flat rooftops on many homes in Israel were places to find a cool breeze in the evening and were considered part of the living quarters." (Arnold 2002, 150) In Jewish homes of those who could afford a multiform house, there was a staircase outside that led to the roof. The poor would have had a ladder in the courtyard, which led to the roof. Therefore, anyone on the housetop of their home, which was very common, could leave without having to enter their home. Moreover, many homes were built side-by-side, and it was possible to walk from one rooftop to the next. These backgrounds fit what Jesus meant by the words that he used. Whether Jesus meant his words in a hyperbolic sense of, 'when you see these things, act immediately, do not delay,' or literally, 'do not even look back, get out,' it is clear that Christians considered Jesus' warning serious, knowing that mere materials were not worth the loss of their lives.

Zondervan's Illustrated Bible Background Commentary on Matthew comments in verse 18 that "The outer coat was an essential garment for traveling, often used as a blanket when sleeping outdoors, and only those in the greatest hurry would think of leaving it behind." (Arnold 2002, 150) ZIBBC comments on Mark 13:18, saying, "Winter is the time of heavy rains in Palestine, flooding roads and wadis.303 Gadarene refugees during the first revolt sought shelter in Jericho but could not cross the swollen Jordan and were slain by the Romans.304 Winter travel is also hazardous if people are to traverse mountain passes." (Arnold 2002, 283)

Matthew 24:19 Update American Standard Version (UASV)

[19] But woe to those who are pregnant and to those who are nursing babies in those days!

41

Certainly, the modern-day woman has taken on some very rigorous activities. Recently, this author saw news of a woman running a marathon in her eighth month of pregnancy. However, in the days of the first century C.E., an extended flight over mountainous terrain on foot would be very difficult and quite dangerous. This would be especially true for any woman close to her due date. When the Romans finally desolated Jerusalem in 70 C.E., pregnant women, and those with young, were shown no mercy by the Roman troops. As the months of laying siege to the city, drug on, feminine prevailed, which for a pregnant woman, the baby would be robbing the woman of nourishment. For example, the baby would take the mother's calcium for bone development, meaning the woman could lose all of her teeth. Moreover, some mothers gave birth and had to watch their child starve to death, and in some cases, the people would take the child, cook it and eat it.

Matthew 24:20 Update American Standard Version (UASV)

20 But pray that your flight will not be in the winter, or on a Sabbath.

This verse is self-explanatory, as we can only imagine the Christians trying to escape over mountainous terrain during the winter. Imagine if they ignored the warning, procrastinated until the Roman troops arrived, and had to make their escape in the winter; when they could have left earlier. *Zondervan's Illustrated Bible Background Commentary* on Matthew comments on verse 18, saying, "Flight in winter, when roads are washed out, and rivers are swollen, presents even more difficulty for those fleeing the horrors of the coming desolation. In prayer the disciples must cling to God's presence and ever-ready help, even though they may have to disrupt even the most devoutly held religious traditions, such as the Jewish Sabbath." (Arnold 2002, 150)

Matthew 24:21 Update American Standard Version (UASV)

21 For then there will be great tribulation, such as has not been from the beginning of the world until now, no, and never will be.

As we look at Matthew 24:15-22 with Luke 21:20-24, the great tribulation of Jesus' prophecy is applicable to what took place in Jerusalem. The fulfillment of these words came in 70 C.E., when General Titus and his Roman armies laid siege to the city, desolating it, killing 1,100,000 Jews, whereas 97,000 who survived were taken into captivity. (Whiston 1987, Wars of the Jews 6.420) Some might argue that the 6,000,000 million Jews killed by Hitler during World War II was certainly a greater tribulation than

70 C.E. However, the difference is God used the Roman army as a tool to judge ("a day of the Lord") the Jews for their 1,500 years of false worship, child sacrifice, murder, and the execution of the Son of God. After 70 C.E., Jerusalem was never again the holy city that it once was, nor were the Jews God's chosen people. Therefore, the suffering that the Jews faced during World War II was not a judgment of God, but rather an unexpected or unforeseen event of human imperfect, as the result of Adamic sin, no different from any other atrocity on humanity.

Matthew 24:22 Update American Standard Version (UASV)

²² And if those days had not been cut short, no flesh would have been saved: but for the chosen ones[62] sake those days shall be shortened.

Again, these words are applicable to a preliminary fulfillment in 66-70 C.E. If we recall the city was under siege by General Cestius Gallus, who had the city, were undermining the Temple wall, with many of the Jews ready to surrender, but for some unknown reason pulled away, suffering great casualties at the hands of the pursuing Jews. Had Gallus not pulled away, leaving several years before Titus would come back and finish the job, the chosen ones, i.e., predominantly Jewish and some Gentile Christians, would not have been saved from the desolation. Yes, they heeded Jesus' words, "But when you see Jerusalem surrounded by armies, then know[63] that its desolation has come near. Then let those who are in Judea flee to the mountains, and let those who are in the midst of the city depart, and let not those who are out in the country enter it." (Luke 21:20-21) Thus, the Christians fled the city that was doomed to suffer destruction in 70 C.E. – **End of Excursion**

Christians Today Must Pay Much Closer Attention

Just as those first century Christians need to pay much closer attention, so it is true of Christians today. We need to pay much closer to the Word of God because there is more destruction on the horizon. Of course, like them, we do not know the day or the hour. However, it is better to be awake when the thief breaks in your house. Moreover, we would not want to be distracted by the things of this world of humankind, who are alienated from God. After foretelling the destruction of Jerusalem, Jesus wrote, "But stay awake at all times, praying that you may have strength to

---

[62] Or *the elect*

[63] Or *then recognize*

escape all these things that are going to take place, and to stand before the Son of Man." Luke 21:36

What can we do to motivate ourselves spiritually, pay much closer attention, and stay awake? Of course, being prepared and regular at our Christian meetings is crucial. Moreover, we do not just want to have a Bible that we carry around, but rather become a student of God's Word. The Psalmist tells us, "Your word is a lamp to my **feet** and a light to my **path**." Psalm 119:105

Consider the Bible can light up the **path** of things to come, things that are distant. On the other hand, the Bible can light up our every **step** into that distant future, helping us to make day-to-day decisions. This is why we need to pay much closer attention as we prepare for Christian services and carry out personal Bible studies at home. The knowledge, understanding, wisdom, and insight that we will acquire will help us make decisions that will please God. (Pro. 27:11; Isa. 48:17) How can we increase our focus during Christian meetings?

Cultivating Our Attentiveness

Many things at a Christian meeting can sap us of our attention. It may be a crying infant just a few aisles over. It may be someone whispering behind us. It may be someone showing up late, trying to find a seat. It may be that we just finished eight hours at an extremely physical job, and both body and mind are tired. Moreover, maybe the speaker or the conductor is not exciting. All or any of this can cause the mind to drift away. In extreme cases, these circumstances could cause us almost to fall asleep. Therefore, how can we cultivate our ability to be attentive during such trying times?

If we had prepared well at home, before the day of the meeting, it would be much easier to follow. Therefore, if we know what will be considered at future meetings, it might be prudent to buy out the time in the convenience of our home to prepare. If we know what is coming in the Bible study class, we can work through that section by reading, meditating, and writing down our thoughts in the margins of our book or on a notepad. We can also look up each cited Scriptures, read them, and even consider them in a commentary volume. If we have a schedule, we could prepare well for all of our meetings. This will be even more efficient in those meetings, where participation is permissible.

Another trick to staying focused is to sit closer to the podium, as all the distractions will be far behind us. Moreover, we can look directly at the speaker as we follow along in our Bible. In addition, we can bring our notepad, add notes from the points the speaker brings out, and comparing them with ours. These techniques should keep our minds from wondering. There is little doubt that a prepared heart is far more beneficial than any guru method of focusing. Moreover, our inner person needs to value why we gather. i.e., to praise and worship the Creator of the universe, the one from who we received life. (Ps. 26:12; Lu 2:36-37) It is also an opportunity to be fed spiritually. (Matt. 5:3) Lastly, the meetings give us an opportunity "to stir up one another to love and good works." (Hebrews 10:24-25)

We can tend to view the Christian services through worldly lenses: if those conducting are skilled, we see it as a good service, but if the conductors lack in any way, we see it as a bad service. Of course, we should expect our religious leaders to give their best to God and us (1 Tim. 4:16), but we should not be overly critical of our leaders, expecting some charismatic personality that moves us more with emotions, as opposed to biblical insights. That is like feeding on junk food instead of a good healthy meal. The former tastes good, but it has no lasting benefits and can do more harm than good. The latter may not have the exhilarating taste of the former but will fill us spiritually, holding us over for the long haul. While the teaching ability of those taking the lead has some significance, it is not the totality of being spiritually fed. If we desire to take in the very knowledge of God, the speaker's abilities will be but a minor bump in the road, which we can easily get over as he grows into his role. (Pro. 2:1-6) Therefore, let us be determined to "pay much closer attention to what we have heard, lest we drift away from it."

Personal Bible Study

We must also "pay much closer attention to what we have heard" through our personal Bible study. The Holy Spirit can call to mind the things that we have fed our mind, but only if we have fed our mind. When we take some time out of each day to meditate on the Bible, using Bible study tools (Bible dictionaries, commentaries, word study, encyclopedias, and the like), it will implant biblical truths within our minds and hearts. This will benefit us, and those who listen to us. It will affect our thinking (biblical worldview), our actions (Christlike), and help us make disciples of those who are reasonable. (Ps. 1:2; 40:8; Matt. 13; 28:19-20) Therefore, we need to cultivate attentiveness when we study on our own as well.

Interruptions are controllable. We can turn off our home phone and cell phone. We can turn off the radio. Then again, it could be that we seem to have a short attention span. We may prepare to study highly excited, but within a few minutes, we may lose our focus, daydreaming or worrying about life's troubles. How can we "pay much closer attention"?

We can do this by having foresight. If we know that we have a short attention span, prepare to cope with such. We can set up a schedule, i.e., set a specific time for each day, one that is less likely to be interrupted. In other words, do not look for a time each day, but rather, have a time each day and do not allow anything to interrupt, except a family emergency. Make sure all family and friends know your seriousness about not being interrupted. Give them examples of things they may interrupt and examples of things for which they may not. (Eph. 5:15-16) If we are morning persons, we may get up before others do. If we are not, or that is impossible, the evening may be best. (John 17:3) We should not neglect a consistent regular study of God's Word, especially if we hope to be effective apologists, and evangelists. For this reason, we need to make a schedule and stick to it.

Meditating is emptying the mind of thoughts (i.e., distractions) to concentrate the mind on one thing to aid mental or spiritual growth. It is the process of thinking about something carefully, calmly, seriously, and for some time to arrive at God's thoughts, not man's thoughts. It will help us apply God's Word in our lives correctly and in a balanced manner. (Jam. 1:22-25) It will help us to draw closer to God as we reflect on his Word. Thus, our focus should be on what the author meant by what he penned, and how this is applicable to my life.

In addition, as an apologist, we are always looking at how we can use Scriptures to reach the heart of others. We want to pause when we come to the text, which seems to be the answer to a question we have read or may have heard. We will want to take some time digging through the Bible study tools, to find out if it is the answer. One thing we do not wish to do is to misinterpret and misapply a verse. There is nothing more humiliating than to reference the text to a Bible critic. He says something like, "that verse does not mean that you are using it out of context. If you look at the historical setting, it means …" Yes, Bible critics are quite well informed and can grasp Scripture well. While we 'study to be approved,' they study to disprove. Generally, we do not waste our time with Bible critics who do not have receptive hearts. However, there may be a time when the conversation is in a public forum or in public, and failing to answer, leaves the impression the Bible critic is correct. This does not mean that we must always have a response. We can simply say, "I must humbly admit, I do not know, but I will study it out and give you an answer if you are genuinely interested."

Review Questions

(1) What illustration makes a point of how distractions can cause a disaster?

(2) What counsel did the apostle Paul give the Hebrew Christians, and why was it beneficial and timely?

(3) Why were some of the Jewish Christians tempted to return to Judaism?

(4) Why was the worship implemented by Jesus superior to that of the Mosaic Law?

(5) What situation on the horizon made it vitally important that the first-century Christians 'pay much closer attention to what they had heard, lest they drift away'?

(6) When Paul penned the letter to the Hebrews, how long was it before the destruction of Jerusalem?

(7) Why is it just as vitally important that Christians today 'pay much closer attention to what they are hearing, lest they drift away'?

(8) What can we do to show that we are cultivating attentiveness to spiritual matters?

(9) How is God's Word like a lamp to our feet and light to our path?

(10) Why can paying attention to our Christian services be difficult at times?

(11) What can we do to improve our being able to pay attention?

(12) What is it that truly makes a Christian meeting successful?

(13) How do personal Bible study and meditation benefit us?

(14) How can we make the most out of our personal Bible study time?

(15) What is meditation, and how does it help us?

(16) What can we do to improve our attentiveness in our personal Bible study?

(17) What does the Holy Spirit need to call things back to our minds?

(18) In summary, what do we need to do to become an effective evangelists, apologist, and help us draw closer to God?

CHAPTER 2 Seeking and Searching the Word of God

Proverbs 2:1-5 Updated American Standard Version (UASV)

2 My son, if **you** receive **my words**[64]
  and treasure up my commandments with you,
2 making **your** ear attentive to wisdom
  and inclining your heart to discernment;[65]
3 For if **you** cry for discernment[66]
  and raise **your** voice for understanding,
4 if **you** seek it like silver
  and search for it as for hidden treasures,
5 then **you** will understand the fear of Jehovah
  and find the knowledge of God.
6 For Jehovah gives wisdom;
  from his mouth come knowledge and understanding;

After reading verses 1-5 of chapter 2, one can clearly see that it is their responsibility to acquire wisdom. *You* or *your* is found eleven times in these first five verses. Each of us is obligated to incline our ear, apply our heart, cry out for, lift our voice, seek, search for wisdom, and then we will understand the fear of Jehovah, the beginning of wisdom, and the knowledge of God we will find. All of this is found in God's Word.

What exactly is wisdom, though? It is the ability to make sensible decisions and judgments based on knowledge and experience; wisdom is sensibly applied knowledge. The genre of wisdom literature is found all throughout the Bible but especially in the book of Job, Psalms, Proverbs, Ecclesiastes, and Song of Solomon. However, Wisdom is found in all of the genres of Scripture, even the life lessons within the narrative accounts. Indeed, we learn a valuable lesson from the account of King David, one of the ancestors of Jesus Christ. He had an extremely close relationship with God, yet we find him committing adultery with Bathsheba and then having

---

[64] "2:1 **my words**. Solomon has embraced God's law and made it his own by faith and obedience, as well as teaching. The wisdom of these words is available to those who, first of all, understand the rich value ("treasure") that wisdom possesses. Appropriating wisdom begins when a person values it above all else." — MacArthur, John (2005-05-09). *The MacArthur Bible Commentary* (Kindle Locations 24768-24770). Thomas Nelson. Kindle Edition.

[65] The Hebrew word rendered here as "discernment" (*tevunah*) is related to the word *binah*, translated "understanding." Both appear at Proverbs 2:3.

[66] See 2.2 ftn.

her husband Uriah murdered. Does this account not teach us that we all are susceptible to stumbling in our walk with God and that innocent appearing situations are to be avoided? A mere walk on his rooftop, and David sees Bathsheba bathing below, to which he could have turned away, but he continued to look and entertain inappropriate thoughts. We can learn from every word of Scripture.

Romans 15:4 Updated American Standard Version (UASV)

⁴ For whatever was written in former days was written for our instruction, that through endurance and through the encouragement of the Scriptures we might have hope.

1 Corinthians 10:11 Updated American Standard Version (UASV)

¹¹ Now these things happened to them as an example, but they were written down for our instruction, on whom the end of the ages has come.

Suppose we are going to become wise truly. In that case, we must understand that even the wisest imperfect man, who ever lived, King Solomon, the man who wrote the book of Proverbs, stumbled in apostasy in the latter parts of his life by not following his own God-inspired counsel. If we are to be wise, we also need to have understanding, and the ability to grasp parts of the bigger picture. We also need to acquire discernment, the ability to distinguish those parts one from the others. This would mean that David and his son Solomon would have been able to distinguish right from wrong and avoid the obstacle that got in their way. David might have looked over his rooftop that night, where he saw Bathsheba's beautiful nude body as he bathed in her tub. Wisely he would have turned from the scene, heart beating, and then he could have spoken out loud, rational self-talk, as he paced his roof, telling himself the possible outcomes of what he may have been thinking. Then, he could have chosen the right course of removing himself from the roof.

Psalm 119:27 Updated American Standard Version (UASV)

²⁷ **Make me understand** the way of your precepts,
so I will meditate on your wondrous works.

119:27 Make me understand. Philip asked the Ethiopian eunuch who was reading Isaiah 53, "Do you understand what you are reading?" (Acts 8:30). The psalmist understood God to be the best source of instruction (cf. vv. 34, 73, 100, 125, 144, 169).[67]

Psalm 119:100 Updated American Standard Version (UASV)

100 I understand more than the aged,[68]
for I keep your instructions.[69]

Psalm 119:104 Updated American Standard Version (UASV)

104 From your instructions I get understanding;
therefore I hate every false way.

True Christians should undeviatingly proclaim the Kingdom of God by Christ as the one and only hope of mankind, instead of any nation on earth, including the United States. There is nothing wrong with being a patriot, but one must realize there is but one kingdom of God. At present, the governing authorities are but a tool used to maintain control until the real King returns.

Psalm 119:130 Updated American Standard Version (UASV)

130 The unfolding of your words gives light;
it gives understanding to the simple.

> **119:130 light . . . understanding**. This refers to illumination in comprehending the meaning of Scripture.[70]

We want to have a part in the outworking of God's will and purposes, so we need to pray that he makes us understand his Word so that we fully grasp it. As we begin to understand things, this means that we will have faith in what we have come to know, so we will start to apply what we know. We will actually begin to love the things that he loves and hate what he hates. There are no written works in the history of man for which we can compare it to the Word of God. Even if we are young, we too can acquire wisdom, understanding, and discernment. Some have sorely

---

[67] MacArthur, John (2005-05-09). *The MacArthur Bible Commentary* (Kindle Locations 23993-23995). Thomas Nelson. Kindle Edition.

[68] IBID., 119:98–100 The wisdom of God always far surpasses the wisdom of man.

[69] **Instructions**: (Heb. *piqqudim*) This Hebrew noun means instructions, precepts, directions, procedures, regulation, i.e., a principle or rule concerning the personal conduct that is to be obeyed within a community.– Ps 19:9; 103:18; 111:7; 119:4, 15, 27, 40, 45, 56, 63, 69, 78, 87, 93-94, 100, 104, 110, 128, 134, 141, 159, 168, 173+

[70] MacArthur, John (2005-05-09). *The MacArthur Bible Commentary* (Kindle Locations 24026-24027). Thomas Nelson. Kindle Edition.

misunderstood the role of the Holy Spirit as to its role in our understanding of Scripture. Some believe that the Holy Spirit miraculously gives them understanding as they read the Bible. Bible Apologist Norman L. Geisler wrote, "I also believe that the role of the Holy Spirit, at least in His special work on believers related to Scripture, is in illuminating our understanding of the significance (not the meaning) of the text. The meaning is clear apart from any special work of the Holy Spirit."

In other words, we are blessed by the Holy Spirit by diving into the Spirit-inspired Word through Bible Study. The more you wish to understand, the deeper things of God, the deeper you dig. However, merely acquiring head knowledge will not be enough. We need to deeply ponder the information we take into our minds to get it down to our heart, the seat of motivation. Yes, we need to meditatively how we can use the information we are discovering through our studies. We need to consider real-life situations where we might use what we know. Every word of the Bible can be used to:

(1) build up our faith or the faith of another,

(2) defend the truth or the Word of God,

(3) save ourselves or another that has begun to doubt,

(4) help us or another pass by something that may have been foolish,

(5) help us or another to take the right course, and on and on.

We Need Solid Food

However, once you understand the "knowledge of God," you must then apply that knowledge in a correct and balanced manner. Paul said Jesus "became the source of eternal salvation to all who obey him." However, take note of those words: "to all who obey him." How can you obey if you do not understand Scripture correctly? What did Paul say to young Timothy? He said, "From childhood you have been acquainted with the sacred writings, which are able to make you wise for salvation through faith in Christ Jesus." (2 Timothy 3:15)

Timothy's faith was grounded in truths, reason, understanding, and trust. It is based on "the knowledge of God." Timothy came to know and understand why Jesus had to offer himself as a ransom and what it resulted in, as all of humanity now has an opportunity at eternal life. Knowledge of God's Word applied results in faith in the things heard. The Bible is the

Book that will build this faith, as it is "living and active, sharper than any two-edged sword, piercing to the division of soul and of spirit, of joints and of marrow, and discerning the thoughts and intentions of the heart." (Hebrews 4:12)

Now, here comes the question that has some confusion. Why are there 41,000 different Christian denominations if the Bible is so powerful? Why is there so much division? Why are so many Christians suffering spiritual shipwreck? It is because of biblical illiteracy. Over 90 percent of Christianity are biblically illiterate. Many pastors do not know how to turn this around because they are actually the ones dumbing the church members down. What I am about to say will hurt the feelings of some and anger others, but it must be told.

True Christians love Christ and will do what is expected of them. We are not looking for imitation Christians, and the churches are full of them, ones looking for a social club to be a part of but are not committed to obeying the Word of God to the greatest extent possible. There is no real Bible education in the churches, as most Bible study classes are studying out of a feel-good booklet written on a sixth-grade level. The church members are not educated in the Bible, about the Bible, or the doctrine of the faith. They are not trained evangelists because most churches believe that their members are not intelligent enough, nor will they buy out the time.

However, the truth is, the Christians that we are looking for are those who will, like Jesus and the apostles, and other first century Christians, will take in knowledge of God's Word and buy out time to understand its true meaning. Then, they will apply that Word as they are taught to be evangelists in their own communities, taking the great commission as serious as the pastor does. (Matt 28:19-20) They will transform their lives as they correctly apply God's Word. Yes, they are 'transformed by the renewal of their mind, that by testing they may discern God's will, what is good and acceptable and perfect.' (Rom 12:2) These one's faith would grow strong, their course would be wise, and if they actually had the knowledge of God and acted on it correctly, they would be 'doing the will of God and abiding forever.' (1 John 2:17) Such faith and knowledge are being withheld from these true Christians, as pastors have low expectations because they are so busy pleasing the world and are merely imitation Christians who keep the core flock as spiritual babes.

Warning Against Immaturity

Hebrews 5:11-6:1 Updated American Standard Version (UASV)

¹¹ Concerning whom we have much to say, and it is hard to explain, since you have become dull of hearing.⁷¹ ¹² For in view of the time you ought to be teachers, you have need again for someone to teach you from the beginning the elementary things of the sayings⁷² of God, and you have come to need milk and not solid food. ¹³ For everyone who partakes of milk is unacquainted with the word of righteousness, for he is an infant. ¹⁴ But solid food belongs to the mature, to those who through practice have their discernment trained to distinguish between good and evil.

6 Therefore, leaving behind the elementary doctrine about the Christ, let us press on to maturity, not laying again a foundation of repentance from dead works and faith in God,

True faith and knowledge come from God's Word. We simply need our pastors to preach and teach, raising the bar of expectations so the true Christians can remain while the imitation Christians can be sifted out. True, some Christians will be sifted out because they will not loyally submit to God's Word nor God's pastor (Heb. 13:17) if the bar of expectation is raised. However, many true Christians will prove obedient to God's Word and be submissive to the pastor taking the lead in the congregation.

How many years have we been serving God? What has been our spiritual growth over those years? Are we still drinking the milk (basic truths), or have we moved on to the meat (the deeper things)? Are we able to use the Bible, logic, and reasoning to defend the Word of God? What about the faith? Can we defend it? Can we use Scripture for someone who has begun to doubt? Are we proficient in using Scripture to evangelize workmates, family, friends, and our community?

Paul said, "**solid food is for the mature**, for those who have their powers of discernment trained by constant practice to distinguish good from evil." In other words, if we are regularly taking in biblical knowledge,

---

⁷¹ **Hearing, Dull of:** (Gr. *Nōthros tais akoais*) This is an idiom, which literally means that one has 'lazy ears.' In other words, they are slow to learn, to understand, to react, lacking intellectual perception, with the implication that this is so because they are lazy. Have we become lethargic in the truth, to the point of having lazy ears? Are we slow to learn, to understand, to react, lacking intellectual perception?–Heb. 5:11.

⁷² **Sayings:** (Gr. *logia, on* [only in the plural]) A saying or message, usually short, especially divine, gathered into a collection.–Acts 7:38; Romans 3:2; Hebrews 5:12; 1 Peter 4:11.

and in turn, we also regularly use that knowledge to make decisions between good and bad, our discerning abilities will be trained to the point of being mature in the faith. We will have the natural inclination to make everyday life decisions based on our biblical worldview, our mind of Christ. (1 Cor. 2:16) We will be able to see what is healthy and what is hurtful morally and spiritually, not to mention physically. By regularly taking in the Word of God and applying that word correctly, they will **no longer be** "unskilled in the word of righteousness."

Regularly Feeding on God's Word

If we have truly given ourselves over to God, we should be moved to take in knowledge of his Word. As we draw closer, our love should move us to want to be better acquainted with the deeper things found in the Bible, helping us better understand him, as well as his will and purposes. This involves deep study and reflection. (Ps.1:1-2; 119:97) Our motivation should not be based on what we can gain from our relationship with God, but rather our "searching the Scriptures" should be driven by love for him and our love of neighbor. (John 5:39-42; Psalm 143:10; Matthew 27:37-40)

Spiritual Health

1. **Proper incentive:** Improve our desire to so as to be better acquainted with God and his Word

2. **Regular Bible Study:** Take advantage of the hundreds of thousands of study tools that we are provided.

3. **Correct Application:** Use the Bible knowledge to help others, such as evangelizing in our own community.

It would be nearly impossible to share the amount of spiritual food available to the Christian today. Bible scholarship has covered every conceivable subject one could want to understand better. We should take advantage of the banquet that has been set before us. We need to find some time to study each day of the week. We should offer a word of caution here, though as not all books are created equal. As conservative Christians, who care deeply about the inerrancy of Scripture, the trustworthiness of the Bible, and the authority of Scripture, we need to look at the Bible scholar's credentials before buying his books. We have far more liberal scholars out there publishing books as well. Once we have added a name that can be trusted, we know any book he pens can generally be trusted.

Three things will help us to grow and maintain our spirituality: (1) proper incentive, (2) regular Bible study, (3) and correct application. These three points will help us see the need to consider the deeper things of God's Word, and it will also help us appreciate the need for having a regular study schedule.

Enjoy You Study

We all love to relax with a good novel, one that is a page-turner. When we get our hands on a good one, hours can pass without our even noticing it. When we come to the point where we begin a Bible study session, and time moves by without our noticing it, it has then become joy. Yes, it is true that productive Bible study requires effort on our part. However, as the saying goes, 'love what you do, and you will never work a day in your life.' If our studies are satisfying and rewarding, they will bring us unimaginable joy and pleasure. Let me offer two examples.

First, there will come a time when we will be witnessing to someone informally, and as we talk, they ask a question, we give answers straight from the Scriptures, and we will see the lights going off in their head (they suddenly understand), and the smile on their face, this will warm our heart. This will be a motivating factor like no other. Second, there will come a time when we will be witnessing to a skeptic, and we find ourselves quite easily overcoming his argument, overturning his false reasoning. This too, will prove to be a great motivator.

If we are going to accomplish tasks like the two above and even more, we must be willing to invest the time needed. The word "study" suggests continued focused attentiveness. When we sit down to study, are we actually studying, or do we find ourselves skimming through the study material? If this is the case, we need to allow sufficient time to consider our material more thoroughly. (Eph. 5:15-17) We might have to take time away from other activities, such as television, movies, social media, and the like. Another surprise that will await us is in improving how we study. Once we find a rhythm and effective way of going about our studies, we will accomplish in one hour what might have taken three before. Lastly, prayer is paramount. We need to open and close our studies with meaningful prayer, asking that our minds and heart be receptive to the material that we are about to cover. (James 1:5-7)

Deeper Studies

Proverbs 2:4-5 Updated American Standard Version (UASV)

⁴ if you seek it like silver
  and search for it as for hidden treasures,
⁵ then you will understand the fear of Jehovah
  and find the knowledge of God.

Verses 1-3 show that it is us who must seek out God's words, "commandments, "wisdom," "understanding," and "insight." If we have watched an old western movie, we know that to search for treasures was no easy task, and it called for much digging with a pickaxe and a shovel. The same is true for the Word of God if we are to find "the knowledge of God." We must dig into the Word of God to discover the gems of truth lying deep beneath word studies, Bible backgrounds, grammar and syntax, historical setting, and the like. We will not find the big nuggets of truth by just skimming the surface of the gold mine.

The Psalmist wrote, "How great are your works, O Lord! Your thoughts are very deep!" (Ps. 92:5) The apostle Paul wrote, "Oh, the depth of the riches and wisdom and knowledge of God! How unsearchable are his judgments and how inscrutable his ways!" (Rom. 11:33) He was not suggesting that it was impossible to discover truths about God, but it will take effort on our part. Paul also wrote, "These things God has revealed to us through the Spirit. For the Spirit searches everything, even the depths of God." (1 Cor. 2:10) Keep in mind that the Bible is inspired (literally, "God-breathed"), and those who penned it was moved along by Holy Spirit. The apostle Peter had this to say about Paul's letters, "As he does in all his letters when he speaks in them of these matters. There are some things in them that are hard to understand, which the ignorant and unstable twist to their own destruction." (2 Pet. 3:15-16) We should be truly grateful for all the study tools that we have, which make digging in God's Word so much easier.

Why do We Study?

We do not acquire the knowledge of God in order to feel superior to those who do not have it. We do not use our knowledge to beat others down or to win a biblical fight. Paul's words remind us to be cautious, "'knowledge' puffs up, but love builds up." (1 Cor. 8:1) We want to use our knowledge to draw closer to God, proclaim the Word to others, teach them, and make disciples. We also want to defend the Word of God against attacks from the enemy and defend the faith. Moreover, we want to use our knowledge to save those who have begun to doubt. We want to use our understanding of Scripture to offer comfort to our neighbors, especially our brothers and sisters in the faith.

Ephesians 4:13-16 Updated American Standard Version (UASV)

¹³ until we all attain to the unity of the faith, and of the accurate knowledge[73] of the Son of God, to a mature man, to the measure of the stature which belongs to the fullness of Christ. ¹⁴ So that we may no longer be children, tossed to and fro by the waves and carried about by every wind of teaching, by the trickery of men, by craftiness with regard to the scheming of deceit; ¹⁵ but speaking the truth in love, we are to grow up in all aspects into him who is the head, Christ, ¹⁶ from whom the whole body, joined together and held together by every supporting ligament, according to the working by measure of each individual part, causes the growth of the body for the building up of itself in love.

4:13. Diverse gifts create and build up one body in unity. This unity is in faith and knowledge of Christ. Christ does not try to build up superstars in his kingdom with superior faith or superior knowledge. He tries to build up a church unified in its faith and knowledge, each member being built up to maturity. All are to reach the **fullness of Christ**. The church's goal is that each member and thus the entire church will show to the world all the attributes and qualities of Christ. Then the church will truly be the one body of Christ.

4:14–16. The result of these spiritually gifted people's equipping the saints is that believers are not to be like children, easily persuaded and confused, jumping from one opinion or belief to the next, like **waves** on the sea being driven by gusting winds of false **teaching**. Rather, the believers are to speaking the truth in love. Speaking the truth in love is a mark of maturity, which will enable us to grow up spiritually. Immature people often fall into one of two opposite errors. They speak the truth, but without love, or they love without speaking the truth. When we do the first, we often brutalize others, pounding them with truth but doing it in an unloving way. When we do the second, we don't tell others the truth, thinking that by shielding them from the truth we are sparing them from

---

[73] *Epignosis* is a strengthened or intensified form of *gnosis* (*epi,* meaning "additional"), meaning, "true," "real," "full," "complete" or "accurate," depending upon the context. Paul and Peter alone use *epignosis.*

pain. We are not, however. All we are doing is delaying their maturation. To share the truth with our fellow believers is a mark of maturity, but to do it with love, with understanding, with compassion. From Christ the whole body is gifted, and as each one uses his gift for the benefit of others, the whole body matures. We must recognize that we belong to one another, we need one another, no matter how insignificant we think our contribution is. There are no little people in the kingdom of God, as Francis Shaeffer used to say, and there are no little jobs. Just as a physical body needs red corpuscles and livers more than it needs a handsome face or beautiful hair, so we all belong; we are all necessary. We all can contribute, and when we do, we all grow to maturity in Christ.

4:14. The Ephesian church, as most of the churches Paul wrote, faced teachers with opposing viewpoints. They divided the church body into factions, each opposing the others. Their presence required the type of spiritual maturity and church unity Paul had described. Without such unity the church would act like a group of babies, each crying out because of his own pains and needs, each inconsistently saying one thing and then another, each at the mercy of cunning, deceitful teachers. To avoid infantile behavior, the church must mature into unity of the faith and of knowledge of Christ.

4:15. Such maturity involves teaching the truth in love. False teachers showed no love or care for the members; they simply wanted to get their own way. Mature believers search for the truth as a united body, loving and caring for the needs of each member. Such loving, caring search for truth allows them to grow as members of the body whose head is Christ, for Christ is the truth.

4:16. The head allows each part of the body to mature and grow, not concentrating on special knowledge and growth for a favored few. Each of the parts of the body is needed to hold the whole body together in unity. The body is truly a maturing, loving body only as each part is encouraged to grow and do its part of the work.[74]

Hebrews 6:1 Updated American Standard Version (UASV)

6 Therefore, leaving behind the elementary doctrine about the Christ, let us press on to maturity, not laying again a foundation of repentance from dead works and faith in God,

---

[74] Max Anders, *Galatians-Colossians*, vol. 8, Holman New Testament Commentary (Nashville, TN: Broadman & Holman Publishers, 1999), 152–153.

We need to continue in our diligent study of God's Word; assured that by God's loving kindness we can continue to grow in our Christian maturity. Achieving Christian maturity does not necessarily take many years. It is true that we should buy out the time spent in study, we need to make sure that the knowledge contributes to our depth of heart devotion to God and appreciation for his "word of righteousness." We need to be humble, teachable, and anxious to make progress.

Review Questions

(1) Where can we find the true source of happiness? Explain.
(2) What did the apostle Paul say about some Christians in Corinth and Judea?
(3) What do we find to be true of some Christians today?
(4) What has been the case with some Christians who have been in the faith for years? What advice does Paul offer them?
(5) Look at Hebrews 5:14, for who is "sold food" for, and how can a Christian become such?
(6) What happens if a Christian simply stays on a "milk" diet when it comes to Bible study?
(7) What should motivate us to want to study the deeper things and increase our Bible knowledge?
(8) What questions should we ask ourselves when it comes to our sitting down to study God's Word?
(9) What is the difference between reading the Bible or a book and studying the Bible or a book?
(10) What can we do to find more joy in our personal studies?
(11) What three things do we need in order to achieve spiritual health?
(12) Who must seek out God's words, "commandments, "wisdom," "understanding," and "insight"?
(13) Why do we study?
(14) Why should we be cautious as we grow in knowledge?

CHAPTER 3 Being Prepared to Make a Defense

1 Peter 3:15 Updated American Standard Version (UASV)

¹⁵ but sanctify Christ as Lord in your hearts, always being prepared to make a defense[75] to anyone who asks you for a reason for the hope that is in you; yet do it with gentleness and respect;

To whom was the apostle Peter talking? Who was Peter saying needed always to be prepared to make a defense? Was he speaking only to the pastors, elders, and servants or all Christians? Peter opens this letter by saying, "to the chosen who are residing temporarily in the dispersion in Pontus, Galatia, Cappadocia, Asia, and Bithynia." Who are these "chosen" ones? The College Press NIV Commentary gives us the answer,

> The Greek text does not include the word "God's," but the translation is a fair one since the clear implication is that God did the choosing. The word Peter uses has a rich biblical heritage. The Jews found their identity and the basis of their lives in the fact that they were God's chosen people (see, e.g., Deut 7:6–8). The New Testament frequently identifies Christians as elect or chosen. In 1 Peter 2:9 Peter will identify Christians as "a chosen people," using the same word ἐκλεκτός (*eklektos*) here translated "elect." The same word is also used of Christ in 2:4 and 6 (where it is translated "chosen"). Christians are chosen or elect through the chosen or elect One, Jesus Christ. The idea that Christians are God's chosen people is fundamental to Peter's thinking, as is apparent in 1:13–2:10. Peter is already laying the foundation for his appeals to these Christians to live up to their holy calling. (Black and Black 1998)

The "chosen who are residing temporarily in the dispersion" were Christians, who were living among **non**-Christian Jews and Gentiles. This letter, then, is addressed to all Christians, but the context of chapters 1:3 to 4:11 is mostly addressed to newly baptized Christians. Therefore, all Christians are obligated to 'be prepared to make a defense to anyone who asks us for a reason for the hope that is in us.' Yes, we are all required to

---

[75] Or *argument*; or *explanation*

defend our hope successfully. If any have not felt they were up to the task, this author, by way of Christian publishing House is publishing books to help along those lines. Here is what is available at present. Those readers who wish to go a little further than the threshold of Apologetics may be glad of some hints on what to read.

THE HOLY BIBLE: Updated American Standard Version (UASV) by Christian Publishing House (Author), Edward Andrews (Chief Editor) (https://www.amazon.com/dp/B09RZDVS2D)

BIBLE STUDY TOOL: Appendices to the Updated American Standard Version by Edward D. Andrews **ISBN-13**: 978-1949586602

(https://www.amazon.com/dp/B09T3R3795)

CHRISTIAN APOLOGETICS [Annotated]: Christianity Defended with Responses to Doubts about the Christian faith by A. B. Bruce (https://www.amazon.com/dp/B0B2SG8D3P) **ISBN-13**: 9798833042045

THE YOUNG CHRISTIAN'S SURVIVAL GUIDE: Common Questions Young Christians Are Asked about God, the Bible, and the Christian Faith Answered by Donald Williams **ISBN-13**: 978-1949586893 (https://www.amazon.com/dp/B07VFR66Z4)

BIBLE DIFFICULTIES: How to Approach Difficulties In the Bible by Edward D. Andrews **ISBN-13**: 979-8611089118

EVIDENCE FOR THE HISTORICAL JESUS: Is the Jesus of History the Christ of Faith by Gary Habermas **ISBN-13**: 978-1949586671 (https://www.amazon.com/dp/B08P9JD6J7)

HOW RELIABLE ARE THE GOSPELS?: The Synoptic Gospels in the Ancient Church: The Testimony to the Priority of the Gospel of Matthew by F. David Farnell **ISBN-13**: 978-1949586657

(https://www.amazon.com/dp/B07KG8SQG9)

FROM SPOKEN WORDS TO SACRED TEXTS: Introduction-Intermediate New Testament Textual Studies by Edward D. Andrews **ISBN-13**: 978-1949586985 (https://www.amazon.com/dp/1949586987)

REASONING WITH THE WORLD'S VARIOUS RELIGIONS Examining and Evangelizing Other Faiths by Edward Andrews **ISBN-13**: (978-1945757815 https://www.amazon.com/dp/B07B44G924)

JEHOVAH'S WITNESSES 101: How Can You Share Your Faith When the Jehovah's Witnesses Come Knocking? By Edward D. Andrews **ISBN-13**: 979-8830002073 (https://www.amazon.com/dp/B0B1P6YQS3)

CONVERSATIONAL EVANGELISM: Defending the Faith, Reasoning from the Scriptures, Explaining and Proving, Instructing in Sound Doctrine, and Overturning False Reasoning by Edward Andrews **ISBN-13**: 978-1945757372 (https://www.amazon.com/dp/B01N7OQY16)

THE EVANGELISM HANDBOOK: How All Christians Can Effectively Share God's Word in Their Community by Edward Andrews **ISBN-13**: 978-1945757389

(https://www.amazon.com/dp/B01N7PWS3R)

CHRISTIAN APOLOGETICS: Christianity Defended with Responses to Doubts about the Christian faith by A. B. Bruce **ISBN-13**: 979-8833042045 (https://www.amazon.com/dp/B0B2TK4VFY)

THE EVANGELISM HANDBOOK: How All Christians Can Effectively Share God's Word in Their Community by Edward Andrews **ISBN-13**: 978-1945757389

(https://www.amazon.com/dp/B01N7PWS3R)

JESUS CHRIST: The Great Teacher by Edward Andrews **ISBN-13**: 978-1949586831 (https://www.amazon.com/dp/B07NRN1MBM)

THE TEACHER THE APOSTLE PAUL: What Made the Apostle Paul's Teaching, Preaching, Evangelism, and Apologetics Outstanding Effective? by Edward D. Andrews **ISBN-13**: 978-1949586039

(https://www.amazon.com/dp/1949586030)

REVIEWING 2013 New World Translation of Jehovah's Witnesses: Examining the History of the Watchtower Translation and the Latest Revision by Edward Andrews **ISBN-13**: 978-1945757785

(https://www.amazon.com/dp/B079DGQF5D)

INVESTIGATING JEHOVAH'S WITNESSES: Why 1914 Is Important to Jehovah's Witnesses by Edward Andrews **ISBN-13**: 978-1945757518

(https://www.amazon.com/dp/B073PJNX15)

FIRST TIMOTHY 2:12: What Does the Bible Really Say About Women Pastors/Preachers? by Edward Andrews **ISBN-13**: 978-1949586947

(https://www.amazon.com/dp/B07X971GK7)

THE 1946 PROJECT: The Supposed Mistranslation of "Homosexual" In 1 Corinthians 6:9 by Edward D. Andrews **ISBN-13**: 978-1949586619

(https://www.amazon.com/dp/1949586618)

FEMINIST CRITICISM: What is Biblical Feminism? by Dianna Newman **ISBN-13**: 978-1688658592

(https://www.amazon.com/dp/1688658599)

DEFENDING EVANGELICALISM: The Apologetics of Norman L. Geisler by William C. Roach **ISBN-13**: 978-1949586145

(https://www.amazon.com/dp/1949586146)

CALVINISM VS. ARMINIANISM: The Bible Answers by Edward D. Andrews **ISBN-13**: 978-1949586992

(https://www.amazon.com/dp/1949586995)

INERRANCY OF SCRIPTURE: How Can We Believe Inerrancy of Scripture In the Originals When We Don't Have the Originals? by Edward Andrews **ISBN-13**: 978-1949586121

(https://www.amazon.com/dp/B08FSXNXNR)

THE NEW TESTAMENT DOCUMENTS: Can They Be Trusted? by Edward D. Andrews **ISBN-13**: 978-1949586091

(https://www.amazon.com/dp/194958609X)

IS THE GIFT OF PROPHECY FOR TODAY?: Why Is It Urgent That We Understand New Testament Prophecy? by F. David Farnell **ISBN-13**: 978-1949586732

(https://www.amazon.com/dp/1949586731)

THE GUIDE TO ANSWERING ISLAM: What Every Christian Needs to Know About Islam and the Rise of Radical Islam by Daniel Janosik **ISBN-13**: 978-1949586763

(https://www.amazon.com/dp/B07N5F82DD)

UNDERSTANDING ISLAM AND TERRORISM: A Biblical Point of View by Kerby Anderson **ISBN-13**: 978-1945757617

(https://www.amazon.com/dp/B075HGTSR8)

IS THE QURAN THE WORD OF GOD?: Is Islam the One True Faith? by Edward Andrews **ISBN-13**: 978-1945757495

(https://www.amazon.com/dp/B073DNM5GC)

DEFENDING THE CHRISTIAN FAITH [Annotated]: The Testimony of Reason by Samuel L. Phillips **ISBN-13**: 979-8833544426

(https://www.amazon.com/dp/B0B32266XT)

DEFENDING CHRISTIANITY: A Handbook of Christian Apologetics by Alfred Ernest Garvie **ISBN-13**: 979-8834274988

(https://www.amazon.com/dp/B0B2TW68RG)

APOLOGETICS Annotated: A Treatise on Christian Evidences by Ezekiel Boring Kephart **ISBN-13**: 9798835032310

These first-century Christians in Asia Minor were in a time of difficulty. At the time of Peter's letter, they were about 62-64 C.E. going through some trials, not knowing that many far more severe lie in the not too distant future. Within a few years, the persecution of Christians by Emperor Nero would begin. These new converts had given up former religions, idols, cults, and superstitions, their 'the futile ways inherited from your forefathers.' (1 Pet. 1:18) These ones were taking off their old person and bringing their lives in harmony with God's Word, such as 'malice and deceit and hypocrisy and envy and slander.' (1 Pet. 2:1) Now they were 'no longer living for the lusts of men, but for the will of God.' (1 Pet. 4:2) Their former pagan friends now hated these new Christians because 'they were surprised when these chosen ones do not join them in the same flood of debauchery, and they maligned them.' (1 Pet. 4:4) In fact, Peter informs us that Satan, the Devil, is enraged when one is converted from their former life of debauchery and conformed instead to the Word of God. Peter warned them, "Be sober-minded; be watchful. Your adversary the devil prowls around like a roaring lion, seeking someone to devour." (1 Peter 5:8)

Christians have never really had it easy to defend their hope. Peter counsels these new ones, who have next to no experience in coping with trials and persecutions, to rejoice, albeit distressed by numerous trials. "**Keep your conduct among the Gentiles honorable**, so that when they speak against you as evildoers, they may see your good deeds and glorify God on the day of visitation." (1 Pet. 2:12) "The end of all things is at hand; therefore **be self-controlled and sober-minded for the sake of your prayers**." 1 Pet. 4:4) "Be sober-minded; be watchful" in the midst of men who continue "living in sensuality, passions, drunkenness, orgies, drinking parties, and lawless idolatry." (1 Pet. 4:3) They should be united under Christ as they 'Have purified their souls by their obedience to the truth for a sincere brotherly love, love one another earnestly from a pure heart." (1 Peter 1:22) "Above all, [they were to] keep loving one another earnestly since love covers a multitude of sins. Show hospitality to one another without grumbling. As each has received a gift, use it to serve one another, as good stewards of God's varied grace." (1 Pet 4:8-10) 'Finally, they all had unity of mind, sympathy, brotherly love, a tender heart, and a humble mind. They did not repay evil for evil or reviling for reviling, but on the contrary, they blessed, for to this they were called, that you may obtain a blessing.' (1 Pet. 3:8-9) If they heeded this counsel, it would have kept them from falling or drifting back into their former ways.

There was one more obligation if they were to preserve on the right path of conduct, namely, being prepared to make a defense for their hope. "It was revealed to [the prophets] that they were serving not themselves but you, in the things that have now been announced to you through those who preached the good news to you by the Holy Spirit sent from heaven, things into which angels long to look. Therefore, preparing your minds for action, and being sober-minded, set your hope fully on the grace that will be brought to you at the revelation of Jesus Christ." (1 Pet. 1:12-13) Peter went on to tell them that they were "a chosen race, a royal priesthood, a holy nation, a people for his own possession, that you may proclaim the excellencies of him who called you out of darkness into his marvelous light." (1 Pet. 2:9) When should they "proclaim these excellencies"? He writes, "but in your hearts honor Christ the Lord as holy, **always being prepared** to make a defense to anyone who asks you for a reason for the hope that is in you; yet do it with gentleness and respect." 1 Peter 3:15

The world in which we live today is much vaster than that of the first century up unto the 21st-century. The trials and persecution today are much more intense, which, unfortunately, we can watch around the world through the media and social media. The greatest threat to Christianity is Islam, which has been an ardent enemy of Christianity since the seventh-century C.E. They are slaughtering Christians the world over. They view Christians as the big Satan and the Jews as little Satan. Their theology is looking to turn the world into one big Islamic state governed by the Quran. For the more radical aspects of Islam, the motto is, 'convert to Islam or be killed as an infidel.'

The second greatest threat to tradition and conservatism is liberal Christianity. Theirs continued dissecting the Scriptures until Moses did not pen the first five books, Isaiah is not the author of the book that bears his name, nor is Daniel the author of the book that bears his name, and the Bible is full of myths and legends, errors and contractions.

Then, there are liberal Bible scholars who are advocates of Historical Criticism Methodology and its sub-criticisms: Source Criticism, Tradition Criticism, Form Criticism, and Redaction Criticism. Here are just ten of the "tip-of-the-iceberg" of the things that these scholars would agree with:

(1) Matthew, not Jesus, Created the Sermon on the Mount.
(2) The commissioning of the Twelve in Matthew 10 is a group of instructions compiled and organized by Matthew, not spoken by Jesus on a single occasion.
(3) The parable accounts of Matthew 13 and Mark 4 are anthologies of parables that Jesus uttered on separate occasions.
(4) Jesus did not preach the Olivet Discourse in its entirety, as found in the gospel accounts.
(5) Jesus gave his teaching on divorce and remarriage without the exception clauses found in Matthew 5:32 and 19:9.
(6) In Matthew 19:16-17, Matthew changed the words of Jesus and the rich man to obtain a different emphasis or to avoid a theological problem involved in the wording of Mark's and Luke's accounts of the same event.
(7) The scribes and the Pharisees were in reality, decent people whom Matthew painted in an entirely negative light because of his personal bias against them.
(8) The genealogies of Jesus in Matthew 1 and Luke 3 are figures of speech and not accurate records of Jesus' physical/and or legal lineage.

(9) According to Matthew 2, the magi who visited the child Jesus after his birth are fictional, not real characters.

(10) Jesus uttered only three or four of the eight or nine beatitudes in Matthew 5:3-12 **The List**: (Thomas and Farnell 1998, 15)

Who needs enemies like Richard Dawkins, Bill Maher, and Jon Stewart when we have liberal Bible scholars, who make up over 80 percent of the seminaries in the United States? It is "our" Bible scholars, who give these atheists, agnostics, and Bible critics their ammo, so they can turn around and shoot us conservative Christians.

Let me say that there are logical and reasonable answers to the things above and any other supposed problem with Scripture. However, in academia today, if you are not dissecting the Scriptures (new hermeneutics), casting doubt on the validity of the bible, you are just some knuckle-dragging Neanderthal. In other words, you are caught in a time **prior to** the enlightenment of secularism, humanism, and any other type of "ism" since the 19th century.

The battle for the Bible is being fought by some outstanding apologists, backed by a generation of layman apologists interested in getting into the fight. They are defenders of God's Word and defenders of the faith. The only mistake they are making right now is they only identify the extreme enemies of God, like Richard Dawkins. Real progress will not be made until they oust the liberal scholars for their attack on God's Word.

A Successful Defense of Our Hope

This hope that we have to be prepared to make a defense of must "be proclaimed throughout the whole world as a testimony to all nations, and then the end will come." (matt. 24:14) Moreover, we must also take it to the point of teaching and making disciples." (Matt. 28:19-20) However, this proclaiming of our hope, teaching, and making disciples must be done effectively and successfully. What is the good if we use our time and vital energy to share biblical truths with our family, friends, coworkers, or in our community if we cannot say the right things when we evangelize? Are we able to offer good reasons, logical reasons, and reasonable reasons for our hopes? While it might be a good thing that we are willing to proclaim, it is sufficient, if we are never able to convince them to accept our teaching, to make them disciples. We want to know the joy of taking an unbeliever from the point of not knowing God or rejecting God to accepting God as they conform themselves to his Word. Like was true of Paul and those he witnessed to, they will become our spiritual children. Let us look at Apollos,

Acts 18:24-28 Updated American Standard Version (UASV)

²⁴ Now a certain Jew named Apollos, a native of Alexandria, an eloquent man, arrived in Ephesus; and **he was** well **versed in the Scriptures.** ²⁵ This man had been orally instructed in the way of the Lord; and being **fervent in spirit**, he was **speaking and teaching accurately** the things concerning Jesus, being **acquainted only with the baptism of John**; ²⁶ and this man began to speak out boldly in the synagogue. But when **Priscilla and Aquila** heard him, they **took him aside and explained to him the way of God more accurately.** ²⁷ And when he wanted to go across to Achaia, the brothers encouraged him and wrote to the disciples to welcome him; and when he had arrived, he greatly helped those who had believed through grace, ²⁸ for **he powerfully refuted the Jews in public**, demonstrating by the Scriptures that Jesus was the Christ.

What do we learn here? Apollos were competent in the Scriptures; he was even fervent in the spirit, but he only knew what John has taught in the beginning. In other words, Apollos was unaware of all that Jesus taught in his three and a half year ministry. He had not seen the Gospel of Matthew. He was unaware all that the apostles and the leading men of Jerusalem taught over the next 20-24 years after Jesus' ascension. In other words, he had not read First and Second Thessalonians or Galatians. Therefore, Priscilla and Aquila took Apollos aside and caught him up to the accurate truth of things of God. This man was such an influential speaker; he thereafter went to Achaia, where he "**powerfully refuted the Jews in public**, showing by the Scriptures that the Christ was Jesus." This is not to suggest that if we spent some time taking in deeper and more accurate knowledge of God, we would be able to overcome all the enemies of God that cross our paths and convert those in our community with a receptive heart. Who knows, maybe we will. However, we do know this for a certainty; while deep Bible study does not guarantee that we will become a modern-day Apollos, shallow study guarantees that we will remain right where we are. Bible study is never truly complete until we have become an evangelist.

We should learn from the account about Apollos twofold: (1) if we are semi-competent in the Scriptures but only know the basics, the foundation, the beginner level, we need to move on to the more accurate, deeper things of God. (2) Like Aquila and Priscilla, all Christian evangelists should be able to teach the truth more fully and more correctly to two different groups. We need to be able to explain the deeper truth correctly to both believers and unbelievers. Why do we need to be able to teach believers? Because, whether we like it or not, 41,000 different denominations call themselves Christian, and they are not all just different paths leading to the same place. Some have, unfortunately, found themselves on the path leading to destruction, and we are in the business of saving eternal lives before the end comes.

18:24. Another Lucan **meanwhile**, this time with the actual word inserted. We need to know what happened in Ephesus before Paul arrived, so Luke breaks into the narrative of Paul's ministry to tell us about a new character, Apollos. A native of Alexandria, he was well-educated and well-versed in the Old Testament text. He had become a Christian evangelist and zealously proclaimed everything he knew about the gospel.

How he came to faith and why he came to Ephesus, Luke does not tell us. Since Luke has repeatedly emphasized God's control over all events related to his people, he probably expects readers to understand Apollos' visit to Ephesus and his encounter with Priscilla and Aquila as very much a part of the divine plan.

18:25. Apollos understood the way of the Lord, spoke with great zeal, and curiously, **taught about Jesus accurately**; yet he only knew about the baptism of John. Presumably, Luke wants us to understand that Apollos' knowledge of the gospel and the messianic truth about Jesus came through disciples of John the Baptist, thereby limiting his understanding to pre-Pentecost Christian theology.

18:26. Like many preachers, what Apollos said was quite true. What he *left out* demonstrated his inadequate understanding of Christian truth. We may assume that he had no idea about the coming of the Holy Spirit, the founding of the church, and certainly the now extensive mission to the Gentiles. Who better to pick up on that deficiency than these stable and mature Christians, Priscilla and Aquila. Together they invited him home, and together they taught him the Word of God. We can only imagine the astonishment and joy with which Apollos received this new information.

18:27–28. Priscilla and Aquila would have been full of stories about the work in Corinth, the decision of Gallio, and the lengthy ministry of Paul in that city. Whatever the motivation, Apollos decided to leave Ephesus, where the ministry seemed clearly to be in capable hands. Carrying letters of recommendation (from Priscilla and Aquila?), he headed for Corinth, where **he was a great help to those who by grace had believed**.

This skilled debater appears again in the early chapters of 1 Corinthians, showing the appreciation of the Corinthian congregation for his ministry. We are not surprised by that, for the constant conflict between Christians and Jews in that city offered a great platform for someone who could eloquently demonstrate messianic Christology from the pages of the Old Testament Scriptures.

Some call Apollos the first Christian apologist, but surely that title must be reserved for Stephen. Others indicate that Apollos may very well have written Hebrews. Though the text of that book may reflect both the content and eloquence evident in this man's public ministry, we have no overt evidence of that authorship.[76]

Colossians 1:9-10 Updated American Standard Version (UASV)

[9] For this reason also, since the day we heard of it, we have not ceased to pray for you and to ask that you may be filled with the accurate knowledge[77] of his will in all spiritual wisdom and understanding, [10] so as to walk in a manner worthy of the Lord, fully pleasing to him bearing fruit in every good work and increasing in the accurate knowledge[78] of God; understanding, [10] so as to walk in a manner worthy of the Lord, fully pleasing to him, bearing fruit in every good work and increasing in the knowledge of God.

If we as Christian evangelists want to be pleasing in the eyes of God, we need to produce some results. The apostle Paul's words to the Corinthians did not just apply to church leadership but all Christians. He wrote, "Now if anyone builds on the foundation with gold, silver, precious stones, wood, hay, straw, each one's work will become manifest, for the

---

[76] Kenneth O. Gangel, *Acts*, vol. 5, Holman New Testament Commentary (Nashville, TN: Broadman & Holman Publishers, 1998), 308–309.

[77] *Epignosis* is a strengthened or intensified form of *gnosis* (*epi*, meaning "additional"), meaning, "true," "real," "full," "complete" or "accurate," depending upon the context. Paul and Peter alone use *epignosis*.

[78] *Epignosis* is a strengthened or intensified form of *gnosis* (*epi*, meaning "additional"), meaning, "true," "real," "full," "complete" or "accurate," depending upon the context. Paul and Peter alone use *epignosis*.

Day will disclose it, because it will be revealed by fire, and the fire will test what sort of work each one has done." (1 Cor. 3:12-13) It is not enough that we use words for witnessing to others. Many words will get us nowhere. Rather, we need words that offer reasonable, logical, good reasons for our hope.

When we evangelize, we cannot allow ourselves to think that 'well, others are better than I am; they will get the work done.' Yes, all of us are in awe of such ones as the late Norman L. Geisler,[79] William Lane Craig,[80] Gary Habermas,[81] John Lennox,[82] and Josh McDowell,[83] to mention just a few.[84] Yes, these ones are exceptional in their evangelism abilities, and their ease of doing things can be a bit intimidating. We might think, 'I could never articulate things like William Lane Craig.' Well, the truth is (1) we will never know until we build on our foundation to see where your skills take us. However, (2) we need not be exactly like them; we use only need to use our potential to the fullest. Lastly, these terrific communicators and much more have penned book after book and produced audios and videos to train us to be a more effective and successful evangelists.

If we want to see out full potential, we must study daily. It may only be one hour a day, but it needs to be daily.[85] Keep in mind, no one is asking us to become a seminary study, just a Bible student. We are obligated to defend the Word and faith, and make disciples of all sorts of men and women. We may be so fortunate one day, to overcome the arguments of an atheist school teacher, or at least lay the groundwork, so another can water what we have planted. In addition, we are neither too old nor too young to get started. It does not matter whether we have a higher education from

---

[79] normangeisler.net.

[80] Reasonable Faith.org

[81] GaryHabermas.com

[82] John Lennox.org

[83] Josh.org

[84] Norm Geisler: normangeisler.com; William Lane Craig: Reasonable Faith.org; J. Warner Wallace: ColdCaseChristianity.com; John Lennox: John Lennox.org; Greg Koukl: STR.org; Paul Copan: PaulCopan.com; Ed Feser: http://edwardfeser.blogspot.com/; Lee Strobel: Lee Strobel.com; Josh McDowell: Josh.org; Discovery Institute (Dembski, Meyer, Richards, Luskin, Wells): www.Discovery.org; C.S. Lewis: CSLewis.org; Gary Habermas: GaryHabermas.com; Timothy McGrew: http://historicalapologetics.org/; Dr. Michael Brown: AskDrBRown.org; Richard Howe: Richardghowe.com; Tim Keller: TimothyKeller.com; J. Budziszewski: Undergroundthomist.org; Hank Hanegraaff: Equip.org; Hugh Ross: Reasons.org; R. C. Sproul: Ligonier.

[85] http://www.biblicaltrainingacademy.com/

some university or we have a high school diploma or a GED.[86] God cannot help us unless we make ourselves available to him. The Holy Spirit cannot draw on an empty or low vessel to enable us to recall how to communicate effectively and successfully with another unless we have first taken in an accurate, correct, full knowledge of God's Word. We need a thorough study of God's Word will, "so that [we] may know how [we] ought to answer each person." Sadly, most times, Christians end up arguing with an unbeliever because they are losing the conversation, which puts them on the defense, a difficult place to be, especially if the other is taking advantage of our inability to answer.

Biblical Defense

The most productive way to defend our hope is by being able to use the Word of God skillfully. Our hope lies in the Scriptures, so we need to be able to defend it with the Scriptures. Paul tells us, "The word of God is living and active, sharper than any two-edged sword, piercing to the division of soul and of spirit, of joints and of marrow, and discerning the thoughts and intentions of the heart." (Heb. 4:12) Thus, the Word of God will convince most interested ones that our hope is genuine. Our ability to communicate efficiently is crucial, but what we communicate is even more important. Like Jesus, our example in this matter, what we say must be grounded in Scripture. When tempted by Satan three times in the wilderness, he responded to each temptation with, "it is written," and then he went on to quote from the Hebrew Old Testament. When asked about a subject, do we have several texts that support our position on it? When someone misinterprets a text, do we know enough to open the Bible and look at the verses before and after to see if they are using it in context? Do we know enough historical settings to see if they are correct? Do we know many of the Scriptures that are commonly misapplied so that we may answer even if we do not have a Bible with us? After we have spoken with someone, he will say, "He showed me straight from the Bible," once he is back with his family or friends.

We need to be able to explain Bible truth correctly and persuasively in a easily understood way. If we do not correctly and fully understand the matter, how are we going to explain it in a simplified manner, so the listener will understand? This means that we must have a comprehensive

---

[86] A GED is a diploma for adults equivalent to a high-school diploma. Full form General Equivalency Diploma.

understanding of Scripture. Can we use the Bible to explain the inerrancy of Scripture, who the Father, Son, and the Holy Spirit is, salvation, angels, Satan and demons, the resurrection hope, and so on? As we go on here, some may be thinking, 'this guy expects me to become a Bible scholar.' Again, we do not expect that any reader has to become a Bible scholar, but a serious Bible student, yes. These things are not that complicated, as the study tools these days are quite easy to understand. Moreover, if taken in small bites, it becomes even easier. We can take just three months, and each week study one of these subjects, and in the end, we will have an in-depth understanding of twelve important issues. We can take it one step further; in that same week, we need to share what we are learning with family and friends. When we read something, it is placed in our short-term memory. When we study something, it is placed in our long-term memory. However, it is reinforced deeply in our long-term memory when we explain something.

If we are going to be a defender of the faith and God's Word, we must be able to refute objections. The good thing is; that we will hear many of the same objections repeatedly. A word of caution, though, we do not want to have refuted the same objections so many times that we become unfeeling in doing so. In other words, we do not want to be on autopilot. The person that we are speaking with does not know that we have refuted this objection a hundred times. We should allow him the satisfaction of feeling that we are emotionally involved in his quest, not being mechanical. If we encounter a new objection, i.e., caught off guard, so to speak, openly admit we have not researched that one, and let him know we will get back with him. Then, go into an in-depth study, so you will not be unprepared for it next time. At first, we will feel like you are doing this all the time. In time, it will just happen on occasion. We can head them off by investing in a book like Norman L. Geisler's Big Book of Bible Difficulties. Another way to get ahead of the objections is to be alert as we carry out our personal Bible study, look for good points to share, or notice what one might use.

If we are going to defend our hope successfully to others, we need more than knowledge. We also need to have tact. Remember, Peter said, "Yet do it with gentleness and respect." (1 Pet. 3:15) We need not shy away from confrontation, i.e., ones who are upset with the current situation. We need rather have empathy for these ones because they have no hope. It can be quite upsetting to get up each morning when one is hopeless. We close this heading with another great example, the apostle Paul, and just how serious he took his obligation as an evangelist,

1 Corinthians 9:16-17 Updated American Standard Version (UASV)

¹⁶ Now if I am proclaiming the good news, it is no reason for me to boast, for necessity is laid upon me. Really, woe to me if I do not proclaim the good news! ¹⁷ For if I do this voluntarily, I have a reward; but if against my will, I have a stewardship entrusted to me.

9:16–17. Paul wanted to continue the practice of preaching without pay. He explained that he could not **boast** simply because he preached the gospel. He insisted, **I am compelled to preach**. In other words, he had no choice. God had called him to preach, and he had to fulfill that obligation or fall under divine judgment.

How did Paul enhance his preaching ministry? He preached **voluntarily** so he might receive **a reward**. Paul frequently spoke of himself and of other Christians being motivated to service by a desire for reward and praise (Rom. 2:29; Gal. 6:4–10; Col. 3:24). Eternal reward motivated him as it should all believers. Paul did not want to lose his eternal rewards for preaching willingly and eagerly and without pay. If he preached begrudgingly or received pay, he believed he would be doing nothing more than **simply discharging the trust committed** to him. To raise his preaching above the level of mere obedience, Paul voluntarily gave up his right to remuneration.[87]

Tearing Down Arguments

Satan is the "father of the lie." (John 8:44) The apostle John, in the book of Revelation, says, "The great dragon was thrown down, that ancient serpent, who is called the devil and Satan, the deceiver of the whole world." (Rev 12:9) The apostle Paul tells us, "our gospel is veiled, it is veiled to those who are perishing. In their case the god of this world has blinded the minds of the unbelievers, to keep them from seeing the light of the gospel of the glory of Christ, who is the image of God." (2 Cor. 4:3-4) Yes, unless we can get the light into the minds and hearts of these ones, they will perish into everlasting destruction. Moreover, think of the ones that these blinded ones are influencing. Paul goes on later to talk about some false apostles, saying, "For such men are false apostles, deceitful workmen, disguising

---

[87] Richard L. Pratt Jr, *I & II Corinthians*, vol. 7, Holman New Testament Commentary (Nashville, TN: Broadman & Holman Publishers, 2000), 148–149.

themselves as apostles of Christ. And no wonder, for even Satan disguises himself as an angel of light." (2 Cor. 11:13-14) What have we learned about Satan in these texts thus far?

- Satan is the father of the lie
- He is the deceiver of the whole world
- He is the god of this world
- blinded the minds of the unbelievers
- Satan disguises himself as an angel of light

Satan is the Father of

- **Atheism** (unbelief in God or deities),
- **Agnosticism** (view that God's existence is unprovable),
- **Empiricism** (the view that all concepts originate in experience, that all concepts are about or applicable to things that can be experienced, or that all rationally acceptable beliefs or propositions are justifiable or knowable only through experience)
- **Humanism** (term freely applied to a variety of beliefs, methods, and philosophies that place central emphasis on the human realm, and generally prefers critical thinking and evidence (rationalism, empiricism) over established doctrine or faith),
- **Liberalism** (a form of religious thought that establishes religious inquiry on the basis of a norm other than the authority of tradition. It was an important influence in Protestantism from about the mid-17th century through the 1920s),
- **Modernism** (a movement in which scholars and theologians attempt to accommodate the contemporary worldview within theology and doctrine),
- **Postmodernism** (a late 20th-century movement characterized by broad skepticism, subjectivism, or relativism; a general suspicion of reason; and an acute sensitivity to the role of ideology),
- **Rationalism** (the view that regards reason as the chief source and test of knowledge. Holding that reality itself has an inherently logical structure, the rationalist asserts that a class of truths exists that the intellect can grasp directly.),
- Reconstructionism (the church imposes religion on the state, in secularism, the state ends up imposing irreligion on the state),

- **Relativism** (the doctrine that there are no absolute truths in ethics and that what is morally right or wrong varies from person to person or from society to society),
- **Secularism** (any movement in society directed away from otherworldliness to life on earth. The belief that religion and religious bodies should have no part in political or civic affairs or in running public institutions, especially schools. The rejection of religion or its exclusion from a philosophical or moral system.),
- **Skepticism** (questioning attitude towards knowledge, facts, or opinions/beliefs stated as facts)[88]

2 Corinthians 11:13-15 Updated American Standard Version (UASV)

[13] For such men are false apostles, deceitful workers, disguising themselves as apostles of Christ. [14] And no wonder, for even Satan disguises himself as an angel of light. [15] Therefore it is not a great thing if his servants also disguise themselves as servants of righteousness, whose end will be according to their deeds.

On these verses Dr. Richard L. Pratt, Jr. writes,

11:13–14. Why was he so determined? Paul explained that these so-called super-apostles were actually **false apostles**. They were **deceitful** and only **masquerading as apostles of Christ**. Of course, those who followed these **false apostles** would have insisted that Paul was wrong. So he countered their anticipated objection by noting that the false apostles' deceit was **no wonder**. After all, even **Satan himself masquerades as an angel of light**.

11:15. Paul accused the false apostles of being **servants** of Satan and of imitating his tactics. They **masquerade[d] as servants of righteousness** (cf. Rev. 2:9; 3:9). The work of these false apostles led many into unrighteousness, as opposed to Paul's apostolic ministry of righteousness (see 2 Cor. 3:9).

Paul asserted that these false apostles would ultimately receive **what their actions deserve[d]**. Although this statement carried serious overtones of final judgment, Paul also had in mind that these opponents

---

[88] http://www.britannica.com/

77

would be exposed before the church and removed from their positions when he arrived. God would judge them.[89]

As we have already stated, today, there are over 41,000 different denominations, who claim to be Christian, and not all are paths leading to the same place. There are false Christian denominations, which are not Christian at all when evaluated with Scripture. Then, there are televangelists, such as Joel Osteen, who has 20 million followers in over 100 countries, whom apologist, evangelist call a false teacher, to say the least.[90] We will not go into details about which denomination is false and which is true. However, just know that evangelism is important for three groups of people (1) unbelievers, (2) believers on the wrong path and (3) helps save believers, who have begun to doubt.

Believers in a false Christian denomination on the wrong path need to hear the truth (e.g., Catholics). However, they have their long-held beliefs, which often involve deep-seated emotions. Some of these ones have had these beliefs their entire life. While we may disagree with their belief, we need to find common ground and evidence while respecting their viewpoint, or at least them as a person. (1 Peter 3:15)

We show them dignity by giving them an opportunity to explain what they believe and why, without our interrupting them, in an attempt at disproving some aspect of that belief. (Jam. 1:19) Perhaps they have prayed to particular saints, and such prayers have given them comfort throughout their lives. On the other hand, maybe they worship Mary, the mother of Jesus, and feel that they have a close, intimate relationship with her as we do with Christ. Maybe they believe in faith healing by charismatic preachers. In Roman Catholic and Eastern Orthodox doctrine, the bread and the wine undergo a change in substance, from bread and wine to the body and blood of Jesus Christ during Communion. If we listen to what they say, merely asking leading questions at first, to discover insight into the details of what they believe and how they feel about what they think, this will help us respond in an effective manner. (Proverbs 16:23)

If we take the time to read Luke 10:25-37, we will have an outstanding example for us when Jesus answered questions from a man versed in the

---

[89] Richard L. Pratt Jr, *I & II Corinthians*, vol. 7, Holman New Testament Commentary (Nashville, TN: Broadman & Holman Publishers, 2000), 423.

[90] www.youtube.com/watch?v=jJQx-zb3kN8

Mosaic Law. Jesus never responded with a direct response to this man's questions. Why? Jesus may have avoided a direct approach because this student of the Law may have had cherished beliefs, at least emotionally involved. Instead, Jesus chose to reference Scripture and then invited him to offer his understanding of the Scripture. Thereafter, Jesus also used an illustration to help him reason on the Scripture.

There are tens of millions of believers on the wrong path, with strongly held false religious beliefs which are no part of the Word of God. (Heb. 4:12) If we appeal to their heart, we might succeed in reaching their mind, helping them set aside the false beliefs, and accepting the truth, which will set them free from the wrong path. John 8:32

Review Questions

(1) To whom was the apostle Peter talking? Who was Peter saying needed always to be prepared to make a defense? Was he speaking only to the pastors, elders, and servants, or to all Christians?

(2) What were the context and historical setting of Asia Minor? 1 Peter 3:15

(3) Who are Christianity's two greatest enemies?

(4) What do we learn from the Apollos account of Acts 18:24-28?

(5) How are we to understand 1 Corinthians 3:12-13?

(6) Who are some of the leading Christian apologists today, and why should we not be intimidated by their presence?

(7) How can we reach our full potential?

(8) How effectively should we be able to use the Bible in defense of our hope?

(9) What have we learned about Satan in the above texts?

(10) What three people groups are we expected to evangelize?

(11) Why are we obligated to evangelize to believers on the wrong path?

(12) What makes it challenging to evangelize to believers on the wrong path?

(13) What is one approach that we might use in our evangelization of believers on the wrong path?

CHAPTER 4 Contend for the Faith

2 Timothy 2:25-26 Updated American Standard Version (UASV)

²⁵ instructing his opponents with gentleness, if perhaps God may grant them repentance leading to accurate knowledge[91] of the truth, ²⁶ and they may come to their senses and escape from the snare of the devil, having been held captive by him to do his will.

2:25–26. If a leader's heart is pure, humbled before God's grace, he can then **gently instruct** those who err, **in the hope that God will grant them repentance**. God's earnest desire to draw all people into loving relationship with himself should motivate the pastor to deal kindly with those who oppose him.

Four players participate in this crucial drama for the human soul: the teacher, the unbeliever, God, and Satan.

The Christian teacher not only proclaims truth; he models godliness and kindness as well. As God's representative, he personifies God and his ways. He also recognizes that the battle for human souls takes place on two fronts—the mind and the heart. Unbelievers do not think clearly in matters of the soul or spirit; they need **to come to their senses**. This is why the teacher must feed the minds of unbelievers, leading them to a **knowledge of the truth**.

The unbeliever must remain open and responsive. He must choose to come to his senses. Each person stands responsible before God for his acceptance or rejection of God's truth as found in Jesus Christ.

Beyond the human sphere, God and Satan enter man's spiritual struggle. Those who refuse God's truth come under the influence of **the devil who has taken them captive to do his will.** Satan traps people into his service through clever arguments, fear, and appeals to selfish pride and ambition. Christians should exercise a healthy awareness of the participation of Satan in the thinking of unbelievers. Contending for truth involves contending with spiritual powers; we must not be so naive as to think we

---

[91] *Epignosis* is a strengthened or intensified form of *gnosis* (*epi*, meaning "additional"), meaning, "true," "real," "full," "complete" or "accurate," depending upon the context. Paul and Peter alone use *epignosis*.

confront on purely human terms.

But God remains faithful. He also contends for human souls and minds. As a measure of his grace, he grants repentance. God is sovereign over the universe and all created beings. We should never become overwhelmed at Satan's methods or power. Satan and God are not equals.

As believers, our responsibility is to speak God's truth, live out his nature, and pray earnestly for the salvation of those who continue in Satan's grip. We ask him, by virtue of his authority, to grant a change of heart to those who are estranged from his truth and love.[92]

Defending Our Faith

Most genuine Christians throughout the world are honest, modestly dressed, good neighbors, tax-paying citizens, and would help a complete stranger if it were in their hand. However, they have seen greater and greater persecution in the last one hundred years. Today, being a genuine, conservative Christian is almost view like one with leprosy. Sadly, they are taught by their Christian leaders, 'this is what you should expect in life.' Jesus said to his followers, "you will be hated by all for my name's sake. But the one who endures to the end will be saved." (Matt. 10:22) In fact, Paul said, "Indeed, all who desire to live a godly life in Christ Jesus will be persecuted." (2 Timothy 3:12)

Christians do not go out of their way to seek persecution. It is not as though they enjoy difficult times, and imprisonment under communist governments. In fact, it is their desire that they "may lead a peaceful and quiet life, godly and dignified in every way." (1 Tim. 2:1-2) Christians seek to 'rejoice with those who rejoice, weep with those who weep. Live in harmony with one another. Do not be haughty, but associate with the lowly. Never be wise in their own sight. They do not repay evil for evil but give thought to doing what is honorable in the sight of all. If possible, so far as it depends on them, they desire to live peaceably with all.' (Rom. 12:15-18) In addition, they are "subject to the governing authorities." (Rom. 13:1) Still, they are 'hated by everyone because of Jesus' name.' (Matt. 10:22) Why?

---

[92] Knute Larson, *I & II Thessalonians, I & II Timothy, Titus, Philemon*, vol. 9, Holman New Testament Commentary (Nashville, TN: Broadman & Holman Publishers, 2000), 289–290.

For truly genuine Christians, they are hated for the same reason the early Christians were hated. First, they live by the principles of God's Word, and this makes them unaccepted by the world that is alienated from God and the liberal "Christian" community. For example, they love to talk about Jesus Christ (See Acts 4:19-20), but the world does not understand their love and dedication but rather sees them as being some zealot who believes in myths as reality.

Second, the atheism of today is not the atheism of 50 years ago. The atheism of today is more evangelistic about their beliefs than most Christians are, and they are highly informed, or should I say misinformed, or maybe it is that they are informed, but are misinforming those seeking to be Christians. These atheists are on the radio, television, in Hollywood movies, mainstream news, newspapers, billboards, and the internet, spreading false allegations, shameless lies, and twisted expositions of Christian beliefs. The atheist campaign is an attack on God, the miracles of the Bible and the trustworthiness of the Scriptures. This onslaught of aggressive campaigns has caused most of the world to see Christians as zealots living in the so-called past before introducing the era of the enlightenment. In the 19th-century, there came a rising tide of atheism and agnosticism. Below are some Atheist quotes which will give us the mindset.

(1) The fact that a believer is happier than a skeptic is no more to the point than the fact that a drunken man is happier than a sober one. The happiness of credulity is a cheap and dangerous quality. – George Bernard Shaw

(2) Faith means not wanting to know what is true. – Friedrich Nietzsche

(3) To surrender to ignorance and call it God has always been premature, and it remains premature today. - Isaac Asimov

(4) With or without religion, you would have good people doing good things and evil people doing evil things. But for good people to do evil things, that takes religion. – Steven Weinberg

(5) The God of the Old Testament is arguably the most unpleasant character in all fiction: jealous and proud of it; a petty, unjust, unforgiving control-freak; a vindictive, bloodthirsty ethnic cleanser; a misogynistic, homophobic, racist, infanticidal, genocidal, filicidal, pestilential, megalomaniacal, sadomasochistic, capriciously malevolent bully. – Richard Dawkins

(6) It is not as in the Bible that God created man in his own image. But, on the contrary, man created God in his own image. – Ludwig Feuerbach

(7) All the biblical miracles will, at last, disappear with the progress of science. – Matthew Arnold

(8) Religion does three things quite effectively: Divides people, Controls people, Deludes people. – Carlespie Mary Alice McKinney

(9) Atheism is nothing more than the noises reasonable people make when in the presence of religious dogma. – Sam Harris

Some of these comments can sting, like any other tirade; even though untrue, it can begin to cause low self-esteem. Every day, a gorgeous woman told by her husband that she is ugly or fat will end up with depression or some eating disorder. Even a lie told often enough can lead to doubt if that is all one hears. Imagine our young ones growing up in schools filled with atheist teachers, followed by universities filled with atheist professors. In these universities, they are consistently beaten down with atheism to the point where they begin to doubt.

Witnessing to an Atheist

Whether we are purposefully evangelizing in our community, or we informally happen to someone who says, "I am an atheist," the conversation should not end there. The short response would be to ask how long they have been an atheist and what moved them to accept atheism? If he answers, make sure that we are very respectful, do not interrupt in an attempt to counter any of his reasons as to why he became an atheist. Allow him to get through it all. We could get through in a few verbal responses to let him know that we are following, like an occasional, "I see." We could ask him if he thought it would be wrong for us as Christians to read a book that attempted to prove creationism wrong. He will likely say no and that we need to hear both sides. Then, ask him if he would be comfortable reading a book that presented evidence that life was created. If he says he would have no problem doing so, we could as him, if we could drop such a book at his home. We should not be witnessing to atheists if we have not read a number of books by such authors as William Lane Craig, John Lennox, William A. Dembski, Jonathan Witt, Stephen C. Meyer, Michael J. Behe, and the like. It does our self-esteem no good, nor the atheist's attitude if we egregiously lose a conversation. Let us also consider why atheists do not believe.

Some Reasons Why Atheists Refuse to Believe

Not every atheist was raised by atheist parents. Many formerly were a part of some religion, meaning they believed in God. Some factors for doubt setting in are tragedies, such as heartbreaking deaths by disease. Others might be one difficulty in life after another. Some were brought up in grade schools, middle schools, high schools, and colleges that were filled with atheist educators. Maybe it was religious hypocrisy that moved him to become an atheist. Many Christian households have an unrealistic expectation of God, which can actually contribute to doubt when severe tragedy hits. Many convey the belief that God steps in and solves our problems every time if we are faithful. For a deeper discussion, please see the Christian Publishing House Blog

(https://christianpublishinghouse.co/): Does God Step in and Solve Our Every Problem Because We are Faithful?

Reaching Sincere Atheists

Behind the scenes of social media, out of earshot of their friends, many atheists would love to have answers to the same tough questions that we would like to have answers to. Why are humans so evil? We can somewhat understand a person getting mad and accidentally hurting another. However, how do we explain a man who rapes and sadistically murders almost a hundred little girls in Russia? How do we explain the Nazi concentration camps? Something must be beyond this. Indeed, the sincere atheist would like to know why bad things happen to good people. For a deeper discussion, please see the Christian Publishing House Blog

(https://christianpublishinghouse.co/): Why Has God Permitted Wickedness and Suffering.

One way to reach sincere atheists is to inquire about life and see if there are any problems that come up. If there are marital issues, children rebelling, potential divorce, and the like, we can possibly reach them through the effectiveness of the Scriptures. If we said something like, "the Bible can help us with any family or life situation that we may be facing," they may say something like, "I doubt it." We could then reply, "Do you have something that we could test this with, and then you could personally see for yourself, it cannot hurt or make things any worse, right? If they bring one up, make sure that we offer to show them from Scripture principles that, if applied, will help them overcome the problem. Also, make sure that they realize it will only help if they apply the counsel fully. They will be overcome with joy when they see the outworking of the practical counsel. We should only approach this type of evangelism if we have covered some books on Christian counseling and in conjunction with the pastor. Please see the recommended books below.[93]

We have to understand that not every atheist is going to accept the truth of God's Word, regardless of how skillful we become in our evangelism. Nevertheless, many are sincere in life and will be open to another viewpoint if he is approached in the right way. We need to use empathy, logic, reason, persuasion, and, above all, the power of God's Word. (Acts 28:23-24; Hebrews 4:12)

Let Our Reasonableness be Known to All Men

In this author's work on the internet, he has seen hundreds, if not thousands, of comments on social media that belittle anyone who refuses to accept Christianity. As Christians, we do not return hateful speech for hateful speech directed at us. We need to be better than this. (Prov. 8:13) In the first century, the Jewish religious leaders were dogmatic in their self-righteous ivory tower, believing they were better than any Gentile (non-Jew) was. As genuine Christians, we do not take such a view, but rather, we let our reasonableness be known to all. We do not treat unbelievers with disdain. If our hope is like that of Paul, all unbelievers who hear the truth accept the truth; then, we must be the truth in our representation. (Acts 26:29; 1 Timothy 2:3-4)

Yes, we are "to speak evil of no one, to avoid quarreling, to be gentle, and to show perfect courtesy toward all people." (Titus 3:2) Paul said this to

---

[93] **Competent Christian Counseling, Volume One: Foundations and Practice of Compassionate Soul Care** Apr 16, 2002 by Timothy Clinton and George Ohlschlager

Caring for People God's Way: Personal and Emotional Issues, Addictions, Grief, and Trauma May 10, 2006 by Tim Clinton

Discipleship Counseling: The Complete Guide to Helping Others Walk in Freedom and Grow in Christ Aug 20, 2003 by Neil T. Anderson

Titus about Crete, people who were known to be "liars, evil beasts, and lazy gluttons." (Titus 1:12) Yes, even such ones as this we do not speak evil of, nor speak to with disdain. This is not to say that we excuse such behavior. We can address people's actions and the behaviors themselves. Nevertheless, it would be against biblical principles to speak disparagingly of ones who are unbelievers. Having a self-righteous attitude will not win anyone over to the Christian side of the aisle.

A Time to be Silent and a Time to Speak

Ecclesiastes 3:7 says that there is "a time to keep silence, and a time to speak." Thus, the question that lies before us is, 'when do I ignore the opposer, and when to I defend the faith by speaking out. Again, we turn to our ultimate example (1 Pet. 2:21) An example of a time when Jesus felt it best "to keep quiet" was when he was before the Roman governor Pilate when the Jewish religious leaders falsely accused him. Jesus "gave him [Pilate] no answer, not even to a single charge, so that the governor was greatly amazed." (Matt. 27:11-14) Jesus was likely remaining quiet, to not interfere with the Father's will for him. If Jesus had spoken up and defended himself, maybe he would have been released, and we would not have had the ransom. He knew the truth would not have changed the closed minds and hearts of the Jewish religious leaders, but maybe they would have influenced Pilate. Instead, he allowed himself to go on record as a blasphemer of God. Therefore, Jesus ignored their questions and slanderous comments, refusing to give them an answer. Isaiah 53:7

An example of a time when Jesus felt it best "to speak," challenging his opponents frankly and openly, disproving their false allegations. For example, we can look at the time when the Scribes and the Pharisees tried to discredit him in front of a crowd for his expelling demons, saying, "He is possessed by Beelzebul,[94]" and "by the prince of demons he casts out the demons." Jesus did not let this accusation pass. On that occasion, he used logic and illustrations to debunk their argument. (Mark 3:20-30; see also Matthew 15:1-11; 22:17-21; John 18:37) On another occasion, Jesus was taken before the Sanhedrin, where High Priest Caiaphas deviously demanded, "I put you under oath by the living God, that you tell us if you are the Christ, the Son of God!" Jesus could not let this pass, as it would appear that he was denying that he was the long-awaited Christ. Therefore, Jesus replied, "I am, and you will see the Son of Man sitting at the right

---

[94] Or Beezebul; others read Beelzebub

86

hand of the Power and coming with the clouds of heaven." (Matthew 26:63-64; Mark 14:61-62)

Then, we have the example of Paul and Barnabas. Acts 14:1-2 states, "Now at Iconium, they entered together into the Jewish synagogue and spoke in such a way that a great number of both Jews and Greeks believed. But the unbelieving Jews stirred up the Gentiles and poisoned their minds against the brothers." The New English Bible says, "But the unconverted Jews stirred up the Gentiles and poisoned their minds against the Christians." Note that the unbelieving Jews rejected the message, but then they also went to the next step of discrediting the Christian messengers. They made sure the Gentile inhabitants had an unfounded hatred, fear, and mistrust of the Christians. (Compare Acts 10:28) Thus, for Paul and Barnabas, this was a "time to speak." If they had not, the new Christians in that community of Iconium might have become disheartened by public criticism. "So they [Paul and Barnabas] remained for a long time, speaking boldly for the Lord, who bore witness to the word of his grace, granting signs and wonders to be done by their hands. But the people of the city were divided; some sided with the Jews and some with the apostles." (Acts 14:3-4)

So, then, which method should we take when we are reproached? Just as it depended on the circumstances with Jesus and the first Christians, it is true with us. In some situations, it is best that we choose "a time to keep quiet." This is especially true when Bible critics try to draw us into arguments, where we are always on the defense, and it is just pointless. We might offer the best response, very informative, very detailed, and maybe very well researched for an inline internet response. Then, the Bible critic responds, "Whatever, I do not believe that you are just ..." Think of that time wasted, the research, putting our heart and mind into it, and it is dismissed as nothing within a few words a few seconds. We must keep in mind (2 Thess. 2:9-12); that most critics do not care if they hear the truth because Satan is able to blind their minds because their hearts are unreceptive. (2 Cor. 4:3-4) Attempting to reason with those whose hearts are arrogantly immovable in unbelief is unproductive. Moreover, if we went all out on every person, debating them for their false attacks, Satan would be diverting us from our true commission: proclaiming, teaching Bible truths, and making disciples of those with a receptive heart. Therefore, when opposed to antagonists who are determined to spread lies about Christians on the Bible, the advice from God's Word is, "turn away from them," (NASB), "avoid them" (ESV). (Romans 16:17-18; Matthew 7:6)

However, this is not an absolute written in stone command but rather relative to the circumstance, as there are times when we need to defend the Bible or the faith. Yes, there is "a time to speak." There will be times when it is very public, in the midst of right-hearted one, open-minded ones, which will only hear one side of the situation if we do not respond. In this case, we can clearly explain the truth for the sake of these ones but would not want to be locked down in a long-drawn-out debate. The apostle Peter wrote, "in your hearts honor Christ the Lord as holy, always being prepared to make a defense to anyone who asks you for a reason for the hope that is in you; yet do it with gentleness and respect." (1 Pet. 3:15) The principle that we have to judge for ourselves each time is, if a genuinely interested one is asking skeptical questions of the hope we hold, when they are raising issues about false claims made by opposers elsewhere (Books, TV, News, etc.), we are obligated take the time to defend the faith, providing sound biblical answers. In this, we are always feeling them out as we go on in the conversation. The moment they go from honest skepticism to antagonistic skepticism, we warn them one time that we are not going to give our time if they are not genuinely interested. 1 Peter 2:12-15

Dealing with Slanderous Publicity

Christianity is often distorted in the media, both purposely and through ignorance. For example, Dr. Bart D. Ehrman, formerly an evangelical Christian who later fell away to Agnosticism. He now goes on any show that will have him tearing down the New Testament to the uninformed through the art and science of textual criticism.[95] He has penned numerous books, some New York Times Bestsellers, misrepresenting the New Testament text by misleading his readers about the evidence. Anyone who has some basic understanding of New Testament textual criticism can recognize his comments and books as nothing more than misleading, misinformation and misrepresenting the truth. Even so, the interviews are on YouTube and all over the internet; his books are everywhere, misinforming hundreds of thousands, if not far more, and this is but one man.

---

[95] Textual criticism is the study of a group of manuscripts, versions, lectionaries, and early church father quotations, in order to determine which reading is the original. This is only done on 25 percent of the NT (the other 75 percent we know what was original), but it has given us a critical text that is 99.99 percent of what would have been in the original.

How can we defend our faith against such misleading information? Must we become a textual scholars? No, but there are books that are but 200-350 pages long that will give us the truth, expose his lies and give us the basic knowledge to respond to any readers of his books, who might not have heard both sides of the story. We could go on about other areas of study as well, but the same would be true, we simply need to familiarize ourselves with these subjects. If we are to be an effective Christian apologist, an effective evangelist, we must love taking in knowledge, to defend God's Word and the faith. God has blessed us with many tools in this area.[96]

Review Questions

(1) Why should opposition, even persecution, not surprise Christians? However, what is it that they desire?
(2) What are some reasons that Christians are hated by the world?
(3) Who have been the primary ones to attack Christians and Christianity?
(4) What is the correct view that Christians should have of unbelievers?
(5) What Bible principles should be kept in mind when we speak about unbelievers, even amongst ourselves?
(6) How can we witness to atheists?
(7) What are some reasons atheists do not believe?
(8) How can we reach sincere atheists?
(9) What examples did Jesus set as to a time "to be quiet" and a "time to speak"?
(10) Why did Paul and Barnabas speak with confidence in Iconium?
(11) How can we let our reasonableness be known to all?
(12) What are some suggestions on when "to speak" and when "to be quiet"?
(13) How can we deal with slanderous publicity?

---

[96] If we want to defend against Dr. Bart D. Ehrman, this author has penned,

MISREPRESENTING JESUS: Debunking Bart D. Ehrman's "Misquoting Jesus" Kindle Edition by Edward Andrews (Author) **ISBN-13**: 978-1949586954

https://www.amazon.com/dp/B07YN24CZY

FROM SPOKEN WORDS TO SACRED TEXTS: Introduction-Intermediate New Testament Textual Studies Paperback – February 21, 2020 by Edward D. Andrews (Author) ISBN-13: 978-1949586985 (paperback) ISBN-13: 978-1949586640 (Hardcover)

https://www.amazon.com/dp/1949586987

CHAPTER 5 Reasoning from the Scriptures

Acts 17:2-3 Updated American Standard Version (UASV)

² And according to Paul's custom, he went to them, and for three Sabbaths **reasoned with them from the Scriptures**, ³ explaining and proving that it was necessary that the Christ had to suffer and rise again from the dead, and saying, "This Jesus whom I am proclaiming to you is the Christ."

To help others understand and appreciate God's Word, follow the pattern of Jesus Christ and the Apostle Paul. The Apostle Paul established himself as an effective teacher as he reasoned from the Scriptures and established himself as one whom we should imitate.

While the Scribes and Pharisees of Jesus' day have taken a beating in the press, as they should, for their part in executing Jesus, they also possessed intelligence, knowledge, and the abilities to convey it. However, Jesus' teaching proved different from theirs. The Jewish religious leaders despised and shunned the common people. In fact, they viewed them as "an accursed people." (John 7:49) On the other hand, when Jesus "saw the crowds, he had compassion for them, because they were harassed and helpless, like sheep without a shepherd." (Matt. 9:36) He was heartfelt, understanding, concerned, and empathetic. Moreover, the Jewish religious leaders demonstrated no real love for God, it looked like a showy display and ritualistic. However, Jesus loved his father and delighted in doing his will. (John 5:19, 30) In addition, the religious leaders perverted God's Word to serve their own ends, but Jesus said, "Blessed rather are those who hear the word of God and keep it!" (Luke 11:28) He taught, explained, defended, and lived by it. Yes, love filled the very person of Christ, moving him to teach nothing but the truth, letting that same Word guide him in his dealings with the common people. Finally, he taught from the Scriptures, which was his source of truth and authority, while the Jewish religious leaders quoted past Rabbis (teachers).

Jesus proved very familiar with the Word of God, the Hebrew Scriptures that we call the Old Testament. He quoted from it over 120 times in about three hours of dialogue that we have in the four Gospels. (Luke 4:4, 8) Yes, the Jewish religious leaders and even Satan quoted from the Scriptures. Jesus, unlike them, applied the Scriptures appropriately, while the Jewish religious leaders and Satan twisted the Scriptures to suit their own selfish ends. Jesus not only knew the legal aspect of the Law but the spirit of it, as well. We too can imitate Jesus by buying out the time to understand the Scriptures correctly, then using them properly, and applying them in our lives.

In addition to his having a correct mental grasp of Scripture, he also shared it with all who would listen. People knew him as the "teacher." (Matthew 12:38) Jesus took his Good News everywhere, such as the temple area, synagogues, cities, and rural areas. (Mark 1:39; Luke 8:1; John 18:20) Moreover, when he taught others, he did so with compassion, empathetic understanding, and kindness, expressing love for the ones whom he helped. (Matt. 4:23) We, too, can imitate this by sharing God's Word with relatives, and coworkers, in the market, on the phone, on the internet, door to door in our community, and in all parts of our lives.

2 Timothy 3:16-17 Updated American Standard Version (UASV)

[16] All Scripture is inspired by God and profitable for teaching, for reproof, for correction, for training in righteousness; [17] so that the man of God may be fully competent, equipped for every good work.

When we engage others about the Word of God, who recognizes the authority of the Bible, we should use the Word of God, as it has the authority. As Paul said in Hebrews, "the word of God is living and active, sharper than any two-edged sword, piercing to the division of soul and of spirit, of joints and of marrow, and discerning the thoughts and intentions of the heart."[97] (Hebrews 4:12)

Thus, some will take the Bible more seriously if they see reasons. Show them God's initial purpose for life in the Garden of Eden, why God has permitted wickedness since the rebellion in Eden,[98] where he places us in the stream of Bible history and the hope of unending life in the Kingdom of God. Some people have practical reasons for their skepticism about the Bible. However, these may not have an impact on the atheist since an atheist does not believe in God. Therefore, you would have to first establish this truth of God's existence with him.

---

[97] "This vivid expression of the power of God's message provides the explanation for the strong warning of verse 11. Because God's message is alive, active, sharp, and discerning, those who listen to God's message can enter his rest," rest from trying to prove oneself righteous before God by our works.—Thomas D. Lea, vol. 10, *Hebrews, James, Holman New Testament Commentary*; Holman Reference (Nashville, TN: Broadman & Holman Publishers, 1999), 71.

[98] See Appendix G.

Psalm 119:130 Updated American Standard Version (UASV)

130 The unfolding of your words gives light;
it imparts understanding to the simple.[99]

What if you engage a person in a conversation about the Bible, and he says to you, "Look, I do not believe the Bible to be nothing more than the word of man;" are you to just throw your hands up and allow the conversation to end? He stated what he believed and has opened the door to the evangelist reasoning with him. He may have learned of the atrocities of Christianity in his history classes at school. He also may have had a bad experience with a religious leader, such as a pastor of a church. This is where the evangelist asks questions to find out why he feels the way he does. You might ask, "If you do not mind my asking, what has moved you to view the Bible as the word of man, while two billion people today see the Bible as the Word of God?'

1 Timothy 2:3-4 Updated American Standard Version (UASV)

3 This is good, and it is acceptable in the sight of God our Savior, 4 who desires all men to be saved and to come to **an accurate knowledge[100] of truth**.

Do not just open the Bible and read Scriptures, but rather help people **come to "an accurate knowledge of truth**." An evangelist wants a listener to feel confident that the believer can do that. In other words, we must speak with authority. If one seems timid, stumbling over words, or unsure of one's self, the listener will conclude we do not have authority on God's Word. Would anyone get heart surgery from a heart surgeon who could not explain the procedure or seemed unsure of himself? Hardly! Why, then, would an evangelist expect someone to invest in the idea of a God, life eternal, and other doctrines like the resurrection hope from someone that comes off as unsure?

---

[99] "As the psalmist looks within God's words, the light of truth, understanding, and discernment is revealed to him. This divine illumination of Scripture increases his desire to pant with longing for more of God's Word."—Anders, Max; Lawson, Steven (2006-04-01). Holman Old Testament Commentary - Psalms 76-150 Holman Reference. Kindle Edition.

[100] *Epignosis* is a strengthened or intensified form of *gnosis* (*epi,* meaning "additional"), meaning, "true," "real," "full," "complete" or "accurate," depending upon the context. Paul and Peter alone use *epignosis*.

Preparation that Leads to the Ability to Reason

One can start by following the Christian Publishing House Blog Next Generation Bible Reading / Study Program.

(https://christianpublishinghouse.co/) Reading the Bible daily will familiarize someone with the content of Scripture, but if we read and study the Bible daily, we will know and understand the content of Scripture. We have devised the ultimate Bible reading and study program, which will train anyone whose desire focuses on knowing the Word of God thoroughly to be more effective in evangelism work.

In addition, prepare for Christian meetings by studying the assigned literature. Sit down, read, and study it, look up every cited Scripture, and see what a commentary says about it. If a teacher sets it up as question-and-answer when one attends a meeting, participate by sharing insights learned from the Scriptures.

Sharing new and interesting items, one learns implants them into one's long-term memory. Consider, for example, when Samson ripped out the gates of Gaza, which likely weighed several hundred pounds, he then carried them to the top of Hebron. One's in-depth study will discover that this proved to be a 37-mile hike, uphill! (Judges 16:3) Knowing these details will undoubtedly affect a believer's heart and mind, moving one to feel awe over the power of God.

When speaking with others about the Bible, use it, and have them read from it or read it in front of them. The listener would know the evangelist does not offer his or her opinion but rather the authority of the Bible. When one goes out with others, prepare what will be said to people to start conversations. Determine what to share from the Bible and how to introduce it. Take care of two points by asking a question that also encompasses what an evangelist does: "When we are out talking to people about the Bible, most are curious about what happens to people when someone dies. Have you ever thought of that?" People have dozens of questions about the Bible, and many of them would love to know what it says.

Literal Bible Translations Preferred

Bible translations range from being very close to the original languages in good English (known as literal or word-for-word, ASV, ESV, NASB, and

UASV), to those that take liberties (known as dynamic equivalent or thought for thought, NLT, GNB, CEV, and TNIV), and others with an interpretation of what authors originally wrote. We will take some space to deal with this subject, as it is truly an important matter. See chapters 18-20. There will be no questions and exercises in chapters 18-20, as these educate readers about the differences in the Bibles available and the translation process.

Expounding on Scripture

While we must refer the listener to the Bible by reading a text, and even better that the evangelist helps him follow along, more is needed. One can build their anticipation of looking into the Bible by asking a question that universally catches people's interest. Stress the Bible's answer to the question, and then leave a little pause. The evangelist could ask, "Have you ever wondered why there is so much pain and suffering when most people, if asked, would wish for peace?" (Pause.) The Bible answers that. (Pause and then read the Scripture.) Another, "Scientists say that every seven years we have new organs from cell regeneration, but in the thirties, it starts to slow down, but they do not know why." (Pause) The Bible answers why. (Pause and then read the Scripture.)

When one reads the text, hit the part that one will focus on reading it differently, slow with a deeper tone. Look at Matthew 24:14, "And this **gospel** of the **kingdom** will be **proclaimed throughout the whole world** as a testimony to **all nations**, and **then** the **end will come**." If the evangelist makes a point about the gospel, hit "gospel" harder. If one makes a point about the kingdom, hit "the kingdom" harder. If one makes a point about the extent of the proclamation, hit "throughout the whole world" and "all nations" harder. Here is an example of great emphasis. If the point centers on the end of times, hit "then," pausing before saying "the," then pounce on "end will come." A word of caution, do not stress more than one aspect of a verse, or the stress will lose its impact on the listener.

When one talks about the Bible, do not say, "I think," "I feel," or "I believe." This gives the evangelist authority and gives the authority to God's Word. You would say, "the Bible says," "Peter says," or, "the Apostle Peter says," or, "the book of Matthew says." If the evangelist knows they are dealing with a person that has absolutely no knowledge of the Bible, it will have no effect to say, "Paul said," or the book of Exodus said." In this case, stick with, "the Bible says."

Use the context of a text to demonstrate the right way to arrive at its correct meaning. A Bible critic may make a point about a verse, thinking he has the evangelist in a bind. Show the listener the context that he is the one mistaken, not the Bible nor the believer.

For example, at times, you may have two writers who write from different points of view.

Numbers 35:14 (NIV): Give three on this side of the Jordan and three in Canaan as cities of refuge.

Joshua 22:4 (NIV): Now that the LORD your God has given your brothers rest as he promised, return to your homes in the land that Moses the servant of the LORD gave you on the other side of the Jordan.

Moses speaks about the east side of the Jordan when he says "on this side of the Jordan." On the other hand, Joshua also speaks about the east side of the Jordan when he says, "on the other side of the Jordan." So, who is correct? Both are. When Moses wrote Numbers, the Israelites had not yet crossed the Jordan River, so the east side was "this side," the side he was located. On the other hand, when Joshua penned his book, the Israelites had crossed the Jordan, so the east side was just as he had said, "on the other side of the Jordan."

Bible Background

Bible background information demonstrates the level of knowledge that an evangelist has with the Scriptures and builds confidence in the one listening to you. However, do not get lost in the Bible background to the point where an evangelist strays from the point.

A common Bible expression is that of placing one's foot on the neck of your enemy. Both the Egyptian and Assyrian monuments have depictions where monarchs are pictured in battle with their foot on the enemy's neck. We find this with Moses' replacement, Joshua, the leader and commander of the Israelites.

Joshua 10:24 New American Standard Bible (NASB)

24 When they brought these kings out to Joshua, Joshua called for all the men of Israel, and said to the chiefs of the men of war who had gone with him, "Come near, **put your feet on the necks of these kings**." So they came near and **put their feet on their necks**.

In addition, the removal of one's hair and beard represented imminent destruction. The Ancient Near East viewed hair and a beard as a prize. The Israelites viewed the beard as manly dignity. (1 Chron. 19:5) Israelites would mutilate or remove their bears only during extreme sorrow, shame, or humiliation (Ezra 9:3; Isa. 15:2; Jer. 41:5; 48:37) Therefore, one can better understand King David's strategy.

1 Samuel 21:13 New American Standard Bible (NASB)

[13] So he disguised his sanity before them, and acted insanely in their hands, and scribbled on the doors of the gate, and **let his saliva run down into his beard**.

Now that we have this Bible background, we can better understand the conquest of Assyria:

Isaiah 7:20 Updated American Standard Version (UASV)

[20] "In that day by means of a hired razor from the region of the River,[101] by means of the king of Assyria, Jehovah will shave the head and the hair of the legs, and it will sweep away the beard as well.

Assyria was going to invade and conquer Judah like they had Samaria and the rest of the region, but for the fact that . . .

Isaiah 37:33-38 Updated American Standard Version (UASV)

[33] "Therefore thus says Jehovah concerning the king of Assyria: He shall not come into this city or shoot an arrow there or come before it with a shield or cast up a siege mound against it. [34] By the way that he came, by the same he will return, and he will not come into this city, declares Jehovah. [35] For I will defend this city to save it, for my own sake and for the sake of my servant David."

[36] Then the angel of Jehovah went out and struck one hundred and eighty-five thousand in the camp of the Assyrians, and when men arose early in the morning, behold, all of these were dead. [37] Then Sennacherib king of Assyria departed and returned home and lived at Nineveh. [38] It came about as he was worshiping in the house of Nisroch his god, that Adrammelech and Sharezer his sons killed him with the sword; and they escaped into the land of Ararat. And Esarhaddon his son became king in his place.

---

[101] I.e., *the Euphrates*

The destruction of Jerusalem had finally arrived at the hands of the Babylonians more than a century later.

Review Questions

(1) Explain why an evangelist would follow the example of the Apostle Paul and Jesus Christ in helping others understand and appreciate the Word of God. What should believers use as the authority when engaging those that recognize the authority of the Bible, and why? How should the evangelist react to someone that rejects the Bible as the Word of God? How does one project confidence to those whom they speak regarding the ability to convey truth?

(2) What are some things that will make evangelists more effective?

(3) Why are literal translations preferred? When one reads a text while witnessing, how should the evangelist do it? When one talks about the Bible, how should it be read? How can context help us? Explain and give an example. What is Bible background, and why is it important? Give an example of a Bible background.

CHAPTER 6 The Reasoning Evangelist

Acts 18:19 Updated American Standard Version (UASV)

19 And they came to Ephesus, and he left them there, but he himself went into the synagogue and **reasoned with the Jews**.

Suppose someone or a church evangelizes their community. In that case, one must be prepared to reason with any culture, and numerous religions, such as the Jewish, Buddhist, Muslim, Hindu, Shinto, Taoism, Confucianism, as well as atheists and agnostics, among others. This can seem overwhelming, but it is not as complicated as it sounds. There are many good Christian books out which will give you the basics of the major religions in just one book, a chapter on each, and demonstrate how to reason with them.[102]

Reasoning with someone means that we use Scripture, questions, and illustrations logically, which causes the listener to think and get the message in their mind and then in their heart. If someone uses a direct, rigid, and unbending approach, one will close off the listener's mind and heart. Meanwhile, a reasoning manner uses logical thinking to get results or draw conclusions, which inspires discussions. The evangelist's desire must be for the conversation to weigh on the mind and heart of the listener, moving them to contemplate the discussion, so they are anxious to engage the evangelist in future discussions.

While it is true that the truth will set one free, it must be received in such a way to do just that. Think of a conversation in terms of two people tossing a ball back and forth. If one tosses the ball so that it is catchable, the odds are better that it will be caught and received well. If one throws a ball like you are trying to take the other person's head off, it will not be received well, and few will catch it. Some people's beliefs remain dear to them, and to have them bluntly disclosed may not be received well.

James 3:17 Updated American Standard Version (UASV)

17 But the wisdom from above is first pure, then peaceable, gentle, **reasonable**, full of mercy and good fruits, impartial, without hypocrisy.

---

[102] http://astore.amazon.com/bibletranslat-20/detail/0736920846

James says that "the wisdom from above is ... reasonable (open to reason), ESV." The Greek word here *eupeithes* "open to reason" means "easily persuaded," "compliant," or "congenial." Some translations render it "obedient," (LEB) "gentle" (HCSB, NASB). On this verse, the Baker New Testament Commentary says, "Another attribute of wisdom is consideration. The person who is 'considerate' is fair, **reasonable**, and gentle in all his deliberations. He quietly gathers all the facts before he gives his opinion. He refrains from placing himself first and always considers others better than himself (Phil. 2:3; 4:5)."[103]

Acts 17:1-3 Updated American Standard Version (UASV)

17 Now when they had passed through Amphipolis and Apollonia, they came to Thessalonica, where there was a synagogue of the Jews. ² And according to Paul's custom, he went to them, and for three Sabbaths reasoned with them **[the Jews]** from the Scriptures, ³ explaining and proving that it was necessary that the Christ had to suffer and rise again from the dead, and saying, "This Jesus whom I am proclaiming to you is the Christ."

The Apostle Paul studied under the renowned Pharisee Gamaliel, who was the grandson of Hillel the Elder (110 B.C.E.[104] – 10 C.E.), the founder of one of the two schools within Judaism. Paul describes himself as "circumcised on the eighth day, of the people of Israel, of the tribe of Benjamin, a Hebrew of Hebrews; as to the law, a Pharisee; as to zeal, a persecutor of the church; as to righteousness under the law, blameless." (Phil. 3:5-6) He also states, "But whatever gain I had, I counted as loss for the sake of Christ. Indeed, I count everything as loss because of the surpassing worth of knowing Christ Jesus my Lord. For his sake I have suffered the loss of all things and count them as rubbish, in order that I may gain Christ" (Phil. 3:7-8) Thus, we note that Paul "reasoned from the Scriptures" when he talked to the Jews in the Jewish Synagogue. His listeners accepted the Hebrew Scriptures as an authority. Therefore, he began his witness with what they knew and accepted.

However, at Acts 17:22-31, we find Paul witnessing to the Greeks at the Areopagus in Athens; he did not turn to the Scriptures as his source of reasoning. "As in Lystra, so in Athens, it would have been futile, to begin

---

[103] Simon J. Kistemaker and William Hendriksen, Exposition of James and the Epistles of John, vol. 14, New Testament Commentary (Grand Rapids: Baker Book House, 1953–2001), 122.

[104] B.C.E. years ran down toward zero, although the Romans had no zero, and C.E. years ran up from zero. (100, 10, 3, 2, 1 ◄B.C.E. | C.E.► 1, 2, 3, 10, and 100)

with the God of the Old Testament choosing a certain people, sending prophets, and promising a Messiah. That was a message for synagogues or Jews gathering by a river. Paul began with the doctrine of God and launched his message with a local object lesson, the altar to *agnosto theo.* [unknown god][105] In "Establishing rapport with his Athenian audience, Paul quotes verbatim from two Greek poets. Both writers extol the virtues of the god Zeus ... By quoting these poets, Paul is not intimating that he agrees with the pagan setting in which the citations flourished. Rather, he uses the words to fit his Christian teaching. From the Old Testament, he is able to draw the evidence that man derives his life, activity, and being from God (Job 12:10; Dan. 5:23)."[106] Paul used information familiar to his audience. Then, he took that information and made a case for the Creator, the only true God. On this, Bible scholar John B. Polhill writes,

> As so often in the speeches of Acts, Paul began his discourse with a point of contact with his audience. In this case it was the altars Paul had already observed in the city (v. 16). One in particular caught his attention. It was dedicated "TO AN UNKNOWN GOD." This gave him the perfect launching pad for his presentation of monotheism to the polytheistic and pantheistic Athenians. Piety had no doubt led the Athenians to erect such an altar for fear they might offend some deity of whom they were unaware and had failed to give the proper worship. Paul would now proclaim a God who was unknown to them. In fact, this God, totally unknown to them, was the only true divinity that exists.[107]

In the 1950s and 1960s, almost everyone that someone would talk to on the street possessed some knowledge of the Bible. If one said Old or New Testament, they understood. If an evangelist spoke of the apostles, the person knew what that meant. However, today billions have almost no knowledge of the Bible other than the name "Bible," and it is still regarded as a holy book. People who do not recognize the Bible, nor have any knowledge of the Bible, have **some commonalities** with Christians: they want to hope for something better. They see violence, pain and suffering, sickness, old age, and death every day, the same as any Christian. They, too,

---

[105] Kenneth O. Gangel, *Acts*, vol. 5, Holman New Testament Commentary (Nashville, TN: Broadman & Holman Publishers, 1998), 289.

[106] Simon J. Kistemaker and William Hendriksen, *Exposition of the Acts of the Apostles*, vol. 17, New Testament Commentary (Grand Rapids: Baker Book House, 1953–2001), 636-7.

[107] John B. Polhill, Acts, vol. 26, The New American Commentary (Nashville: Broadman & Holman Publishers, 1995), 371.

want a better life for themselves and their children. Thus, the ability to reason requires finding common ground such as this. Then, open the Scriptures by explaining how we got here and how there is hope for something better in Jesus Christ. This reasoning might offer them hope that they have not had, or hope that is more real and legitimate than any they have now.

Even those who have a vast knowledge of the Bible, but atheists, agnostics or other critics of the Bible, have as their mission in life to evangelize their message, "God is dead!" In the last 50-60-years, atheists have made many disciples for themselves. Millions of Christians and those from other religions have become atheists because they have succumbed to the misleading propaganda of the books, videos, movies, websites, television shows, and other tools of the atheistic machine. We certainly must reason from the Scriptures, but there must be more with these enemies of the faith.

God is rational, and he has created us as rational beings. The Bible urges us to give the reason for the hope that is in us (1 Pet. 3:15, NIV). Indeed, Jesus declared that the greatest commandment is: "You shall love the Lord your God with all ... your mind" (Matt. 22:37). The Apostle Paul added, "whatever is true, ... think on ...° (Phil. 4:8). Thinking is not an option for a Christian; it is an imperative.[108]

Ephesians 6:17 Updated American Standard Version (UASV)

[17] And take the helmet of salvation, and the sword of the Spirit, which is the word of God.

2 Corinthians 10:4-5 Updated American Standard Version (UASV)

[4] For the weapons of our warfare are not of the flesh[109] but powerful to God for destroying strongholds.[110] [5] We are destroying speculations and every lofty thing raised up against the knowledge of God, and we are taking every thought captive to the obedience of Christ,

In Christian spiritual warfare, the mind can help us wield "the sword of the Spirit, which is the word of God." However, a blank mind will do us

---

[108] Ronald M. Brooks; Norman L. Geisler. *Come, Let Us Reason: An Introduction to Logical Thinking* (Kindle Locations 12-14). Kindle Edition.

[109] That is *merely human*

[110] That is *tearing down false arguments*

no good. If we have not taken in the knowledge of God, there is nothing to recall that can be used in the battle for the Bible that lies ahead. Do we want to free those brothers and sisters by the tens of millions who have been taken captive by the world? One could have the absolute best sword ever made, but if he or she does not have the skills to use it, the sword is worthless to use. My prayer is that all Christians will awaken from their stupor and join the fight that some have taken up these last few decades. May they use the mind that God gave them, use their power of reason, and equip themselves to defend the faith?

Believers live in a time when certain critics of Christianity have abandoned all delicacy and decorum in debate. Rather than sticking to rational, carefully reasoned arguments, they have taken off the gloves to launch angry, sarcastic, and sloppily argued attacks. They lob their rhetorical grenades in hopes of creating the (incorrect) impression that belief in God is for intellectual lightweights who believe ridiculous, incoherent doctrines and who also are opposed to all scientific endeavor and discovery. These objectors are writing books—indeed, best sellers—that tend to be more bluster and emotion than substance. New Atheists such as Richard Dawkins, Sam Harris, and Christopher Hitchens characterize this tone of debate. On another front, textual critic Bart Ehrman misleadingly raises doubts about the New Testament text's reliability, while novelist Dan Brown's *Da Vinci Code* and Jesus Seminar co-founder John Dominic Crossan mislead many into thinking that various Gnostic Gospels give us more reliable information about the historical Jesus than do the canonical Gospels. From various angles the public is being told that we cannot trust what the New Testament, and the Gospels in particular, say about Jesus of Nazareth.[111]

It is no longer a matter of preaching on Sunday and hoping that some new faces show up. It is as though most Christians hide in their fort, the Church, watching as lives are taken one by one, hoping that the enemy will go away or that they can hold out until the return of Christ. The enemy takes one life after the other, and few are lifting themselves to join the fight. There is a need for a knowledge of the deeper things of God's Word, the need to reason with the enemy and his victims so that they can see that our message is more important, why it involves them as well, and just how they

---

[111] Craig, William Lane; Copan, Paul (2009-08-01). *Contending with Christianity's Critics: Answering New Atheists and Other Objectors* (Kindle Locations 47-56). B&H Publishing. Kindle Edition.

are going to be affected personally. If Christians prove effective in this, we must have the ability to reason with the enemy, defeating him on the battlefield, not hiding in the church waiting for dawn. One of the leading apologists of the 20ᵗʰ and 21ˢᵗ centuries, Dr. William Lane Craig, wrote the following:

> This is a war we cannot afford to lose. The great Princeton theologian J. Gresham Machen warned on the eve of the fundamentalist controversy that if the church loses the intellectual battle in one generation, then evangelism would become immeasurably more difficult in the next:
>
> False ideas are the greatest obstacles to the reception of the gospel. We may preach with all the fervor of a reformer and yet succeed only in winning a straggler here and there, if we permit the whole collective thought of the nation or of the world to be controlled by ideas which, by the resistless force of logic, prevent Christianity from being regarded as anything more than a harmless delusion. Under such circumstances, what God desires us to do is to destroy the obstacle at its root.[112]
>
> The root of the obstacle is to be found in the university, and it is there that it must be attacked. Unfortunately, Machen's warning went unheeded, and biblical Christianity retreated into the intellectual closets of Fundamentalism, from which it has only recently begun to re-emerge. The war is not yet lost, and it is one which we must not lose: souls of men and women hang in the balance. So what are evangelicals doing to win this war?
> [113]

Biblical and Christian Apologetics

When "false apostles, deceitful workmen, disguising themselves as apostles of Christ" caused trouble in the congregation in Corinth, the Apostle Paul wrote that we are to tear down their arguments and take every thought captive under such circumstances. (2 Cor. 10:4, 5; 11:13–15) All who present critical arguments against God's Word, or contrary to it, can

---

[112] J. Gresham Machen, *"Christianity and Culture," Princeton Theological Review* 11 (1913): 7.

[113] Craig, William Lane; Copan, Paul (2007-10-01). Passionate Conviction: Modern Discourses on Christian Apologetics (pp. 8-9). B&H Publishing. Kindle Edition.

have their arguments overturned by the Christian who is able and ready to defend that Word in mildness. (2 Tim. 2:24–26)

1 Peter 3:15 Updated American Standard Version (UASV)

[15] but sanctify Christ as Lord in your hearts, always being prepared to make a defense[114] to anyone who asks you for a reason for the hope that is in you; yet do it with gentleness and respect;

Peter says that we must be prepared to make a *defense.* The Greek word behind the English "defense" is *apologia* (apologia), which is actually a legal term that refers to the defense of a defendant in court. Our English apologetics is just what Peter spoke of, having the ability to give a reason to any who may challenge us, or to answer those who are not challenging us but who have honest questions that deserve to be answered.

2 Timothy 2:24-25 Updated American Standard Version (UASV)

[24] For a slave of the Lord does not need to fight, but needs to be kind to all, qualified to teach, showing restraint when wronged, [25] instructing his opponents with gentleness, if perhaps God may grant them repentance leading to accurate knowledge[115] of the truth,

Look at the Greek word (*epignosis*) behind the English "knowledge" from above. "It is more intensive than *gnosis*, knowledge, because it expresses a more thorough participation in the acquiring of knowledge on the part of the learner."[116] The requirement of all of the Lord's servants is that they be able to teach, but not in a quarrelsome way, but in a way to correct opponents with mildness. Why? The purpose of it all is that by God, yet through the Christian teacher, one may come to repentance and begin taking in an accurate knowledge of the truth.

Some Christians see apologetics as pre-evangelism; it is not the gospel, but it prepares the soil for the gospel.[117] Others make no such distinction,

---

[114] Or *argument*, or *explanation*

[115] *Epignosis* is a strengthened or intensified form of *gnosis* (*epi,* meaning "additional"), meaning, "true," "real," "full," "complete" or "accurate," depending upon the context. Paul and Peter alone use *epignosis.*

116. Spiros Zodhiates, *The Complete Word Study Dictionary: New Testament,* Electronic ed. (Chattanooga, TN: AMG Publishers, 2000, c1992, c1993), S. G1922.

[117] Norman Geisler and Ron Brooks, When Skeptics Ask (Grand Rapids: Baker Books, 1996), 11.

seeing apologetics, theology, philosophy, and evangelism as deeply entwined facets of the gospel.[118] Whatever its relation to the gospel, apologetics **is an extremely important enterprise that can profoundly impact unbelievers** and be used as the tool that clears the way to faith in Jesus Christ. (Bold mine.)

Many Christians did not come to believe as a result of investigating the Bible's authority, the evidence for the resurrection, or as a response to the philosophical arguments for God's existence. They responded to the proclamation of the gospel. Although these people have reasons for their belief, they are deeply personal reasons that often do not make sense to unbelievers. **They know the truth but are not necessarily equipped to share or articulate the truth in a way that is understandable** to those who have questions about their faith. It is quite possible to believe something is true without having a proper understanding of it or the ability to articulate it. (Bold mine.)

Christians who believe but do not know why are often insecure and comfortable only around other Christians. Defensiveness can quickly surface when challenges arise on issues of faith, morality, and truth because of a lack of information regarding the rational grounds for Christianity. At its worst, this can lead to either a fortress mentality or a belligerent faith, precisely the opposite of the Great Commission Jesus gave in Matthew 28:19–20. The Christian's charge is not to withdraw from the world and lead an insular life. Rather, we must be engaged in the culture, to be salt and light.

The solution to this problem requires believers to become informed in doctrine, the history of their faith, philosophy, logic, and other disciplines as they relate to Christianity. Believers must know the facts, arguments and theology and understand how to employ them in a way that will effectively engage the culture. Believers need Christian apologetics. One of the first tasks of Christian apologetics provides information. A number of widely held assumptions about Christianity can be easily challenged with a little information. This is even true for persons who are generally well-educated.[119]

---

[118] Greg Bahnsen, Van Til Apologetic (Phillipsburg, NJ: Presbyterian and Reformed, 1998), 43.

[119] Powell, Doug (2006-07-01). *Holman QuickSource Guide to Christian Apologetics* (Holman Quicksource Guides) (p. 6-7). B&H Publishing. Kindle Edition.

The ability to reason with others will take time, practice and patience. For example, if someone reasons with others successfully, that person must be reasonable. In a discussion about the historicity about Jesus, a believer knows the other person denying the existence of Jesus is wrong. Moreover, believers possess a truckload of evidence to support this position. However, it is best sometimes to not unload the truck by dumping the entire load at a listener's feet in one conversation, or in one breath. Being reasonable does not mean that a believer compromises the truth because he or she does not unload on the listener.

The other person will likely make many wrong statements in the conversation, and we should let most of them go unchallenged; rather, focus on a handful of the most crucial pieces of evidence and do not get lost by refuting every wrong statement. He may make bold condemnatory statements about many Christian beliefs, but we need to remain calm and not make a big deal of those statements. Listen carefully to the other person, and stay within the boundaries of the evidence in the conversation. For example, in a conversation on the historicity of Jesus when the listener states, "The New Testament manuscripts were completely corrupted in the copying process for a millennium, to the point that we do not even have the supposed Word of God." The evidence for the historicity of Jesus rests in the first and second centuries, so it would be a fool's errand to get into an extensive side subject about the restoration of the New Testament text, which took place over the centuries that followed the first two centuries C.E. There will be another day to talk about the history of the Greek New Testament, but today focus on the historicity of Jesus Christ.

God has given humanity free will, meaning each human has the right to choose, even if that choice is unwise. Believers have the assignment of proclaiming "the good news of the kingdom," as well as "making disciples" of redeemable humankind. Therefore, we must not pressure, coerce, or force people to accept the truth of that "Good News." However, all Christians have an obligation to reason with anyone by respectfully, gently, and mildly overturning their false reasoning in the attempt that being used by God we may save some.

Joshua 24:15 Updated American Standard Version (UASV)

15 "And if it is evil in your eyes to serve Jehovah, choose this day whom you will serve, whether the gods your fathers served in the region beyond the River, or the gods of the Amorites in whose land you dwell. But as for me and my house, we will serve Jehovah."

Effective Questions

Luke 10:25 Updated American Standard Version (UASV)

25 And behold, a lawyer[120] stood up to put him to the test, saying, "Teacher, what shall I do to inherit eternal life?"

A historical note here, "an expert in the law," or "lawyer" as some translations have it, is not a lawyer as we would think of one today. A lawyer was someone that was an expert in the Mosaic Law. However, this person would have the same level of education in the law as a lawyer would today, many years of study and memorization. Thus, this man would undoubtedly know the answer to such an easy question like the one he asked. Now, if a believer is asked an easy Bible question, we might be tempted to just offer an answer. Indeed, as the wisest man ever to live, Jesus could have easily answered the question. Instead, Jesus wanted the man to offer his own thoughts, insights, or understanding. However, Jesus knew this man was "an expert in the law," and he recognized the man would have had a certain perspective on his question. In other words, the man was not asked because he did not know. Thus, Jesus asked:

Luke 10:26 Updated American Standard Version (UASV)

26 And he said to him, "What is written in the Law? How do you read it?"

The man answered correctly,

Luke 10:27 Updated American Standard Version (UASV)

27 And he answered, "You shall love the Lord your God with all your heart and with all your soul and with all your strength and with all your mind, and your neighbor as yourself."

The conversation could have ended there. Again, the man knew the Mosaic Law but seemingly wanted to see if Jesus would agree with what he knew. Jesus gratified him, letting him feel good, by giving the correct answer. Jesus responded:

Luke 10:28-29 Updated American Standard Version (UASV)

28 And he said to him, "You have answered correctly; do this, and you will live."

---

120 That is an expert in the Mosaic Law

²⁹ But he, desiring to justify himself, said to Jesus, "And who is my neighbor?"

Here again, the man looks to prove himself righteous, and Jesus could have simply stated the truth, even the Samaritan. However, Jesus having insight into the setting, the Jews detested the Samaritans; so, while he would give the correct answer, it would be disputed in a long, back-and-forth conversation, and the Jews who listened would have sided with the man. Thus Jesus boxed the man into giving an answer by having him reason on an illustration.

The Parable of the Good Samaritan

Luke 10:30-37 Updated American Standard Version (UASV)

³⁰ Jesus replied and said, "A man was going down from Jerusalem to Jericho, and he fell among robbers, who stripped him and laid blows upon and departed, leaving him half dead. ³¹ Now by coincidence a certain priest was going down on that road, and when he saw him, he passed by on the other side. ³² Likewise a Levite also, when he came to the place and saw him, passed by on the other side. ³³ But a Samaritan, who was on a journey, came upon him; and when he saw him, he felt compassion, ³⁴ and came to him and bandaged up his wounds, pouring oil and wine on them; and he put him on his own beast, and brought him to an inn and took care of him. ³⁵ And on the next day, he took out two denarii[121] and gave them to the innkeeper, and said, "Take care of him; and whatever more you spend, when I return I will repay you.' ³⁶ Which of these three, do you think, proved to be a neighbor to the man who fell among the robbers?" ³⁷ And he said, "The one who showed mercy toward him." Then Jesus said to him, "Go and do likewise."

This man had to admit the elite in the Jewish religion, the priest, and the Levite, had not been neighborly, but the Samaritan proved to be a good neighbor. Jesus moved him to reason out a new way of viewing exactly what "neighbor" meant. Instead of letting the man walk him into a long debate, Jesus made the man do all of the reasoning in the conversation and moved him to admit something no Jew would ever utter and grasp a whole new understanding of what it meant to be a neighbor. Jesus took this approach because the circumstances called for it. However, on another occasion, a scribe, another expert in the law, asked him the same question

---

[121] The denarius was equivalent to a day's wages for a laborer

and on that occasion, he chose to give the direct answer. (Mark 12:28-31) Circumstances vary.

What lessons can we take in from the example that Luke provided us? **(1)** Jesus **used the Scriptures** initially to answer the man's question. **(2)** Jesus proved **perceptive** enough to **take notice** of the man's agenda. **(3)** Jesus did not simply answer the easy Bible question but **shifted the responsibility** to **a question** of his own by asking the man how he understood the law, giving him a chance to express himself. **(4)** Jesus **complimented** the man for discerning the correct answer. **(5)** Jesus made sure the man and the listeners **made the connection** between the initial question and the Scriptures. **(6)** Jesus **used an illustration** that was able to **reach the heart and mind**, where the answer was kept to the forefront. **(7)** Jesus moved the man **to reason** beyond his basic understanding of a neighbor. We need to revisit our theme text, Acts 17:2-3.

Explaining and Proving

Acts 17:2-3 Updated American Standard Version (UASV)

² And according to Paul's custom, he went to them, and for three Sabbaths reasoned with them **[the Jews]** from the Scriptures, ³ **explaining and proving** that it was necessary that the Christ had to suffer and rise again from the dead, and saying, "This Jesus whom I am proclaiming to you is the Christ."

We have already spoken about the fact that Paul reasoned from the Scriptures. However, he did more, as one can see from the above, that he explained, proved, and made an application. You often may read a Scripture to someone, and while it seems straightforward enough to you, the listener fails to see the point. As we mentioned previously, you may highlight a word or phrase or a part of the text and then explain the verse, that is, what the Bible author meant by the words that he used. We are doing that with Acts 17:2-3, as we highlight **explaining and proving**. You could also offer to walk them through the context like we also did previously with Acts 17:2-3, when we backed up to verse 1, to show that Paul reasoned from the Scriptures because he talked with Jews in the Synagogue, people who would be familiar with the Hebrew Scriptures. Another option is offering them additional texts that support the one the evangelist used. If the listener does not grasp the text and the explanation, add an illustration like Jesus did over forty times. Then again, asking the right questions might get the listener to reason about things further.

The person who makes a claim has the burden of proving it by offering sound arguments. As stated previously, one must give evidence that reasonably satisfies any statements that are made. Never be troubled over a listener asking for proof, as they have every right to do so. By thorough arguments, rational reasoning, and serious appeal, you can overturn any faulty reasoning of the one who is listening.

When the person an evangelist talks to makes a claim, he is then responsible for proving it. He may begin with a wrong proposition that forms the basis of his argument or from which a conclusion is drawn. Maybe, the sources he is using are biased, which can be pointed out to him. Additionally, you might point out that part of his argument is superficial. Moreover, if you know the issue well enough, one may notice the listener offering evidence yet failing to mention any facts that support his argument. Then again, one might point out that his evidence is not really evidence at all but simply appeals to emotion instead of reasons.

The Bible is the primary evidence for Christians, while other sources are secondary. However, as already stated, the majority of people no longer hold the Bible as an authority. Therefore, the evangelist must be versatile by being able to use both in conjunction with each other or depend on the secondary evidence until the listener begins to see the value and reasonableness of Scripture. For example, one may use the universe as evidence of a Creator.

The universe reveals God's existence. It is evident that the things which constituted the universe could not have made themselves (see Cosmological Argument). There must be "a first cause eternally existing, of a nature totally different to any material existence we know of, and by the power of which all things exist; and this first cause, man calls God" (ibid. 26; cf. 28). Paine also argued from motion. Since the universe consists of matter that cannot move itself, the origin of the rotation of the planets is impossible unless there exists an external first cause which set them in motion. This First Cause must be God (Aldridge, 6:17). He also argued from design (see Teleological Argument). Since the "work of man's hands is a proof of the existence of man," and since a watch is "positive evidence of the existence of a watch-maker," then "in like manner the creation is

evidence to our reason and our senses of the existence of a Creator"
(*Complete Works*, 310).[122]

If an evangelist witnesses to someone who sees the Bible as the word
of man, not the word of God, how should one respond? Seeing what Bible
scholars such as Dr. Norman L. Geisler or Dr. Gleason L. Archer have to
say may be helpful. However, the evidence is not the fact that they are
saying it is the Word of God, but rather what they provide as evidence.
Support from someone that agrees with you, especially the like of the above
scholars, is evidence, but it is low-level evidence. One could use science by
starting with what Scripture says first and then use science to confirm or
give support.

Regardless of whatever one attempts to prove, the level of evidence
required will be dependent on the person to whom you are talking. With
some outside sources, the average person may not need more than
Scriptural proof. Some may require a tremendous amount of evidence. A
few people will not be convinced as no amount of evidence will persuade
them to change their minds. Their heart and mind are closed to the light of
truth. They are mentally blind. The evidence that will satisfy this person
may not be enough to satisfy another. Therefore, one must pay attention to
the listener to meet their needs sufficiently.

One must appreciate that the evangelist seeks redeemable ones, one's
who hearts and minds are open to truth or can be opened to the truth.
Believers do not seek people with closed minds and hearts. Jesus said, "Do
not give dogs what is holy, and do not throw your pearls before pigs, lest
they trample them underfoot and turn to attack you." (Matt 7:6) One will
recognize these after some experience in witnessing. One sign is that they
present a claim that the Bible is man's word, not God, and is full of errors
and contradictions. Ask for one, and they provide one that they feel is the
nail in the coffin of the Bible. The evangelist offers them a reasonable
answer, which they cannot dispute, so they act as though they never raised
that issue and go on to another. The evangelist then gives them a
reasonable answer to that one, which they cannot dispute. Instead of
showing appreciation that they have received answers to these supposed
issues, they act as though they never asked and move on to the next.

---

[122] Norman L. Geisler, *Baker Encyclopedia of Christian Apologetics*, Baker Reference Library (Grand
Rapids, MI: Baker Books, 1999), 573.

Therefore, the pattern will continue, as they do not seek answers, as they have a closed mind and heart.

How can any Christian obtain or develop more fully the skill to reason from the Scriptures? Several things are essential: **(1)** One must accurately understand what the Scriptures say and mean. One must prepare for Christian meetings that one regularly attends. Regular personal Bible study, every day is necessary. **(2)** One must have a complete picture of the history of the Bible from Genesis 1:1 to Revelation 22:21. This can be accomplished by studying through a book like the *Holman Bible Handbook* by David S. Dockery (Nov 2, 1992). **(3)** One must have an understanding of Bible difficulties, which run from Genesis 1:1 to Revelation 22:21. This can be accomplished by studying through *The Big Book of Bible Difficulties: Clear and Concise Answers from Genesis to Revelation* by Norman L. Geisler and Thomas Howe (Jun 1, 2008). **(4)** One must have an accurate understanding of the Bible background of Bible times. One can accomplish this by studying through *Nelson's New Illustrated Bible Manners And Customs How The People Of The Bible Really Lived* by Vos, Howard (May 15, 1999). **(5)** One definitely must understand how to interpret the Bible correctly. This can be accomplished by studying *Basic Bible Interpretation* by Roy B. Zuck (Jan 1991). **(6)** One must meditate and ponder the things he or she learns, mentally exploring the information from various perspectives and appreciate their significance. **(7)** While one studies the Bible, look for not only clarifications of Scriptures but also Scriptural whys and wherefores for those clarifications. **(8)** As one studies, consider how to use the verses to explain biblical truths to different groups of people. **(9)** Contemplate and ponder what kind of illustrations might be used to make biblical points.

Review Questions

(1) Who must we be prepared to reason with? What does reasoning mean? How is a conversation like tossing a ball? What did James mean by "open to reason?" Explain how Paul reasoned differently, depending on his audience. How did Paul use information differently, depending on his audience? How do we find commonalities with people who do not know the Bible or those who do not recognize its authority?

(2) Why is the Christian mind so critical in spiritual warfare? Why are Bible critics getting away with offering misleading and false information? If Christians are to be effective in evangelism work,

what ability do they need? Where are most Christians hiding today? What ideas are the greatest obstacle to one receiving the gospel?

(3) What is biblical and Christian apologetics? What does the Greek word (epignosis) mean? Christians who come into the faith outside of apologetics usually are unable to do what? Christians who believe but do not know why are often what? The solution to this problem is for believers to do what? When reasoning with others, why should we not unload all of the evidence?

(4) How did Jesus use questions effectively? What lessons can one take in from the example that Luke provides in 28:25-37? Based on Paul in Acts 17, what more is needed than reasoning from the Scriptures? Who is responsible for providing the evidence? If the Bible critic makes a claim, what weaknesses may the evangelist look for being used? If one witnesses to someone who sees the Bible as the word of man, not the word of God, how should one respond? Why will someone have to provide different levels of evidence? How can any Christian obtain or fully develop the skill to reason from the Scriptures?

CHAPTER 7 Effectively Communicating With Others

Whether you are gathering to go out into your community, to share the good news with the locals, or staying at the church to make calls, your frame of mind is essential. If you have a negative attitude that day, you must get it right. You need to go to God in prayer before ever leaving the house, asking him for the strength to set aside any mental disposition that may hamper your communication and help you endure and overturn any potential negativity from others.

Negative Attitudes

The way you approach others while communicating biblical truths to them will determine if they will be receptive or unreceptive to your message. People love to share their perspectives on everything. So you are bound to hear some whom you will be witnessing to, who will offer incorrect information, irrational thoughts, misconceptions about the Bible, even criticism of the Bible and Christianity as a whole, among other things. We are the ones that must maintain our composure because "A soft answer turns away wrath, but a harsh word stirs up anger." (Proverbs 15:1)

Finding Fault

First, you do not want to **find fault** with every incorrect statement that they may make. If you are correcting everything they say, you will come across as negative. It is best to choose your battles, so to speak. Then, if you **word things thoughtfully**, they will fall on receptive ears. The one you are talking with says, "I have read a few books that claim the Bible has thousands of errors and contradictions; it then listed dozens throughout." First, they are the victim of the Bible critic, so you will need to choose your words carefully.

'Yes, this is a common comment that I hear, and I would add that they are more along the lines of what we call Bible difficulties, not contradictions and errors. A Bible difficulty is something in the Bible that is difficult to understand because we are thousands of years removed from their culture, because it was written in ancient languages. After all, the reader has not noticed that two writers are looking at things from two different points of view, among many other things." Then you offer to give an example. "May I give you an example?" He responds with a yes, and you offer an example.

You tell him, "If you were to speak to officers who take accident reports for their police department, you would find cohesion in the accounts, but each person has merely witnessed aspects that have stood out to them. We will see that this is the case as we look at the same account by two different Bible writers." You open your Bible and have him read,

Matthew 8:5: When he entered Capernaum, *a centurion* came forward to him, appealing to him.

Then have him read,

Luke 7:3: When *the centurion* heard about Jesus, he sent to him *elders of the Jews*, asking him to come and heal his servant.

You then say, "Immediately, you likely noticed the problem of whether **the centurion** or the **elders of the Jews** spoke with Jesus." He nods his head in agreement. You then say, "The solution is not really hidden from us." You then ask, "Which of the two accounts is the more detailed account?" He responds with, "Luke." "Correct," you respond. Then you explain to him, "The centurion sent the elders of the Jews to represent him to Jesus so that whatever response Jesus might give, it would be as though he were addressing the centurion; therefore, Matthew gave his readers the basic thought, not seeing the need of mentioning the elders of the Jews aspect. This is how a representative was viewed in the first century, just as some countries see ambassadors today as being the person they represent. Therefore, both Matthew and Luke are correct."

Respecting the Person

People will have their own views, but you must come across **respectfully**. You respect the person, not necessarily their view. The person you are talking with may ask, "Why do Christians hate homosexuals?" You would respond with something like, "Christians should not have an irrational hatred for those that struggle with same-sex attraction. We are to respect all people. Anyone spewing hatred, he is not truly acting like Jesus. (Matt. 7:12) We are to reject same-sex relationships, the conduct, not the person. For those that are advocates for gay rights, this is their viewpoint, and we **respectfully** disagree and **respectfully** articulate as to why."

She responds with another question: "Did Jesus not visit sinners and was he not tolerant of others?" You then reply with something like, "Yes, this is partially true, but the inference is mistaken. Jesus spent time with sinners, but he did not ever condone their sin."

"You are right,[123] the Bible does not condone hating those who struggle with same-sex attraction, but we are to hate the sin, not the one who may be practicing the sin. However, we are to make a stand against sin that is against the moral code of our Creator, and we are not to cave to public opinion. The moral code reflects our Christian lifestyle within Scripture, and we have a right to our position by the Creator himself. There is no reason that we should be ashamed of our viewpoint."

Good Communication

Your objective is to share the truth without giving in to popular opinion. However, the truth you want to share will be better received when you afford them the opportunity to share their thoughts and ideas. Then, you express your respectful appreciation for sharing their time with you. You engender trust when they feel that you are listening and that they are involved in a two-way conversation instead of being on the receiving end of a lecture.

Take Notice of Your Surroundings

If you are going to share your Bible beliefs effectively, you will have to be observant of your surroundings. Taking note of what you hear and see will help you have far more success. You may be witnessing from house to house, so you should note when the person answers the door or comes from the backyard to greet you. Are there toys, meaning they have children? Is the house immaculately clean? Are there trophies on mantles? Does the house look like it is going through some restoration? Is the newspaper or a magazine lying there with a current affair on the cover? These types of things can be used to generate conversations. However, at the same time, do not come across as being too curious. You should make eye contact, letting them know that you are listening, but not to the point of making them uncomfortable. You may also note body language and the pitch and tone of their words, helping you to know their interest level.

---

[123] You want to say that they are right at every opportunity where that is the case, which helps them to see that you do not just disagree blindly, because not everything is always bland and white.

How You Can Be Clear

Do not rush your words, and express them so that the other person can easily understand you. This means that you should be aware of the pace of your speech, and you may want to slow down and pronounce your words more distinctly in private reading. You can practice this in your private Bible reading, where you can read aloud, speaking clearly. However, do not let this become a habit.

Being clear with what you mean to convey can be accomplished by not being bogged down in many unnecessary words but rather being more concise. In other words, if you need to make a point that has multiple parts, it is best that the initial basis of your argument is short and clearly written or stated. Thereafter, you follow it with rational arguments that are mentally clear in their meaning or intention, which your reader or listener can easily understand. Jesus was the greatest teacher who ever lived, and he on many occasions, took the incredibly complex Mosaic Law and made it easier to understand for his audience.

To effectively teach someone, you must have a solid understanding of the subject yourself, to then help others understand the material. You are ready to teach a subject when you are, in your own words, able to offer reasons as to why it is or is not so. Jesus was able to get his points across by keeping things simple, using indisputable reasoning, stimulating questions, remarkable figures of speech, and discernible illustrations are taken from his listener's everyday life. (Matt. 6:25-30; 7:3-5, 24-27) Jesus was also known for his taking an incident occurring around him and his disciples, which he would then use as an opportunity to teach a lesson. (John 13:2-16)

Sadly, some Bible scholars have placed their books out of the hands of the typical person, as they use language that requires the reader to hold their book in one hand and a Webster's Dictionary in the other. By their nature, these individuals are a polysyllabricator who uses sesquipedalian words. In other words, they use long words with many syllables. Sadly, these individuals spend hundreds, if not thousands, of hours researching and writing a book that five people are going to read. In the Sermon on the Mount, Matthew 5:3–7:27, Jesus spoke for a mere half hour, covering anger, lust, divorce, retaliation, helping the needy, prayer, fasting, anxiety, and judging others, materialism. He did not use long words with many syllables here and could be understood by children, farmers, fishermen, and shepherds. (Matt. 7:28)

Jesus expressed word pictures that conveyed the riches of meaning, even today. For example, "No one can serve two masters ... You cannot serve God and money." (Matt. 6:24) "You will recognize them by their fruits." (Matt. 7:20) "Judge not, that you be not judged." (Matt. 7:21) But when he heard it, he said, "Those who are well have no need of a physician, but those who are sick." (Matt. 9:12) Then Jesus said to him, "Put your sword back into its place. For all who take the sword will perish by the sword. (Matt. 26:52) Jesus said to them, "Render to Caesar the things that are Caesar's, and to God the things that are God's." (Mark 12:17)

Effective Use of Questions

On many occasions, Jesus could have simply told his listeners the point that he wanted to get across, but instead, he chose to ask them questions. For those that were looking to make him look a fool, Jesus asked questions to expose these people. (Matt. 12:24-30; 21:23-27; 22:41-46) However, he often used his questions to convey the point he wanted to make, and he wanted them to remember.

Matthew 17:24-27 Updated American Standard Version (UASV)

[24] When they arrived in Capernaum, the ones who collected the double drachma tax[124] came up to Peter and said, "Does your teacher not pay the double drachma tax?"[125] [25] He said, "Yes." And when he came into the house, Jesus spoke to him first, saying, "What do you think, Simon? From whom do kings of the earth collect tolls or tax? From their sons or from strangers?" [26] And when he said, "From strangers," Jesus said to him, "Then the sons are free. [27] However, so that we do not cause them to stumble, go to the sea and throw in a hook, and take the first fish that comes up; and when you open its mouth, you will find a shekel.[126] Take that and give it to them for you and me."

---

[124] This was two drachmas paid by each male Jew as a yearly temple tax.

[125] This was two drachmas paid by each male Jew as a yearly temple tax.

[126] A stater coin, a silver coin worth two didrachma or approximately one shekel.

Effective Use of Hyperbole

Again, Jesus is by far the most effective teacher of all time, and hyperbole is one method he often used. Hyperbole is a deliberate and obvious exaggeration used for effect, e.g., "I could eat a million of these." The objective is to add emphasis and importance to what is being said. Moreover, like other special literary forms, hyperbole imprints a mental picture in your mind, one that is hard to forget.

There are actually two different types of exaggerations: **(1)** the first being an overstatement but possible, and **(2)** hyperbole, which is a statement that is impossible. Our concern is that we might have the ability to recognize either of these when we see them. Let us look at a few examples.

Matthew 7:1-3 Updated American Standard Version (UASV)

7 "Do not judge so that you will not be judged. ² For with the judgment you are judging you will be judged, and by what measure you are measuring, it will be measured to you. ³ Why do you look <u>at the speck that is in your brother's eye, but do not notice the **log** that is in your own eye</u>?

Try to picture what is being emphasized. You have a person who is continuously and aggressively judging others, who goes up to a brother that is seldom critical, to offer advice on not being critical. A brother with a log's worth of being judgmental to him is advising the brother that has a mere straw of judgmentalism. Is this not a beautiful way to illustrate how a brother, who has immense problems in a particular area, should be slow to offer advice to another brother, who seldom offends in this area? Below Jesus is rebuking some Pharisees, Jewish religious leaders.

Matthew 23:24 Updated American Standard Version (UASV)

²⁴ Blind guides, who strain out a gnat and swallow a camel!

This was the foremost way to use hyperbole. Take note of the fact that he is contrasting a small gnat with a huge camel, which represents the largest animal known to his audience. One religious magazine stated, "It is estimated that it would take up to 70 million gnats to equal the weight of an average camel!" Jesus was also very much aware that the Pharisees strained their wine through a cloth sieve to avoid ceremonial uncleanness by accidentally drinking a gnat. However, they were quite eager to gulp down the figurative camel, it also being unclean. (Lev. 11:4, 21-24) How? The

Pharisees were very quick to follow the minor points of the Mosaic Law but set aside the weightier laws, like "justice and mercy and faithfulness." (Matt. 23:23) This one point makes using hyperbole all too clear and exposes them for the hypocrites they were.

Matthew 17:20 Updated American Standard Version (UASV)

20 And he said to them, "Because of your little faith. For truly I say to you, if you have faith like a mustard seed, you will say to this mountain, 'Move from here to there,' and it will move, and nothing will be impossible for you."

Jesus could have simply said that they need more faith, but that would not have made the impact this figurative comment did. He only stressed the need for a little faith in an effective manner, making the point that a small amount of faith can move mountain-like objects.

Matthew 19:24 Updated American Standard Version (UASV)

24 Again I say to you, it is easier for a camel to go through the eye of a needle than for a rich man to enter the Kingdom of God."

Try if you will to picture a camel fitting through the eye of a sewing needle. It is impossible, not difficult! Of course, this does not mean that rich people are excluded from the kingdom of God. The context is about people, who have a greater love for money than their love of the kingdom. It is their love of money, which makes them ineligible. Jesus' colorful, vivid idioms have an effect so powerful that literally hundreds of millions of people have used them over the last 2,000 years.

Throughout his three and a half years of ministry, Jesus masterfully used hyperbole. Are you not in awe of Jesus' exciting figures of speech and his skill of accomplishing a maximum effect without long words with many syllables?

Overcoming Dismissive Comments

Many today are just not interested in your desire to share the Good News with them. They will attempt to shut you down with one good dismissive comment in the beginning. Your objective is to become effective in your ability to overcome or get around these walls of disinterest. They may hold up their hand, which is a dismissive gesture, and say in a dismissive tone,

- "I am not interested."
- "I am not interested in religion."
- "I am busy."
- "Why do Christians feel the need to share?"
- "I am a Buddhist, a Hindu, a Muslim, or a Jew."
- "I don't believe the Bible."
- "Everyone interprets the Bible differently."
- "The Bible is not practical in today's scientific world."
- "The Bible contradicts itself."
- The Bible is a good book by man, but there is no such thing as absolute truth."

These quick comments are meant to stop us in our tracks. These dismissive comments can be general, "I am not interested," or they could be based on the subject you start the conversation with. People have many reasons as to why they do not want to talk, and most are misconceptions.

- They had a bad experience in a congregation they had attended before.
- They have taken many liberal classes throughout their high school and college years.
- They are aware of Christian history, like crusades, inquisitions, or immoral Popes in church history.
- They are aware of major church scandals.
- They have read popular books that tear down the Bible as being full of historical, geographical, and scientific errors and contradictions. To them, the book is by imperfect men, not inspired by God.
- Maybe their life has been filled with one tragedy after another, and they cannot grasp how a loving God would allow such suffering.

These are some of the reasons why they use dismissive comments. They have issues that are not well-founded and need to be reasoned on further. That is why, many times, if you can get beyond the comment, you can get at what really troubles them and help them reason through it. Below is an example of one trying to be dismissive, using the Bible to shut down the conversation.

'The Bible contains contradictions, mistakes, and errors'

Whoever makes a claim carries the responsibility, so tactfully inquire, "Yes, this is a common claim. Could you take my Bible and point to an example?" Most will not take the Bible because they are just repeating a common complaint about the Bible. However, for the sake of those few who will, he takes your Bible and turns to Matthew 27:5 and says, "It states that Judas hanged himself," whereas Acts 1:18 says that "falling headlong he burst open in the middle and all his bowels gushed out."

Matthew 27:5 Updated American Standard Version (UASV)

⁵ And he threw the pieces of silver into the temple and departed; and he went away and **hanged himself**.

Acts 1:18 Updated American Standard Version (UASV)

¹⁸ (Now this man acquired a field with the price of his wickedness, and **falling headlong**, he burst open in the middle and all his intestines gushed out.

You Respond: "Neither Matthew nor Luke made a mistake. What you have is Matthew giving the reader the manner in which Judas committed suicide. On the other hand, Luke is giving the reader of Acts the result of that suicide. Therefore, instead of a mistake, we have two texts that complement each other, really giving the reader the full picture. Judas came to a tree alongside a cliff that had rocks below. He tied the rope to a branch and the other end around his neck and jumped over the edge of the cliff in an attempt to hang himself. One of two things could have happened: (1) the limb broke, plunging him to the rocks below, or (2) the rope broke with the same result, and he burst open onto the rocks below."

Then you could add, "Generally, it comes down to many books that criticize the Bible, pointing to Scriptures, showing what they call errors, contradictions, and mistakes. However, they do not show the reader that there are reasonable answers for ninety-nine percent of these complaints.'

A longer response might be, "Considering that there are 31,000 plus verses in the Bible, encompassing 66 books written by about 40 writers, ranging from shepherds, to kings, an army general, fishermen, tax collector, a physician and on and on, and being penned over a 1,600 year period, one does find a few hundred *Bible difficulties* (about one percent). However, 99 percent of those are explainable. Yet no one wants to be so arrogant to say that he can explain them all. It has nothing to do with the inadequacy of

God's Word but is based on human understanding. In many cases, science or archaeology and the field of custom and culture of ancient peoples has helped explain difficulties in hundreds of passages. Therefore, there may be less than one percent left to be answered, yet our knowledge of God's Word continues to grow. R. A. Torrey said about 100 years ago, "Some people are surprised and staggered because there are difficulties in the Bible. For my part, I would be more surprised and staggered if there were not."

You explain that these are not contradictions, errors, or mistakes but are Bible difficulties, which are difficult because the Bible was written in dozens of different cultures and times that range from 2,000 to 3,500 years ago. In addition, the Bible was written in three different ancient languages. Moreover, the Bible was written with the intention of human authors back then, and we should not impose our modern world on that author. Today, in our news reports, we say that the sun rises and sets at certain times, even though we know this is scientifically inaccurate. However, it is human observation. Today, we round numbers because it simplifies things if we are trying to make a point, like how many people live in America. We would just say 316 million, not 315,940,341, unless we were doing a census. Jesus spoke of mustard seeds as the smallest of all seeds. This is not accurate. However, was Jesus giving a lesson on botany? No, he was making a point to people who knew this seed as being the smallest. Therefore, considering Jesus' audience, the point that he was making, and how the mustard seed was commonly used as a figure of speech, this was the tiniest seed in that setting and circumstance.

Either this person raising issues about the Bible is going to be more receptive to the conversation, or he will ignore your insight as though you never made it, moving on to the next criticism that he has memorized. His response is a way for you to read his heart attitude. You will not want to throw your pearls before the swine of Bible criticism, so move on if it is evident that no answer will satisfy this one. However, far more right-hearted ones are going to be receptive to your insightful words. This brings us to our next point, how they listen to you.

How the Unbeliever Listens to Us

Getting a sense of how one is listening to us will enable us to determine if more time should be given to this one. The person we are talking with may very well be what is known as a **judgmental listener**. They are listening to us to ascertain whether we are right or wrong and are labeling us in their mind ('that was foolish') instead of hearing what we are saying. Then, there is what is known as the **distorted listener**. In other words, this one does not hear us clearly, because he is viewing us in a biased and prejudiced way ('Christians are such fools!'). There is the **stereotype listener**, who also fails to hear our real message because they are labeling us in their mind as "just a woman," "Bible thumper," "so naïve," and so on.

Then, the resistive listener will not be receptive to anything that is not a part of his worldview. Moreover, anyone in opposition to their worldview is viewed as the enemy, and they resist anything they say, no matter how reasonable it may be. They think things like, 'Why do these people not see that science has displaced the Bible as a book by man." We also have the **interpretive listener**. These view everything through their preconceptions, ideas based on little or no information, just personal bias. They incorporate their life experience into what they are hearing, making snap interpretations of our every word. They filter everything through their worldview, their knowledge, and understanding.

Then, the association listener evaluates our Christian visit with everything bad they have ever heard of Christianity and the Bible, and we are guilty by association. No matter what we say, it is ignored because they see us as a member of a group that they perceive a certain way. Of course, this could go the other way if they have a favorable view of Christianity. While these are the negative side of listening, they can give us an idea of why and how we could be shut out before getting started. If we feel unfairly dismissed, we could ask open-ended questions such as 'how do you feel,' 'what do you think,' 'what do you believe,' or 'how do you see these questions.' Open-ended questions enable us to get to their heart condition, enabling us to formulate our arguments better.

Lastly, there are the persons that all Christian evangelizers are looking for, which is the **receptive heart listener**. One who has a receptive heart will let us reason from the Scriptures receptively, which will build confidence that what we are saying is true. We will be able to plant seeds of truth within this person's heart, which God will make grow. In writing to the Corinthians, who were caught up in arguing over who was greater (Paul or Apollos), Paul made the comparison of a Christian evangelist with that of a farmer. The Apostle Paul planted the Corinthian congregation. Apollos came later on the scene and watered the Bible truths that Paul had already planted. With his passion and force and his authoritative Scriptural refutations of the arguments that the unbelieving Jews had raised, Apollos was very beneficial to the Corinthian Christians. However, it was God, who made those truths grow.

1 Corinthians 3:1-9 Updated American Standard Version (UASV)

Corinthians Still Fleshly

3 And I, brothers, was not able to speak to you as to spiritual men, but as to fleshly men, as to infants in Christ. ² I gave you milk to drink, not solid food, for you were not yet ready. But now you are still not able, ³ for you are still fleshly. For since there is jealousy and strife among you, are you not fleshly, and are you not walking like mere men? ⁴ For when one says, "I am of Paul," and another, "I am of Apollos," are you not mere men?

God Makes It Grow

⁵ What then is Apollos? And what is Paul? Servants through whom you believed, as the Lord assigned to each. ⁶ I planted, Apollos watered, but God gave the growth. ⁷ So then neither the one who plants nor the one who waters is anything, but only God who gives the growth. ⁸ Now he who plants and he who waters are one; but each will receive his own reward according to his own labor. ⁹ For we are God's fellow workers; you are God's field, God's building.

Keep in mind that the receptive heart listener is not just the person, who shakes his head yes, as he agrees with your every word. Peter was sent to the Ethiopian Eunuch (Acts 8:26-38), who had rapid spiritual progress, while the Apostle Paul was sent to the Greek philosophers on Mars Hill.

Mars Hill (Areopagus) was a "prominent rise overlooking the city of Athens where the philosophers of the city gathered to discuss their ideas, some of which revolutionized modern thought. Paul discussed religion with the leading minds of Athens on Mars Hill. He used the altar to an 'unknown god' to present Jesus to them (Acts 17:22)."[127]

The point is that the Apostle Paul was sent to people who were very knowledgeable, intelligent, and wise, who only lacked the light to see where the real truth lies. This was no easy assignment, but in the end, "some men joined [Paul] and believed, among whom also were Dionysius the Areopagite and a woman named Damaris and others with them." (Acts 17:34) Yes, Paul reasoned from the Scriptures in the synagogue with the Jews, and he reasoned with Epicurean and Stoic philosophers, who also

---

[127] "Mars Hill", in Holman Illustrated Bible Dictionary, ed. Chad Brand, Charles Draper, Archie England et al., 1084 (Nashville, TN: Holman Bible Publishers, 2003).

conversed with him. It says that he was "explaining and proving." This illustrates that a receptive heart listener also includes those who require us to reason from the Scriptures; therefore, we have to have the ability to reason from the Scriptures. (Acts 17: 2-3, 17-18)

Effective Listening and Responding

It can be quite a challenge in trying to communicate with strangers at times. We may deal with biases, prejudices, a person in the middle of life trauma, someone who has had bad experiences, someone who just lost a loved one, and many more communication challenges. We will be able to overcome some of the anxieties of starting a conversation by taking a moment to consider some of these challenges.

One of the ways to deal with a challenge is empathy. We, in our hearts, must place ourselves in their shoes, getting their mindset. Just because a person comes across abrasively about talking about the Bible, this does not mean that we let them go. There may very well be a reason as to why they are not open to a Bible conversation. This is where insightful, thought-provoking questions can get at the significant part that has closed them down.

By employing active listening and allowing them to vent, we will understand whatever issues we need to overcome. We might ask, 'tell me, what have you to where you are unable to talk about the Bible.' This will let them know that we are open to listening. While they are expressing themselves, do not be tempted to resolve their issue; just listen as they fully explain. First, make sure we respond in a calm voice. Then reiterate what they said in a summary point, which will let them know we were listening, and it helps us to know we understand what it is. In the end, we may not agree, but we can empathetically understand in some way.

Now, if we have a solution to what was mentioned, offer it at this time. If we do not have a biblical answer, be honest, saying something like, "I can understand, and while I do not have a ready answer for you at this time, I will research it at home, and we can talk again." This lets them know that we are going beyond what one would expect and that we are very concerned about them.

Review Questions

(1) Why is it important that we pray about our mindset before we ever go out to evangelize our community?

(2) What balance should someone have if the unbeliever to whom one witnesses to is mistaken on almost everything they believe about the Bible? How might you respond to an unbeliever that has heard that the Bible is full of errors and contradictions?

(3) What does it mean to respect the person, but possibly not their view? How might you respond to a person that claims that Christians hate homosexuals? How would you respond to a person who uses Jesus visiting sinners and tolerating others as a means to rationalize and accept practicing homosexuals?

(4) What is the benefit of being observant when witnessing to others?

(5) Why is clear pronunciation important? What should you do if an unbeliever asks you a Bible question that requires a complex answer? Why have some Bible scholars found themselves out of touch with most people? How did Jesus usually express himself?

(6) Who set the example of effective use of questions? Give an example.

(7) What are some dismissive comments that the unbeliever might make, and what is his purpose for making such comments? What are some legitimate reasons the Bible critic might not be interested in talking about Christianity or the Bible?

(8) How might you respond to someone that claims the Bible contains contradictions, mistakes, and errors? How might you explain why there are no contradictions, errors, or mistakes in the Bible, just Bible difficulties?

(9) What type of listeners is there, and which one is the evangelist seeking? Are Christians expected only to evangelize those who are easy to convince?

CHAPTER 8 Becoming a Better Communicator

We cannot participate in the Great Commission that Jesus assigned every Christian without effectively communicating with others. (Matt. 24:14; 28:19, 20; Acts 1:8) Suppose an intimate family of husband and wife, father and children, mother and children, struggle to communicate with each other. How are we to be expected to communicate well with strangers?

We must empathize with the people whom we are trying to evangelize. Individuals live busy lives, and then they face people trying to sell them things, people trying to get their vote, people trying to debate and argue ideologies, people trying to do them harm, and the list continues. This can force most people to shut out the noise by not talking with strangers. The good thing is we as Christians can communicate a message to strangers even before we say one word. How? We send a nonverbal sign to others just by being different in our appearance, conduct, or behavior. If we were to go to a very big mall [128] and sit watching people for a few hours, would we be able to pick out the Christians in the crowd? Therefore, we communicate by displaying a humble, unassuming personal appearance before we say one word.

In addition, to communicate effectively, we must not be anxious or appear worried. If we are anxious, then the stranger we approach will be apprehensive. If we display a sense of calm and ease, he will more likely listen to us. What makes us less anxious? The Apostle Peter said that we must "**always to be prepared** to make a defense to anyone who asks you for a reason for the hope." (1 Pet. 3:15) Certainly, a well-prepared person is going to be less nervous than someone not prepared. We will draw people to the Good News when they sense this peace of mind that dwells in us.

Communication is a two-way street. If someone tends to dominate a conversation, others will not want to listen to us and may leave. Christ-followers need to learn how to be better listeners. If we ask a question, the other person must have the opportunity to speak, not be overcome by

---

[128] A mall is a large enclosed building complex containing stores, restaurants, and other businesses and facilities serving the general public.

one's zeal to share our message.[129] Moreover, we must demonstrate evidence that we are listening by looking the other person in the eyes and nodding our heads in agreement. You can also ask to clarify questions that dig deeper based on what the person said. Obviously, we go out to talk to others, and we have planned the things that we want to discuss. However, those whom we speak with may have things they want to talk about, so we must be flexible.

One of the most challenging adjustments that must be made is one's attitude. If one views himself as superior in any way, the other person will notice it. Christianity is the truth and the way, but one cannot be dogmatic in their expressions. Moreover, one will talk to liberal Christians,[130] who must be witnessed to just as any unbeliever because they must be led back to the flock. Therefore, suppose one witnesses to a liberal Christian who is repeatedly making unbiblical comments. Correct his unbiblical view, but one ought to not go on a rampage of one correction after another. If this is the first time, one speaks to him, overlook correcting him now. Build a rapport and establish a comfort level by finding common ground if possible. Yes, this may require a measure of self-control and skillful tact. When you meet a second time, choose a topic that you know he raised the first time, and see if you can get him to reason on that one matter. If the other person jumps from subject to subject, it would be best to confine it to one area with discernment and sensitivity.

Reason With Them from the Scriptures

Again, do not sound dogmatic in communicating, but instead, reason with them from the Scriptures, just as Paul did on many occasions. In fact, it says, "**As was his custom,**" meaning that Paul regularly went to the "synagogue of the Jews" to reason with them from the Scriptures, trying to convert them to Christianity. (Acts 17:2, 17; 18:19) To do this, one must be well prepared, which is exactly what any believer must do when one faces liberal or progressive Christians or others who have fallen away because of doubt. (Jude 1:3, 22-23) As one sees much wickedness in the world today,

---

[129] However, people can get off the subject at hand, and begin jumping from one topic to the next. If this proves the case, do not overtake the conversation; just lovingly guide them back on topic.

[130] Christian liberalism is based on a departure from the traditional tenets of biblical Christianity. Often, liberalism within Christian groups begins with a denial of the absolute reliability and historical accuracy of the Word of God. Hindson, Ed (2008-05-01). The Popular Encyclopedia of Apologetics (Kindle Locations 11793-11795). Harvest House Publishers. Kindle Edition.

the pain, the suffering, and death have caused many to doubt the very existence of God.[131]

To resolve the issues Satan raises, God has tolerated evil, sickness, pain, suffering, and death until today. People become self-centered in thinking that this has only pained us. Imagine that one holds a rope on a sinking ship that 20 other men, women, and children are clinging to when your child loses her grip and falls into the ocean. Either hold the rope, saving 20 people, or let go of the rope and attempt to rescue your child. God has been watching the suffering of billions from the day of Adam's and Eve's sin. Moreover, it has been his great love for us that causes him to cling to the rope that saves us from a future of the same issues.

Nevertheless, he will not allow this evil to remain forever. He has set a fixed time when he will end this wicked system of Satan's rule. (Eccles. 3:1-8) Galatians 4:4 says, "But when the fullness of time had come, God sent forth his Son, born of woman." However, this was over 4,000 years after he had made the promise to do just that. (Gen. 3:15) Similarly, it has been 2,000 years since God's Word has made the promise to end pain, suffering, and death. When the fullness of time comes, he will do that. One can take the person back to the beginning and establish that it was man who willfully entered human beings into this world of imperfection. The issues raised, offering illustrations of why those must be settled first, reasoning from the Scriptures.

What It Takes for Effective Communication

Matthew 11:28-30 Updated American Standard Version (UASV)

Jesus' Yoke Is Refreshing

[28] "Come to me, all you who are laboring and loaded down, and I will give you rest. [29] Take my yoke upon you and learn from me, for I am **gentle** and **lowly in heart**, and you will find rest for your souls. [30] For my yoke is easy,[132] and my burden is light."

Yes, if we are going to be effective communicators, we must learn from Jesus. What do we learn from Jesus? First, Jesus is "gentle," which is the English for the Greek word *praus* that is found "three times in Matthew and once in 1 Peter ... means 'gentle, humble, considerate, meek in the

---

[131] IF GOD IS GOOD: Why Does God Allow Suffering? Paperback – March 24, 2015 by Edward D Andrews. ISBN-13: 978-0692414620 (https://www.amazon.com/dp/0692414622)

[132] I.e. *easy to bear*

older favorable sense' (BAGD)."[133] In what sense was Jesus, "lowly in heart"?[134] With his knowledge and understanding, as the Son of God, he could have taught in Jewish schools, having some of the greatest Jewish minds as students. He could have taught the Jewish teachers themselves if he so desired.

However, Jesus chose to teach the lowliest of the Jewish world, from the seaside, fishermen. He lived and taught among the poor and the low in social position. It is a privilege to pattern ourselves after such a teacher as he was. This humility and lowliness of heart qualified him as the greatest teacher ever, so it will qualify us, as he teaches us, to be teachers of others. When we are lowly in heart, following in the footsteps of Jesus, we too will refresh others. A gentle, humble, considerate, and meek teacher will appeal to both the low and high in social standing. As those with a receptive heart found Jesus refreshing, this will be the case with us as well.

In Acts 20:19, it says that the Apostle Paul served the Lord "with all humility," with "humble-mindedness" or "humility of mind." The Greek (*tapeinophrosune*) literally reads "lowliness of mind."[135] It is derived from the words *tapeinos*, which means to "make low," "lowly, "humble" and *phren*, "the mind." Paul told the Philippians that they were to "do nothing from selfish ambition or conceit, but in humility **["lowliness of mind"]** count others more significant than yourselves." (Phil. 2:3-4) Paul also told the Corinthians, "Let no one seek his own good but the good of the other." (1 Cor. 10:24) This quality of "lowliness of mind" will stop us from assuming a superior attitude or tone when we speak to others about God's Word.

Additionally, if you want to be effective in your communication, one must follow Paul's counsel found at Colossians 4:6,

Colossians 4:6 Updated American Standard Version (UASV)

⁶ Let your speech always be gracious, seasoned with salt, so that you may know how you ought to answer each person.

---

[133] Leon Morris, The Gospel According to Matthew, The Pillar New Testament Commentary (Grand Rapids, MI; Leicester, England: W.B. Eerdmans; Inter-Varsity Press, 1992).

[134] The heart ([kardia]) is the core and center of man's being, the mainspring of dispositions as well as of feelings and thoughts. It is the very hub of the wheel of man's existence, the center from which all the spokes radiate (Prov. 4:23; cf. 1 Sam. 16:7). All of this also applies to Christ's human nature.—William Hendriksen and Simon J. Kistemaker, vol. 9, Exposition of the Gospel According to Matthew, New Testament Commentary (Grand Rapids: Baker Book House, 1953-2001).

[135] W. E. Vine, Merrill F. Unger and William White, Jr., vol. 2, Vine's Complete Expository Dictionary of Old and New Testament Words, 314 (Nashville, TN: T. Nelson, 1996).

Yes, this is the reason that anyone has purchased *The Evangelism Handbook*, to "study how best to talk with each person you meet." Certainly, patience and tact, which is skillfully expressing oneself when another person's feelings are involved, are two qualities that establish effective communication. When one communicates with others, one's words must be in good taste. Good speech will keep lines of communication open, but unwise, foolish, and careless comments will close those lines of communication.

A prepared person will not be anxious but will be relaxed, which will have a calming effect on the listener. But allow the listener to do most of the talking, to get at the heart of their thinking. One can never adjust another's thinking because one does not know what is going through their mind. For example, someone could comment, and one could choose a phrase and give several minutes of feedback, which proves irrelevant to what the person meant. It would have been better to ask, "What do you mean by …?" Once the person explains themselves, then we can offer our thoughts.

Loving Communication

The characteristics of being gentle, humble, considerate, meek, modest, lowliness of mind, tactfulness, and patience make the qualities of a good communicator. When a person also has selfless love, he or she becomes a great communicator.

Matthew 9:36 Updated American Standard Version (UASV)

36 When he saw the crowds, he had compassion for them, because they were **harassed** and **scattered**, like sheep without a shepherd.

Mark 6:34 Updated American Standard Version (UASV)

34 When he went ashore he saw a great crowd, and he had compassion on them, because they were like sheep without a shepherd. And he began to teach them many things.

"Harassed is from a verb meaning "to trouble," "distress." **Scattered** is from a verb meaning to throw down. The past tense used here implies the thoroughness of their oppression and its persistent effect on the people. These people were completely and perpetually discouraged."[136] The Jewish religious leaders of Jesus' day did next to nothing in offering enough to

---

136 Stuart K. Weber, vol. 1, Matthew, Holman New Testament Commentary, 130 (Nashville, TN: Broadman & Holman Publishers, 2000).

make common people feel pleased or content in their spiritual hunger. Rather, they made their lives even more burdensome with all of the rules and regulations that they tacked on to the Mosaic Law. (Matt. 12:1, 2; 15:1-9; 23:4, 23) The religious leaders revealed their true heart condition when they said about those listening to Jesus, "this crowd who does not know the law is accursed!" (John 7:49) Jesus' selfless love moved him to "find rest for their souls," getting on the road to life. Today, we have a message that is filled with love, and believers must offer love to people in a selfless way.

1 Thessalonians 2:7-8 Updated American Standard Version (UASV)

[7] But we became gentle[137] in the midst of you, as a nursing mother tenderly care for[138] her own children. [8] So, being affectionately desirous of you, we were well-pleased to impart to you not only the gospel of God but also our own souls,[139] because you became beloved to us.

2:7. Instead, Paul and Silas chose to be **gentle**. There is no tenderness quite like a mother's, and Paul dared to identify with maternal love and care. Greek writers used the term *gentleness* to describe those who dealt patiently and with a mild manner toward those who were difficult—obstinate children, unmanageable students, those who had not reached maturity and were experiencing the inconsistencies and struggles of development. Whatever difficulties the Thessalonians may have presented, Paul and Silas recognized that these new Christians were not yet "grown up." So rather than dealing with these people in an authoritarian manner, they chose to be patient—like a mother.

It is a great lesson for the church today, because we have not always been patient with new or young believers. Sometimes we have cut a mold and demanded that they fit it—now. Instead of this approach, we need to see each individual's need for help and encouragement as he or she struggles to conform to the image of Christ.

2:8. Here is a classic understanding of biblical love. To Paul, love is always a verb, it is doing. Feelings may accompany love, but they do not define it. Instead, the commitment of acting in the best interest of another opens the way for feelings: **We loved you so much that we were delighted to share ... our lives.**

It is easier to teach theology than to love, easier to share lists than time. Paul gave not only the message of the gospel, but the example of it as

---

[137] Some MSS read *babes*

[138] Or *cherishes*

[139] Or *lives*

well. He spent time. He shared joys and headaches. Parents and teachers, coaches and mentors, pastors and leaders know what it means to give part of their heart away to others. Love is not just a job. It is a way of life.

But note that Paul did *share* the gospel of God. He was balanced. He gave his life and love. He gave content as well. It is not enough to visit people in the hospital or prison, or to show compassion to the poor or those new in the faith. Somewhere, carefully and candidly, they must also hear the truth of the cross and what it means to trust and follow Christ.

Arguing whether the church should meet people's physical needs or whether it should limit itself to preaching the gospel is like debating which wing of an airplane is more important. Both are essential![140]

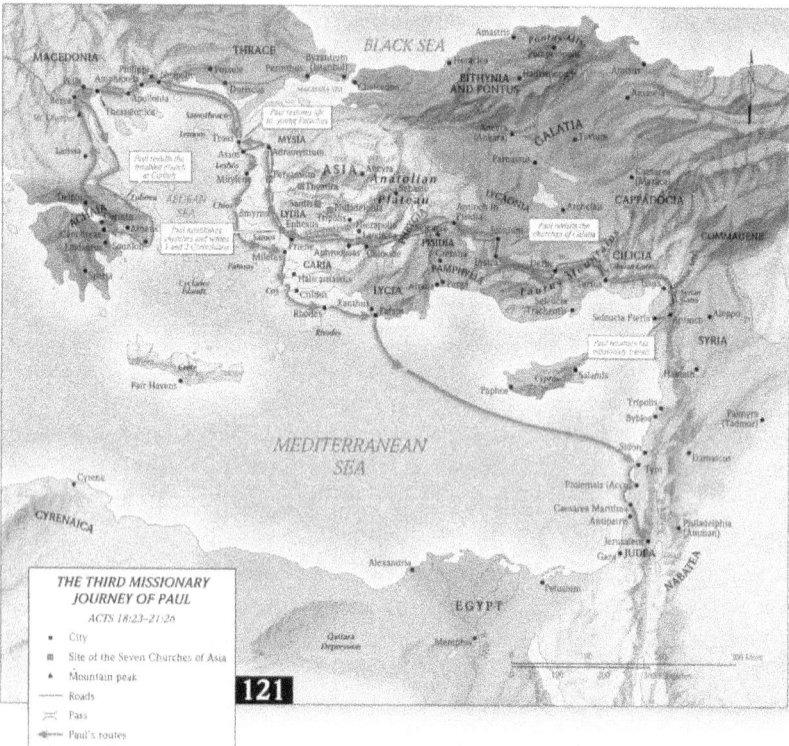

THE THIRD MISSIONARY
JOURNEY OF PAUL
ACTS 18:23–21:26

121

[140] Knute Larson, *I & II Thessalonians, I & II Timothy, Titus, Philemon*, vol. 9, Holman New Testament Commentary (Nashville, TN: Broadman & Holman Publishers, 2000), 23–24.

The Apostle Paul started numerous congregations, one right after the other, from Antioch of Syria, throughout Asia, into Macedonia, down through Greece and Achaia. What made Paul such an effective evangelist? Was it his zeal for spreading the Good News? Yes! The above says that Paul was "**affectionately desirous**" of the new Thessalonian congregation. "Here is a classic understanding of biblical love. To Paul, love is always a verb; it is doing. Feelings may accompany love, but they do not define it. Instead, the commitment to acting in the best interest of another opens the way for feelings: **We loved you so much that we were delighted to share ... our lives**."[141] Paul's love for God and his neighbor made him a successful evangelist.

If our message is repeatedly rejected, is this a sign of poor communication skills? It could be, but keep in mind; that most are going to reject the Christian message. The majority of the world will not be converted to true Christianity by the time of Christ's second coming. In addition, when we consider Christianity as a whole, most are false. We are only after a select few, which are actually many when we consider there are seven billion in the world. Believers must be in search of those that are open and true, modest, and seeking. Have you done your best to be an effective communicator of God's Word when an opportunity presents itself? If you answered yes, and people still have rejected the message, they are not rejecting you, but they are rejecting God. If you answered no, then there is work to do.

Review Questions

(1) Why must we be emphatic to the people whom we evangelize? What does the Apostle Peter exhort us to do which will help us overcome the anxiety of witnessing to others? How is communication a two-way street? How do you address repeated comments that are unbiblical?

(2) Why is it important that we improve our reasoning skills from the Scriptures?

(3) How was Jesus lowly in heart?

(4) How did Paul serve the Lord? Expound on the Greek behind the English translation.

---

[141] Knute Larson, vol. 9, I & II Thessalonians, I & II Timothy, Titus, Philemon, Holman New Testament Commentary, 24 (Nashville, TN: Broadman & Holman Publishers, 2000).

(5) What does it mean to "study how best to talk with each person you meet?" How can we get a correct understanding of what the other person means?

(6) How did Jesus, as a teacher and disciple maker, differ from the religious leaders of his day?

(7) What made Paul such an effective and influential evangelist? Why may we not be at fault if many reject our message?

CHAPTER 9 Active Listening to Fully Understand

Luke 8:18 Updated American Standard Version (UASV)

[18] Therefore, take care how you listen; for whoever has, to him more shall be given; and whoever does not have, even what he thinks he has shall be taken away from him."

Jesus' caution to his audience about how they listen proves just as relevant today as it was 2,000 years ago. If one only hears the words but not what lies behind those words, he will find himself in trouble with his spouse, children, employer, and everyone else he communicates with daily. More importantly, it could jeopardize one's hope of eternal life. We need to consider more than the words themselves.

We must hear the words that are spoken, as well as the way it is said, the tone, and the body language to get a sense of what someone means. A common complaint of wives to husbands is that they passively listen to them, blocking out much of what they do not want to hear because they oppose or are not interested in what she is saying. Sadly, we tend to be less appreciative of those who are closest to us than total strangers. Active listening is a form of listening that results in the speaker and listener are fully understanding what is meant. There are seven points to active listening:

(1) Pay close attention to what is being said; listen for the ideas behind the words. Do not just hear but also feel the words. Let the speaker know that you are listening by leaning forward a little, looking at him, not staring, but having sufficient eye contact.

(2) Look at a facial expression, the tone of the voice, the inflection of the voice, the mood, and body language. Get at the feelings behind the words. People generally do not say all that is on their minds or convey their true feelings, so the listener must pay close attention to the non-verbal signs.

(3) Turn off your internal thinking as much as possible. In other words, do not think of how to respond to certain points while he is still talking, because you will miss the whole of what he has said.

(4) Let the speaker know you are paying attention by **nodding from time to time** and acknowledging with verbal gestures.

(5) Reiterate is not a common word, but it means to repeat what you think the person meant by what they said, but in your own words, to see if you understood them correctly. "So, you mean … right?"

(6) The person you are speaking with will acknowledge that you are correct, or he will correct you and will restate what they meant, and likely in a more comprehensive way since you misunderstood. **Pay even closer attention** as they explain again what they meant.

(7) When they have explained their message again, you must **repeat your reiteration**.

Considering how to listen proves vital if we are going to be effective evangelists. There has been no greater teacher than Jesus Christ because he was an effective communicator and an active listener. While some may be effective speakers, very motivational and moving, they lack teaching skills. Every time we open our mouths to share the Good News with another person, be it five minutes or an ongoing study with them, we must build a relationship with them.

Jesus in the Temple at Twelve Years Old

Luke 2:41-47 Updated American Standard Version (UASV)

[41] Now his parents went to Jerusalem every year at the Feast of the Passover. [42] And when he was twelve years old, they went up according to the custom of the feast. [43] And after the days were completed, while they were returning, the boy Jesus stayed behind in Jerusalem. And his parents did not know it, [44] but supposing him to be in the company, they went a day's journey; and they began looking for him among their relatives and acquaintances. [45] and when they did not find him, they returned to Jerusalem, looking for him. [46] Then, it occurred, after three days they found him in the temple, sitting in the midst of the teachers and listening to them and questioning them. [47] And all those listening to him were amazed at his understanding and his answers.

This incident develops into something far more magnificent than one might first realize. Kittel's *Theological Dictionary of the New Testament* helps the reader appreciate that the Greek word *eperotao*, which means to ask, to question, to demand of, for "questioning" was far more than the Greek word *erotao* to ask, to request, to entreat, for a boy's inquisitiveness. *Eperotao* can refer to questioning, which one might hear in a judicial hearing, such as a scrutiny, inquiry, counter questioning, even the "probing and cunning questions of the Pharisees and Sadducees," for instance those we find in Mark 10:2 and 12:18-23.

The same dictionary continues: "In [the] face of this usage it may be asked whether ... [Luke] 2:46 denotes, not so much the questioning curiosity of the boy, but rather His successful disputing. [Verse] 47 would fit in well with the latter view." Rotherham's translation of verse 47 presents it as a dramatic confrontation: "Now all who heard him were beside themselves, because of his understanding and his answers." Robertson's Word Pictures in the New Testament says that their constant amazement means, "They stood out of themselves as if their eyes were bulging out."

After returning to Jerusalem, and after three days of searching, they found young Jesus in the Temple, questioning the Jewish religious leaders, to which "they were astounded." (Luke 2:48) Robertson said of this, "(The) second aorist passive indicative of an old Greek word [*ekplesso*]), to strike out, drive out by a blow. Joseph and Mary 'were struck out' by what they saw and heard. Even they had not fully realized the power in this wonderful boy."[142] Thus, at twelve years old, Jesus, but a boy, is already demonstrating he is a great teacher and defender of truth. BDAG says, "To cause to be filled with amazement to the point of being overwhelmed, amaze, astound, overwhelm (lit., strike out of one's senses)."[143]

The Jewish culture, especially Jesus' Jewish family, displayed an effective listening ability. On the other hand, the Jewish religious leaders seemed eager to speak, not listen. Jesus was not in the temple to win conversations with the greatest teachers of Jewish Law but rather to listen. It says in verse 46 that the twelve-year-old Jesus was "listening to them." Once he listened to them, he then knew what they meant, their motives for what they said, and it was at that time, that he proceeded in "**asking them questions.**" Good listening leads to good questions.

---

[142] A.T. Robertson, Word Pictures in the New Testament (Nashville, TN: Broadman Press, 1933), Lk 2:48.

[143] William Arndt, Frederick W. Danker and Walter Bauer, A Greek-English Lexicon of the New Testament and Other Early Christian Literature, 3rd ed. (Chicago: University of Chicago Press, 2000), 308.

Verse 47 says, "All who heard him were amazed at his insight and his answers," which means that Jesus' questions were intensely insightful and even penetrating. We must listen if one finds himself in a conversation with a Bible critic in a public setting, where others are listening. If one discerns that the Bible critic does not have a receptive heart, and nothing we say will open his eyes to the truth of God's Word, we must consider others who may be listening. Because of that larger audience, one will then do as Jesus did, use effective practical questions to put the Bible critic on defense so that those around know we do have answers for the criticisms, giving them faith in the message they heard.

Do Not Allow Yourself to Get in the Way

Passive involvement in a discussion can get in the way of our own objective. One must be aware that not everyone has taken the time to read a book on effective communication. Therefore, a person in the conversation may be someone who goes on for some time and gets lost or sidetracked with other subjects not relevant to the discussion. If that occurs, respectfully stop them and briefly explain that it would be best to stay on topic and offer that person the point that they were making.

Overzealousness also proves another way that we get in the way of our own objective. One can fall into a trap with a very active mind by anticipating what the speaker will say. It can be rude to interrupt them by finishing their thoughts, or worse, to assume what they will say and then offer feedback on one's assumption. That often leads to the response, "I was not going to say that at all; what I was going to say was ...." Each time one interrupts the other speaker *unnecessarily*, that person withdraws further and further from being an active participant in the conversation. Rather, let the person finish their thoughts and hold off for a few seconds to see if they will start again before you respond.

The person, who may seem like a Bible critic, can make a believer defensive, which can unnerve most evangelists. What should we do if someone approaches a believer with an alleged error or contradiction? We should be frank and honest. If we do not have an answer, we should admit such. If the text in question gives the appearance of difficulty, we should admit this as well. If a believer remains unsure how to answer, simply say that you will look into it and return to them, returning with a reasonable answer.

However, do not express disbelief and doubt to people who have legitimate concerns about the Bible because they will be moved even further in their disbelief. Moreover, it will put them on offense and place the believer on defense. With great confidence, tell them there is an answer. The Bible has withstood the test of 2,000 years of persecution and is the most printed book of all time, currently being translated into 2,287 languages. If these critical questions threatened its credibility, the Bible would not be the book that it is.

The evangelist must keep Paul's words "knowledge puffs up" at the fore of his thinking because as one grows in knowledge and understanding, it is too easy to fall prey to a haughty spirit. After the evangelist has spent hundreds of hours listening to unbelievers talk about the Bible, one will hear the same thing many times. This is like watching the same uninteresting movie dozens of times. This can cause the evangelist to start speaking in a disdainful tone to the person who is speaking. It may be blatant, or even subtle, but the unbeliever will notice it, and while they may respectfully finish the conversation with the evangelist, they will not care what the believer said before the end of the conversation.

Proverbs 16:18 Updated American Standard Version (UASV)

[18] Pride goes before destruction,
and a haughty spirit before a fall.

In the end, God has given each of us the right to make our own decisions. The evangelist that respects another person's right to their views may win the day in the end. If a Bible critic goes through a conversation with both speakers having an equal time, they will feel that they were respected, and they will be open to speaking to another Christian at another time. We must keep in mind that we are planting seeds of truth. Life experiences have a way of altering heart conditions. One unbeliever may have something happen in their life, which makes them more receptive to Bible truths, and the next Christian they engage will have success in watering those seeds.

Getting Beneath the Surface

In witnessing to others, there will come times when one feels the other person is holding back. The unbeliever really does not want to go deeper into the conversation because she may not want to offend. Maybe she views the Bible or God as foolish, and anyone who holds them as truth is just as foolish. Therefore, they just give surface answers to finish the conversation. Gently and respectfully ask some questions that will probe beneath the surface answers she has been supplying. One could ask, "Can you tell me more about ...? What has brought you to this conclusion?"

In some cases, people hold back because of past hurts. Maybe their child died, and this has only reinforced that there cannot be a loving God. They may not feel like sharing the hurt, so he attempts to get out of the conversation. If a couple of discreet, tactful questions might get them to open up, go ahead. However, if it seems that additional questions will do more damage than good, let it go because they will respect the believer for handling the conservation that way. On the other hand, if the searching questions prove effective, and the person becomes emotional in explaining why they have not been able to accept God, do not get analytical; rather, be a comforter who is an empathetic and understanding listener.

How questions are asked can make all the difference. If one seeks answers that lie beneath the surface, we should avoid the "why" questions because they come across more like an interrogation. This may make the other person close down even further. You can use qualifiers to get deeper. Thus, it would not be, "Why do you not believe in God?" Instead, it would be, "What has contributed to your understanding of God?" Another way might be to ask, "How have you come to your current position on God?" Searching questions at the right time come about because a believer has been an active listener.

Review Questions

(1) Why should we "consider how we listen?" What are the five points to active listening?

(2) Why might we address a Bible critic's questions in a public setting?

(3) Why is it best to stop a person who is jumping from subject to subject? What is the result of being too active in the conversation, and unnecessarily interrupting? How should we handle a question on the Bible when we do not know the answer? Why can we express confidence in the trustworthiness of the Bible, even if we do not have an answer to the current question? Even though we may have heard it all before, why should we approach a person's concerns as though it were the first time? Even though we may not

overturn false reasoning, what might a respectful attitude accomplish in the end?

(4) Why may some people hold back in the conversation? How can we get beneath the surface? Why is it important to consider how we ask questions?

CHAPTER 10 Look for Opportunities to Establish Rapport

Rapport is pronounced ra•páwr, as the "t" is silent. The *Encarta Dictionary* defines rapport as "an emotional bond or friendly relationship between people based on mutual liking, trust, and a sense that they understand and share each other's concerns." There likely have been times when you connected with someone the first time you met them, and it seemed as though you were of the same mind, the same line of thought. Some synonyms to rapport are "understanding, bond, link, affinity, fellow feeling, connection, empathy, camaraderie, affiliation, and fellowship." People need this bond in every walk of life. It proves especially important in the family, with your friends, church, workplace, and any new connections. This ability to build rapport or bond with others is paramount in the work of an evangelist.

Rapport in the Life of the Evangelist

One must establish a genuine connection with those whom one witness to; otherwise, they will notice the lack of sincerity. Everyone loves to share their thoughts on this, which means open-ended questions are the best way to move the conversation. As a believer begins a conversation, invite them to express themselves, and take note of their home if that is where you are talking with them. Do they have pets? Has something just been remolded? Do they have children? Are there things sitting out that show a university someone attended? The objective is to get to know the person to whom you are witnessing by showing interest in them. The believer must have some idea of what that person believes, which will build an even stronger bond. Perhaps the believer notices that she is wearing a cross, but is she Catholic or Protestant? What denomination is she a part of, and how often does she attend? Bring these observations to the surface; however, the believer must be willing to share some of their life. There must be a balance because you do not want to leave the unbeliever feeling they have been interrogated.

Current Affairs

Once a believer has done that, ask a question about some troubling current event. This will let one know their beliefs and values as they address your questions. If you are at their home and have magazines lying around, showing they follow world events, you might ask: "Have you been following the unrest in the Middle East (2016 news, Ukraine-Russia 2022)? If it does not appear that they follow world events, think of something local. It should be within their state or a neighboring state, but that has made national news, such as the George Zimmerman trial in the death of Trayvon Martin. These insights that one gains will determine if they are conservative or liberal. It is important to remember that how one asks a question is just as important as what is asked. Try to be neutral in the question, not giving away how you may feel about the current affair because the believer wants an accurate assessment.

Scriptural Beliefs

Answers to these questions help a believer know how to move the discussion into more of a biblical conversation. Starting with the Bible may compel the listener to say, "I do not discuss religion." Because one has gained the listener's trust, they will feel more comfortable talking about the Bible. When a believer engages a person, be prepared not to judge them on their views. Facial expressions and body language will give away feelings. If an unbeliever has issues with Christianity, religion, or even certain segments of Christianity, there may be genuine reasons why the person has those views. Maybe the person believes the Bible is just a book by men. Maybe he or she dislikes the hypocrisy within religion. Maybe the only Christianity the person knows is the televangelists they catch on television.

Whatever the unbeliever displays, be empathetic to their circumstances. However, this also is the time to share a couple of Scriptural thoughts, which will differ based on what has been learned about him. However, share some texts that demonstrate understanding and let your loving kindness and tact shine through at this time. (Gal. 5:22; 2 Cor. 6:3, 4, 6) Get these interested ones to open up to gain a sense of whom they are, and then use a couple of applicable texts in the conversation, leaving an opening to visit with them again.

Open-Ended Questions

Open-ended questions allow an answer that is more than a simple yes or no. These usually include: "Whom would you say …?"; "What do you think …?"; "Where did you …?"; "Why do you think …?"; "How did you …?" or "Tell me more about …." These questions or statements open things up, enabling the believer to discover their worldview. You may ask, "Do you think all of this hideous violence in the world suggests that something more than man has a role in these events?" This may just result in a simple yes or no. One could also ask, "With everyone wanting happiness, yet there is so much evil in the world, why do you think that is the case?"

Ask questions that generate a sense of an invitation, not pressure. One could ask, "What do you believe will bring about world peace?" Once the person gives their response, push on with, "What makes you feel that way?" In street witnessing, one could ask those with children, "What do you think life will be like for them when they are adults?" Then follow with, "What is it that concerns you the most about their future?" None of these questions should make the listener feel uncomfortable.

Draw It Out

Proverbs 20:5 Updated American Standard Version (UASV)

[5] Counsel in a man's heart is like deep water,
  but a man of understanding draws it out.

Everyone is different. The melting pot[144] of races, cultures, and worldviews has seen an explosion over the last 30 years and seems far removed from the Christian community by way of language, customs, and lifestyle. You may live in a community that has numerous cultures. So, be prepared to adjust the approach to suit the person and circumstances, such as the topic and tone. How does one draw people out? This is done by allowing them to speak while you serve as the guide of the conversation, merely keeping the other person on the subject or involving them in numerous topics. If one wants a deep discussion on just one issue, let the other person speak, but make sure they stay on topic. Their thoughts must

---

[144] A melting pot is "a place where a variety of races, cultures, or individuals assimilate into a cohesive whole.—Inc Merriam-Webster, Merriam-Webster's Collegiate Dictionary., Eleventh ed. (Springfield, MA: Merriam-Webster, Inc., 2003).

be appreciated, so attach the appropriate facial expression and body language to what the other person says, with comments such as "interesting," true," "I never thought of it that way," and so on. Acknowledge each time you are on common ground: "Yes, I feel that way too." To interject a Scripture, one could add, "You know the Bible touches on that. Let me share the verse ..." Most importantly, never water down Bible truth, but do not be unbending or confrontational.

Success in generating rapport depends on *listening skills*. An Unbeliever will be able to sense if one's heart is in the conversation. By giving that person space and time to unload their thoughts and react to them from the heart. This will serve as another point of attraction. Showing another person respect and honor by active listening will make them more likely to listen to biblical truths shared with them.

Making Contact

Certain gestures will contribute to others being attracted to your biblical message. We have discussed active listening at length, but there is also physical contact, eye contact, and expressing deep respect in our voice and body language. You must be very cautious when touching others, but laying your hand on their shoulder a couple of times in a conversation, can truly make some feel your warmth toward them. Shaking their hand is also an appropriate gesture. Women should not touch men, and men should not touch women. If a woman touches a man, this may send the wrong signal. If a man touches a woman, this may startle her, pushing her away, not drawing her in. We return to the cultures as well because some Asians do not like to be touched, as is true of some Jewish cultures as well.

Learning to Listen

As discussed above, the more one uncovers about the person to whom one witnesses to, the greater the bond that will form. To learn more, one must listen to the way the person acts and reacts in the conversation. But we know that humans typically do not listen well. Wives can attest to this based on their husband's selective listening habits. However, listening can be improved. Not only does one want to hear the other person's words, but what does he mean by the words he uses. This would include noticing what he does not say as much as what he says.

Guiding the Conversation

Either a believer can allow a conversation to branch off and flow in whatever natural direction it takes you, or one can guide the conversation in the intended direction. The first time one speaks with someone about God's Word, choose the former over the latter because the believer collects an understanding of the other person: a Protestant, a Catholic, an atheist, an agnostic, a person who follows Eastern religions, a conservative, a liberal, or somewhere in between. Once you understand the other person, you may wish to move to guide the conversation's direction.

To build the bond with the listener, stay at the pace of the listener's behavior and body language. By this, one will gain their trust and attention. They will begin to trust the believer and naturally allow him or her to lead in the conversation. The same pace simply means the believer reflects the person who listens. This means that if they stand or sit casually, the believer stands or sits casually. If they are serious in conversation, the believer displays seriousness in conversation. If they exhibit light-heartedness, the believer becomes light-hearted. If they act warm and friendly, the believer returns warmth and friendliness, which should happen at all times. If they act lively and energetic, the believer becomes lively and energetic. However, if they become agitated, the believer would not reflect that. Witnessing cannot be the childhood game of mocking the other person by repeating what he says or does. Develop a natural bond with one another.

In order to appreciate why you are pacing the listener, we might think of the Old West and the cowboy and the cow.[145] The cowboy is skilled at keeping pace with the cow to guide it where the cowboy wants the cow to go. When the cow goes where it wants, the horse moves him where the cowboy directs. If the cow horse does not keep pace but instead falls behind or gets ahead, he can never take the lead and guide the cow.[146] Once the believer comfortably matches the listener, begin guiding him or her. In this, you set the pace and direction. However, do not rush because the guide's transition must be taken slowly.

---

[145] http://www.youtube.com/watch?v=yIBo8E3UXMw

[146] IBID

Review Questions

(1) What is rapport? How can one get beneath the surface? Why is it important to consider what is happening around the person who may be an unbeliever?

(2) How can current affairs assist you in building rapport?

(3) Why is it essential to gain their trust before venturing in to talk about the Bible? How should we feel if the listener is hostile toward God's Word and Christianity? Why do we want the listener to open up?

(4) What is the difference between an open-ended and a close-ended question, and which is preferable?

(5) What does it mean to "draw it out?" How can we get beneath the surface? What does listening have to do with "drawing it out?"

(6) Why is listening being emphasized?

(7) What two ways can a conversation move along, and which is preferable in the beginning and later? What does it mean to keep pace with and reflect on the listener?

CHAPTER 11 Fighting for the Truth

1 Timothy 1:18-19 Updated American Standard Version (UASV)

[18] This charge I am setting before you, child, Timothy, in accordance with the prophecies spoken long ago about you, that by them you might fight as a soldier the fine warfare, [19] having trust and a good conscience, which some have rejected and suffered shipwreck in regard to their faith.

Ponder for a moment; think of our walk as Christians thus far. Have we indeed had a share as a fighter for the truth? We all need to enter the battle, whether man or woman, young or old, as long as we fit the requirements. Paul spoke of our need to be "a good soldier of Christ Jesus." Just as we must fight the right warfare, we too must be the kind of soldier if we are to find God's support. We have to devote our lives to the evangelism of biblical truths and be willing to be part of the adversities and maltreatments that come with it along with numerous pleasures and blessings. The whole of 2 Timothy 2:3 reads, "Share in suffering as a good soldier of Christ Jesus." During training, we can only imagine what kind of soldier we will be, but it is not until we face battle that we cannot truly know. Will we be faithful, trustworthy, steadfast, and dedicated, or will we miss many weekly Christian meetings or not partake in the evangelizing of unbelievers? Will we be reliable and stable, or more like a wandering mercenary who is thinking of his own interests? In reality, as our leaders, the men we serve are representatives of God, so in the end, it will be God who examines us. (1 Corinthians 4:1-4)

For those who have acquired a measure of skill in fighting for the truth as a Christian apologist, we need to carry our own weight in this spiritual warfare, but all that of the new believers, who are not battle-ready as of yet. The most significant number of casualties in a real war are those new recruits that did not have the fighting skills to survive. Just as Paul looked after his spiritual children, so the experienced Christian apologists of today must look after the new ones so they can walk deservingly with God until they have the necessary skills to walk on their own. This responsibility needs to be carried out with a humble spirit, leaving the pride for those in the world. We need to appreciate and value the responsibilities God has given us. (2 Tim. 1:7-8) The apostle Paul tells us that we need to be worthy to be among the Christian fighters for the truth through such qualifications.

He stresses another qualification with his student, Young Timothy, i.e., live accord to the faith.

1 Timothy 1:18-20 Updated American Standard Version (UASV)

¹⁸ This charge I am setting before you, child, Timothy, in accordance with the prophecies spoken long ago about you, that by them **you might fight as a soldier the fine warfare**, ¹⁹ having trust and **a good conscience**, which <u>some have rejected</u> and <u>suffered shipwreck</u> in regard to their faith. ²⁰ among whom are Hymenaeus and Alexander, whom I have handed over to Satan that they may be taught not to blaspheme.

There was a good reason for Paul's exhortation because some in his day attempted to undermine the faith, fighting back against the truth to an extreme degree, and he cautioned that such ideas would be as deadly as gangrene if allowed to take hold. In the same way that a soldier who is uncertain or faltering or lacking resolution may very well pay with his life, so may we if we do not embrace steadfastly to our faith. We have to let God prove to be true by evidencing our faith and confidence in the Word. We must cling to it as we would a life preserver in the midst of a rushing river. Some in those early days lost their way and attempted to bring others down with them. Paul wrote, "among whom are Hymenaeus and Alexander, whom I have handed over to Satan that they may learn not to blaspheme."

If we are to be effective in our fight for the truth, we must be spiritually clean, morally clean, mentally clean, and physically clean.[147] "Only let your manner of life be worthy of the gospel of Christ, so that whether I come and see you or am absent, I may hear of you that you are standing firm in one spirit, with one mind striving side by side for the faith of the gospel." (Phil. 1:27) Yes, Paul 'urges us to walk in a manner worthy of the calling to which we have been called, with all humility and gentleness, with patience, bearing with one another in love, eager to maintain the unity of the Spirit in the bond of peace." (Ephesians 4:1-3)

Other criteria for qualifying as fighters for the truth would be avoiding "the works of the flesh are evident: sexual immorality, impurity, sensuality, idolatry, sorcery, enmity, strife, jealousy, fits of anger, rivalries, dissensions, divisions, envy, drunkenness, orgies, and things like these." As 'Paul warns us, as he warned others before, that those who do such things will not

---

[147] See 2 Corinthians 6:14-18; Revelation 18:4; 1 Peter 2:12; Hebrews 4:13; 1 Corinthians 6:9-11; Philippians 4:8; (Matthew 15:18-20; Deuteronomy 23:12-13; Ephesians 4:25, 29, 31; 5:3; Revelation 21:8

inherit the kingdom of God.' (Gal. 5:19-21) Thus, if we are to qualify as fighters in this spiritual warfare under our leader Jesus Christ, we must have no part in any way of the fruitages of the flesh but rather evidence the fruitages of the Spirit. "The fruit of the Spirit is love, joy, peace, patience, kindness, goodness, faithfulness, gentleness, self-control; against such things, there is no law." (Gal 5:22-23) We cannot be a fighter in name only, but rather, we must maintain the faith in good conscience, namely, a conscience that is trained in keeping the Word of God.

1 Peter 3:16-17, 21 Updated American Standard Version (UASV)

[16] having a good conscience, so that, when you are slandered, those who revile your good behavior in Christ may be put to shame. [17] For it is better to suffer because you are doing good, if the will of God wishes it, than because you are doing evil. [21] Baptism, which corresponds to this, now saves you, not as a removal of dirt from the flesh but as an appeal to God for a good conscience, through the resurrection of Jesus Christ,

We can uphold God's sovereignty and maintain our integrity, for the apostle Paul wrote,

1 Corinthians 10:13 Updated American Standard Version (UASV)

[13] No temptation has overtaken you but such as is common to man; and God is faithful, who will not allow you to be tempted beyond what you are able, but with the temptation will provide the way of escape also, so that you will be able to endure it.

The apostle Paul describes the war waged within the Christian between "the law of sin" and "the law of God," or "the law of my mind" (the Christian's mind must be in harmony with God). (Romans 7:15-25)

Paul does not want us to be among those that run the race of faith and share in proclaiming biblical truths to others, only to find ourselves eliminated from the prize of life.

1 Corinthians 9:24-27 Updated American Standard Version (UASV)

[24] Do you not know that those who run in the stadium all run, but one receives the prize? Run in such a way that you may win. [25] Everyone who competes in the games exercises self-control in all things. They then do it to receive a perishable wreath, but we an imperishable. [26] Therefore, the way I am running is not aimlessly; the way I am aiming my blows is so as not to be striking the air; [27] but I discipline my body and make it my slave, so that, after I have preached to others, I myself will not be disqualified.

Army of Fighters Going into Action

No army is made up of one soldier. It must be an effort of many units, a subdivision of a larger body, if the battle, and eventually, the war is to be one. We need to stand 'firm in one spirit, with one soul contending side by side for the faith of the gospel, and not letting ourselves be intimidated by anything by our opponents, which is a sign of destruction to them, but of our salvation, and this from God, because to us has been graciously granted on behalf of Christ not only to believe in him but also to suffer on behalf of him.' (Phil. 1:27-29) We depend on our spiritual brothers and sisters, just as real soldiers would fellow soldiers. However, our greatest trust is in God. "For it is not the one who commends himself who is approved, but the one whom the Lord commends." (2 Cor. 10:18) That is why Paul wrote, "Let the one who boasts, boast in the Lord." (2 Corinthians 10:17-18; Jeremiah 1:19; Psalm 35:1-10)

Pilate said to Jesus, "So you are a king?" Jesus answered, "You say that I am a king. For this purpose, I was born, and for this purpose, I have come into the world, **to bear witness to the truth**. Everyone who **is of the truth** listens to my voice." Pilate said to him, "**What is truth?**" (John 18:37-38)

The Roman Governor Pontius Pilate cynically posed that question to Jesus. He was not looking for an answer, nor did Jesus give him one. It might be that Pilate viewed "truth" as too abstract or relative to understand.

Many share this disdainful attitude toward truth today, including liberal Bible scholarship, educators of our children and young adults, and politicians. They do not accept that truth, especially moral and spiritual truth, is absolute but relative and always changing from one person to the next. Yes, they believe that each person can determine what is right and what is wrong for themselves. (Isa. 5:20-21) Moreover, these progressive liberals vehemently reject past values and moral standards as out-of-date.

The statement that provoked Pilate's question is worth repeating. Jesus had said, "For this purpose, I was born, and for this purpose, I have come into the world, **to bear witness to the truth**." (John 18:37) Truth to Jesus was no ambiguous, beyond our understanding notion. He assured his disciples, "you will know the truth, and the truth will set you free." (John 8:32)

We know exactly where that truth can be found. On one occasion, when Jesus was praying to his Father, he said, "your word is truth." (John 17:17) The Word of God in sixty-six books, is inspired and fully inerrant, with each author being moved along by Holy Spirit. This is what makes known truth that makes available both trustworthy guidance and a sure hope for the future, life everlasting. 2 Timothy 3:15-17, 2 Peter 1:21; John 3:16, 36

Pilate uninterestedly rejected the occasion to learn the truth. This is what we have to offer as Christian apologists, which we readily make available to all.

Evade Being a Casualty of War

Jesus has given us the privilege to be his evangelists, something that will never be repeated in the eternity to come. We definitely want to take advantage of this opportunity and make him proud. If we are to succeed, it means we must become serious students of God's Word, acquire full knowledge (epignosis), and full discernment, so that we do not teach things that are biblically untrue so that we do not stumble anyone. We need to have the zeal as Paul had for the truth. We do not want to have the spirit like some that Paul referred to, "For I bear them witness that they have a zeal for God, but not according to knowledge. 3 For, being ignorant of the righteousness of God, and seeking to establish their own, they did not submit to God's righteousness." (Romans 10:2-3)

Philippians 1:9-11 Updated American Standard Version (UASV)

9 And this I pray, that your love may abound yet more and more in accurate knowledge[148] and all discernment;[149] 10 so that you may approve[150] what is excellent, and so be sincere and blameless for the day of Christ, 11 being filled with the fruit of righteousness which comes through Jesus Christ, to the glory and praise of God.

We need to have the correct knowledge, and if we find that we do not have the correct knowledge of a particular belief, we need to adjust our thinking and use the truth rightly and humbly. We may recall that Paul went by Saul prior to Paul, and Jesus introduced him to the truth and the way. Paul was a proud Pharisee, who refused to adjust, so Jesus had to make a personal visit. We now make personal visits to believers on the wrong path on behalf of Jesus Christ.

---

[148] *Epignosis* is a strengthened or intensified form of *gnosis* (*epi,* meaning "additional"), meaning, "true," "real," "full," "complete" or "accurate," depending upon the context. Paul and Peter alone use *epignosis.*

[149] Or insight, experience (Gr, *aisthesei*)

[150] Or *discover,* or *differing*

Ecclesiastes 7:12 Updated American Standard Version (UASV)

¹² For wisdom is a protection just as money is a protection,
  but the advantage of knowledge is this: wisdom preserves the life of its owner.

There are just as many casualties in spiritual warfare, if not more. God has seen fit to give us his Word, to give us teachers of that Word, and has provided us with a storehouse of biblical study tools in these end times, and yet many fall by the wayside and become indifferent to the truth. This may cause us concern to hear, but we are very safe as long as we keep the right mental attitude. We need not fear any opposer, as our God is greater than everything in existence is, as he brought it into existence. (Isa. 41:11-12) However, as long as Satan exists, up until the return of Christ, the fight for the truth still wages. Like Paul, 'a wide door for effective work has opened to us, and there are many adversaries.' (1 Cor. 16:9) By choosing to be a Christian apologists; we have boldly stepped through that door to fight for the truth!

Review Questions

(1) Who can qualify to be a Christian apologetic evangelist?
(2) What are some of the requirements or qualifications for being an evangelist?
(3) How may some have fallen victim to being disqualified as a fighter for the truth?
(4) Why do we need to become one if we will defeat the enemy?
(5) Describe the Satanic, demonic army that we face.
(6) How do we evidence our love for Christ?
(7) How can we resist Satan and his tactics?
(8) Why must we come together as an army?
(9) What is truth?
(10) How can we evade being a casualty of this spiritual warfare?

CHAPTER 12 Fighting the Right Warfare

2 Corinthians 10:4 Updated American Standard Version (UASV)

[4] For the weapons of our warfare are not of the flesh[151] but powerful to God for destroying strongholds.[152]

Wise King Solomon tells us, "For everything there is a season, and a time for every matter under heaven: … a time to love, and a time to hate; a time for war, and a time for peace." (Eccl. 3:1, 8, RSV) For almost immediately after the flood of Noah, man has been in one war after another, to the point eventually; it became nation against nation, and eventually two World Wars. Certainly, the return of the prince of peace will be a long-awaited relief. (Isaiah 9:6)

Many Christians have struggled with all of the bloodshed and genocide, wondering if it is God's will that these things take place, did he bring them about? No, this would not be reasonable thinking. Of course, by allowing sin to enter the world instead of destroying Satan, Adam, and Eve, he has allowed these things to take place.   God does not cause evil and suffering. Romans 9:14. The fact that God has allowed evil, pain, and suffering has shown that independence from God has not brought about a better world. (Jer. 8:5-6, 9). God's permission of evil, pain and suffering has also proved that Satan has not been able to turn all humans away from God. (Ex. 9:16; 1 Sam. 12:22; Heb. 12:1). The fact that God has permitted evil, pain, and suffering to continue has provided proof that only God, the Creator, has the capability and the right to rule over humankind for their eternal blessing and happiness. (Eccl. 8:9). Satan has been the god of this world since the sin in Eden (over 6,000 years); and how has that worked out for man, and what has been the result of man's course of independence from God and his rule? (Matthew 4:8-9; John 16:11; 2 Corinthians 4:3-4; 1 John 5:19; Psalm 127:1)

Satan's impact on the earth's activities has carried with it conflict, evil, and death, and his rulership has been by means of deception, power, and his own self-interest. He has demonstrated himself as an unfit ruler of everything. Therefore, God is now completely vindicated in putting an end to this corrupted rebel along with all who have shared in his evil deeds.

---

[151] That is *merely human*

[152] That is *tearing down arguments*

(Rom. 16:20) God has tolerated evil, sickness, pain, suffering, and death until our day in order to resolve all the issues raised by Satan. We are self-centered in thinking that this has only pained us. If you desire a deeper look, please read the Christian Publishing House Blog

(https://christianpublishinghouse.co/): Why Has God Permitted Wickedness and Suffering.

Over the past 4,000 years, the wars have not brought any peace and security. These wars are against blood and flesh. The apostle Paul tells us "For the weapons of our warfare are not of the flesh but powerful to God for destroying strongholds." Our spiritual warfare is for tearing down arguments. Let us pause to consider why we are fighting and against whom for a moment. Paul tells us by way of Ephesians, that our fight is not "against flesh and blood, but against the rulers, against the authorities, against the cosmic powers over this present darkness, against the spiritual forces of evil in the heavenly places." (6:12) This verse is not saying that Christians are to rise up and fight human governments. On this, Max Anders writes, "The picture of warfare here implies that we do not face a physical army. We face a spiritual army. Therefore, our weapons must be spiritual. **Against the rulers, against the authorities, against the powers of this dark world and against the spiritual forces of evil in the heavenly realms** seems to suggest a hierarchy of evil spirit-beings who do the bidding of Satan in opposing the will of God on earth." (Anders, Holman New Testament Commentary: vol. 8, Galatians, Ephesians, Philippians, Colossians 1999, 190)

In fact, we are told to pray for rulers so that their decisions may allow us to carry out our evangelism work. (1 Tim. 2:1-3) Jesus said, "My kingdom is not of this world. If my kingdom were of this world, my servants would have been fighting, that I might not be delivered over to the Jews. But my kingdom is not from the world." (John 8:36) As Anders brought out, this fight is against Satan's organization of demonic angels, which have been in control of the earth for centuries. Revelation 12:9-12

What has been the effect of Satan's rule over the earth? He has blinded the minds of the unbelievers to the light of biblical truths. Yes, for those with an unreceptive mind and heart, Satan has been allowed to place a veil over the gospel, which keeps these particular unbelievers from discerning or comprehending the truth. Therefore, Christ's servants on the earth are shining the light of truth from the darkest corner of the demonically controlled earth.

Blinded the Minds of the Unbelievers

2 Corinthians 4:3-4 Updated American Standard Version (UASV)

³ And even if our gospel is **veiled**, it is veiled to those who are **perishing**. ⁴ In their case **the god** of this world has **blinded the minds** of the **unbelievers**, to keep them from seeing the light of the gospel of the glory of Christ, who is the image of God.

2 Corinthians 3:12-18 Updated American Standard Version (UASV)

¹² Therefore having such a hope, we use great boldness in our speech, ¹³ and are not like Moses, who used to put a veil over his face so that the sons of Israel would not look intently at the end of what was fading away. ¹⁴ But **their minds were <u>hardened</u>**; for until this very day at the reading of the old covenant the same **veil remains unlifted**, because it is **taken away only by means of Christ**. ¹⁵ But to this day whenever Moses is read, a **veil lies over their <u>hearts</u>**; ¹⁶ but whenever **one turns to** the Lord, the **veil is taken away**. ¹⁷ Now the Lord is the Spirit, and where the Spirit of the Lord is, there is freedom. ¹⁸ But we all, with unveiled face, beholding as in a mirror the glory of the Lord, are being transformed into the same image from glory to glory, just as from the Lord, the Spirit.

Let us start by looking at an example of blind minds within Scripture. This was not a case of physical blindness but mental blindness. A Syrian military force came after Elisha, and God **blinded them <u>mentally</u>**. If it had been physical blindness, they would have to have been led by the hand. However, what does the account say?

2 Kings 6:18-20 Updated American Standard Version (UASV)

¹⁸ And when the Syrians came down against him, Elisha prayed to Jehovah and said, "Please strike this nation[153] with blindness." So he struck them with blindness in accordance with the prayer of Elisha. ¹⁹ Then Elisha said to them, "This is not the way, nor is this the city; follow me and I will bring you to the man whom you seek." And he brought them to Samaria.

²⁰ When they had come into Samaria, Elisha said, "O Jehovah, open the eyes of these men, that they may see." So Jehovah opened their eyes and they saw; and behold, they were in the midst of Samaria.

---

[153] Or *people*

Do we believe that one man led the entire Syrian military force to Samaria? If they were physically blind, they would have to have all held hands. Were the Syrian military forces not able physically to see the images that were before them? No, rather, it was more of an inability to understand them. This must have been some form of mental blindness, where we see everything that everyone else sees, but something just does not register. Another example can be found in the account about the men of Sodom. When they were blinded, they did not become distressed, running into each other.

Definitely, Paul is speaking of people who are not receptive to truth because their heart is hardened to it, callused, and unfeeling. They are not responding because their figurative heart is opposed. It is as though God handed them over to Satan to be mentally blinded from the truth, not because he disliked them per se, but because they had closed their hearts and minds to the gospel. Thus, no manner of argumentation is **likely** to bring them back to their senses.

HOWEVER, Saul (Paul) was one of these at one time. Until he met the risen Jesus on the road to Damascus, he was mentally blind to the truth. He was well aware of what the coming Messiah was to do, but Jesus did none of these things because it was not time. Thus, Paul was blinded by his love for the Law, Jewish tradition, and history. So much so that he was unable to grasp the Gospel. He lived during the days of Jesus' ministry and studied under Gamaliel, who was likely there in the area. He could have even been there when Jesus amazed the Jewish religious leaders at the age of twelve. Therefore, Saul (Paul) needed a real wake-up call to get through the veil that blinded him from the gospel. Hence, a mentally blind person sees the same information as another, but the truth will normally cannot or will not get down into their heart. This is not saying that an unbeliever cannot understand the Bible; it is simply that they see no significance in it, as it is foolishness to them.

Staying with the spiritual warfare aspect, we must think of those who have been taken captive by Satan and his world. Like in any war, prisoners of war can be released. Our being able to teach the truth of God's Word to all unbelievers and believers, who have found the wrong path, is how this freeing of Satanic captives is accomplished. Gradually, with some, we are able to pull aside the veil of darkness, allowing the light to shine. Once they see the knowledge of the truth, their joy is just as great as any blind person who has had their sight restored. In real-life warfare, freed prisoners can come home angry, holding to hate and bitterness. However, in the spiritual warfare unites men and women of all kinds and from all nations in the connections of lasting love, joy, and peace, having shared understanding through the Word of God.

We need to change the face of Christianity as Christians the world over, sharing in the battle for the Bible, advancing Bible knowledge, defending the Word of God, defending the faith, and saving those who have begun to doubt. We need to take the fight into our communities, effectively sharing biblical truths with our neighbors in our villages, towns, and cities. The apostle Paul was a madman for the truth. Listen, as he had to defend himself against false apostles.

2 Corinthians 11:23-27 Updated American Standard Version (UASV)[154]

[23] Are they servants of Christ? I reply like a madman, I am more outstandingly one: I have done more work, been imprisoned more often, with countless beatings, and often near deaths. [24] Five times I received 40 strokes less one from the Jews, [25] three times I was beaten with rods, once I was stoned, three times I experienced shipwreck, a night and a day I have spent in the open sea; [26] in journeys often, in dangers from rivers, in dangers from robbers, in dangers from my own people, in dangers from the nations, in dangers in the city, in dangers in the wilderness, in dangers at sea, in dangers among false brothers, [27] in labor and toil, in sleepless nights often, in hunger and thirst, frequently without food, in cold and lacking clothing.[155]

Our Struggle against Dark Spiritual Forces

Living in the modern scientific-minded world of the 21st century, most no longer believe in wicked spirit forces and demons. If such spirit creatures exist, their belief in them is irrelevant, and the effect is felt on every living person on earth. Even for those of us, who accept the demons as being true, we are not immune from their activity because we are disciples of Jesus Christ. In reality, we have an even bigger target on our backs because we do not give in to their influences and are the enemy of their fight against Jehovah God. Listen to the words of Paul:

---

[154] "**11:22–33** The third and most comprehensive list recorded in this letter of Paul's sufferings for the cause of Christ (cf. 4:8–12; 6:4–10)." – MacArthur, John (2005-05-09). *The MacArthur Bible Commentary* (Kindle Locations 55700-55701). Thomas Nelson. Kindle Edition.

[155] Lit *and in nakedness*

The Whole Armor of God

Ephesians 6:10-20 Updated American Standard Version (UASV)

[10] Finally, be strong in the Lord and in the strength of his might. [11] Put on the full armor of God, so that you will be able to stand firm against the schemes of the devil. [12] For our wrestling[156] is not against flesh and blood, but against the rulers, against the powers, against the world-rulers of this darkness, against the wicked spirit forces in the heavenly places.

[13] Therefore, take up the whole armor of God so that you will be able to resist in the evil day, and having done everything, to stand firm. [14] Stand firm, therefore, with your **loins girded[157] about with truth**, and having put on the **breastplate of righteousness**, [15] and with your feet shod with **the preparation of the gospel of peace**; [16] in all things, taking up the **shield of faith** with which you will be able to extinguish all the flaming arrows of the evil one. [17] And take the **helmet of salvation**, and the **sword of the Spirit**, which is the **word of God**.

[18] Through all **prayer and petition** praying at all times in the Spirit, and with this in view, keep awake with all perseverance and making supplication for all the holy ones. [19] Pray also for me, that the words may be given to me when I open my mouth, so that I may be able to speak boldly in making known the mystery of the gospel, [20] for which I am an ambassador in chains;[158] that in it I may speak boldly, as I ought to speak.

We may be thinking that it seems very unlikely that any human can be at odds with a demonic spirit creature and come out victorious as they have unimaginable superhuman abilities. It is only possible by our reliance on Christ Jesus. We must have a complete grasp of God's Word and apply it in a balanced manner in our lives each day. Only by doing so can we be freed from the bodily, moral, emotional, and mental harm that those under demonic or satanic control have gone through. (Ephesians 6:11; James 4:7)[159]

---

[156] Or struggle

[157] (an idiom, literally 'to gird up the loins') to cause oneself to be in a state of readiness—'to get ready, to prepare oneself.'—GELNTBSD

[158] Lit *a chain*

[159] Paul made sure believers recognized that as new people who have been granted new life in a new family with new relationships they still would endure spiritual warfare. The closing portion of Paul's letter explained his account of the Christian's conflict with evil forces.

Defending the Loins, the Breast, and the Feet

Girding Your Loins with Truth

The loins are the area on each side of the backbone of a human between the ribs and hips. When the Apostle Paul wrote this to the Ephesians, soldiers wore a belt or girdle-like, you see in the image of Roman soldiers. It was 2 to 6 inches in width. This belt served double duty: (1) to protect the soldier's loins and (2) to support his sword. When a soldier girded up his loins, this meant he was getting ready to go into battle. This soldier and his belt served as the perfect analogy of how a Christian is to put on the belt of biblical truth to protect his life. The truths of Scripture should be pulled tight around us, helping us to live a life that is reflective of that truth and so that we can use that Bible truth to defend the faith, contend for the faith, and save those who doubt. (1 Pet. 3:15, Jude 3, 21-22) If we accomplish these tasks, we will have to study the Bible and consider its contents carefully. Prophetically, it was said of Jesus, "your law is within my heart." (Psalm 40:8) If Jesus came under attack by the enemy of truth, he was able to refer to biblical truth from memory. (Matthew 19:3-6; 22:23-32)

Isaiah 30:20-21 Updated American Standard Version (UASV)

20 And though Jehovah[160] give you the bread of distress and the water of oppression, yet your Teacher[161] will no longer hide himself, but your eyes shall behold your Teacher. **21** And your ears shall hear a word behind you, saying, "This is the way, walk in it," when you turn to the right or when you turn to the left.

30:20–22 The text emphasizes that God "gives" (*nātan*) his people different experiences (also in v. 23; cf. Eccl 3:1–12), including times of

---

Believers must adorn themselves with the armor of God in order to stand against the devil's schemes. Five defensive weapons are identified: (1) the enabling nature of truth that resists lying and false doctrine; (2) the covering quality of righteousness that resists accusations of conscience and despondency; (3) the stabilizing quality of peace that resists slander and selfishness; (4) the protective ability of faith that resists prayerlessness and doubt; and (5) the encouraging nature of salvation that resists fear and disappointment.

Two offensive weapons are included in the armor of God: (1) the sword of the Spirit, which is the word of God, and (2) prayer. It is fitting that this prayerful and meditative letter concludes with an exhortation to prayer and a request for prayer. (Dockery 1998, 581)

[160] One of 134 scribal changes from *YHWH* to *Adhonai*.

[161] Lit *your teachers*. The Hebrew verb is plural to denote grandeur or excellence.

adversity or punishment for sin. In Isaiah's situation he did not intervene immediately when the Assyrians invaded: instead, he allowed the Assyrian attack on Judah to defeat 46 walled cities and take 200,150 people captive. But in the future some "teachers/a Teacher" will instruct the people in the way that they should walk.[155] NIV takes these as teachers (probably prophets) who will guide the people in God's ways, but Oswalt argues that the singular verb points to a divine Teacher, God himself, who will instruct his people. God will no longer hide himself in the sense of seeming distant or of a failure to act on their behalf (45:15; 59:1–2; Ps 27:8–9; 4:3–4; 102:1–2). His presence will be seen, for he will be active among them, instructing in the way they should walk. This pictures God, the teacher, giving moral instruction to his people with his own voice (cf. 2:2–4; Ps 25:8–14) so that they will stay out of trouble. The Lord will gently teach his disciples in "the way" (*haderek*) of God, instructing them in the disciplines of godliness so they will not turn in any other moral directions (right or left). This reminds one of God's original instructions for his people to follow his instructions (Deut 5:32–33; 17:19–20; Josh 1:7–8; 23:6–7).

God's presence and his teaching will result in the total rejection of idols (30:22) covered with a thin layer of gold or silver to make them look important. Once the people's eyes are opened and they hear God's instructions, the people will see the foolishness of trusting in lifeless images that can do nothing. The people became defiled (*ṭimmē'tem* Lev 15:31; 20:3; 2 Kgs 23:16; Jer. 7:30) by these idols, but in the future their defilement or desecration of these statues of wood will show an utter disrespect for the gods these idols represent (cf. 2:20; 13:17; 31:7; 44:15–17). They will no longer reverence or treat these idols as holy, but will reject them and throw them out, as if they were getting rid of an object that was repulsive. As Oswalt suggests, "blessings can be received only after the abandonment of one's own efforts and a complete commitment to God."[162]

Breastplate of Righteousness

The breastplate of the soldier was a piece of armor that covered the chest, protecting one of the most important organs, the heart. As all Christians likely know, we have a figurative heart, which is our inner person, and it needs special protection because it leans toward wrongdoing. (Gen. 8:21) Therefore, we must cultivate a love for God's Word and the

---

[162] Gary V. Smith, *Isaiah 1–39*, ed. E. Ray Clendenen, The New American Commentary (Nashville: B & H Publishing Group, 2007), 520–522.

standards and values that lie within. (Ps 119:97, 105) Our love for the Word of God should be to such a depth that we would reject "the desires of the flesh and the desires of the eyes and pride of life." (1 John 2:15-17) In addition, once we have developed such a desire for right over wrong, we will be able to avoid paths that would have otherwise led us to ruination. (Ps 119:99-101; Amos 5:15) Our greatest example in everything, Jesus Christ, evidenced this to such an extent that Paul could say, "You have loved righteousness and hated wickedness." (Hebrews 1:9)

Shod Your Feet with the Preparation of the Gospel of Peace

Roman soldiers needed suitable footwear, which (1) kept the soldier's footing sure in battle, and (2) allowed them to march some 20 miles during a campaign while wearing or carrying some 60 pounds of armor and equipment. Thus, Paul's ongoing analogy of the armor of a Roman soldier was right on target, as the appropriate footwear for the readiness of a Christian evangelizer active in spreading the gospel message is even more relevant. The importance is shown by Paul again in his letters to the Roman congregation when he asks how the people will get to know God if the Christian is not willing and ready to bring it to him as he preaches and teaches? (Romans 10:13-15)

Once again, we must look to our exemplar Jesus Christ as he said to the Roman Governor Pontius Pilate, "For this purpose I was born and for this purpose I have come into the world, to bear witness to the truth. Everyone who is of the truth listens to my voice." For three and a half years, Jesus walked throughout the land of Palestine, preaching to all who would listen, giving the ministry a top priority in his life. (John 4:5-34; 18:37) If we, like Jesus, are eager to declare the good news, we will find many opportunities to share it with others. Furthermore, our being absorbed in our ministry will help keep us spiritually strong. (Acts 18:5)

The Shield of Faith, the Helmet of Salvation, and the Sword of the Spirit

Thureon is the Greek word rendered "shield," which refers to a shield that was "large and oblong, protecting every part of the soldier; the word is used metaphorically of faith."[163] This shield of faith would and will protect the Christian from the "the fiery darts of the wicked one." In ancient times,

---

[163] W. E. Vine, Merrill F. Unger and William White, Jr., vol. 2, Vine's Complete Expository Dictionary of Old and New Testament Words (Nashville, TN: T. Nelson, 1996), 571.

the darts[164] of the soldiers were often hollowed out, having small iron receptacles, which were filled with a clear colorless, flammable mixture of light hydrocarbons that burned. This was one of the most lethal weapons as it caused havoc among the enemy troops unless the soldiers had the large body shields that had been drenched in water and could quench the fiery darts. In fact, the earliest manuscripts repeat the definite article, literally "the darts of the evil one, the fiery (darts)," emphasizing the fact that they were, above all, destructive. If a soldier's shield caught fire, he would be tempted to throw it down, leaving himself open to the enemy's spear.

What does the highly metaphorical language of the fiery darts depict and how does this weaken or undercut our faith? It may come in the form of minor persecution if we live in the Western world, such as being ridiculed for our Christian faith or even verbally assaulted by Bible critics. Another fiery dart may be the temptation to put money over the ministry. Then, Satan's world has a constant temptation to lure us into immorality. You would have to be blindfolded not to see sexually-explicit images hundreds of times per day as it is used to sell everything. It is not only the images but also the mindset. I will give you just one example, and please excuse the graphic nature. The modern-day junior high school children (13 and 14 years old); literally view oral sex as being no different than kissing one another on the lips.

If we are to protect our Christian family, our congregation of brothers and sisters, and ourselves, we must possess "**the shield of faith.**" Faith is not a simple belief in Jesus Christ as some misinformed ones might tell us; rather, it is an active faith in Jesus Christ. James says at 1:19, "You believe that God is one; you do well. Even the demons believe and shudder!" The demons and Satan believe in the existence of Jesus Christ, and yet this brings them no salvation whatsoever. Faith comes from taking in an active knowledge of the Father and the Son to building a relationship, a friendship based on the deepest love, and committing oneself to the point of turning your life over completely. It is regular prayerful communication, understanding, and valuing how he protects us. (Joshua 23:14; Luke 17:5; Romans 10:17)

Again, we turn to our great exemplar, Jesus Christ, who demonstrated his faith throughout some very trying times. He completely trusted the

---

[164] 6.36 belos, ous n: a missile, including arrows (propelled by a bow) or darts (hurled by hand)— 'arrow, dart.' In the NT belos occurs only in a highly figurative context, to bele … peporomena 'flaming arrows (or darts)' Eph 6:16, and refers to temptations by the Devil.—Louw and Nida 6.36.

Father to accomplish his will and purposes. (Matt. 26:42, 53, 54; John 6:38) A great example of this trust can be found when Jesus was in the garden of Gethsemane. He was in great anguish because he knew that he was going to be executed as a blasphemer of his Father, and even then, he fell with his face to the ground and prayed, "My Father, if it is possible, may this cup be taken from me. Yet not as I will, but as you will." (Matthew 26:39) Not that he was backing out of the execution, the ransom that is, but he wanted to be executed for another reason, other than a blasphemer. Jesus was an integrity keeper, which brought great joy to the Father. (Pro. 27:11) As we face difficult times in the world that is alienated from God, we will do well to imitate Jesus' great faith and not give ours under the pressures of the world that lies in the hands of the evil one. Moreover, our faith will be refined if we trust God, evidencing our love for him, by applying his Word in our daily walking with him. (Ps 19:7-11; 1 John 5:3) The immediate gratification that this world offers could never compare with the blessings that lie ahead. (Pro. 10:22)

Not long ago, those trying to curb the use of drugs among the American youth had the saying, "the mind is a terrible thing to waste." Our next piece of the armor of God would be a very useful tool for protecting the Christian mind, **the helmet of salvation**. The Apostle Paul said to the Thessalonians, "we must stay sober and let our faith and love be like a suit of armor. Our firm hope that we will be saved is our helmet," because it protects our Christian mind. (1 Thess. 5:8) Even though we may have accepted Christ and have entered onto the path of salvation, we still suffer from imperfect human weaknesses. Even though our foremost desire is to do good, our thinking can be corrupted by this fleshly world that surrounds us. We need **not** be like this world but rather openly allow God to alter the way we think through his Word, the Bible, which will help us fully to grasp everything that is good and pleasing to him. (Rom. 7:18; 12:2) You likely recall the test that Jesus faced, where Satan offered him "all the kingdoms of the world and their glory." (Matt. 4:8-10) Jesus' response was to refer to Scripture, "Be gone, Satan! For it is written, 'you shall worship the Lord your God, and him only shall you serve.'" Paul had this to say about Jesus, "looking to Jesus, the founder and perfecter of our faith, who for the joy that was set before him endured the cross, despising the shame and is seated at the right hand of the throne of God." (Hebrews 12:2)

We need to understand that the above examples of faith do not come to us automatically. If we are focusing on what this current system of things has to offer, as opposed to focusing on the hopes that are plainly laid out in

Scripture, we will be weak in the face of any severe trial. After a few stumbles, it may be that we suffer spiritual shipwreck and lose our hope altogether. Then again, if we frequently feed our minds or concentrate our minds on the promises of God, we will carry on delighting in the hope that has been offered to us. (Romans 12:12)

If we are to keep our Christian mind in the hope that lies ahead, we need to possess the Sword of the Spirit. The book that reveals the heavenly Father, his will, and purposes, i.e., the Bible, is stated to be "living and active, sharper than any two-edged sword, piercing to the division of soul and of spirit, of joints and of marrow, and discerning the thoughts and intentions of the heart." This Word, if understood correctly, and applied in a balanced manner, can transform our lives and help us avoid or minimalize the pitfalls of this imperfect life. We can depend on that Word when we are overwhelmed, or temple to give way to the flesh, and when the Bible critics of this world attempt to do away with our faith. (2 Cor. 10:4-5) We need to heed the words of the Apostle Paul to his spiritual son, Timothy:

2 Timothy 3:14-17 Updated American Standard Version (UASV)

[14] You, however **[Timothy]**, continue in the things you have learned and were persuaded to believe, knowing from whom you have learned them **[Paul, who Timothy traveled with and studied under for 15 years]**, [15] and that from infancy[165] you have known the sacred writings **[the whole Old Testament]**, which are able to make you wise for salvation through trust[166] in Christ Jesus. [16] All Scripture is inspired by God and profitable for teaching, for reproof, for correction, for training in righteousness; [17] so that the man of God may be fully competent, equipped for every good work.

3:14–15. Each of us is susceptible to this dangerous trap of deception unless we obey Scripture vigilantly. Following Christ is more than a one-time decision or an occasional church service or kind act. True Christianity involves continual dependence and obedience to Christ the king. Paul told Timothy to **continue in what you have learned and have become convinced of.** Our faith is proved by its endurance.

Two elements are necessary for faithful living. First, we must possess

---

[165] *Brephos* is the period of time when one is very young—'childhood (probably implying a time when a child is still nursing), infancy.

[166] *Pisteuo* is "to believe to the extent of complete trust and reliance—'to believe in, to have confidence in, to have faith in, to trust, faith, trust.'

knowledge of the truth. Truth enlightens a person about what is right and wrong, what constitutes purpose and happiness. We cannot trust or love which we do not know. The second element is conviction or belief. We express our belief system in the daily decisions we make and the behaviors in which we engage. No one acts contrary to belief (though we may act contrary to our professions of belief).

Paul also wanted Timothy to consider **those from whom you learned [truth], and how from infancy you have known the holy Scriptures**. Once again he had Timothy's mother and grandmother in mind (see 2 Tim. 1:5). Timothy was schooled in the Old Testament writings and had learned the need for forgiveness, the provision of God, and the necessity of faith. He had also been discipled by Paul, learning Christ and the church. In each case, Timothy had not only been given knowledge; he had been witness to godly lives.

These people served as examples to Timothy about the truth of God, the need for endurance, and the reward of faithfulness. Each person had staked his or her life on the revelation of the Scriptures which, according to Paul, **are able to make you wise for salvation through faith in Christ Jesus**.

3:16. The power of the Bible to affect change and demand obedience resides in the fact that **all Scripture is God-breathed**. The Bible originates with God. Claims of origins carry great significance because authority lives in the Creator. This is why people invest such Herculean efforts in trying to disprove God as the earth's Creator and in questioning the authenticity of the Bible. Admitting to God's authorship is an acceptance of his authority over every aspect of life. By stating that Scriptures are God breathed, Paul established the Bible's claim as God's authoritative Word over all people.

The Scriptures were written by men "as they were carried along by the Holy Spirit" (2 Pet. 1:21). The picture is that of a sailboat being moved along by the wind. Indeed, men wrote the Bible, but the words and substance of what they wrote came from God. This makes the Bible **useful**. Paul listed four main uses of Scripture, all of which intertwine with one another.

Teaching involves instruction. Since Timothy was feeling the attacks of false teachers, Paul encouraged the young pastor to continue in teaching correct doctrine and correct living. The Scriptures must be known so people will grasp their need of salvation and so the confessing community will adhere to its instructions on proper Christian conduct.

Rebuking and **correcting** are the disciplinary authority of Scripture. Because the Bible is God's Word and because it reveals truth, it exercises authority over those who deviate from its standard. "Rebuking" points out sin and confronts disobedience. "Correcting" recognizes that a person has strayed from the truth. Graciously, lovingly, yet firmly, we should try to guide the errant individual back into obedience.

Many times the Old Testament relates Israel's disobedience to God, how the people suffered God's chastisement for their rebellion, and how God corrected their sinful habits. The New Testament continues with stories and instructions, warnings regarding disobedience, disciplinary actions for those who fail to heed God's revelation, and teachings on proper conduct.

Training in righteousness is the counterpoint to correction. The Scriptures give us positive guidance for maturing in faith and acceptable conduct.

3:17. The goal of all this instruction, discipline, and training is not to keep us busy. God intends **that the man of God may be thoroughly equipped for every good work**. We study the Bible, we rely upon God's Spirit, his revelation, and the community of the faithful to keep us on track—obedient and maturing in faith. Continuing in this commitment will enable us to do whatever God calls us to do. Timothy could withstand the attacks of false teachers, the abandonment of professing believers, and the persecution that surrounded him because God had equipped him for the task. God never calls us to do something without first enabling us through his Spirit and the power of his truth to accomplish the task.

We neglect the Scriptures at our own peril. Through them we gain the ability to serve God and others. The Scriptures not only point the way; through the mysterious union of God's Word and faith, they give us the ability to serve.[167]

John MacArthur says, "Whether confronting Satan's efforts to distrust God, forsaking obedience, producing doctrinal confusion and falsehood, hindering service to God, bringing division, serving God in the flesh, living

---

[167] Knute Larson, *I & II Thessalonians, I & II Timothy, Titus, Philemon*, vol. 9, Holman New Testament Commentary (Nashville, TN: Broadman & Holman Publishers, 2000), 305–307.

hypocritically, being worldly, or in any other way rejecting biblical obedience, this armor is our defense.[168]

After his baptism by John the Baptist, Jesus went out into the wilderness for forty days and forty nights, which left him weak and hungry. Then, Satan tempted Jesus, waiting until he was in a weakened condition. Read carefully as Satan offers the first temptation to Jesus:

Luke 4:3 Updated American Standard Version (UASV)

[3] And the devil said to him, "**If you are** the Son of God, command this stone to become bread."

Jesus' First Temptation

First, Satan played on Jesus' natural desire for food as he deliberately waited until Jesus was in a weakened state from fasting. In addition, Satan knew that Jesus was the Son of God, as he had been in heaven with him. Notice how he is attempting to attack Jesus' hunger by starting his accusation with "if" to get Jesus to use his powers for selfish gain. In other words, he wanted Jesus to be annoyed and say, 'You know I am the Son of God, so watch as I turn these stones into bread!' Was Jesus tempted into a selfish act, a needful feeling of proving himself right? No, Jesus did not permit Satan to bait him into rebellion.

Luke 4:4 Updated American Standard Version (UASV)

[4] And Jesus answered him, "It is written, 'Man shall not live on bread alone.'"[169]

Jesus' Second Temptation

Luke 4:5-7 Updated American Standard Version (UASV)

[5] And he led him up and showed him all the kingdoms of the inhabited earth in a moment of time. [6] And the devil said to him, "**To you** I will give all this authority and their glory; for it has been handed over to me, and I give it to whomever I wish. [7] Therefore if you bow down before me, it shall all be yours."

One way of being emphatic in the Greek language is to front word(s) before others, and in this case, the second person pronoun (*soi*, "to you")

---

[168] MacArthur, John (2005-05-09). *The MacArthur Bible Commentary* (Kindle Locations 57514-57516). Thomas Nelson. Kindle Edition.

[169] Quotation from Deuteronomy 8:3

was fronted to the beginning of the Greek sentence by Luke to show just how important this question was. The English cannot bring this out well, but the Greek makes it all too clear. Satan said a bit like what a car salesperson might say,[170] 'Look, this deal is for you and you alone!' Did Jesus even slightly consider Satan's offer? No, he responds,

Luke 4:8 Updated American Standard Version (UASV)

[8] Jesus answered him, "It is written, 'You shall worship the Lord your God and serve him only.'"

Jesus' Third Temptation,

Luke 4:9-10 Updated American Standard Version (UASV)

[9] And he led him to Jerusalem and had him stand on the pinnacle of the temple, and said to him, "If you are the Son of God, throw yourself down from here; [10] for **it is written,**

"'He will command his angels concerning you,
to guard you,'

Notice that Satan even quotes Scripture but of course, twists it to suit his misleading benefits. This temptation is much more subtle than one might think. Satan wanted Jesus to get caught up in himself and take the easy way out instead of the humble three and half years of ministry that lay ahead. If Jesus had stood on the top of the pinnacle of the temple, at a time of the day when everyone was out, with all gathered to see him there, it would have made his ministry easier. Because if he had leaped in front of thousands of onlookers and angels came to rescue him before he hit the ground, many would have had faith in him based on his showmanship. However, Jesus knew his Father's will was for him to have an education ministry of three and a half years, a ministry of humility. Moreover, how did Jesus feel about doing the will of the Father? Here are his own words, "My food is to do the will of him who sent me and to accomplish his work." (John 4:34)

Matthew 4:7 Updated American Standard Version (UASV)

[7] Jesus said to him, "Again it is written, 'You shall not put the Lord your God to the test.'"[171]

On many other occasions, Jesus used the Scriptures to help unsuspecting people escape Satan's influences, as well as those of the

---

[170] I borrowed the car salesman analogy off of Dr. Darrell Bock, but it is a bit revised.

[171] A quotation from Deut. 6:16

overbearing Jewish religious leaders, who were twisting the Scriptures for their ill-gotten gains. Jesus made more than 120 references or quotations from the Old Testament Scriptures, from over half the books of the Hebrew Old Testament, in his three and half year ministry. This may appear to be trivial when you think of a three and half year ministry. However, notice what John says about Jesus, "Now Jesus did many other signs in the presence of the disciples, which are not written in this book." (John 20:30)

John also said, "Now there are also many other things that Jesus did. Were every one of them to be written, I suppose that the world itself could not contain the books that would be written." (John 21:25) Thus, if we take everything Jesus said in the Gospels, it would only amount to 3-4 hours of speaking. Now imagine four speakers at a religious assembly, giving an hour talk each, and each of them referencing or quoting some 30 Scriptures in their allotted hour. These would be considered highly biblical talks. Moreover, Jesus usually never had any scrolls in front of him. Therefore, his quotes and references were from memory. In the famous Sermon on the Mount, he directly or indirectly referenced dozens of Scriptures from memory.

Our Need to Pray

After giving us the complete suit of spiritual armor, Paul goes on to tell us,

Ephesians 6:18 Updated American Standard Version (UASV)

[18] Through all prayer and petition praying at all times in the Spirit, and with this in view, keep awake with all perseverance and making supplication for all the holy ones.

6:18 And pray in the Spirit

The soldier must maintain contact with his commanding officer. Prayer helps keep one in tune with the Lord and his purposes. Perhaps prayer should even be considered a part of the "full armor," because a consistent prayer life is a defense against attacks of Satan and prayer strengthens against temptation. Prayer is said to be "in the Spirit," since it is the Spirit who helps us pray, interceding "with groans that words cannot express" (Rom 8:26). To pray "in the Spirit" in 1 Cor 14:15 is to pray under the influence of the Spirit.

---

on all occasions with all kinds of prayers and requests.

Paul told the Thessalonians to "pray continually" (1 Thess 5:17). Whatever the occasion, God wants his children to pray regularly, consistently, and frequently. "Prayer" (προσευχή, *proseuchē*) is the general word for communication with God, including all aspects of asking, praising, and giving thanks. "Request" (δέησις, *deēsis*) is a more specific word, indicating a special request or entreaty to God. When this word for "request" is found in the N.T., it is most often used in the context of making an entreaty on behalf of someone else.

With this in mind, be alert and always keep on praying for all the saints.

To "be alert" (ἀγρυπνέω, *agrypneō*) is literally to "keep from falling asleep." Its use in Mark 13:33 shows that the word is synonymous with the word γρηγορέω (*grēgoreō*) ("watch," "stand guard duty") in Mark 13:35, 37. There is a sense, then, in which the praying Christian is standing guard to ensure the safety of his fellow soldiers. In Samuel's farewell speech to his people he caught the essence of this duty when he said, "And as for me, far be it from me that I should sin against God by failing to pray for you" (1 Sam 12:23).[172]

Prayer can strengthen us immeasurably when we are enticed by our flesh, come upon a trial, or find ourselves discouraged. (Matthew 26:41) Jesus "offered up prayers and supplications, with loud cries and tears, to him who was able to save him from death, and he was heard because of his reverence." (Hebrews 5:7)

Review Questions

(1) Why should the Scriptures guide us?

(2) What is spiritual warfare?

(3) Who has blinded many to the truth, and how can we help them?

(4) What are the benefits of Christian warfare?

---

[172] Kenneth L. Boles, *Galatians & Ephesians*, The College Press NIV Commentary (Joplin, MO: College Press, 1993), Eph 6:18.

(5) What are three primary forms of protection that every Christian must have? (Phil. 3:1; 4:8, 9; 1 Cor. 10:12, 13; 2 Cor. 13:5; 1 Pet. 1:13)

(6) Whose standards of righteousness are we obligated to follow, and why is it for our best interests? (Rev. 15:3)

(7) If we disobey God because we have not formed a longing for his Word, what could be the outcome? (1 Sam 15:22, 23; Deut. 7:3, 4)

(8) What should we keep our feet busy doing? (Matt 28:19, 20; Rom. 10:15; Ps. 73:2, 3; 1 Tim. 5:13)

(9) How will firmly grounded faith help us when faced with tragedy or attacks from Bible critics? (2 Tim 1:12; 2 Ki 6:15-17)

(10) How does our hope of salvation help us to avoid being entangled by disproportionate concern with material possessions? (1 Tim. 6:7-10, 19)

(11) On what should we at all times rely when fighting off attacks against our spirituality or that of others? (Ps. 119:98; Pro 3:5, 6; Matt 4:3, 4)

CHAPTER 13 How to Develop Interest When Evangelizing

Many Christian evangelists may be struggling with gathering and holding the interest of prospective disciples. Do we find that we are struggling even to get a few words into the conversation? Are we being dismissed in the middle of our introduction or right afterward? If so, let us look to our exemplar, Jesus Christ,

Luke 10:5 Updated American Standard Version (UASV)

⁵ Whatever house you enter, first say, 'Peace be to this house!'

Most are thinking, 'this comment will not go over too well today,' and that would be correct. Nevertheless, it gives us the foundation for an introduction, getting us into the Bible discussion we so much desire. They need to see us as their friend, who comes with information that will be encouraging and bring them peace of mind in this wicked world. We could begin with, "I am very pleased that I found you at home. I have brought you a gift today, which I believe will make this day the best day of your year." This is a friendly opening, which is encouraging regardless of the person. Of course, whatever brief Scriptural message we have must come across as being beneficial, not superficial. Below are more introductions that may get us into a good conversation.

Many Christians are struggling to capture and hold the interest of an unbeliever when starting a conversation. They need to have an effective introduction, which will enable them to arouse interest.

Jesus said that whatever house [or conversation] you enter, first say, 'Peace be to this house!' (Lu 10:5) This is not a common way of greeting someone in the Western world; rather, it is more the Eastern way. However, let us consider its principle, which may give us introductions into a conversation. We are looking to introduce ourselves in a very friendly and respectful way, with the sense of something that may bring them a measure of peace now.

We might have a Bible tract that deals with what Christian life can be like in a wicked world, what life will be like under Christ, or how living a Christian way can bring joy even now. If we cannot find such a Bible tract, have 3-4 verses ready to be read. We might say, "Hello, my name is

_____, and I am sharing some very good news with my neighbors. What if I could read you a message in 90 seconds that would give you peace of mind today, tomorrow, and the rest of your life?" This message is warm, friendly, and has two aspects that the unbeliever will appreciate: (1) we mention how short our comments will be, and (2) a question that is so intriguing that few would walk away without the answer. Below are some other introductions that may work for us.

Warm Introductions

We might start by introducing ourselves and say, "I have a gift for you that is certainly going to make life far more interesting; it is encouraging, to say the least; do you have 90 seconds?

If we shake their hand and introduce ourselves by giving our name, and as we are doing so, we see they **are smiling**, we might say,

"It certainly is nice to see someone smiling in these difficult times; you must have found a measure of happiness. This is what I am sharing with others. May I add to the happiness you apparently already have? It will take but a minute or two."

If we shake their hand and introduce ourselves by giving our name, and as we are doing so, we see they **are <u>not</u> smiling**, we might say,

I know life in this world of evil, lack of love, crime, and violence, not to mention selfishness, can be overwhelming. May I take 1-2 minutes to offer you hope that can bring joy and happiness now."

These are warm; they are thought-provoking, very short ways of introducing unbelievers to the Word of God.

Hello, I am _____. Have you ever wondered why Christians such as myself risk themselves to share Bible messages with such persons as yourself?" Allow a response and build from there. If they say yes, they have wondered why tell them why. If they respond with a sarcastic remark, treat it like a joke, and smile as you reason your way out of his trying to end your conversation. If more sarcasm is repeated, simply offer a Bible tract and move on, as we cannot reason with the unreasonable.

Subject Introductions

A great way to break the ice is by introducing a subject that may be of interest to the unbeliever. We have to be cautious here because we do not know their worldview. Are the liberal, moderate, or conservative? These titles are not just a political position but also relate to one's worldview as well. If we interject a topic by immediately taking a Christian worldview, and the unbeliever is liberal, we will have ended the conversation before it has begun. Topics can be local, national, or even the world over, but they must be something that the unbeliever would have likely heard. One thing is certain about human nature; people love to share their views with others, even strangers. Therefore, introduce the subject as a question.

Another way to generate interest is to ask the unbeliever questions that we might not want to hear the answers to but will give us an opportunity at a lengthy conversation.

- "Why do you think that so many people no longer believe the Bible to be the Word of God?"

- We would like to get your view on, "Is the Bible inspired of God, or is it just 66 books written by men?"

- "What do you think about Christianity today?"

- "Do you think Armageddon is a real thing that we need to worry about?"

- "Do you believe the Bible is really the Word of God?"

Whatever way we decide to start a conversation, we must be prepared for the responses. Are we able to defend the Word of God as inspired and fully inerrant?[173] Are we able to defend the faith? Are we able to defend the Christian worldview? Can we effectively communicate without losing our temper or letting it get into a debate?

---

[173] We recommend, IS THE BIBLE REALLY THE WORD OF GOD? Myths? Errors? Contradictions? Scientifically Inaccurate? [Second Edition] by Edward D. Andrews

http://www.christianpublishers.org/apps/webstore/products/show/7138936

Jumpstarting with a Subject

We might say, "We all thought that technology would give us more time, but would you not agree that our lives are even busier than ever, wishing we had more time?" Allow for a response, and then say, "Well, I do have some good news for you. Did you know that the Bible actually has counsel on how we can buy out more time? May I share it with you?"

Another approach is to mention a local problem that is affecting their community. We might say, "We would love to hear your insights on _____, it is greatly impacting our community." People love to offer advice, and letting them speak at length is a way to build rapport. However, if their insights are not even close to being rational, do not attack their thoughts. Simply find an ounce of common ground within them, and move on into the biblical message we prepared. The objective of starting with the local problem was to jumpstart our biblical message, not debate.

Another conversation starter might be, "Have you ever contemplated what it might be like to live forever in a perfect world, with a perfect body and mind?"

Work with other Christians in your church, and generate some great conversation starters based on the biblical message that you are seeking to convey. Then, create a Bible insert so that it is handy when members are out evangelizing in the community.

Remember that a well-prepared introduction does not mean that a person of interest will not go off in another direction. Do not be so prepared that we are thrown off our mission because they are not interested in what we came to talk about. Simply be happy that they are willing to talk, and take advantage of whatever subject they want to discuss.

Simple Introductions

We could simply start by asking them, 'how is your day going? I have brought something that will undoubtedly make it even better."

If we notice at the very beginning that he or she is a friendly person, because they are smiling and offering their hand, we might say, "It is so nice to meet someone with a pleasant disposition, which means you are making the best of this stressful world we live in. Would you not agree that there is little in the world where we can find true happiness?" Allow a response, and then share, "I have come to bring you even more happiness."

On the other hand, if you clearly see the other that you are about to engage is not in a good mood, say, "I have stopped you today because we are offering encouraging information and hope for a better future. As you read or listen to the news, there is not much to encourage us to believe life will be better for our children or grandchildren. Do you have a very brief moment so that I might share some good news with you?"

Introductions need to be simple, short, and encouraging. They are designed as a stepping-stone into the biblical message that we want to share. We might simply say, "I am a Christian, and we are speaking with our neighbors about some good news. We do this because we love and care for our neighbors."

Make Every Effort to See Them Again

We live in a world of skepticism, agnostics, and atheists, who carry hopelessness around with them 24/7. Thus, one cannot just bring someone into Christianity overnight. Thus, when we engage someone in our evangelism work within our community, we need to make every effort to see them again. At first, it may be by sharing emails or cell phone numbers, and hopefully, their address, so we can make a personal visit. Once we are regularly visiting them at their homes, we need to buy out the time to see them at least weekly, even for just a few minutes; otherwise, all is for not. We **(1)** look for interested ones, and then **(2)** we cultivate the interest of those we have already found.

We might ask ourselves, 'am I open to developing disciples, or have I only been stuck in the mode of initiating interest?' Once we discover one, who has a love for righteousness, ones who are upset over world conditions, who are receptive to biblical truths, we need to grow that one into a disciple. Simply because a person is dismissive in an initial discussion, this does not mean they are not open to biblical truths. We have to learn how to overcome those dismissive thoughts, which takes skill and practice. (Luke 19:3-5) How can we do this?

We have to be as skilled with our Bible as one is with and tool from a professional trade. We can be in awe if we are able to see a skilled worker at work, thinking, 'it must have taken a very long time to develop their skills.' In some cases, maybe so, but we can draw comfort in the fact that the human body and mind are very receptive to learning new skills. One way to begin is to have a regular Bible study program at home, studying (1) the

Bible from cover to cover with commentary volumes, (2) how to interpret Scripture, (3) foundational doctrines, and (4) effective evangelism.

The more we know, the better we know, the more we practice, the more confident we will be, and the more effective we will be. There are many good books out there on how to become a better evangelist, communicate effectively with others, reason from the Scripture, overcome false reasoning and explain truths. Yes, the head knowledge of how is very important, but it must be followed up by practice and repetition. We can begin by having a full share in commenting at any Christian meeting that is designed for such. We can also share things that we learn with our spiritual brothers and sisters. We can also invite fellow spiritual brothers and sisters to role-play and work on better communication. Like any skilled person, it takes dedication, patience, and love to become good, or better yet, effective.

Whenever we do have an opportunity to spend some quality time with one who truly wants to talk about the Bible, how should we approach it? First, the first few times, let him do most of the talking if he is so inclined, and be an active listener, discovering how he feels, thinks, and believes. We also are building rapport, because he feels as though we are truly interested in him. In this stage, he is likely to make many unbiblical statements and dismiss the urge to correct him constantly. If you are commenting to help him move along, find some aspect of what is said to agree with, making a brief statement. Once things are developed, it is time to be more structured.

It is always best to use ourselves in this next approach of helping him appreciate that things must be biblically correct. Start with, "'when I first started showing interest in the Bible, I would say things like, 'I think, I feel, or I believe.'" I was shown Matthew 7:21, which reads, "Not everyone who says to me, 'Lord, Lord,' will enter the kingdom of heaven, but the one who does the will of my Father who is in heaven." State, 'clearly, you would agree, it is not our will, what we think, what we believe, or how we feel, but the will of the father, what he thinks, believes, and feels that is important?' If we read on in verse 23, it makes the point that we must always keep in mind. If we are only doing our will, Jesus will say to us, "'I never knew you; depart from me, you workers of lawlessness.'" Then say, "You would agree that our thinking must be biblically correct, right?"

This mindset of being biblical will be our guiding force until he has made it his own. We will have to keep sharing that point as we help him understand some of his beliefs are unbiblical. It is best to move a person into seeing the need to get the correct understanding by having them see that is what the Bible requires, as the Bible carries the authority and power.

Hebrews 4:12 Updated American Standard Version (UASV)

¹² For the word of God is living and active and sharper than any two-edged sword, and piercing as far as the division of soul and spirit, of both joints and marrow, and able to judge the thoughts and intentions of the heart.

However, when it comes down to it, we have to be realistic, the world we live in has little interest, so we must address how we are to cope with such an environment.

Evangelizing in a World of Little Interest

How can we respectfully bow out of a conversation when we conclude that an unbeliever is not truly interested? (Pro. 15:23; 25:11) Should we try to overcome their attempts to reject the message until they tell us to leave them alone? Would it not be better to end the conversation with them still having a measure of respect for us, a representative of Christianity? Ecclesiastes 3:7

We need to be able to discern between sharing biblical truths clearly and understandably, giving the unbeliever the ability to make a choice, as opposed to forcing our truths on another. We are not some worldly salesperson. God never forced us to be his servants; rather, he allowed us the freedom to whom or what we wanted to serve. (Josh. 24:15) We can feel good that we have carried out the Great Commission that Jesus gave all of us (Matt. 28:19-20), as long as we gave the unbeliever a clear and understandable message, even if he rejects that message.

Moreover, if someone rejects our message, he is not rejecting us he is rejecting God. If he merely rejects us for personal reasons or out of hand, we should not view him as an enemy of the truth; he may be reached somewhere down the road. However, suppose this one seems well prepared with antichrist type answers, with anti-biblical, with anti-Christian answers. In that case, he may very well be an enemy of the truth who actually proactively evangelizes against the truth. We should respect both of them, and we should move on either way. However, with the latter, even though he seems interested in dialoguing, his goal is to stumble us, so we should not continue on but rather respectfully bow out of the conversation.

For the one that is simply not interested, we can simply say, "I am grateful for the opportunity of speaking with you. Maybe a future conversation will go a little longer; nevertheless, I appreciate your time that you have given today. "May I simply leave you with this Bible tract?" If he says no, respect that too. Why should we take this approach?

The unbeliever will have gained respect for Christianity where it might have been lacking before. He will be impressed with the fact that you respected his right to choose. The reasonableness that we showed him may mean the next Christian he talks to will get a better response. Thus, we watered and cultivated, and God will use another to make the seeds of truth grow.

In instances where we are shut down before we ever get started, we need to have a Bible tract that we can offer. "Sir, may I at least leave you with this tract that takes but 1-2 minutes to read." On the back of that tract should be some kind of contact information to help the unbeliever get back in touch with us. We have to be balanced, both having the ability to win over those not wanting to talk and knowing when not to try out of respect.

We do not know why some are not interested. They simply may have had somewhere to be, or he was too busy. Another may be his experiences of Christians arguing with him, not respecting him, and even insulting him. Alternatively, it could simply be he is available or even wants to get into a lengthy conversation. The last reason is that it is important to always quality our conversation openers with some adjective: brief, short, or a couple of minutes. If we say such a thing, we need to honor what we said and be brief.

Doing any of the above does not mean that we never may an effort to overcome objections, or that we do not do as the apostle Paul did, persuading one to listen to the truth. (Ac 18:4; 26:28; 2 Cor. 5:20) We make allowances for those who show little or no interest, as they may be affected by time or circumstances, so we should not judge them as an enemy of the truth. If we get any indication that we are trying to reason with the unreasonable, i.e., persuade a closed mind, we do not push ahead until we cause offense. Rather, we must use our God-given discernment to warmly and respectfully bow out of the conversation, leaving the unbeliever with one morsel of rapport.

We must also keep in mind that our ministry is more than winning souls for Christ. Another aspect of our ministry is warning the wicked, even though almost none will accept the truth because they have a closed heart and minds. Nevertheless, even though this chapter started quite optimistically, we must also be realistic as to the other side of our evangelism job. If I have made one point clear in the entirety of this book, may it be this? We are not doomsayers like the Westboro Baptist Church. We do not get loud and yell, nor do we threaten them with eternal torment. This type of rhetoric wins no souls that last. They end up serving God out of fear, not love.

God's people willingly offer themselves to their heavenly Father just before the return of Jesus Christ.

Psalm 110:3 Updated American Standard Version (UASV)

³ Your people will offer themselves willingly
on the day of your power,
in holy array;
from the womb of the dawn,
the dew of Your youth belongs to you.

Our heavenly Father and his Son, Jesus Christ will be well pleased with those who offer themselves willingly, evangelizing with their whole soul, mind, heart and spirit.

2 Corinthians 9:7 Updated American Standard Version (UASV)

⁷ Each one must give as he has decided in his heart, not reluctantly or under compulsion, for God loves a cheerful giver.

If God loves a cheerful giver, one that is not under compulsion or reluctant, why did Paul say in his previous letter to the Corinthians, "For if I preach the gospel, that gives me no ground for boasting. For necessity is laid upon me. Woe to me if I do not preach the gospel!" Here Paul is saying, "Necessity is laid upon" him, and 'Woe to me if I do not preach the gospel!' Which is it?

On the other hand, did Paul change his mind in the few months between First and Second Corinthians? It is not a contradiction, or change of mind, as they both agree. A necessity is laid upon us, but God wants us to do it willingly, not under compulsion. The "woe" that Paul felt was not out of some fear of reprisal if he did not carry out his ministry of evangelism. Rather, it was a feeling of "woe" because he felt the same as God, the love for the people fear that they would miss the hope of "life." Paul was well aware of and empathetic to the Hebrew Old Testament texts, such as

Ezekiel 3:18 Updated American Standard Version (UASV)

¹⁸ When I say to the wicked, 'You shall surely die,' and you give him no warning, nor speak to warn the wicked from his wicked way, in order to save his life, that wicked person shall die in his iniquity, but his blood I will require at your hand.

Warning the Wicked

It is our responsibility to give a warning to the wicked people, just as it was Ezekiel's responsibility to give a warning to Judah. Ezekiel, Paul and us realize that God's love for humanity, who suffers from imperfection and the desire to do wicked things, needs to be warned. Yes, Paul loved the people he witnessed to, and so should we. If we go ahead and look at the next verse, we will see that Paul willingly carried out his ministry, making a personal sacrifice to do so.

1 Corinthians 9:17 English Standard Version (ESV)

¹⁷ For if I do this voluntarily, I have a reward; but if against my will, I have a stewardship entrusted to me.

It should sadden all of us that so many out of so-called conservative Christianity are not arranging their lives around an evangelism program because their church is not carrying out the work. Nevertheless, an author on evangelism cannot judge the hearts of its readers. However, Paul himself clearly said, "each one tests his own work, and then his reason to boast will be in himself alone and not in his neighbor." (Gal. 6:4) We are well aware of the fact that many of us have families, and Paul was quite clear about our need to care for them too. He wrote, "But if anyone does not provide for his relatives, and especially for members of his household, he has denied the faith and is worse than an unbeliever." (1 Tim. 5:8) Regardless, our love of our neighbor and even our enemy (Matt. 5:43-44), should move us to have some share in the evangelism work, we simply need to buy out the time. If our church has nothing along these lines, we may want to ask why.

If we find joy in the fact we have offered a used coat to a homeless person or a meal to a hungry family at a shelter, imagine what our joy will be if we play a role in getting another person on the path to eternal life. Imagine how our inner person will shine as we see this unbeliever become a believer. Imagine each time they learn something new or finally grasp something that they have been struggling with; we will have a continued joy as they grow in the truth and make it their own.

Review Questions

(1) How does the principle behind Luke 10:5 help us with introductions?

(2) Why are warm introductions so effective?

(3) What are subject introductions, and why are they so effective?

(4) Why are simple introductions effective?

(5) Why is it important that we make every effort to see them again?

(6) How are we to evangelize in a world with little interest?

(7) What are some reasons why some may not engage us in a conversation?

(8) We win souls for Christ, but what else are we doing while evangelizing?

CHAPTER 14 Being Faithful to the Truth

2 Thessalonians 2:3-12 Updated American Standard Version (UASV)

³ Let no one deceive[174] you in any way, for it will not come unless the apostasy[175] comes first, and the man of lawlessness is revealed, the son of destruction, ⁴ who opposes and exalts himself against every so-called god or object of worship, so that he takes his seat in the temple of God, showing himself as being God. ⁵ Do you not remember that while I was still with you, I was telling you these things? ⁶ And now you know the thing restraining him, so that in his time he will be revealed. ⁷ For the mystery of lawlessness is already at work; but only until the one who is right now acting as a restraint is out of the way. ⁸ Then the lawless one will be revealed, whom the Lord Jesus will do away with by the spirit of his mouth, and wipe out by the appearance of his presence, ⁹ but the one whose coming is in accordance with the activity of Satan, with all power and signs and false wonders, ¹⁰ and with every unrighteous deception[176] for those who are perishing, because **they did not receive <u>the love of the truth</u>** so as to be saved. ¹¹ For this reason God is sending upon them a working of error[177] so that they will believe the lie, ¹² in order that they all may be judged because **they did not <u>believe the truth</u>** but took pleasure in unrighteousness.

Those in the Thessalonica Christian congregation had thought the day of the Lord was already upon them. However, Paul begins chapter 2 by offering them a word of comfort and caution. He says, "Now we request you, brothers, with regard to the presence of our Lord Jesus Christ and our gathering together to him, that you not be quickly shaken from your composure or be disturbed either by a spirit or a word or a letter as if from us, to the effect that the day of the Lord has come." – 2 Thessalonians 2:1-2.

[2:3, 8] Who is "the man of lawlessness," and what does it mean that the Lord Jesus will do away with him by the spirit of his mouth?

---

[174] Or *seduce*

[175] Namely, to stand off from the truth, i.e., to not only fall away from the faith, but to then turn on the faith, rebellion.

[176] Lit *seduction*

[177] Or *a deluding influence*

Many Bible scholars would agree with Knute Larson, who says, "The **man of lawlessness** will be a person so given to sin that he will become the embodiment of it. Here is a man so overcome with evil that no flicker of light can be detected. It is hard to imagine how horrible that will be, especially in light of some of the diabolical figures throughout history which this man will overshadow." (Larson 2000, p. 106) Yes, most believe that the **man of lawlessness** is one person or man, as they believe that the antichrist will be just one person. However, they are mistaken on both counts. The apostle John clearly states there are many antichrists, which is simply anyone, any group, or organization that is against Christ. Similarly, the **man of lawlessness** is a composite man, made up of many individuals from the days of the apostles up unto **the day of the Lord**. Paul said the man of lawlessness was already at work in his day. However, he also says that this lawless one will be destroyed be Jesus in the day of the Lord. (2 Thess. 2:2, 7-8) How could one human live over 2,000 years? The lawless one will be false teachers, false prophets, and atheists, i.e., anyone trying to stand in the way of **the truth**. These ones **stand off from the truth** (i.e., apostasy), to the point that it is a defection, a revolt, a planned, deliberate rebellion. Jesus does away with the composite man [many individual rebels] of lawlessness by **the spirit of his mouth**, which is a figure of speech that evidently represents his commanding call to destroy the wicked in the day of the Lord.

Apostasy Foretold

The apostasy was foretold by Jesus Christ, Paul, and Peter.

Jesus Christ himself warned of this apostasy, in his parable of the wheat and the weeds (Matt. 13:24-30, 34-43), with the wheat picturing those who are truly Christian and an enemy [i.e., Satan] sowed the weeds picturing false Christians. Speaking of the wheat [true Christians] and weeds [false Christians], Jesus said that they are both to grow together until the end of the age, namely, in the day of the Lord. However, when the two are separated, the weeds are burned, that is destroyed. (2 Thess. 1:9) Then, in the book of Acts, we have the apostle Paul warned the Ephesian elders,

Acts 20:28-30 Updated American Standard Version (UASV)

28 Pay careful attention to yourselves and to all the flock, in which the Holy Spirit has made you overseers, to care for the congregation of

God, which he obtained with the blood of his own Son.[178] [29] I know that after my departure fierce wolves will come in among you, not sparing the flock; [30] and from among your own selves men will arise, speaking twisted things, to draw away the disciples after them.

The apostle Paul's words show that the true Christian congregation would be attacked on two fronts. First, false Christians ("weeds") would "come in among" true Christians. Second, "from among your own selves," i.e., true Christians; some would become apostates [stand off from the truth, attack the truth], "speaking twisted things." These apostates will "draw away the disciples [that is, Jesus' disciples] after them," not looking to make their own disciples. The apostle Paul also wrote,

1 Timothy 4:1-3 Updated American Standard Version (UASV) **[c. 61-64 C.E.]**	**2 Timothy** 4:2-4 Updated American Standard Version (UASV) **[c. 65 C.E.]**
[1] But the Spirit explicitly says that **in later times** some will **fall away from the faith**, paying attention to deceitful spirits and doctrines of demons, [2] by means of the hypocrisy of men who speak lies, whose conscience is seared as with a branding iron, [3] men who forbid marriage and command to abstain from foods that God created to be partaken of with thanksgiving by those who have faith and accurately know the truth.	[2] preach the word; be ready in season and out of season; reprove, rebuke, exhort, with complete patience and teaching. [3] For there will be **a time when** they will **not put up with sound teaching**, but in accordance with their own desires, they will **accumulate teachers for themselves** to have their ears tickled,[179] [4] and will **turn away** their ears **from the truth** and will turn aside to myths.

The apostle Peter also spoke of these things about **64 C.E.**, "there will be false teachers among you, who will secretly bring in destructive heresies … in their greed they will exploit you with false words." (2 Pet. 2:1, 3) These abandoned the faithful words, and became false teachers, rising within the Christian congregation, sharing their corrupting influence, intending to hide, disguise, or misleading.

---

[178] Lit *with the blood of his Own.*

[179] Or *to tell them what they want to hear*

These dire warnings by Jesus and the New Testament Authors had their beginnings in the first century C.E. Yes, they began small but burst forth on the scene in the second century.

"[Paul says it] Is Already at Work"

About **51 C.E.**, some 18-years after Jesus' death, resurrection and ascension, division was already starting to creep into the faith, "the mystery of lawlessness is already at work." (2 Thess. 2:7) Yes, the power of **the man of lawlessness** was already present, which is the power of Satan, the god of this world (2 Cor. 4:3-4), and his tens of millions of demons, are hard at work behind the scenes.

There were even some divisions beginning as early as **49 C.E.**, when the elders wrote a letter to the Gentile believers, saying,

Since we have heard that some persons have gone out from us and troubled you with words, unsettling your minds, although we gave them no instructions (Ac 15:24)

Here we see that some *within*, was being very vocal about their opposition to the direction the faith was heading. Here, it was over whether the Gentiles needed to be circumcised, suggesting that they needed to be obedient to the Mosaic Law. – Acts 15:1, 5.

As the years progressed throughout the first-century, this divisive "talk [would] spread like gangrene." (2 Tim. 2:17, **c. 65 C.E.**) About **51 C.E.**, As we already saw above, some in Thessalonica, at worst, going ahead of, or at best, misunderstanding Paul, and wrongly stating by word and a bogus letter "that the day of the Lord has come." (2 Thess. 2:1-2) In Corinth, about **55 C.E.**, "some of [were saying] that there is no resurrection of the dead. (1 Cor. 15:12) About **65 C.E.**, some were "saying that the resurrection has already happened. They [were] upsetting the faith of some." – 2 Timothy 2:16-18.

Throughout the next three decades, no inspired books were written. However, around **96-98 C.E.**, the apostle John pens three letters, wherein he tells us, "**Now** many antichrists have come. Therefore we know that it is the last hour." (1 John 2:18) These are ones, "who denies that Jesus is the Christ" and ones who do not confess "Jesus Christ has come in the flesh is from God." – 1 John 2:22; 4:2-3.

We must keep in mind that the meaning of any given text is what the author meant by the words that he used, as it should have been understood by his audience and had some relevance/meaning for his audience. The rebellion [apostasy] began slowly in the first century and would break forth after the last apostle's death, i.e., John. Historians Ariel and Will Durant inform us that by 187 C.E., there were 20 varieties of Christianity, and by 384 C.E., there were 80 varieties of Christianity. Christianity would become one again, a universal religion, i.e., Catholicism. However, that oneness was a false imitation, as it was by threat of torture and death.

Rebellion Against God

The man of lawlessness places himself in opposition against God, being used as a tool by the great resister- adversary, Satan himself. Paul warns us that this lawless one was/is "coming is in accordance with the activity of Satan." (2 Thess. 2:9) Paul also told the Thessalonians, "the mystery of lawlessness is already at work." The identity of the man of lawlessness has been shrouded in mystery, with many scholars supposing it is one evil man who will appear just before the day of the Lord. However, as Paul stated above, the lawless one was already at work in Paul's day. Again, the lawless one is a composite man [many individual rebels], meaning anyone in opposition against God, some worse than others. Some of these lawless ones set themselves up over God by their lies and false teachings, which they place above God's Word and place themselves in opposition to those who are truly Christian. (See 2Pet. 2:10-13) This lawless one is an imitation, a false Christian, who claims that he is truly Christ "so that he takes his seat in the temple of God, showing himself as being God." – 2 Thessalonians 2:4.

Restraining the Man of Lawlessness

What or who is acting as a **restraint** to the man of lawlessness and the apostasy? It would seem that the apostles of the first century were preventing this great apostasy **from taking hold** while they were alive. In the above, we saw Paul warning that wolf-like men would be infiltrating the congregation after Paul was gone. (Ac 20:29) Paul spoke of the apostasy in many of his writings. In order to keep the congregations clean, Paul taught all over the then known world, teaching people like Timothy and Titus, whom he left behind after he was martyred, to teach other qualified men in Paul's place. Paul called "the household of God, which is the church of the living God, a pillar, and buttress of the truth." (1 Tim. 3:15) Paul and the rest of the apostles grew the Christian congregation all over the then known

190

world, going from 120 disciples at Pentecost 33 C.E. to over a million in the beginning of the second century C.E. They wanted to build the purest church possible, **to withstand** centuries of the apostasy that began in full earnest in the second century C.E.

However, the **restraint** of the apostasy and the man of lawlessness (rebels against the truth) were not the apostles alone back in the first century C.E. The restraint of the apostasy and the lawless ones has been those who are truly Christian spread through these last 2,000 years, right up unto the day of the Lord. We have had both men and women who have stood out and stood up for the truth from the time of the martyrdom of Polycarp (69 – 155 C.E.), who had been a student of the apostle John. Keep in mind that throughout the Dark Ages 500 – 1500 C.E., they may not have taught everything that was biblically true, but they were living in a world of spiritual darkness. Catholicism was the dominant influence on Western civilization from late antiquity to the dawn of the modern age (Medieval and Renaissance Periods, 4th – 17th century C.E.). The Catholic Church would like us to forget the good "seeds" of discontent that were present in their midst many years before the Waldenses of the 12th century C.E., 200 years before John Wycliffe (1330-84) and Jan Hus (1369-1415) and 350 years before Martin Luther (1483-1546) and John Calvin (1509-64). (Matt. 13:24) These men's seeds sought the truth even in the darkest of periods, even if it meant their life.

Pre-Reformation Seeds of Truth Seekers

- **Bishop Agobard** of Lyons, France (779-840), was against image worship, churches dedicated to saints, and church liturgy that was contrary to Scripture.

- **Bishop Claudius** (d. between 827 and 839 C.E.)

- **Archdeacon Bérenger**, or Berengarius, of Tours, France (11th century C.E.), excommunicated as a heretic in 1050

- **Peter of Bruys** (1117-c. 1131), left the church because he disagreed with infant baptism, transubstantiation, prayers for the dead, worship of the cross, and the need for church buildings.

- **Henry of Lausanne** (who died imprisoned around 1148) spoke out against church liturgy, the corrupt clergy, and the religious hierarchy.

- **Peter Waldo** (c. 1140–c. 1218) and the Waldenses rejected purgatory, Masses for the dead, papal pardons and indulgences, and the worship of Mary and the saints.

- **John Wycliffe** (c. 1330-1384) preached against corruption in the monastic orders, papal taxation, the doctrine of transubstantiation (the doctrine that the bread and wine of Communion become, in substance, but not appearance, the body and blood of Jesus Christ at consecration), the confession, and church involvement in temporal affairs.

- **Jan Hus** (c. 1369-1415) preached against the corruption of the Roman Church and stressed the importance of reading the Bible. This swiftly fetched the anger of the hierarchy upon him. In 1403, the church leaders ordered him to stop preaching the antipapal notions of Wycliffe, whose books they had openly burned. Hus, nevertheless, went on to pen some of the most hurtful impeachments against the Church and its practices, such as the sale of indulgences. He was condemned and excommunicated in 1410.

Reformation Seeds of Truth Seekers

- **Girolamo Savonarola** (1452-98) was of the San Marcos monastery in Florence, Italy, who spoke out against the corruption in the Church.

- **Martin Luther** (1483-1546) was a monk-scholar who was also a doctor of theology and a professor of Biblical studies at the University of Wittenberg. Luther disagreed with or argued against papal indulgences, power, purgatory, and plenary remission of all penalties of the pope, among many others.

- **Ulrich Zwingli** (1484-1531) was a Catholic priest, who agreed with Luther in many doctrinal areas, and the removal of all vestiges of the Roman Church: images, crucifixes, clerical garb, and even liturgical music. However, he disagreed with Luther's literal interpretation of the Eucharist, or Mass (Communion), as he said it "must be taken figuratively or metaphorically; 'This is my body,' means, 'The bread signifies my body,' or 'is a figure of my body.'" This one issue caused them to part ways.

- **Anabaptists** (i.e., rejected infant baptism, so rebaptized adults, *ana* meaning "again" in Greek), **Mennonites** (Dutch Reformer Menno Simons), and **Hutterites** (Tyrolean Jacob Hutter), felt that the

Reformers did not go far enough in rejecting the failings of the Catholic Church.

- **John Calvin** (1509-64) published *Institutes of the Christian Religion*, in which he summarized the ideas of the early church fathers and medieval theologians, as well as those of Luther and Zwingli. His theological views would take too much space. John Calvin had Michael Servetus burned to death as a heretic. Calvin defended his actions in these words: "When the papists are so harsh and violent in defense of their superstitions that they rage cruelly to shed innocent blood, are not Christian magistrates shamed to show themselves less ardent in defense of the sure truth?" Calvin's religious extremism and personal hatred made him unwilling to see and understand the radicalness of his judgments and choked out any Christian principles.

- **William Tyndale** (1494-1536) had to flee from England, published his New Testament in 1526, and completed most of the Old Testament after his betrayal and arrest in a dungeon. He would be strangled at the stake, and his body was burned. The 1611 King James Version was actually 97 percent Tyndale's translation. He denounced the practice of prayer to saints. He taught justification by faith, the return of Christ, and mortality of the soul.

- **Jacobus Arminius** (1560-1609), graduated from Holland's Leiden University, after which he spent six years in Switzerland, studying theology under Théodore de Bèze, the successor to Protestant Reformer John Calvin. Rather than support Calvinism, he went against it, especially the doctrine of predestination, which was at the core of Calvinism.

The Darnel[180] Seed of Catholicism

Roman Catholicism has tainted itself with its history of immorality and bloodshed and its pagan-tainted religious ideas and practices. The centuries-

---

[180] "Darnel, the weed [in Jesus' parable of the Wheat and the Weeds] (species name Lolium temulentum,) is an annual plant that grows in the same areas as wheat. Darnel is nearly indistinguishable from wheat until the ear appears. Wheat ears are heavy and make the entire plant droop downward but darnel's light ears stand up straight. Ripe wheat is light brown but darnel is black. Jesus' parable of the weeds among the wheat in Matt. 13:24–40 builds on the early stage resemblance between darnel and wheat. Hos 10:4, Matt 13:24–40" – (Logos Bible Images by Richard Myers) It should be added that in the roots of these weeds entangle themselves with the wheat, which would make it inadvisable to pull the weed early.

long oppression, torture, rape, pillage, and murder of tens of millions of men, women, and children cannot come from true Christianity. They were the biggest offenders of the apostasy that Paul said had to come before **the day of the Lord**.

The Good Seed Protestantism

The Reformation gave us a return to the Bible in the common person's languages, which the Catholic Church had locked up in the dead language of Latin for 500-years. The Reformers brought the common folk freedom from papal authority but also from many erroneous Bible doctrines and dogmas that had gone on for a thousand years. However, the Protestant denominations have found themselves so fragmented and divided; one can only wonder where the truth and the Way are to be found. All 41,000 plus denominations that call themselves Christian cannot be just different roads leading to the same place.

Over eighty percent of Protestant Christianity is liberal-progressive as to their biblical and social beliefs, which began in the late 18th century up until the present. This covers too much area for a summary, but to mention just a few, they treat the Bible as being from man, not inspired and fully inerrant. They prefer to explain away the Bible accounts of miracles as myths, legends, or folk tales. They do not believe in the historicity of Bible characters such as Adam, Eve, and Job. They say that Moses did not write the first five books of the Bible but that they were written by several authors from the tenth to the fifth centuries B.C.E. and were compiled after that. They say Isaiah did not author the book bearing his name in the early eighth century B.C.E. However, two or three authors penned it, centuries later. They claim that Daniel did not write his book in the sixth century B.C.E., but rather it was written in the second-century B.C.E. They claim that the Bible is full of errors, mistakes, and contradictions regarding its history, science, and geography. They claim that the Antichrist is merely good versus evil and is not to be taken literally. Higher criticism has opened Pandora's Box to an overflow of pseudo-scholarly works whose result has been to weaken, challenge and destabilize people's assurance in the trustworthiness of the Bible. Who needs enemies like agnostics and atheists when we have liberal Bible scholars? We have not even delved into their unbiblical views of social justice, gay marriage, homosexual priests, abortion, women in the pulpits, etc.

Some may ask what about the remaining twenty percent of Christian denominations. Most of those are moderate in beliefs, which cast doubt on the trustworthiness of the Scriptures and give fodder to the liberal-progressive denominations. These are fence-riders who have abandoned **the Truth** and the Way of true, pure worship within Christianity. Before delving into the so-called conservative parts of Christianity, let us look at the charismatics.

We have charismatic Christianity, the fastest-growing segment, which emphasizes the work of the Holy Spirit, spiritual gifts, and modern-day miracles, speaking in tongues[181] and miraculous healing, and even fringe groups that perform snake handling in some areas. All of this is **un**biblical and based on emotionalism.

Those who believe that charismatic Christianity is false Christianity, persons such as this author, are said to be overly critical. Supporters of Charismatic Christianity say we "should be focusing on the fact that while many in the church continue to abandon our Christian faith, the Pentecostal/Charismatic community continues to offer the church a legitimate growth mechanism."[182] I would respond that a denomination founded on **un**biblical beliefs is not true Christianity and are the false teachers and prophets that we were warned were coming by Jesus and the New Testament writers. Therefore, charismatic Christianity is no Christianity at all, and all who are being brought in those groups are being obscured from finding the path of true Christianity. Further, Catholicism brought in almost the whole world from 400 to 1600 C.E. based on the same false, illogical reasoning from above; this oneness would supposedly be a sign of their being genuine Christianity. However, conservative Protestant denominations would fail to give them a pass.

So-called conservative Christianity is so minuscule that it barely gets press. We should not confuse radical Christianity, such as the Westboro Baptist Church,[183] with truly conservative, fundamentalist Christianity. However, even here within conservative Christianity, we find differences doctrinally and, yes, even in the so-called salvation doctrines.

Are all of the 41,000 different varieties of Christianity just different roads leading to the same place? Are all of the various conservative

---

[181] http://www.christianpublishers.org/speaking-in-tongues-truth

[182] http://tiny.cc/j5d7mx

[183] www.godhatesfags.com/

churches the Truth and the Way? There is no way of knowing for certain, but we know that Christ will bring back the oneness that the first century church experienced before the day of the Lord. We need to return to the question that Jesus asked, "When the Son of Man comes, will he find faith on earth?" (Lu 18:8) Jesus would not find faith on earth at present, not at the level that one might expect, not at present. However, he would find many good seeds, those who are truly Christian, who act as a restraint against imitation, false Christianity, agnosticism, atheism, and every other man of lawlessness.

DIVERSITY OF BIBLICAL INTERPRETATION
DIVERSITY OF CHRISTIAN BELIEFS

In his forward to R. C. Sproul's Knowing Scripture, J. I. Packer observes that Protestant theologians are in conflict about biblical interpretation. To illustrate the diversity of biblical interpretations, William Yarchin pictures a shelf full of religious books saying different things, but all claiming to be faithful interpretations of the Bible. Bernard Ramm observed that such diverse interpretations underlie the "doctrinal variations in Christendom." A mid-19th century book on biblical-interpretation observed that even those who believe the Bible to be "the word of God" hold "the most discordant views" about fundamental doctrines." Below are just a few examples.

Four Views of Hell	Four Views of Salvation	Two Views of Inspiration	Three Views of Atonement
Four Views of creation	Four Views of Eternal Security	Four Views of Inspiration	Four Views of Works in Final Judgment
Four Views of Inerrancy	Four Views of Sanctification	Two Views of Fasting	Four Views of the Book of Revelation
Two Views of Christology	Three Views of Image of God	Three Views of Grace	Three Views of Human Constitution
Four Views of Providence	Two Views of Lord's Supper	Four Views of Free Will	Two Views of Charismatic Gifts
Two Views of Baptism	Three Views of Jesus' Return	Two Views of Sabbath	Four Views of Predestination
Three Views of Purgatory	Four Views of the Church	Four Views of End Times	Four Views of Christian Spirituality
Four Views of Antichrist	Three Views of Neutrality	Three Views of Heaven	Two Views of Foreknowledge

Believe the Truth

2 Thessalonians 2:9-12 Updated American Standard Version (UASV)

⁹ but the one whose coming is in accordance with the activity of Satan, with all power and signs and false wonders, ¹⁰ and with every unrighteous deception[184] for those who are perishing, because **they did not receive the love of the truth** so as to be saved. ¹¹ For this reason God is sending upon them a working of error[185] so that they will believe the lie, ¹² in order that they all may be judged because **they did not believe the truth** but took pleasure in unrighteousness.

---

[184] Lit *seduction*

[185] Or *a deluding influence*

Here Paul uses **truth** (*aletheia*) as something *factual*, a *truth statement* that deals what a fact or reality is. Our eternal future is dependent upon whether we **love the truth**, i.e., what is true. If we do not accept and love the truth, there is no salvation for us. How can we really know whether we love the truth, or that Satan is using unrighteous deception (deluding influence) on us? (2:9) The first question is, "Can we say that we are truly seeking the truth?" Proverbs 23:23 says, "Buy truth, and do not sell it." Dave Bland writes, "To **buy the truth** (v. 23) does not mean to pay money for it. Rather it means for one to invest mental, emotional, and spiritual resources in pursuing it." (Bland 2002, p. 213) 'Buying truth' is not as straightforward as one might think. In many cases, it means that we are paying a price; it is coming at a cost to us personally.

What if we discover that a Bible doctrine that is accepted by many denominations is not **the truth**? Suppose that we have spent months, even years, privately poring over this doctrine and find that it is just not biblically true. Do we simply hide that truth and not bring it up, and if it is commented on at a meeting, do we just not participate that day? What if we read a verse in the KJV and decide to compare the ESV, RSV, UASV, and the NASB to find that all of these recent translations read differently than the King James Version? Do we just drop it and ignore that fact because their reading does not support our doctrinal position, a favorite verse in our beloved KJV that we have often used? What if we do investigate and we find two articles, one that supports the reading in the KJV and one that supports the reading in the newer translations, and we find that the article for the KJV reading seems to be rationalizing and justifying as it really misrepresents the evidence?

Remember, the apostle Paul was known by his Jewish name Saul before he ever met Jesus on the road to Damascus. Young Saul had studied under the renowned Pharisee Gamaliel, one of the greatest Jewish teachers, who may have been there in the area when Jesus was amazing the Jewish religious leaders, at the age of twelve. Gamaliel was the grandson of Hillel, the Elder (110 B.C.E.[186] – 10 C.E.), the founder of one of the two schools within Judaism. Paul describes himself as "circumcised on the eighth day, of the people of Israel, of the tribe of Benjamin, a Hebrew of Hebrews; as to the law, a Pharisee; as to zeal, a persecutor of the church; as to righteousness under the law, blameless." (Phil 3:5-6) Why was Paul so slow

---

[186] B.C.E. years ran down toward zero, although the Romans had no zero, and C.E. years ran up from zero. (100, 10, 3, 2, 1 ◄B.C.E. | C.E.► 1, 2, 3, 10, and 100)

to accept the truth of Christianity, even to the point of his persecuting Christians and being there when Stephen was stoned to death?

Paul saw Christianity as an apostate, false religion, a break off from Judaism, as it was made up of only Jews before he was converted. Paul had been part of the only true way to God, the Israelite nation, which had existed and received miraculous protection from God for 1,500 years, not to mention the 39 books of the Old Testament. He knew that Deuteronomy said that anyone hung on a tree would be accursed by God. Well, Jesus was executed by being hung on (i.e., nailed to) a wood cross. Paul knew that Daniel and other books said that Jesus would set up a kingdom that would crush all other kingdoms and never be brought to ruin. Jesus did no such thing and was executed for treason and as a blasphemer of God. Thus, we can see why Saul/Paul was slow to be receptive to **the truth**.

Nevertheless, Paul did convert. Did Paul buy the truth? Did it cost Paul anything? Yes, Paul had studied under the renowned Gamaliel, meaning he would have been a prominent leader and teacher within Judaism, leading to much wealth. However, in Paul's own words, what did he suffer for the truth? Paul told the Corinthians that he was "in far more labors, in far more imprisonments, beaten times without number, often in danger of death. Five times, I received from the Jews thirty-nine lashes. Three times, I was beaten with rods, once I was stoned; three times I was shipwrecked, a night and a day I have spent in the deep. I have been on frequent journeys, in dangers from rivers, dangers from robbers, dangers from my countrymen, dangers from the Gentiles, dangers in the city, dangers in the wilderness, dangers on the sea, dangers among false brethren; I have been in labor and hardship, through many sleepless nights, in hunger and thirst, often without food, in cold and exposure.[187]" (2 Cor. 11:23-27, NASB; See also 6:4-10; 7:5; 12:7). Sadly, this was in 55 C.E., so Paul had ten more years of even more pain and suffering before he would be martyred for the truth. So, yes, Paul paid a heavy price for the truth, it cost him much. Yet, concerning such a life as a wealthy, prominent Pharisee, Paul wrote, "But whatever gain I had, I counted as loss for the sake of Christ. Indeed, I count everything as loss because of the surpassing worth of knowing Christ Jesus, my Lord. For his sake I have suffered the loss of all things and count them as rubbish, in order that I may gain Christ." – Philippians 3:7-8.

---

[187] i.e., *in cold and nakedness*

Looking at Saul/Paul, we can establish whether we really have a **love for the truth**. Do we have such love for a doctrinal truth that we will accept it when it is contrary to what we thought was a doctrinal truth? When a long-held cherished belief is exposed as false, do we have such real love for the truth?

Imagine the courage that Paul, Barnabas, Timothy, and hundreds of others must have had in the first century Christian congregation. Imagine what is needed today with a liberal-progressive world, Islam being favored over Christianity, many thousands of false Christian denominations that claim to be the truth and the way, with liberal and moderate Bible scholars aiding atheism, not to mention some conservative scholars standing on the line, refusing to take a stand. Again, Paul warned, "the time is coming when people will not endure sound teaching, but having itching ears they will accumulate for themselves teachers to suit their own passions, and will turn away from listening to the truth and wander off into myths."[188] (2 Tim. 4:3-4) He also warned, "even if our gospel is veiled, it is veiled to those who are perishing. In their case, the god of this world has blinded the minds of the unbelievers, to keep them from seeing the light of the gospel of the glory of Christ, who is the image of God." In the same letter, "And no wonder, for even Satan disguises himself as an angel of light. So it is no surprise if his servants, also, disguise themselves as servants of righteousness. Their end will correspond to their deeds." (2 Cor. 4:3-4; 11:14-15) Many false and imitation Christians prefer to take the path of least resistance, as they possess the spirit of "go along to get along," which means to conform in order to have acceptance and security, i.e., **not** standing up for the love of the truth just to avoid confrontation. Yes, they turn away from the truth of God's Word. Thus, since most are turning away from the truth, do we have the courage of Christ, of Paul, and other faithful ones, to buy the truth, to seek the trust, no matter the cost to us?

---

[188] "**4:3 not endure**. This refers to holding up under adversity, and can be translated "tolerate." Paul here warns Timothy that, in the dangerous seasons of this age, many people would become intolerant of the confrontive, demanding preaching of God's Word (1:13, 14; 1 Tim. 1:9, 10; 6:3–5). ... **their own desires . . . itching ears**. Professing Christians and nominal believers in the church follow their own desires and flock to preachers who offer them God's blessings apart from His forgiveness, and His salvation apart from their repentance. They have an itch to be entertained by teachings that will produce pleasant sensations and leave them with good feelings about themselves. Their goal is that men preach "according to their own desires." Under those conditions, people will dictate what men preach, rather than God dictating it by His Word. **4:4 fables**. This refers to false idealogies, viewpoints, and philosophies in various forms that oppose sound doctrine." – MacArthur, John (2005-05-09). *The MacArthur Bible Commentary* (Kindle Locations 60854-60860). Thomas Nelson. Kindle Edition.

In addition, we can tell if we have a **love for the truth** by our heart attitude. The truth should appeal to both our hearts and our heads. The disciples of Jesus said to each other, "Did not our hearts burn within us while he talked to us on the road while he opened to us the Scriptures?" (Lu 24:32) It is only when we have true love for the truth; we will follow it no matter where it leads and regardless of who is on the other side of the truth. If our hearts, like the disciples of Jesus Christ, burn within us, we will be motivated to action because our salvation is dependent upon whether we really **love the truth.**

Walk in the Truth and Be Taught

Psalm 25:5 Updated American Standard Version (UASV)

⁵ Lead me in **your truth** and teach me,
for you are the God of my salvation;
for you I wait all the day long.

Mounce's *Complete Expository Dictionary of Old & New Testament Words* defines the Hebrew term (ᶜ*met*) "truth" as "faithfulness, reliability, trustworthiness; truth, what conforms to reality in contrast to what is false." (Mounce 2006, 896) Jehovah God, the Creator of heaven and earth is our only true source of information about humanity's current circumstances (i.e., our imperfect condition). He has a complete understanding of everything he has created, including humankind. He knows our design, which means our optimum circumstances for enjoying the life that he gave us. He is also well aware of how to deal with the rebellion of our first parents, Adam and Eve. He is also aware of what the future holds as well.

Psalm 31:5 Updated American Standard Version (UASV)

⁵ Into your hand I commit my spirit;
you have redeemed me, O Jehovah, **God of truth.**

Jesus himself said to the Father in a prayer of the disciples, "Sanctify them in the truth; your word is truth." (John 17:17) Since we are able to place complete trust in every word God has inspired, we need to heed his direction about human behavior, as it is entirely trustworthy. Young Prince Hezekiah says of Jehovah, "all your commandments are true." (Ps. 119:151) The promises that he lays out with his Word the Bible are dependable. After a lifetime of trusting Jehovah, Joshua said, "nothing failed from all the good things that Yahweh promised to the house of Israel; everything came to pass." (Josh. 21:45) Thus, from the books of Moses to the book of

Revelation, we see that God is 'righteous and true in all his ways.' – Revelation 15:3.

Walking In the Truth

Adam and Eve were created in the image of God and were a reflection of his qualities and attributes. Even after the fall, in humanity's state of imperfection, we still maintain a good measure of that image. For that reason, there is little surprise that the Creator of humankind would expect us to continue to walk in his truth or that the **lovers of truth** would want to walk in his truth. How are we to accomplish this in our imperfection? The Apostle Paul provided that answer when he wrote, "this is good and acceptable before God our Savior, who wants all people to be saved and to come to an accurate knowledge[189] of the truth." (1 Tim. 2:4) We need to acquire an accurate knowledge of who God is, why he created the earth, humans, and his will and purpose for us and the earth. What does he expect of us, his followers? (John 17:3; 1 John 2:3-4) Walking in the truth is far more than mere knowledge of who, what, where, why, and how. This knowledge will lead to what Luke called the early Christians "the Way." (Acts 9:2) This taking in knowledge of the Father and the Son will be life-altering, becoming a Way of life.

Certainly, what is true of our human parents would be even more accurate of our heavenly Father as well. God finds great joy, satisfaction and happiness when imperfect humans choose to imitate his qualities and attributes over their fleshly desires, which lean toward wrongdoing, and over the god of this system of things, Satan the Devil. (Gen. 1:26-27; Pro. 23:24-25) As the Creator and Designer of us, 'he teaches us what is best for us, leads us in the way you should go.' (Isa. 48:17) It is a privilege to work with hundreds of millions of others who want to walk in the truth, be used in the Great Commission, helping millions more to move from death to life. – Matthew 28:19-20; John 5:24.

We also bring glory to God when we **walk in the truth**. Satan challenged his sovereignty, the rightfulness of his rulership, and our choosing to walk with him means we support him as ruler. (Gen. 3:1-4; Rev. 12:9) Part of Satan's challenge was that created persons would only love him for what they can get out of him; if opposition to their loyalty arises, they will abandon him. (Job 1:6-12) Thus, our continuously,

---

[189] Greek *epignosis*, accurate or full knowledge

steadfastly walking in the truth, evidence that lies, because we refuse to compromise what is right for some immediate gratification. (Pro. 27:11) Those who have chosen not to walk in the truth, but have followed the path of independence, like Adam and Eve, unwittingly align themselves with Satan. He is the "father of the lie," "who deceives the whole world," as he is "the god of this age [and] has blinded the minds of the unbelievers." (Jn. 8:44; Rev. 12:9; 2 Cor. 4:4) These have a closed heart and mind and are unable to see the path of truth. May we maintain the mindset of the Psalmist and the prophet Samuel,

Psalm 25:4-5 Updated American Standard Version (UASV)

⁴ Make me to know your ways, O Jehovah;
   teach me your paths.
⁵ Lead me in your truth and teach me,
   for you are the God of my salvation;
   for you I wait all the day long.

1 Samuel 12:21 Updated American Standard Version (UASV)

²¹ You must not turn aside, for then you would go after futile things which cannot profit or deliver, because they are futile. ²⁴ Only fear Jehovah, and serve him faithfully with all your heart, for see what great things he has done for you.

Written for Our Instruction

We can learn some object lessons from what God has disclosed to us in his Word. Paul told the Corinthians, "these things happened to those people as an example but are written for our instruction." (1 Cor. 10:11) He also told the congregation in Rome, "For whatever was written beforehand was written for our instruction, in order that through patient endurance and through the encouragement of the scriptures we may have hope." (Rom. 15:4) Israelite history is a great opportunity for us to learn. God personally chose Abraham, Isaac, and Jacob because they walked with him while others chose to abandon him. The nation of Israel was the descendants of Jacob's 12 sons.

The Israelites became God's chosen people, of whom he made a covenant, which they agreed to follow. If they walked in the truth, they would be blessed by God's presence. If they abandoned that walk like the pagan nations, they would lose his presence, resulting in the difficulties that came with living in this fallen world. While they maintained their loyalty, they never became victims to enemy nations. (Deut. 28:7) Furthermore, they could depend on crop growth that was exceptional year after year and their flocks of animals. (Ex. 22:1-15) Additionally, they had no reason to build jails to house criminals because they had the perfect social system. (Ex. 22:1-15) In addition, they did not suffer from diseases like other nations (Deut. 7:15). Moreover, while they had an army, it would have never needed to be used if they had obeyed because God fought in their behalf. (2 Ki 19:35) He promised them that they would "be blessed more than all of the peoples," and when they walked in the truth, this proved to be true.

Deuteronomy 7:14 Updated American Standard Version (UASV)

[14] You shall be blessed above all peoples; there will be no male or female barren among you or among your cattle.

We all have the history before us of how Israel just **refused to walk in the truth**. They would walk in the truth for a number of years, and then they would abandon that truth until life was impossibly difficult, moving them to return to the Father. This walking in the truth, abandoning the truth, and repenting to return to the truth, went on for some 1,500 years. The final difficulty in this back and forth was their rejection of the Son of God. His words to them were quite clear:

Matthew 21:43 Updated American Standard Version (UASV)

[43] Therefore I say to you, the kingdom of God will be taken away from you and **given to a nation,**[190] producing the fruit of it.

Matthew 23:37-38 Updated American Standard Version (UASV)

[37] "Jerusalem, Jerusalem, who kills the prophets and stones those who are sent to her! How often I wanted to gather your children together, the way a hen gathers her chicks under her wings, and you were unwilling.

[38] Behold, your house is being left to you desolate!

Just who are **the people or nation** that the Kingdom was to be given to after the Israelites fell out of favor with God? He chose for himself a new spiritual nation, which became the Christian congregation that Jesus established between 29 and 33 C.E. He no longer had the descendants of

---

[190] Or *people*

Abraham, Isaac, and Jacob as his chosen people, by which other nations would bless themselves.

Acts 10:34-35 Updated American Standard Version (UASV)

[34] So Peter opened his mouth and said: "Truly I understand that God shows no partiality, [35] but in every nation anyone who fears[191] him and works righteousness[192] is acceptable to him.

Acts 13:46 Updated American Standard Version (UASV)

[46] And Paul and Barnabas spoke out boldly and said, "It was necessary that the word of God be spoken to you first; since you thrust it aside and judge yourselves unworthy of eternal life, behold, we are turning to the Gentiles.

Did this mean that no Jewish person could be a part of the Kingdom? Hardly! For seven years, 29 C.E. to 36 C.E., the first disciples of that Kingdom were only Jewish people. After 36 C.E. and the baptism of the first Gentile, Cornelius, anyone, including the Jews, could be a part of this Kingdom, as long as they accepted the King, Jesus Christ. Jesus said, "I am the way, and the truth, and the life. No one comes to the Father except through me." (John 14:6) At Jesus' Baptism, a voice from heaven said, "This is my beloved Son, with whom I am well pleased." (Matt.3:16-17) Jesus' teaching, miraculous signs, his ransom sacrifice, and resurrection established him as the truth, having the authority and power of the Father.[193] The Christians in the first century were given the position of being God's chosen people. (Acts 1:8; 2:1-4, 43) **The truth** would now flow through Jesus to the Christian congregation. As Paul told the Corinthians, "For to us God has revealed them through the Spirit. For the Spirit searches all things, even the depths of God." (1 Cor. 2:10) It happened just as Jesus had said it would, "I praise you, Father, Lord of heaven and earth, because you have hidden these things from the wise and intelligent, and have revealed them to young children." – Matthew 11:25.

However, more truth was on the horizon with the birth of the Christian congregation. There had been 39 books written by the Jewish writers of the Hebrew Old Testament (2 Tim. 3:16-17), and now there were

---

[191] This is a reverential fear of displeasing God because of one's great love for him. It is not a dreadful fear.

[192] I.e., *does what is right*

[193] Matt. 15:30-31; 20:28; John 4:34; 5:19, 27, 30; 6:38, 40; 7:16-17; 17:1-2; Acts 2:22

to be added an additional 27 books by Jewish Christians, making up the Greek New Testament (2 Peter 2:15-16). Thus, there were 66 small books written over a 1,600-year period that would make one book, which we hold today in our modern-day translations. Yes, some 40-plus Bible writers were, as Peter put it, "men carried along by the Holy Spirit spoke from God." – 2 Peter 1:21.

True and False Disciples

The question that begs to be asked is, 'how do we know, who is walking in the truth and who only appears to be walking in the truth?' Who truly is the dispenser of truth these days? As has been mentioned, we have some 41,000 different denominations that all claim to be Christian, and each would argue that they are doing just that.

Matthew 7:21-23 Updated American Standard Version (UASV)

21 "Not everyone who says to me, 'Lord, Lord,' will enter the kingdom of heaven, but **the one who does the will of my Father** who is in heaven. 22 On that day many will say to me, 'Lord, Lord, did we not prophesy in your name, and cast out demons in your name, and do many mighty works in your name?' 23 And then I will declare to them, 'I never knew you; depart from me, you who practice lawlessness.'[194]

The primary concern of any true disciple of Christ is that he is "**one who does the will of my Father.**" We often hear Christians saying, "I think, I feel, I believe," when in reality, this is not the right path. We need to establish what the will of the Father is, as opposed to our will, or the will of our pastor, or the will of the people, or the popular will. Maybe we are accomplishing some very good deeds that are done in the name of Christ, but if it is not the will of the Father, then it is being done in vain. We need

---

[194] **7:21 Not everyone who says . . . but he who does.** The faith that says but does not do is really barren unbelief (cf. v. 20). Jesus is not suggesting that works merit salvation but that true faith will not fail to produce the fruit of good works. This point is also precisely the point of James 1:22–25; 2:26. **7:22 7:22 have we not prophesied . . . cast out demons . . .** and done many wonders. Note that far from being totally devoid of works of any kind, these people were claiming to have done some remarkable signs and wonders. In fact, their whole confidence was in these works—further proof that these works, spectacular as they might have appeared, could not have been authentic. No one so bereft of genuine faith could possibly produce true good works. A bad tree cannot bear good fruit (v. 18). **7:23 lawlessness.** All sin is lawlessness (1 John 3:4), i.e., rebellion against the law of God (cf. 13:41). – MacArthur, John (2005-05-09). *The MacArthur Bible Commentary* (Kindle Locations 39114-39118). Thomas Nelson. Kindle Edition.

to appreciate that the Father has placed all authority into the hands of the Son.

John 17:1-3 Updated American Standard Version (UASV)

¹ Jesus spoke these things; and lifting up his eyes to heaven, He said, "Father, the hour has come; glorify your Son, that the Son may glorify you, ² just as **you have given him authority over all flesh**, so that he may give eternal life to all those whom you have given to him. ³ This is eternal life, that they may know you, the only true God, and the one whom you sent, Jesus Christ.

Matthew 28:18-20 Updated American Standard Version (UASV)

¹⁸ And Jesus came up and spoke to them, saying, "**All authority has been given to me** in heaven and on earth. ¹⁹ Go therefore and **make disciples** of all the nations, baptizing them in the name of the Father and the Son and the Holy Spirit, ²⁰ **teaching them** to observe all that I commanded you; and behold, I am with you always, even to the end of the age."

Matthew 24:14 Updated American Standard Version (UASV)

¹⁴ And this gospel of the kingdom **will be proclaimed in all the inhabited earth**[195] as a testimony to all the nations, and then the end will come.

John 6:38 Updated American Standard Version (UASV)

³⁸ because I have come down from heaven not that I should do my will, but the will of the one who sent me.

John 5:24 Updated American Standard Version (UASV)

²⁴ Truly, truly, I say to you, whoever hears my word and believes him who sent me has eternal life. He does not come into judgment, but has **passed from death to life**.

What do we learn from the above texts? **(1)** We need to do the will of the Father if we are to be walking in the truth. **(2)** The Father gave all authority to the Son. **(3)** The Son, Jesus, does not do his will, but the will of the Father. **(4)** Therefore, to do the will of the Father is to obey the Son,

---

[195] Or *in the whole world*

who is doing the will of the Father. Jesus specifically told his disciples before his ascension that he had "all authority in heaven and on earth." Then, he gave them one commission to obey: to preach, teach, and make disciples. In other words, a disciple walking in the truth is one who is being used as a tool to bring people from all nations over from death into life.

Faithfully Walking in the Truth

3 John 1:4 Updated American Standard Version (UASV)

⁴ No greater joy do I have than this, to hear of my children walking in the truth.

The Apostle John penned these words about 96-98 C.E. when he was almost 100 years old. He had spent a lifetime making disciples and helping them maintain their walk in the truth. This writer has spoken many times about the number of denominations today, numbering around 41,000. Those denominations that are walking in the truth today are those that reflect Scripture as though it were a fingerprint. When a detective lifts a fingerprint from a crime scene and there is a match to a criminal, it is done by determining how many points within the print match up. We can use this as an analogy for those who are walking in the truth. How many points match up if we use the Bible as lines in a fingerprint? However, for the sake of argument, let us assume that the reader is in a denomination that highly reflects the Bible and first century Christianity. How can we be certain that we will be able to maintain our walk in the truth?

There are many difficulties in this life that can sap us of our strength to continue our walk. Maybe we have grown discouraged because of serious health problems or family difficulties. Then, some have become distracted chasing after the lifestyles that this world has to offer. What can we do so as not to drift away, fall away, turn away, refuse, or become sluggish in our walk in the truth?

Consider Jesus Christ

Jesus did not live in an ideal time. He lived under the Roman Empire, which expected taxes from its citizen, and he lived under the Jewish system, which demanded their taxes as well. Many Jews were very poor, and the Jewish Law was very oppressive to its people because the religious leaders added so many oral traditions. When Jesus finally started his ministry, he was tempted personally by Satan. In addition, those who chose to follow him were very difficult to deal with because Jewish pride kept them seeking their own interests. Furthermore, Jesus faced those that mocked him for his message and Jewish religious leaders who were trying to kill him for that message. Moreover, he knew how things were going to end, how he was going to be betrayed by one of the twelve, arrested, beaten within an inch of his life, and executed as a blasphemer. (Matt. 4:8-11; John 6:14, 15) Regardless of all the difficulties that came his way, Jesus continued walking in the truth. What was it that gave him the ability to persevere?

Hebrews 12:1-2 Updated American Standard Version (UASV)

[1] Therefore, since we have so great a cloud of witnesses surrounding us, let us also lay aside every weight and the sin which so easily entangles us, and let us run with endurance the race that is set before us, [2] fixing our eyes on Jesus, the author and perfecter of faith, who for the joy set before him endured the cross, despising the shame, and has sat down at the right hand of the throne of God.

Paul informs us what it was that enabled Jesus to endure. It was 'the joy set before him." He knew the result of his obedience right up to the very end, and so he kept walking in the truth, as should we. We too can keep in mind the reward of eternal life. (Rev. 22:12) As we are walking through life, there may be, some very atrociously difficult times, where getting up each morning seems overwhelming. If one can focus in on the destination of this journey, it will make each step of the way, just a little easier. Therefore, we can find our walk in the truth, somewhat easier, if we see the life that awaits us.

Consider the Apostle Paul

2 Corinthians 11:23-29 Updated American Standard Version (UASV)

[23] Are they servants of Christ? I reply like a madman, I am more outstandingly one: I have done more work, been imprisoned more often, with countless beatings, and often near deaths. [24] Five times I received 40 strokes less one from the Jews, [25] three times I was beaten with rods, once I was stoned, three times I experienced shipwreck, a night and a day I have spent in the open sea; [26] in journeys often, in dangers from rivers, in dangers from robbers, in dangers from my own people, in dangers from the nations, in dangers in the city, in dangers in the wilderness, in dangers at sea, in dangers among false brothers, [27] in labor and toil, in sleepless nights often, in hunger and thirst, frequently without food, in cold and lacking

clothing.[196] [28] Besides those things of an external kind, there is what rushes in on me from day to day: the anxiety for all the congregations. [29] Who is weak, and I am not weak? Who is made to stumble, and I am not incensed?[197]

Philippians 4:11-13 Updated American Standard Version (UASV)

[11] Not that I speak from want, for I have learned to be content[198] in whatever circumstances I am. [12] I know how to be made lowly, and I know also how to be abounding; in everything and in all things I have learned the secret *of* both being filled and going hungry, both to abound and to be lacking. [13] I can do all things through[199] him who strengthens me. [14] Nevertheless, you have done well to share[200] *with me* in my affliction.

We have to appreciate the power that is offered to us, just as it was offered to Jesus and Paul and other servants from the Hebrew Old Testament (Ps. 55:12). It is not the power to fulfill our wishes or desires but the power to carry out the will and purpose of the Father and the Son. Our ability to walk in the truth through such things as that, which Jesus and Paul walked through, does not come to us naturally. However, this power to endure is very much available to us today as well.

Isaiah 40:29-31 Updated American Standard Version (UASV)

[29] He gives power to the tired one,
    and full might to those lacking strength.
[30] Youths will tire out and grow weary,
    And young men will stumble and fall;
[31] But those hoping in Jehovah will regain power;
    they will soar on wings like eagles;
they will run and not grow weary;
    they will walk and not tire out.

What kinds of things would be in harmony with the will and purposes of God, by which we may be empowered? The world requires so much of our strength to cover the necessities of food, housing, and clothing. We may be worn out from work, so we need the strength to carry out our daily

---

196 Lit *and in nakedness*

197 Lit *I am not on fire*

198 Or *"self-sufficient"*

199 Lit *in*

200 Or *have fellowship with*

personal Bible study, going to Christian meetings, Christian activities, and especially our evangelism of the Good News.[201] We may need strength to maintain our Christian walk in the face of temptations, discouragement, or some form of persecution. – Psalm 1:1-3; Romans 10:10; 1 Thessalonians 5:16, 17; Hebrews 10:23-25.

Satan is the god of this wicked age.' (2 Cor. 4:4) Christians are his primary targets, as we are alien residents of his world. Therefore, we should not be at all startled that there is the extra difficulty of living a righteous life in an unrighteous world. When we accept Christ, it is as though we have arrived in a new land, the land of Christianity. It is not an isolated nation but is embedded with a world of nations that are contrary to its very essence of God. It is no easy task to pick up stakes in the land of worldliness. We must let go of old friends and begin to discover new ones. We must learn a completely new culture. In this land, we are the minority, and most people see us as though we are a stranger in their land. As Christians, our walk in the truth can take us through many difficulties in life, but our destination is life in a renewed world, not this wicked fallen one.

How does this analogy play out for the Christian? We must now learn how to live according to the Spirit, not the flesh, an entirely new moral code. Shortly thereafter, we will develop a new personality that is reflective of our new land of Christianity. "For at that time I will change the speech of the peoples to a pure speech, that all of them may call upon the name of [Jehovah] and serve him with one accord." (Zeph. 3:9) As a new member of Christ's Kingdom, we will have already given up our former ways.

1 Corinthians 6:9-11 Updated American Standard Version (UASV)

[9] Or do you not know that the unrighteous will not inherit the kingdom of God? Do not be deceived; neither fornicators, nor idolaters, nor adulterers, nor men of passive homosexual acts, nor men of active homosexual acts,[202] [10] nor thieves, nor the covetous, nor drunkards, nor revilers, nor swindlers, will inherit the kingdom of God. [11] And such were

---

[201] I am not of the mind of the rest of Christianity, who believe that sharing their conversion, or what God has done in their life is our "evangelism." Our evangelism is to preach the Good News, to teach Bible doctrine, and to make disciples by conversion, much of which is not being done in Christianity at this point and time.

[202] The two Greek terms refer to passive men partners and active men partners in consensual homosexual acts

some of you; but you were washed, you were sanctified, you were justified in the name of the Lord Jesus Christ and by the Spirit of our God.

There are far more benefits to this move from the land of worldliness to the land of Christianity. First, the land of Christianity has a population of persons that live a morally clean life, who accept and love us for who we are, not who we were. (Lu 18:29-30) Second, there is the strength that we are given to cope with this new life as an alien resident in the land of worldliness. Third, there is God's Word, the Bible, which, if followed will generally lead to a far better outcome than the former days of being led by the flesh. Fourth, we now have the hope of life, while before, it was the inevitability of death. (Phil. 4:8-9) Most importantly, we will now be a friend of the Creator of heaven and earth. – James 2:23; Matthew 7:13, 14; 1 John 2:15-17

Consider Your Spiritual Health

It is generally true that if we take care of your physical health, we will seldom fall ill, and should we fall ill, the recovery is easier and faster. The same is true of spiritual health. If we fall sick spiritually, the recovery will be easier and faster, if we were healthy to begin with. We need to keep the benefits that we have received from obeying Scripture and the hope that awaits us at the forefront of our minds. Of course, we cannot completely sidestep the difficulties of this imperfect world or its people, but if we have maintained our spiritual health, they will not overcome us entirely because there is the resurrection hope, which no one can take from us.

Review Questions

(1) What is the apostasy that was foretold, and how long was it to run?

(2) Who is the man of lawlessness, and how will this lawless one be destroyed?

(3) What rebellion against God has taken place?

(4) Who has been acting as the restraint against the apostasy and the man of lawlessness from the first century until now?

(5) What two different types of seeds have grown up together?

(6) What is the darnel seed of Catholicism?

(7) What does it mean to believe the truth?

(8) What does it mean to walk in the truth?

(9) How can we know if we truly love the truth?

CHAPTER 15 Knowing When Not to Give God's Word Away

Proverbs 15:23 Updated American Standard Version (UASV)

²³ A man has joy in the answer of his mouth,
and a word in season, how good it is!

Proverbs 25:11 Updated American Standard Version (UASV)

¹¹ Like apples of gold in silver settings
is a word spoken at the right time.

What do we do when we determine that the one we are witnessing to is just not interested? How can we disengage? Should we continue on trying to reach the heart and mind, hoping that we may eventually stimulate interest? Alternatively, would it simply be best to terminate the discussion? It is all about having respect for the person we are trying to evangelize and God himself. We cannot reason with the unreasonable.

Ecclesiastes 3:7 Updated American Standard Version (UASV)

⁷ a time to tear apart, and a time to sew together;
a time to be silent and a time to speak;

Matthew 7:6 Updated American Standard Version (UASV)

⁶ "Do not give what is holy [Word of God] to dogs, and do not throw your pearls [Word of God] before swine, or they will trample them under their feet, and turn and tear you to pieces.

We must realize that there is a difference between sharing the Good News in an easy-to-understand way, allowing the listener to determine what his or her reaction will be, as opposed to trying to force the message on someone. We are not salespeople who use pressure tactics to get a sale. We do not force others to accept the truth, as God would not accept anyone who does not come to him freely.

Joshua 24:15 Updated American Standard Version (UASV)

¹⁵ And if it seems evil to you to serve Jehovah, choose for yourselves today whom you will serve; whether the gods, which your fathers served which were beyond the River, or the gods of the Amorites in whose land you are living; but as for me and my house, we will serve Jehovah.

Our task is to present our message as clearly and understandable as possible so the person knows what we are saying, and then he states explicitly that he is uninterested; we can walk away, knowing that we have served God well and have done our best. Moreover, as we are walking away, we should never view the uninterested (indifferent or apathetic) one as an enemy. Life circumstances can alter his outlook in time, causing him to view things differently. Therefore, a future visit from a fellow Christian may bring about better results. If we leave him respectfully, he can sense that he will be more open to future discussions. We could say, "I really appreciate your time; maybe another time."

Why do we not press on? What do we gain by not doing so? First, the person we are speaking to will be impressed that we were respectful instead of being pushy. Second, our being reasonable with him, not forcing him to get upset, may make him more inclined toward a future visit.

If we are abruptly shut down with "I am busy," what can we do? We simply offer a brief comment about the lack of time in the modern-day world, and give him a Bible tract, saying, "This takes a mere two minutes to read; I hope that you might consider it when you get a moment. Then, we might discuss it at another time."

This person may genuinely have been busy. On the other hand, he may fear a lengthy conversation. Alternatively, he may have had many bad experiences with other Christians who lacked tact and respect. On the other hand, he may feel that his best defense does not let us get started. However, our respectful (courteous or polite) disposition may leave him impressed, which may cause him to reconsider and talk with us or be more open in the future.

Just because we have spoken of how to end uneventful witnessing opportunities, this does not mean that we do not ever look for ways to overcome objections. We are not the type to give up easily in our efforts to make disciples, but we are the type to respect no when they sincerely mean no. The time of a person's life may very well be why they are inclined toward ignoring the Gospel, so we should not be so quick to judge them by this one encounter. Many young people, for example, are not pressed to talk about eternal life when it seems that they will live forever.

Ambassadors of Christ

2 Corinthians 5:20-21 Updated American Standard Version (UASV)

20 Therefore, we are ambassadors for Christ, as though God were making an appeal through us; we beg you on behalf of Christ, be reconciled

214

to God. ²¹ He made him who knew no sin to be sin on our behalf, so that we might become the righteousness of God in him.

5:20a. Paul's role in the divine plan of reconciliation led him to a remarkable claim. He and his company were **Christ's ambassadors.** "Ambassadors" was a technical political term used in Paul's day that closely parallels our English word "ambassadors." An ambassador represented a nation or kingdom in communication with other nations. Paul had in mind his apostolic call to represent the kingdom of Christ to the nations of the earth. Ambassadors held positions of great honor in the ancient world because they represented the authority of the kings on whose behalf they spoke.

This was also true for Paul as the ambassador of Christ. When he spoke the message of reconciliation, it was **as though God were making his appeal through** him. Rather than speaking directly to the nations of earth, God ordained that human spokespersons would speak for him. As an apostle, Paul had authority to lead and guide the church (2 Cor. 13:3, 10). Yet, this description applies to all who bear the gospel of Christ to others— even to those who do not bear apostolic authority (1 Pet. 4:11). Though we may not present the gospel as perfectly as Paul did, we do speak on God's behalf when we bring the message of grace to others. But Paul and his company were to be received as mouthpieces of God in the most authoritative sense.

5:20b–21. In these verses Paul summarized the content of the message of reconciliation. His summary includes an expression of his heart, an appeal, and an explanation.

First, Paul introduced his message in emotional terms, expressing his heart. He spoke **on Christ's behalf** because he was an ambassador. But as ordinary ambassadors often sought reconciliation between national enemies with intensity, Paul **implore[d]** others to be reconciled to God. The term *implored* (*deomai*) often connotes beseeching or begging. In imitation of the passionate ministry of Christ himself (Matt. 23:37), Paul so desired to see people come to Christ that he thought of his ministry as begging.

Paul did not actually beg people to have saving faith. He spoke metaphorically in an attempt to convey the motivations behind his ministry. Paul appealed to others for their own sake, even when he was firm or harsh. He knew the enemies of God would suffer divine wrath (Eph. 5:6; Col. 3:5–6). For this reason, his ministry was not impersonal or emotionally disconnected. He desired to see people come to Christ, as should all who minister the gospel on Christ's behalf.

Second, Paul summarized the content of his message of reconciliation in a short appeal. His practice was to tell others to **be reconciled to God**. Since Paul had to appeal to others to be reconciled, he did not believe that the work of Christ automatically reconciled every human being to God. Christ's saving work on the cross is sufficient for every human being, but it is effective only for those who believe. As the imperative (**be reconciled**, from *katallasso*) indicates, those who hear the gospel are responsible to believe in Christ in order to become reconciled to God.

Third, Paul explained that sinful people, who are the enemies of God, can be reconciled to God only through Christ and his work on behalf of the human race. Paul summarized Christ's work in two elements. On the one hand, **God made** Christ, **who had no sin, to be sin**. Paul did not mean that Christ actually became a sinner. Throughout his humiliation, Christ remained faithful and righteous. It is likely that Paul followed the Septuagint's practice of using the term *sin* (*harmartia*) as a circumlocution for "sin offering" (e.g., Num. 6:14). The New Testament frequently refers to Isaiah 53 in which the Messiah's death is declared to be "an offering for sin" (Isa. 53:10, NRSV). This language stems from the Old Testament sacrificial system and identifies the sacrifice that brought forgiveness to those for whom it was made (Lev. 4:5–10).

In this sense, Christ became the sin offering **for us**—for all who believe in him. In the gospel of the New Testament, salvation comes to enemies of God because Christ himself became the perfect and final substitutionary sacrifice on behalf of those who have saving faith in him.

Paul then pointed to the purpose of Christ's sacrifice. It was **so that in him we** (all who have saving faith) **might become the righteousness of God**. Note first that it is **in him** (in Christ) that reconciliation takes place. The concept of "in Christ" formed one of Paul's central teachings. To be "in Christ" was to be joined with him in his death and resurrection and thus to receive the benefits of his salvation. In this passage Paul summarized the benefits received in Christ by stating that the believer becomes **the righteousness of God**.

The precise meaning of this expression has been the source of much controversy. Paul probably intended the expression **of God** to be taken as "from God," as Romans 1:17 suggests. Yet, is this righteousness that is infused into believers as they live the Christian life (sanctification)? Or is it the righteousness that is imputed to believers when they turn in faith toward Christ (justification)? Probably Paul's emphasis is on imputed righteousness, since it was by imputation of our sin to Christ, and not by infusion, that Christ was **made ... to be sin for us**.

Still, it is best not to divide these issues so sharply as we approach this passage. As Romans 1:17 suggests, the **righteousness from God** is by faith from first to last. Believers become the righteousness from God when they first receive the imputation of Christ's righteousness in justification, but they also receive the continuous blessing of the experience of righteousness in their lives as they grow in their sanctification (cf. Gal. 3:1–5).

6:1. Paul concluded this section by making the implications of his ministry evident. He and his company appealed to the Corinthians **as God's fellow workers**. In the preceding verses, Paul had spoken of his ministry "as though God were making his appeal" (5:20) through him and his company. The apostle and his company served alongside God as "Christ's ambassadors" (5:20). Because Paul and his company spoke the true gospel as God ambassadors, the Corinthians should have received and honored them, especially by complying with their petition that the Corinthians be reconciled to God. So Paul **urge[d]** them **not to receive God's grace in vain**.

Paul had warned the Corinthians several times not to falter in their faith. He did not believe that true believers could lose their salvation (Eph. 4:30; Phil. 1:6), but he was not convinced that everyone in the Corinthian church was a true believer. During this life, it is necessary for all who profess faith in Christ to make certain that their faith endures. Otherwise, the mercy shown to them in the preaching and reception of the word of God will be **in vain**.

6:2. To support his appeal, Paul referred to Isaiah 49:8. This prophecy focused on the restoration of God's people after the exile. God promised that he would respond to the cries of the exile, **in the time of** his **favor** and **in the day of salvation**. Paul focused attention on Isaiah's emphasis that in God's timing salvation from the judgment of exile would come.

As a result, Paul pressed the significance of this prophecy on the Corinthian situation. The days in which they lived, the days of the New Testament, were not to be ignored or taken for granted. Those days were, as our own days are, **the time of [God's] favor** and **the day of salvation**. When Christ came to earth, he began to restore God's people from exile. After Christ ascended into the heavenly places, we continue to see him fulfilling the hopes of restoration. Christ will complete his saving work when he returns in glory. In the meantime, everyone must recognize the urgency of the times in which we live.

We are in the day of great opportunity because the final saving work of God has come to earth. Yet, we are in a day of great danger because failing to receive this salvation through enduring faith will bring a severe judgment. The New Testament age is the climax of history. There will be no possibility of salvation beyond the New Testament. Paul wanted the Corinthians to prove faithful because of the critical moment in history that they occupied.[203]

Review Questions

(1) What do we do when we determine that the one we are witnessing to is just not interested?

(2) How do we view the uninterested?

(3) Why do we not press on? What do we gain by not doing so?

(4) If we are abruptly shut down with "I am busy," what can we do?

(5) Does this mean we never try to overcome objections?

(6) What does it mean that we are ambassadors of Christ?

---

[203] Richard L. Pratt Jr, *I & II Corinthians*, vol. 7, Holman New Testament Commentary (Nashville, TN: Broadman & Holman Publishers, 2000), 359–362.

CHAPTER 16 Using the Bible When We Evangelize

The Word of God employs incredible power upon those who hear it, but only if they have a receptive heart or the evangelist was able to adjust that one's thinking. Once a person accepts the Bible as being the Word of God, it will carry more of an impact than anything that man has ever written. Therefore, we must become proficient in using our Bible when witnessing to others. God's Word will enable us to sift through those not really wanting to know the truth, helping us to develop or discover right-hearted ones, enabling them to get on the path of salvation.

2 Timothy 3:16-17 Updated American Standard Version (UASV)

16 All Scripture is inspired by God and profitable for teaching, for reproof, for correction, for training in righteousness; 17 so that the man of God may be fully competent, equipped for every good work.

Are we using the Bible while we do our personal study? Are we looking up the Scripture every time one is cited? Are we using the Bible when we are preparing for our congregation meetings? Are we then using the Bible once at the congregation meetings? Are we using the Bible when we try to witness informally to others? While this may not apply to you the reader, one survey after another shows that ninety percent of Christians are biblically illiterate. This means **(1)** they cannot use the book that they claim to be the Word of God. This means **(2)** that they are unable to look up Scriptures when talking with unbelievers. This means **(3)** they cannot defend the Bible as truly being the Word of God. This means **(4)** they are unable to explain the foundation beliefs of Scripture correctly. This means **(5)** they are unable to reason from the Scriptures, explaining and proving what is necessary for the listener to accept a belief as true. This means **(6)** that their church has not trained them to effectively communicate the Word of God.

If we are going to accomplish the things above, it means preparation on our part. Are we buying out the time to develop the skills needed to accomplish all six of the above points? If we are reading this book, then our heart is seeking to do just that. We might think that the above seems quite difficult to ascertain, but it is not as difficult as expected. If we will do the following for the next year of our Christian walk, we will be on our way to achieving all six of the above.

(1) Have a personal Bible study time of at least thirty minutes a day, preferably one hour.[204]

(2) Prepare for all Christian meetings.

(3) Look up Scriptures when they are not cited within the literature.

(4) Participate in the congregation meetings if that particular meeting allows it (e.g., Bible study class).

(5) Use the Bible whenever the opportunity presents itself. Do not paraphrase a Scripture, pull out the Bible, look it up, and hold it in front of the person, read it aloud.

(6) Every time we learn something new, share it with at least one person, and not on the internet. Explain it as though it were a teaching moment. Try to do this with as many Christian friends as possible, making it a different person each time.

(7) At least once a week, find a relatively or completely new person at the meeting, and pull them aside to share something biblically exciting.[205] See the example below about Samson.

(8) Continue to read this series, *The Christian Evangelist*, as it will help us to develop our skills in effective communication.

(9) Look for opportunities to witness to unbelievers after a few months of doing the above. If possible, find a friend, who will be doing the above as well. The best-case scenario is that the congregation might choose to start an evangelism program.

Something New to Share

Judges 16:2-3 Updated American Standard Version (UASV)

2 The **Gazites** were told, "Samson has come here." And they surrounded the place and set an ambush for him all night at **the gate of the city**. They kept quiet all night, saying, "Let us wait untill the light of the morning; then we will kill him." 3 But Samson lay till midnight, and at

---

[204] In this study, you will be working through the Holman Old and New Testament Commentary volumes, as well as Bible Difficulties in the Book of Genesis: Answering the Bible Critics. These Bible Difficulty volumes will enable you to have answers to defend the Bible as the Word of God.

[205] This will give you the experience of talking to strangers about the Bible, and develop your skills as a teacher, because you have to hone them to be effective on one with little Bible knowledge.

midnight he arose and **took hold of the doors of the gate of the city and the two posts, and pulled them up**, bar and all, and **put them on his shoulders** and **carried them to the top of the hill that is in front of Hebron**.

City gate from Balawat—Zondervan Illustrated Bible Backgrounds

Every Christian is aware of Samson's superhuman strength that he received through God. However, some biblical accounts come to life when the reader is aware of the background information. What Samson pulled out of the ground and threw on his shoulders at Judges 16:2-3, it weighed a minimum of 400-500 pounds, with some suggesting closer to 2,000 pounds. If this feat of strength is not enough to grow our appreciation of Samson's great power, the simple statement that he "carried them to the top of the hill in front of Hebron" will do just that. Gaza, the city, mentioned here is at sea level, while Hebron is about 3,000 feet above sea level, a serious climb indeed! However, there is more. Hebron is 37 miles from Gaza, uphill all the way! Knowing the weight of the gate and posts, the distance traveled, and that it was uphill, makes Samson's colossal feat take on a completely new magnitude, does it not?

If the reader carries out the above for one year, which is really nothing more than four things every Christian should be doing anyway: (1) have a personal Bible study, (2) prepare for Christian meetings, (3) share the things we are learning, and (4) use our Bible. If we do not put knowledge in our heads, there will be nothing to draw on when it comes time to share biblical truths.

There is no joy or excitement when we are unprepared, no matter what it is. Take a moment to remember the first day on any job. It was so frightening, and we were tense all day. Now, remember one year into that job. After just one year, we were completely competent and experienced to the point that we did most things subconsciously, not even giving much thought to them. Now, after one year of the above-suggested nine practices, imagine that we are sitting at a food court reading our Bible in the shopping mall when a person at the next table says, 'I don't believe in the Bible.' Your heart does not even miss a beat; you simply respond, 'Why, have you always felt that way?' He responds with several reasons,

(1) 'the Bible contradicts itself,'

(2) 'It is full of errors,'

(3) 'it is a book by men nothing more,'

(4) 'everyone has his own interpretation of the Bible,'

(5) 'it is not practical for our day,'

(6) 'and while I agree that the Bible offers good advice on some things, I do not believe there is such thing as absolute truth.'

Even his extensive list of criticisms of the Bible does not intimidate us at this point. From his perspective, all of these seem true. He does not seem to be one looking to argue, but rather one who wishes his list was not true. We take a deep breath and ask, 'can I address at least one of these concerns?' He says, 'sure, I would like to have answers to all of the errors and contradictions.' We pick up our lunch, move over to his table, and offer to address a few.

Over the next hour, we find that we can flip through the Bible, sharing one Scripture after another, referring to several archaeological points, giving some in-depth Bible backgrounds, and even referring to a few original language words. Moreover, we gave him the gist of how these so-called errors and contradictions are really Bible difficulties. In the end, we resolved four major Bible difficulties for him. He was so moved by our ability to effectively reason from the Scriptures; he is the one that asked, 'can I talk with you again?' The conversation ended with an exchange of contact information.

Psalm 119:162 Updated American Standard Version (UASV)

162 I rejoice at your word
like one who finds great spoil.

Review Questions

(1) What questions about Bible use should we ask ourselves? What is the circumstances as to biblical illiteracy, and what does that mean?

(2) What do we need to be accomplishing in our Bible studies?

(3) What do we learn from Judges 16:2-3?

(4) How do we feel when we are unprepared?

(5) What illustration is given?

(6) How should we feel about God's Word?

CHAPTER 17 Effectively Communicating the Truth to Others

1 Timothy 2:3-4 Updated American Standard Version (UASV)

³ This is good, and it is acceptable in the sight of God our Savior, ⁴ who desires all men to be saved and to come to an accurate knowledge[206] of truth.

Communicating the Truth to Muslims

Many have not had many opportunities to witness to a Muslim. Most of us, because of radical Islam (e.g., ISIS and Al Qaeda) over the past 15-years, have gotten to know that they have a fervent belief in Allah, the Islamic name of God. However, most Muslims are not that familiar with what the Bible truly teaches. It is our hope that we can share our faith with Muslims when the opportunity presents itself. (1 Tim. 2:3-4) The following is a simple introduction to that process. For more on this subject, please see the following book that will be out in 2020. THE GUIDE TO ANSWERING ISLAM: What Every Christian Needs to Know About Islam and the Rise of Radical Islam by Daniel Janosik (Author) **ISBN-13**: 978-1949586763

Islamic Worldview

A worldview in the simplest terms, is "the sum total of a person's answers to the most important questions in life."[207] Ironically, while everyone has a worldview in today's world, most are unaware of what it is and how it may affect their lives. For this reason, most worldviews are deficient, contradictory, and seldom are they united in thought with their many different pieces. (Nash 1999, 13)

While most of the earth's seven billion residents are walking around unaware that they are carrying an insufficient worldview; it actually affects

---

[206] *Epignosis* is a strengthened or intensified form of *gnosis* (*epi,* meaning "additional"), meaning, "true," "real," "full," "complete" or "accurate," depending upon the context. Paul and Peter alone use *epignosis.*

[207] Zondervan (2010-06-19). Life's Ultimate Questions: An Introduction to Philosophy . Zondervan. Kindle Edition.

every facet of their lives. Moreover, it is actually a matter of life and death that one not only become better aware of their worldview. However, it must be brought into alignment with the only worldview that matters, the thinking of the Creator of humankind himself as he has revealed to us through his loving revelation, the Bible.

What is of supreme importance, then, is that the Christians continuously evaluate their own worldview, making sure that it is in harmony with God's Word. Nevertheless, it is just as important to familiarize ourselves with the worldview of others: Buddhism, Hinduism, Shintoism, and Islam, to mention a few. "Converts and immigrant [of Islamic] communities are found in almost every part of the world. With about 1.62 billion followers or 23% of the global population, Islam is the second-largest religion by the number of adherents and, according to many sources, the fastest-growing major religion in the world."[208]

Evangelism is the obligation of every Christian to teach and preach the gospel to the ends of the earth. (Matt 24:14; 28:19-20; Ac 1:8) For this reason, we will look at the worldview of Islam and contrast it with the Christian belief system. Initially, we will offer a brief overview of how Islam got its start and explain some terms that should help us better understand the Islamic mindset. Next, we will look at a short overview of every worldview's five facets: Islam's view of God, view reality, knowledge, moral code, and religious character. Finally, we will contrast the beliefs systems of Islam with Christianity before ending with a brief overview of what has been said herein.

Short Overview of Islam[209]

Muhammad bin [son of] Abdullah, was born about 570 C.E. in the prosperous trade city of Mecca. Young Muhammad was very much dissatisfied with the religious system of his day; it became known as the 'time of ignorance.' His people were steeped in idolatry and the worship of hundreds of local deities. Through his interactions with local Christian and Jewish traders, Muhammad had become just as disappointed with their approach to God. As far as he was concerned, both Judaism and

---

[208] Islam - Wikipedia, the free encyclopedia, http://en.wikipedia.org/wiki/Islam (accessed September 14, 2015).

[209] [Ar *islām* submission (to the will of God)] 1817.—*Merriam-Webster's Collegiate Dictionary.* Eleventh ed. Springfield, Mass.: Merriam-Webster, Inc., 2003

Christianity had abandoned Allah,[210] and for this reason, the God of the Bible was raising up one last prophet to restore the pure religion of Abraham.

According to *A Christian's Pocket Guide to Islam* "the Jews, the Arabs gained a superficial knowledge of the Old Testament stories and Jewish folklore, which is seen in the pages of the Quran. The Christianity that Muhammad encountered was brought to Arabia chiefly by Christians who had fled from the Byzantine Empire, victims of the intricate Christological controversies of those days, who had been condemned as heretics. Muhammad's very imperfect understanding of Christian doctrine was probably due to the nature of these informants." (Sookhdeo 2001, 10)

Muhammad's marriage into a wealthy family afforded him the opportunity to engage in meditative thought as to his religious environment. On one of these occasioned trips, Allah or Gabriel began to come to him while he was in his trance. The inhabitants of Mecca were not receptive to these visions, believing Muhammad to be "demon-possessed." It is at this point, about 622 C.E.; that Muhammad made his flight to Medina. This also corresponds with the start of the Muslim[211] calendar. As a result, dates are known as A.H.[212] (Sookhdeo 2001, 12, 80)

The Arabic word *jihad*[213] was given birth to in about 624 C.E. after the battle of Badr, in which it was decided that the Muslims had an obligation to perform a jihad whenever they perceived a threat of any sort. Further, it was here in Medina that the Quran, a sacred textbook, was further developed into the final revelation from Allah. It is here, too, that many of the traditions of Islam had their beginning: prayer toward Jerusalem, Friday as the day of worship, and the fast of Ramadan.[214] In Muhammad's lifetime, he managed to conquer all of Arabia, being the first to unite all Muslims as one, into the religion of Islam. Muhammad died in 632 C.E. and was

---

[210] (Arab. *Allāh*, a contraction of *al-Ilāh*, "the God")—*The Encyclopedia of Christianity*, 749

[211] [Ar *muslim*, lit., one who submits (to God)] ca.1615—*Merriam-Webster's Collegiate Dictionary*. Eleventh ed. Springfield, Mass.: Merriam-Webster, Inc., 2003

[212] Anno Hegirae, year of the flight

[213] [Ar *jihād*] 1869: a holy war waged on behalf of Islam as a religious duty *also*: a personal struggle in devotion to Islam esp. involving spiritual discipline—ibid.

[214] [Ar *Ramaḍān*] ca. 1595: the ninth month of the Islamic year observed as sacred with fasting practiced daily from dawn to sunset—ibid.

succeeded by Caliph[215] Abu Bakr in 634 C.E. and Caliph Umar in 644 C.E. Throughout this initial period of unity, Syria, Iraq, Persia, and Egypt fell to the newly founded Islamic empire. (Sookhdeo 2001, 13)

There are the two major divisions of Islam, the Sunni and the Shiah. This came apart back at the time of Muhammad's successors and is based on a discrepancy of understanding as to who is his lawful religious heirs. Does the procession come after Muhammad's lineage as the Shiite Muslims assert or is it based on elective office as the majority Sunni claim? The argument continues to this day, with no resolution in sight. The Sunni Muslims are in the majority by about ninety percent, with most of the ten percent of Shiah being found in Iran. Of course, with the Shiah being in the minority, they are under constant persecution by the Sunnis. (Sookhdeo 2001, 65)

Five Facets of the Islamic Worldview[216]

Unlike most religious systems that exist today, Islam has accomplished a way of life that many other institutions only dream of, a unity to the point that the Quran and the hadith[217] govern their religious system, state laws, and all social settings Shariah law.[218] It is sacrilege to violate any of the religious norms, and one Muslim will correct another, and in many cases, it can mean death in Islamic countries.

View of God

Allah is the God of Islam. The Quran states: "So believe in God and His apostles. Say not 'Trinity': desist: it will be better for you: for God is One God." (Surah 4:171, *AYA*) The Quran does not dispute the reality of God's existence, like the Bible, it simply speaks as though he is. For the Muslim, Allah is almighty, all-powerful, all-knowing, and has no equal. Allah is the God of judgment and is to be feared in the sense of dread, not a

---

[215] [*caliphe*, Ar *khalīfa* successor] 14c: a successor of Muhammad as temporal and spiritual head of Islam —ibid.

[216] As the Sunni are in the vast majority, this worldview will largely reflect their belief system. The hadith is the narrative record of the sayings or customs of Muhammad and his companions; and the collective body of traditions relating to Muhammad and his companions.—*Merriam-Webster's Collegiate Dictionary*. Eleventh ed. Springfield, Mass.: Merriam-Webster, Inc., 2003

[217] The hadith is the narrative record of the sayings or customs of Muhammad and his companions; and the collective body of traditions relating to Muhammad and his companions.—*Merriam-Webster's Collegiate Dictionary*. Eleventh ed. Springfield, Mass.: Merriam-Webster, Inc., 2003

[218] Shariah law is the immensely detailed body of rules and regulations, instructions for religious practice and daily life.—*A Christian's Pocket Guide to Islam*. Pewsey, Wiltshire: Isaac Publishing, 2001, p. 19.

reverential fear. As Abraham was God's friend, the concept of a Muslim being the friend of Allah would be foreign to his mindset.

View of Reality

Islam believes Allah, the "Almighty God" is the One who created the universe. They believe that the universe we are living in is not eternal as on the Day of Judgment, there will be new Heaven and new earth. "On the Day when the earth will be changed to another earth and so will be the heavens, and they (all creatures) will appear before Allah, the One, the Irresistible." (Quran 14:48) Further, they believe the universe to be material, as the earth is under your feet and is directed by God.

Knowledge

Aristotle's work greatly influenced the Arab world. Arabian scholars, such as Avicenna and Averroes, expanded on and built on Aristotelian thinking in their attempts to bring into line Greek thought with the Muslim teaching. Setting aside the philosophical aspect of epistemology, and looking at the knowledge of Islam as it pertains to their religious institution, one will find that it has predominately been borrowed from late Judaism and Christianity and fused into Muhammad's understanding, as later interpreted by the Arabian scholars. For example:

- **Quran**: "Allah receiveth (men's) souls at the time of their death, and that (soul) which dieth not (yet) in its sleep. He keepeth that (soul) for which He hath ordained death."

- **Quran**: "I do call to witness the Resurrection Day ... Does man think that We cannot assemble his bones? ... He questions: 'When is the Day of Resurrection?' ... Has not He [Allāh] the power to give life to the dead?" (75:1, 3, 6, 40)

- **Quran**: "They ask: When is the Day of Judgement? (It is) the day when they will be tormented at the Fire, (and it will be said unto them): Taste your torment (which ye inflicted)." (51:12-14)

- **Quran**: "And as for those who believe and do good works, We shall make them enter Gardens underneath which rivers flow to dwell therein forever." (4:57) "On that day the dwellers of Paradise shall think of nothing but their bliss. Together with their wives, they shall recline in shady groves upon soft couches." (36:55, 56)

- **Quran:** "And if ye fear that ye will not deal fairly by the orphans, marry of the women, who seem good to you, two or three or four; and if ye fear that ye cannot do justice (to so many) then one (only) or (the captives) that your right hands possess." (Surah 4:3)

Christian Moral Code vs Islam

Each human descended from Adam and Eve has a moral code (conscience) that is inherent in them from birth, which corresponds to the words found in Genesis when God said, "Let us make man in our image." This moral code is an internal awareness that enables one to choose between what is right and what is wrong, "and their conflicting thoughts accuse or even excuse them." – Romans 2:15.

While inherent from birth, this inner moral code must be trained; if not, it can be deceptive. It can serve as a guide to one's life. However, it can become dangerous or even treacherous if it has not been enlightened under the correct standards, being in harmony with its maker. As this moral code develops over time, it can be influenced for the good or bad by one's environment, worship, and behavior. It is the correct understanding of the Word of God which trains the moral code.

On the surface, the moral values of the Muslims may seem to be humane and selfless in nature. Even many similarities further the misbelief that the Christian and the Muslim worship the same God, similarly, but by different names. Islam believes that faith is dead without evidence of good works; God will punish any worship that is not directed at him, rights against crime against your fellow man, adultery and fornication are wrong, similar abhorrence to the seven deadly sins, the obeying of the law of the land, drunkenness, suicide, and homosexuality are forbidden.

This section does not contain the space to look at all facets of the Islamic moral code; therefore, we will briefly consider how the women of Islam are treated. Unlike the West, it is the woman, who brings honor to the family, thus, there are many restrictions on the women of Islam in order to protect the family honor. Islam has an equation: the greater the restriction, the greater the honor. For example, a girl must retain her virginity for marriage without exception. The woman must have someone, even a child, who accompanies and supervises her everywhere she goes. The woman's role in the house is to be the caretaker, and no Muslim husband would dare lift a hand, even if the wife has a full-time job outside the home. In the name of modesty, the woman is to be covered from the 'neck to wrist and ankle and her hair.' The marriage is arranged, and while the female may refuse, the pressure is usually insurmountable. While it is permissible for a man to marry a Christian or a Jew (as they would then be Muslim), a Muslim woman can only marry a Muslim man. Divorce in the Islamic community is very similar to the Jewish religious leaders of Jesus day: the man can divorce the woman for any reason by simply saying three times, in front of witnesses: "I divorce you." The woman, on the hand, is largely unable to divorce the husband. The rape of Christian women within Islamic countries, while being a dishonor to the woman, it is a means for a Muslim man to proliferate the Muslim population because a child is Muslim if born of a Muslim man. While many today are attempting a progressive liberal approach in looking at similarities between Islam and Christianity, it has its dark side, and any syncretism attempts are seriously misplaced. (Sookhdeo 2001, 59-64)

Religious Character

As opposed to delving into Islam's highly developed religious rituals and traditions; we will take a brief look at how Islam's tolerance, or lack thereof for other religious institutions. Actually, Islamic scholars who are behind the footnotes in the Quran and articles dealing with Islam's view of Christianity and Judaism have begun a campaign to conceal their hatred for these religious institutions, viewing them as infidels.[219] For example, while the word *fight* may be found in the writings, it actually means *kill*. The end game for Islam is to convert the world to Islam and to rule from Jerusalem, under Shariah law. This can be done by preaching, or by terrorism and killing the infidel. The words of the infamous Osama bin Laden bring this point home with a chilling affect: "I was ordered to fight the people until they say there is no god but Allah, and his prophet Muhammad."

Islam versus Christianity

ISLAM	CHRISTIANITY
View of God: Islam considers the Trinity to blasphemous. (Q:	**View of God**: Trinity—one God on three persons—separate in

[219] Suras 2:190-193, 2:216, 2:244, 3:56, 3:151, 4:56, 4:74, 4:76, 4:89, 4:91, 4:95, 4:104, 5:51, 5:32-38, 7:96-99, 8:12-14, 8:39, 8:60, 8:65, 9:5, 9:14, 9:23-30, 9:38-41, 9:111, 9:123, 22:18-22, 25:52, 47:4, 47:35, 48:16, 48:29, 61:4, and 66:8-10.

4:171, 5:17, 5:72-75)

person, equal in nature and subordinate in duty. (John 1:1; Isa 44:8)

View of Man: While man may be may be weak, he is capable of righteousness before God.

View of Man: Man is fallen and sinful by nature, as inherited from Adam. (Rom 5:15)

View of Salvation: Islamic belief is that we can attain a righteous standing before God by works, and the denial of Christ's ransom sacrifice. (Q: 4:157)

View of Salvation: Man, who is fallen cannot save himself, and is in need of a savior, and salvation is by faith alone. (John 3:16; Matt 20:28)

View of Heaven: The Islamic perception of heaven is very carnal as they will drink wine and have sexual relations with dozens of virgins. (Q: 2:25, 4:57, 13:35, 36:55-57, 37:39-48, 47:15, 52:20-23, 55:46-78, 56:12-40)

View of Heaven: The Christian perception of heaven is that we are no longer troubled with the concern of eating and drinking, there being no one getting married, for we will be like angels and drinking and with our new bodies, pain and suffering will be no more. (Rom 14:17; Matt 22:30; Rev 21:4)

View of Predestination: Ironically, while Islam believes that man cannot be held responsible for his actions; Shariah law is very quick to exact justice for certain actions, many of which result in death. (Q: 35:8)

View of Predestination: This term is really dealt with under doctrines, such as: foreknowledge, salvation, eternal security, the destiny of the unevangelized. Under these doctrinal positions, you have numerous views, but the majority consensus is that man is to be held responsible for his actions.

View of the Qur'an: Islam believes that the Qur'an is the very word of God through Muhammad and inerrant, never attaining copying errors. (Q: 61:6)

View of the Bible: Conservative Christianity believes the Bible to be the inspired, inerrant Word of God. (2 Tim 3:16; 2 Pet 1:21)

231

View of the Bible: Islam believes the Bible to have been the inspired Word of God, but has been corrupted beyond all trustworthiness.

View of the Qur'an: Early collections of Muhammad's writings came in several different variations because they were retrieved from memory. Around 650-656 there was an attempt to deal with this by creating a standard edition.

(Sookhdeo 2001, 25-48)

While it is paramount that the Christian, who attempts to engage the Muslim in his ministry, be very much aware of the belief system of Islam, it is best to accept that, it is very difficult to disprove Islam based on knowledge alone. It is God alone who will help the message grown within the Muslim heart. (1 Cor. 3:5-9) However, this knowledge of Islam will enable the evangelizer to counter, explain, and overturn the wrong beliefs that the Muslim may raise. It should be understood that most Muslims are like most Christians in that; they are not that familiar with their Quran, like the Christian with his Bible.

To the Muslims, Muhammad is the greatest prophet that has ever lived, and it will bring the conversation to a complete stop if it should be perceived that the Christian is criticizing him in any way. While the Christian cannot honor Muhammad in a conversation with such honorifics as 'the blessed Muhammad,' it is fine to say, 'the prophet Muhammad.' Instead of attempting to dethrone Muhammad, it is the wisest course to educate them about Christ, which they do not view as being the Son of God, but rather a great prophet like Muhammad.

Islam has circled the earth with its presence, and it would be a mistake to assume that every Muslim is the same. Many Muslims are only Muslim in a very basic sense: prayer, Ramadan, and occasioned visits to the mask. They may have been westernized and feel ousted by the conservative Islamic community. However, Islamic extremism is just as prevalent, and caution is the word of the day. Until one realizes who they are speaking with, it is best to be very cautious about what is said and how it is said. It must also be kept in mind that his objective is to evangelize his visitor, as much as it is the Christian's objective to evangelize him.

A white Christian attempting to evangelize a non-white Muslim is at a disadvantage from the start because they are lumped in with the immoral western world. It is best to address this immediately with, "I know that the western world is immoral in the extreme, and even within the Christian community, there are such cases, but would you agree that all major religions have those who do not represent themselves well?' (Sookhdeo 2001, 73-75)

Some final suggestions are to be friendly and tactful. (Pro. 25:15) Keep in mind that while Most Muslims do not know their Quran well, what they do know is deeply entrenched and has been learned by rote. Part of the Muslim development is repeatedly hearing the fundamental Muslim teachings, which is part of their spiritual development. If we are to reach the heart of a Muslim, it will be through patience and understanding. Arguing with a Muslim will serve us no better than arguing with any other person over religious matters. Instead of using the word "Bible," refer to it as the book of God. Muslims also do not like the phrase "Son of God," but they have great regard for Jesus as a prophet or messenger, so avoid the phrase "Son of God" until you have a long record of rapport. It is best to witness to just one person and avoid talking with a group. Most importantly, women should witness to women and men to men. If a female Muslim were caught talking with a westerner for an extended time, her life could be in danger, as honor killings are becoming the norm even in the West. In addition, keep in mind that modestly dressed in the West is not necessarily modestly dressed in the Muslim world. Some things to build rapport on are the greatness of God and the love of God. We could speak on the wrongness of idol worship, the wickedness found in the world today, wars, uprisings, racial hatred, as well as the hypocrisy of religion. If we sense any anger, it is best to excuse ourselves from the conversation as soon as possible.

Each of us is affected by the diversity of our world, and it has come to almost every neighborhood. With this variety of beliefs, it is no longer the case of a Christian attempting to share his gospel with unbelievers. Thus, we need to educate ourselves and broaden our understanding of what others' worldviews are, which may very well open up the opportunity of one receiving life. As Islam makes up 23 percent of the earth's population (1.62 billion followers), we have given more space to them, which will not be the case with other groups below.

Another Islamic Overview by Encyclopedia of apologetics

Islam. *Islam* means "submission." A follower of this religion is called a *Muslim*, "a submitted one." Muhammad, the founder of the Islamic faith, was an Arabian trader from Mecca who was born around 570 and died in 632. As Christians measure history from the birth of Christ, so Muslims set the hinge date of history at 622, the year Muhammad fled from Mecca to Medina. This *Hijra* (*hijj* means "flight" in Arabic) marked Muhammad's turning point of submission to God and his proclamation of a new revelation from God. Muslims believe Muhammad to be the last prophet of God, superseding Christ, the prophet who was before him.

Muslims believe in submitting to the one and only one God, named *Allah*. They are categorically opposed to the Christian belief in the triunity of God (*see* Trinity). To believe that there is more than one person in God is an idolatry and blasphemy called *shirk*.

Beliefs. *The Word of God.* Although Muslims hold that God revealed himself in the Jewish Law (*tawrat*), the Psalms (*zabur*), and the Gospels (*injil*), they claim that today's Christian Bible is corrupted, or *tahrif*. They assert that the *Qur'an* is the final Word of God (*see* Qur'an, Alleged Divine Origin of). It is divided into 114 chapters or *suras* and is about the size of the New Testament.

Doctrines. There are five basic Muslim doctrines:

1.   There is one and only one God.

2.   There have been many prophets, including Noah, Abraham, Moses, Jesus, and Muhammad.

3.   God created angels (jinn), some of which are good and others evil.

4.   The *Qur'an* is God's full and final revelation.

5.   A final day of judgment is coming, followed by heaven for the faithful and hell for the lost.

Besides these five central beliefs, there are five basic pillars of Islamic practice:

1.   All that is necessary to become a Muslim is to confess the *shahadah*: "There is no God but Allah, and Muhammad is his messenger."

2.   One must pray the *salat*, usually five times a day.

3.   One keeps an annual fast (*sawn*) through the ninth lunar month of *Ramadan*.

4. One gives alms (*zakat*) to the needy, one-fortieth of one's income.

5. Every able Muslim must make one pilgrimage during life to Mecca.

Muslims also believe in jihad or holy war, which some radical groups have exalted to the level of a pillar. While this may involve killing infidels for their faith, more moderate Muslims think of it as being a sacred struggle with the word, not necessarily with the sword.

Many doctrines are shared with Christianity, such as creation (*see* Creation, Views of), angels, heaven, hell, and the resurrection of all people. As for Christ, they affirm his prophethood, virgin birth, physical ascension, second coming, sinlessness (*see* Christ, Uniqueness of), miracles, and messiahship.

Muslims deny the heart of the Christian message, namely, that Christ died on the cross for our sins (*see* Christ, death of; Christ's Death, Moral Objections to; Christ's Death, Substitution Legend) and that he arose from the grave physically three days later (*see* Resurrection, Evidence for; Resurrection, Physical Nature of).

God as Absolute One. Allah is described by Muslims in terms of several basic attributes. Fundamental to all is the attribute of absolute unity. Of all the Islamic God's attributes, the most important is his undivided unity. To deny this is blasphemous.

The Islamic God is his absolute and indivisible unity. In sura 112, Muhammad defines God in these words: "Say: He is God, The One and Only; God, the Eternal, Absolute; He begetteth not, Nor is He begotten; And there is none Like unto Him." This sura is held to be worth a third of the whole *Qur'an*. The seven heavens and the seven earths are founded upon it. Islamic tradition affirms that to confess this verse sheds one's sins "as a man might strip a tree in autumn of its leaves" (Cragg, 39).

Two words are used in the *Qur'an* to describe the oneness of God: *ahad* and *wahid*. *Ahad* is used to deny that God has any partner or companion. In Arabic, this means the negation of any other number. The word *wahid* may mean the same as the first word or it may also mean "the One, Same God for all." That is to say, there is only one God for Muslims, and he is the same God for all peoples. God is a unity and a singularity.

God's Oneness is such a fundamental aspect of Islam that, as one Muslim author put it, "Islam, like other religions before it in their original clarity and purity, is nothing other than the declaration of the Unity of God, and its message is a call to testify to this Unity" (Mahmud, 20). Another Muslim writer adds, "The Unity of Allah is the distinguishing characteristic of Islam. This is the purest form of monotheism, that is, the worship of Allah Who was neither begotten nor beget nor had any associates with Him in His Godhead. Islam teaches this in the most unequivocal terms" (Ajijola, 55).

It is because of this uncompromising emphasis on God's absolute unity that the greatest of all sins in Islam is the sin of *shirk*, or assigning partners to God. The *Qur'an* sternly declares "God forgiveth not (the sin of) joining other gods with Him; but He forgiveth whom He pleaseth other sins than this: one who joins other gods with God, hath strayed far, far away (from the Right)" (sura 4:116).

God as Absolute Ruler. In the words of the *Qur'an*,

God—there is no god but He—the Living, The Self-subsisting, Eternal. No slumber can seize Him nor sleep. His are all things In the heavens and on the earth. Who is there that can intercede in His presence except As He permitteth? He knoweth What (appears to His creatures As) Before or After Or Behind them. Nor shall they compass Aught His knowledge Except as He willeth. His Throne doth extend Over the heavens and the earth, and He feeleth no fatigue in guarding and preserving them For He is Most High, The Supreme (in glory). [sura 2:255]

God is self-sustaining and does not need anything but everything needs him. This attribute is known as aseity, or self-existence. God is The Mighty and The Almighty. He is The Willer of existing things and the things which will exist; and nothing happens apart from his will. He is the Knower of all that can be known. His knowledge encompasses the whole universe which he has created and he alone sustains. God is completely sovereign over all his creation.

Many of God's ninety-nine Islamic names speak of his sovereignty. He is:

Al-Adl, the Just, whose word is perfect in veracity and justice (6:115);

Al-Ali, the High One, he who is high and mighty (2:225–26);

Al-Aziz, the Sublime, mighty in his sublime sovereignty (59:23);

Al-Badi, the Contriver, who contrived the whole art of creation (2:117);

Al-Hakim, the Judge, who gives judgment among his servants (40:48–51);

Al-Hasib, the Accounter, who is sufficient as a reckoner (4:6–7);

Al-Jabbar, the Mighty One, whose might and power are absolute (59:23);

Al-Jalil, the Majestic, mighty and majestic is he;

Al-Jami, the Gatherer, who gathers all men to an appointed day (3:9);

Al-Malik, the King, who is King of kings (59:23);.

Al-Muizz, the Honorer, who honors or abases whom he will (3:26);

Al-Muntaqim, the Avenger, who wreaks vengeance on sinners and succors the believers (30:47);

Al-Muqsit, the Observer of Justice, who will set up the balances with justice (21:47–48);

Al-Mutaali, the Self-Exalted, who has set himself high above all (13:9–10);

Al-Qadir, the Able, who has the power to do what he pleases (17:99–101);

Al-Quddus, the Most Holy One, to whom all in heaven and on earth ascribe holiness (62:1);

Al-Wahid, the One, unique in his divine sovereignty (13:16); the Unique, who alone has created (74:11);

Al-Wakil, the Administrator, who has charge of everything (6:102);

Malik al-Mulk, Possessor of the Kingdom, who grants sovereignty to whom he will (3:26).

God as Absolute Justice. Several of God's names bespeak his absolute justice: the Majestic, the Gatherer, the Accounter, the Judge, the Just, the Most Holy One, to whom all in heaven and on earth ascribe holiness, the Observer of Justice, and the Avenger.

God as Absolute Love. Contrary to a popular misunderstanding, Allah is a God of love. Indeed, some of God's names depict this very characteristic.

237

For example, God is *Ar-Rahman*, the Merciful, the most merciful of those who show mercy (sura 1:3; 12:64), and *Al-Wadud*, the Loving, compassionate and loving to his servants (11:90, 92). He has imposed the law of mercy upon himself (sura 6:12). He says, "My mercy comprehends all" (7:156). Muhammad said in the *Qur'an*, "If you do love God, Follow me:, and God will love you And forgive you your sins. For God is Oft-Forgiving, Most Merciful" (sura 3:31).

God as Absolute Will. There is a certain mystery about God's names. Historian Kenneth Cragg affirms that these names "are to be understood as characteristics of the divine will, rather than laws of his nature. Action, that is arising from such descriptives, may be expected, but not as a matter of necessity." What gives unity to all God's actions is that he wills them all. As Willer he may be recognized by the descriptions given him, but he does not conform to any. The action of his will may be identified from its effects, but his will of itself is inscrutable. This accounts for the antithesis in certain of God's names (see below). For example, God is "the One Who leads astray," as well as "the One Who guides."

God as Absolutely Unknowable. Since everything is based in God's will and since his effects are sometimes contradictory and do not reflect any absolute essence, God's nature is utterly unknowable. Indeed, "the divine will is an ultimate beyond which neither reason nor revelation go. In the Unity of the single will, however, these descriptions co-exist with those that relate to mercy, compassion, and glory" (Cragg, 64) God is named from his effects, but he is not to be identified with any of them. The relation between the Ultimate Cause (God) and his creatures is extrinsic, not intrinsic. That is, God is called good because he causes good, but goodness is not part of his essence.

Evaluation. Muslim monotheism is vulnerable to many criticisms, particularly from a Christian perspective. Crucial is their rigid idea of absolute unity.

The Problem of Absolute Unity. Islamic monotheism is rigid and inflexible. Its view of God's unity is so strong that it allows for no plurality at all in God. Hence, it sees nothing between monotheism and tritheism (three gods), and Christians are placed in the latter category. There are several reasons for this misunderstanding. For one thing there appears to be a misunderstanding of the biblical text related to God (Muhammad, Alleged Biblical Predictions of). Muslims also have a rather grossly anthropomorphic view of what it means for Christ to be a "Son" of God.

This often seems to demand some kind of sexual generation, according to their thinking. But the terms "Father" and "Son" no more necessitate physical generation than the term *alma mater* implies that the school from which we were graduated was our physical womb. Paternity can be understood in more than a biological sense.

There is a deeper and more basic philosophical problem. In the final analysis God has no (knowable) essence or nature from which one can distinguish his three persons or centers of consciousness (*see* Trinity). This position is known as nominalism. God is absolute will, and absolute will must be absolutely one. A plurality of wills (persons) would make it impossible to have any absolute unity. And Muslims believe God is absolutely one (both from revelation and by reason). Reason informed Muhammad that unity is prior to plurality. As Plotinus put it several centuries earlier (205–70), all plurality is made up of unities. Thus unity is the most ultimate of all. Accepting this neoplatonic way of thinking leads logically to a denial of the possibility for any plurality of persons in God. Hence, by the very nature of his philosophical commitment to the kind of neo-Platonism prevalent in the Middle Ages, Islamic thought about God was solidified into an intractable singularity which allowed no form of trinitarianism.

This rigid monotheism is not entirely consistent with some of Islam's own distinctions. Muslim scholars, consistent with certain teachings in the *Qur'an*, have made distinctions within God's unity. For example, they believe the *Qur'an* is the eternal Word of God. Sura 85:21–22 declares, "Nay, this is a Glorious *Qur'an*, (Inscribed) in a Tablet Preserved! [in heaven]" And in sura 43:3–4, we read, "We have made it a *Qur'an* in Arabic, that ye may able to understand (and learn wisdom). And verily, it is in the Mother of the Book, in Our Presence, high (in dignity), full of wisdom" (cf. sura 13:39). This eternal original is the template of the earthly book we know as the *Qur'an*.

Muslims insist the true *Qur'an* in heaven is uncreated, and perfectly expresses the mind of God. Yet they acknowledge that the *Qur'an* is not identical to the essence of God. Some Muslim scholars even liken the *Qur'an* to the divine *logos* view of Christ, held by orthodox Christians (*see* Christ, Deity of). As Professor Yusuf K. Ibish stated of the *Qur'an*, "It is not a book in the ordinary sense, nor is it comparable to the Bible, either the Old or New Testaments. It is an expression of Divine Will. If you want to compare it with anything in Christianity, you must compare it with Christ

Himself." He adds, "Christ was the expression of the Divine among men, the revelation of the Divine Will. That is what the *Qur'an* is" (Waddy, 14).

Orthodox Islam describes the relation between God and the *Qur'an* by noting that speech is an eternal attribute of God, which as such is without beginning or intermission, exactly like His knowledge, His might, and other characteristics of His infinite being (see Golziher, 97). But if speech is an eternal attribute of God that is not identical to God but is somehow distinguishable from him, then does not this allow the very kind of plurality within unity which Christians claim for the Trinity? Thus, it would seem that the Islamic view of God's absolute unity is, by their own distinction, not incompatible with Christian trinitarianism. The basic Muslim logic of either monotheism or polytheism is invalid. They themselves allow that something can be an eternal expression of God without being numerically identical to him. Thus, to use their own illustration, why can't Christ be the eternal "expression of Divine Will" without being the same person as this Divine Will?

The Problem of Voluntarism. At the very basis of the Islamic view of God is a radical voluntarism (*see* Essentialism) and nominalism. For traditional Islam, properly speaking, God does not have an essence, at least not a knowable one (*see* God, Nature of). Rather, he is Will. True enough, God is said to be just and loving, but he is not essentially just or loving. And he is merciful only because "He has imposed the law of mercy upon Himself" (sura 6:12). But since God is Absolute Will, had he chosen to be otherwise he would not be merciful. There is no nature or essence in God according to which he must act.

There are two basic problems with this radical nominalism: one metaphysical and one moral.

The metaphysical problem. The orthodox Islamic view of God claims, as we have seen, that God is an absolutely Necessary Being. He is self-existent, and he cannot not exist. But if God is by nature a necessary kind of being, then it is of his nature to exist. He must have a nature. Orthodox Islam believes that there are other essential attributes of God, such as, self-existence, uncreatedness, and eternality. But if these are all essential characteristics of God, then God must have an essence. Otherwise the attributes could not be essential. This is precisely how essence is defined, namely, as the essential attributes or characteristics of a being.

The moral problem. Islamic voluntarism poses a serious moral problem. If God is only will, without an essence, then he does not do things because

240

they are right; rather, they are right because he does them. God is arbitrary about what is right and wrong. He does not have to do good. He does not have to be loving to all; he could hate, if he chose to do so. Indeed, in sura 3:31 we read, "God will love you.... God is Oft-Forgiving, Most Merciful," but verse 32 says that "God loveth not those Who reject Faith." So love and mercy are not of the essence of God. God could choose not to be loving. This is why Muslim scholars have such difficulty with the question of God's predestination.

The problems of agnosticism. Since God has no essence, at least not one that the names (or attributes) of God really describe, the Islamic view of God involves a form of agnosticism. Indeed, the heart of Islam is not to *know* God but to *obey* him. It is not to *meditate* on his essence but to *submit* to his will. As Pfander correctly observed of Muslims, "If they think at all deeply, they find themselves absolutely unable to know God.... Thus Islam leads to Agnosticism" (Pfander, 187).

Islamic agnosticism arises because Muslims believe God caused the world by extrinsic causality. Indeed, "the Divine will is an ultimate, beyond which neither reason nor revelation go. In the Unity of the single Will, however, these descriptions co-exist with those that relate to mercy, compassion, and glory" (Cragg, 42–43). God is named from his effects, but he is not to be identified with any of them. The relation between the Ultimate Cause (God) and his creatures is extrinsic, not intrinsic. That is, God is called good because he causes good, but not because goodness is part of his essence.

Among the significant weaknesses inherent in this agnosticism, a moral, a philosophical, and a religious problem stand out immediately.

First, if God is not essentially good, but only called good because he does good, why not also call God evil, since he causes evil? (*see* Evil, Problem of) Why not call him sinful and faithless, since he causes people not to believe? It would seem consistent to do so, since God is named from his actions. If Muslims reply that something in God is the basis for calling him good, but nothing in him is the basis for calling him evil, then they admit that God's names do tell us something about his essence. In fact, they admit an intrinsic relation between the cause (Creator) and the effect (creation). This leads to a metaphysical problem with the Islamic view of God.

Second, at the root of medieval views of God, an entrenched neo-Platonism springs from Plotinus. Plotinus' belief that the Ultimate [God] was absolutely an indivisible One heavily influenced Muslim monotheism. Further, Plotinus held that the One is so utterly transcendent (above and beyond all) that it cannot be known, except by mystical experience. This influenced both orthodox Muslim agnosticism and Sufi mysticism. The fundamental reason there can be no similarity between the One [God] and what flows from It (the universe) is because God is beyond being, and there is no similarity between being and what is beyond it.

Thomas Aquinas provided the definitive answer to plotinian agnosticism and mysticism. Aquinas argued that an effect must resemble its cause. "You cannot give what you have not got." Hence, if God causes goodness, he must be good. If he caused being, he must be (Geisler, *Thomas Aquinas*, chap. 9).

Objections to this view generally confuse either a material or instrumental cause with an efficient cause. The efficient cause of something is that *by which* it comes to be. The instrumental cause is that *through which* it comes to be. And the material cause it that *out of which* it is made. Material and instrumental causes do not necessarily resemble their effects, but efficient causes do. The painting does not resemble the artist's paint brush, but it does resemble the artist's mind. The brush is the instrumental cause, whereas the artist is the efficient cause.

Another mistake is to confuse material and efficient causality. Hot water is soft, yet it can cause an egg to get hard, because of properties in the egg. The same hot water softens wax. The difference is the material receiving the causality. Thus an infinite God can and does cause a finite world. God is not thereby finite because he caused a finite cosmos. Nor is he contingent because he, as a Necessary Being, caused a contingent universe. Finiteness and contingency are part of the very material nature of a created being. God is unlike creation in these kinds of ways. On the other hand, everything that exists *has* being, and God *is* Being. There must be a similarity between Being and being (*see* Analogy, Principle of). God is pure actuality, with no potentiality whatsoever. Everything else that exists has the potential not to exist. So all created things have actuality, since they actually exist, and potentiality, since they could possibly not exist. God is like creatures in their actuality but unlike them in their potentiality. This is why when we name God from his effects we must negate whatever implies finitude and limitation or imperfection, and attribute to him only the pure attribute or perfection. This is the reason that evil cannot be attributed to God but good can. Evil implies imperfection or privation of some good characteristic. Good, on the other hand, does not in itself imply either limitation or imperfection (*see* Evil, Problem of). So God is good by his very nature but he cannot be or do evil.

Third, religious experience within a monotheistic context involves the relation between two persons, the worshiper and God. It is, as Martin Buber correctly observed, an "I-Thou" relationship. But how can a person worship someone about which he can know nothing? Even in Islam, one is supposed to love God. But how do we fall in love with someone of which we know nothing? As atheist Ludwig Feuerbach put it, "The truly religious man can't worship a purely negative being.... Only when a man loses his taste for religion does the existence of God become one without qualities, an unknowable God" (Feuerbach, 15).

Some critics have suggested that the extremely transcendent Muslim view of God has led some Muslim sects to deify Muhammad. Since relationship with the transcendent God is seen to be distant, it is only through Muhammad that one even dares to approach the throne of God. In *Qawwalis* (a popular cultural event), Muhammad is praised in verse. This often takes the form of deification: "If *Muhammad* had not been, God himself would not have existed!" This is an allusion to the close relationship Muhammad is supposed to have with God. Muhammad is often given titles like "Savior of the World" and "Lord of the Universe." The popular deification of Muhammad, who so violently opposed any such idolatry, only shows the theological bankruptcy of the Muslim view of a God so distant and so unknowable that the devotee must make contact with something they can understand, even to the extent of deifying the prophet who condemned idolatry.

The problems of extreme determinism. Since in Islam the relationship between God and human beings is that of Master and slave, God is the Sovereign Monarch and humans must submit (*see* Determinism; Free Will). This overpowering picture of God in the *Qur'an* has created its own tension in Muslim theology regarding God's absolute sovereignty and human free will. Despite protests to the contrary, Orthodox Islam teaches the absolute predestination of both good and evil, that all our thoughts, words and deeds, whether good or evil, were foreseen, foreordained, determined, and decreed from all eternity, and that everything that happens takes place according to what has been written for it. Sura 6:18 says "He is the Irresistible." Commenting on these kinds of *Qur'anic* statements, Cragg points out that God is the *Qadar*, or "determination," of all things and his *taqdir*, or "subjection," covers all people and all history. Nature, whether animate or inanimate, is subject to his command and all that comes into existence—a summer flower or a murderer's deed, a newborn child or a sinner's disbelief—is from Him and of Him." In fact if "God so willed, there need have been no creation, there need have been no idolatry, there need have been no Hell, there need have been no escape from Hell" (Cragg, 44–45).

There are four basic problems with this extreme form of predetermination: logical, moral, theological, and metaphysical. In order, it involves a contradiction; it eliminates human responsibility; it makes God the author of evil, and it gives rise to pantheism.

The logical problem with Islamic determinism is that even Muslim commentators are forced to acknowledge that God performs contradictory actions (*see* First Principles). Islamicist Ignaz Golziher summarizes the situation, "There is probably no other point of doctrine on which equally contradictory teachings can be derived from the *Qur'an* as on this one" (Golziher, 78). One Muslim scholar notes, "The *Qur'anic* doctrine of Predestination is very explicit though not very logical" (Stanton, 54–55). For example, God is "the One Who leads astray," as well as "the One Who guides." He is "the One Who brings damage," as also does Satan. He is "the Bringer-down," "the Compeller" or "Tyrant," and "the Haughty." When describing people, all these concepts have an evil sense.

Muslim scholars sometimes attempt to reconcile this by pointing out that these contradictions are not in God's nature (since he does not really have one), but are in the realm of his will. They are not in his essence but in his actions. However, this is an inadequate explanation. God does have a knowable nature or essence. Hence, Muslim scholars cannot avoid the contradiction that God has logically opposed characteristics by placing them outside his essence within the mystery of his will. Further, actions flow from nature and represent it, so there must be something in the nature that corresponds to the action. Salt water does not flow from a fresh stream.

Others attempt to downplay the harsh extremes of Muslim determinism by creating a distinction, not found in the *Qur'an*, between what God *does* and what he *allows* his creatures to do by free choice. This solves the problem, but, only through rejecting clear statements of the *Qur'an*, tradition, and creeds.

These statements can be seen in connection with the moral problem with Islamic determinism. While Muslim scholars wish to preserve human responsibility, they can only succeed in doing so by modifying what the

Qur'an actually says. Sura 9:51 declares: "Say, Nothing will ever befall us save what Allah has written for us." Sura 7:177–79 adds, "He whom Allah guides is he who is rightly guided, but whom he leads astray, those are the losers. Indeed, We have assuredly created for Gehenna many of both jinn and men." Sura 36:6–10 reads: "Verily the sentence comes true on most of them, so they will not believe. We, indeed, have set shackles on their necks which reach to the chins so that they perforce hold up [their heads]. And We have set a barrier in front of them, and a barrier behind them, and We have covered them over so that they do not see. Thus it is alike to them whether thou warn them or dost not warn them; they will not believe."

The *Qur'an* frankly admits that God could have saved all, but did not desire to do so. Sura 32:13 declares: "Had we so willed We should have brought every soul its guidance, but true is that saying of Mine: 'I shall assuredly fill up Gehenna with jinn and men together.'" It is extremely difficult to understand how, holding such a view, one can consistently maintain any kind of human responsibility.

There is also a theological problem with this severe view of God's sovereign determination of all events: It makes God the author of evil. In the *Hadith* traditions Muhammad declares "the decree necessarily determines all that is good and all that is sweet and all that is bitter, and that is my decision between you." According to one tradition, Muhammad slapped Abu Bakr on the shoulder and said: "O Abu Bakr, if Allah Most High had not willed that there be disobedience, he would not have created the Devil." Indeed, one of the most respected Muslim theologians of all time, Al-Ghazzali, frankly acknowledges that "He [God] willeth also the unbelief of the unbeliever and the irreligion of the wicked and, without that will, there would neither be unbelief nor irreligion. All we do we do by His will: what He willeth not does not come to pass." And if one should ask why God does not will that men should believe, Al-Ghazzali responds, "'We have no right to enquire about what God wills or does. He is perfectly free to will and to do what He pleases.' In creating unbelievers, in willing that they should remain in that state; … in willing, in short, all that is evil, God has wise ends in view which it is not necessary that we should know" (Haqq, 152).

In the metaphysical problem with Islamic determinism, this extreme view led some Muslim scholars to the logical conclusion that there is really only one agent in the universe—God. One Muslim theologian wrote, "Not only can He (God) do anything, He actually is the only One Who does anything. When a man writes, it is Allah who has created in his mind the will to write. Allah at the same time gives power to write, then brings about the motion of the hand and the pen and the appearance upon paper. All other things are passive, Allah alone is active" (Nehls, 21). This pantheism is at the heart of much of medieval thought. Thomas Aquinas wrote *Summa contra Gentiles* to help Christian missionaries dealing with Islam in Spain.

This radical predeterminism is expressed in Muslim creedal statements. One reads: "God Most High is the Creator of all actions of His creatures whether of unbelief or belief, of obedience or of rebellion: all of them are by the Will of God and His sentence and His conclusion and His decreeing" (Cragg, 60–61). Another confesses:

God's one possible quality is His power to create good or evil at any time He wishes, that is His decree.... Both good things and evil things are the result of God's decree. It is the duty of every Muslim to believe this.... It is He who causes harm and good. Rather the good works of some and the evil of others are signs that God wishes to punish some and to reward others. If God wishes to draw someone close to Himself, then He will give him the grace which will make that person do good works. If He wishes to reject someone and put that person to shame, then He will create sin in him. God creates all things, good and evil. God creates people as well as their actions: *He created you as well as what you do* (*Qur'an* 37:94). [Rippin & Knappert, 133; emphasis added]

Conclusion. The attitude of God's absolute control over every aspect of his creation profoundly influences Islamic theology and culture. Persian poet, Omar Khayyam, reflected the fatalistic strain of Muslim theology when he wrote:

'Tis all a chequer-board of night and days Where destiny with men for pieces plays; Hither and thither moves and mates and slays,

And one by one back in the closet lays.[220]

EXCURSION Islam and the Bible

Bible, Islamic View of. Muslims believe that the *Qur'an* is the Word of God, superseding all previous revelations. To maintain this belief, they

---

[220] Norman L. Geisler, "Islam," *Baker Encyclopedia of Christian Apologetics*, Baker Reference Library (Grand Rapids, MI: Baker Books, 1999), 368–374.

must sustain an attack upon the competing claims of their chief rival, the Bible.

The Attack on the Bible. Muslim accusations against the Bible fall into two basic categories: first, the text of Scripture has been changed or forged; second, doctrinal mistakes have crept into Christian teaching, such as the belief in the incarnation of Christ, the triunity of the Godhead, and the doctrine of original sin (Waardenburg, 261–63).

Praise for the Original Bible. Strangely, sometimes the *Qur'an* gives the Judeo-Christian Scriptures such noble titles as: "the Book of God," "the Word of God," "a light and guidance to man," "a decision for all matters," "a guidance and mercy," "the lucid Book," "the illumination *(al-furqan)*," "the gospel with its guidance and light, confirming the preceding Law," and "a guidance and warning to those who fear God" (Takle, 217). Christians are told to look into their own Scriptures to find God's revelation for them (5:50). And even Muhammad himself at one point is exhorted to test the truthfulness of his own message by the contents of the previous divine revelations to Jews and Christians (10:94).

The Bible Set Aside. This praise for the Bible is misleading, since Muslims hasten to claim that the *Qur'an* supersedes previous revelations, based on their concept of progressive revelation. By this they hope to show that the *Qur'an* fulfills and sets aside the less complete revelations, such as the Bible. One Islamic theologian echoes this conviction by stating that while a Muslim needs to believe in the Torah (Law of Moses), the *Zabur* (the Psalms of David), and the *Injil* (Gospels), nevertheless "according to the most eminent theologians" the books in their present state "have been tampered with." He goes on to say, "It is to be believed that the *Qur'an* is the noblest of the books.... It is the last of the God-given scriptures to come down, it abrogates all the books which preceded it.... It is impossible for it to suffer any change or alteration" (Jeffery, 126–28). Even though this is the most common view among Islamic scholars, still many Muslims claim to believe in the sacredness and truthfulness of the present-day Bible. This, however, is largely lip-service due to their firm belief in the all-sufficiency of the *Qur'an*. Very few ever study the Bible.

Against the Old Testament. Muslims often show a less favorable view of the Old Testament, which they believe has been distorted by the teachers of the law. The charges include: concealing God's Word (sura 2:42; 3:71), verbally distorting the message in their books (sura 3:78; 4:46), not believing in all the parts of their Scriptures (sura 2:85), and not knowing what their own Scriptures really teach (sura 2:78). Muslims have included Christians in these criticisms.

Due to the ambiguities in the qur'anic accounts, Muslims hold various views (that are sometimes in conflict) regarding the Bible. For instance, the well-known Muslim reformer, Muhammad Abduh writes, "The Bible, the New Testament and the *Qur'an* are three concordant books; religious men study all three and respect them equally. Thus the divine teaching is completed, and the true religion shines across the centuries" (Dermenghem, 138). Another Muslim author tries to harmonize the three great world religions in this way: "Judaism lays stress on Justice and Right; Christianity, on Love and Charity; Islam, on Brotherhood and Peace" (Waddy, 116). However, the most typical Islamic approach to this subject is characterized by comments of the Muslim apologist, Ajijola:

> The first five books of the Old Testament do not constitute the original Torah, but parts of the Torah have been mingled up with other narratives written by human beings and the original guidance of the Lord is lost in that quagmire. Similarly, the four Gospels of Christ are not the original Gospels as they came from Prophet Jesus … the original and the fictitious, the Divine and the human are so intermingled that the grain cannot be separated from the chaff. The fact is that the original Word of God is preserved neither with the Jews nor with the Christians. The Qur'an, on the other hand, is fully preserved and not a jot or tittle has been changed or left out in it. [Ajijola, 79]

These charges bring us once again to the Islamic doctrine of tahrif, or corruption of the Judeo-Christian Scriptures. Based on some of the above qur'anic verses and, more important, exposure to the actual contents of other scriptures, Muslim theologians have generally formulated two responses. According to Nazir-Ali "the early Muslim commentators (e.g., Al-Tabari and Ar-Razi) believed that the alteration is tahrif bi'al ma'ni, a corruption of the meaning of the text without tampering with the text itself. Gradually, the dominant view changed to tahrif bi'al-lafz, corruption of the text itself" (Nazir-Ali, 46). The Spanish theologians Ibn-Hazm, and Al-Biruni, along with most Muslims, hold this view.

Another qur'anic scholar claims that "the biblical Torah was apparently not identical with the pure *tawrat* [law] given as a revelation to Moses, but there was considerable variation in opinion on the question to what extent the former scriptures were corrupted." On the one hand, "Ibn-

Hazm, who was the first thinker to consider the problem of *tabdil* [change] systematically, contended ... that the text itself had been changed or forged (*taghyr*), and he drew attention to immoral stories which had found a place within the corpus." On the other hand, "Ibn-Khaldun held that the text itself had not been forged but that Jews and Christians had misinterpreted their scripture, especially those texts which predicted or announced the mission of Muhammad and the coming of Islam" (Waardenburg, 257).

Whether a Muslim scholar shows more or less respect for the Bible, and whether or how he will quote from it depends on his particular interpretation of *tabdil*. Ibn-Hazm, for instance, rejects nearly the whole Old Testament as a forgery, but cheerfully quotes the *tawrat*'s bad reports of the faith and behavior of the *Banu Isra'il* as proofs against the Jews and their religion.

Against the New Testament. Noted Muslim commentator Yusuf Ali contends that "the *Injil* spoken of by the *Qur'an* is not the New Testament. It is not the four Gospels now received as canonical. It is the single Gospel which, Islam teaches, was revealed to Jesus, and which he taught. Fragments of it survive in the received canonical Gospels and in some others of which traces survive" (Ali, 287). Direct allegations against New Testament and Christian teaching are made. These include the charges that there have been a change and forgery of textual divine revelation, and that there have been doctrinal mistakes, such as the belief in the incarnation of Christ, the Trinity, the godhead, and the doctrine of original sin (Waardenburg, 261–63).

Debated among Muslim theologians is the question of the eternal destiny of the people of the Book. Although the average Muslim might consider anyone who has been a "good person" worthy of salvation, accounting for all the qur'anic evidences on this subject has created much uncertainty.

Among classical Muslim theologians, Jews and Christians were generally regarded as unbelievers (*kafar*) because of their rejection of Muhammad as a true prophet of God. For example, in the qur'anic commentary of Tabari, one of the most respected Muslim commentators of all time, we notice that, even though the author distinguishes between the people of the book and the polytheists (*mushrikun*) and expresses a higher opinion of the former, he clearly declares that the majority of Jews and Christians are in unbelief and transgression because of their refusal to acknowledge Muhammad's truthfulness (Antes, 104–5).

Added to this is the charge against Christian belief in the divinity of Christ as the Son of God (*see* Christ, Deity of), a belief that amounts to committing the unpardonable sin of *shirk*, and is emphatically condemned throughout the *Qur'an*. The condemnation of Christians is captured in 5:75: "They do blaspheme who say: 'God is Christ the son of Mary.' … Whoever joins other gods with God, God will forbid him the Garden, and the Fire will be his abode."

On the other hand the contemporary Muslim theologian, Falzur Rahman, goes against what he admits is "the vast majority of Muslim commentators." He champions the opinion that salvation is not acquired by formally joining the Muslim faith, but as the *Qur'an* points out, by believing in God and the last day and doing good deeds (Rahman, 166–67). The debate continues and each individual Muslim can take a different side of this issue based on his own understanding.

A Response to Islamic Charges. One evidence that these Islamic views are critically flawed is the internal inconsistency within the Muslim view of Scripture itself. Another is that it is contrary to the facts.

Tension within the Islamic View of the Bible. There is serious tension in the Islamic rejection of the authenticity of the current New Testament. This tension can be focused by the following teachings from the *Qur'an*:

The original New Testament ("Gospel") is a revelation of God (sura 5:46, 67, 69, 71).

Jesus was a prophet and his words should be believed by Muslims (sura 4:171; 5:78). As the Muslim scholar Mufassir notes, "Muslims believe all prophets to be truthful because they are commissioned in the service of humanity by Almighty God (Allah)" (Mufassir, i).

Christians were obligated to accept the New Testament of Muhammad's day (a.d. seventh century; sura 10:94).

In sura 10, Muhammad is told: "If thou wert in doubt as to what We have revealed unto thee, then ask those who have been reading the Book [the Bible] from before thee; the truth hath indeed come to thee from thy Lord; so be in no wise of those in doubt." Abdul-Haqq notes that "the learned doctors of Islam are sadly embarrassed by this verse, referring the prophet as it does to the people of the Book who would solve his doubts" (Abdul-Haqq, 23). One of the strangest interpretations is that the sura is actually addressed to those who question his claim. Others claim that "it was Muhammad himself who is addressed, but, however much they change

250

and turn the compass, it ever points to the same celestial pole—the purity and preservation of the Scriptures." However, Abdul-Haqq adds, "If again, we take the party addressed to be those who doubted the truth of Islam, this throws open the whole foundation of the prophet's mission; regarding which they are referred to the Jews [or Christians] for an answer to their doubts; which would only strengthen the argument for the authority of the Scripture—a result the Muslim critics would hardly be prepared for" (ibid., 100).

Christians respond that Muhammad would not have asked them to accept a corrupted version of the New Testament. Also, the New Testament of Muhammad's day is substantially identical to the New Testament today, since today's New Testament is based on manuscripts that go back several centuries before Muhammad (*see* New Testament Manuscripts). Hence, by the logic of this verse, Muslims should accept the authenticity of today's Bible. But if they do, then they should accept the doctrines of the deity of Christ (*see* Christ, Deity of) and the Trinity, since that is what the New Testament teaches. However, Muslims categorically reject these teachings, creating a dilemma within the Islamic view.

Another inconsistency within the qur'anic view of the Bible is that Muslims claim the Bible to be "the Word of God" (2:75). Muslims also insist that God's words cannot be altered or changed. But, as Pfander points out, "if both these statements are correct ... then it follows that the Bible has not been changed and corrupted either before or since Muhammad's time" (Pfander, 101). However, Islamic teaching insists that the Bible has been corrupted, thus the contradiction.

As Islamic scholar Richard Bell pointed out, it is unreasonable to suppose that Jews and Christians would conspire to change the Old Testament. For "their [the Jews'] feeling towards the Christians had always been hostile" (Bell, 164–65). Why would two hostile parties (Jews and Christians), who shared a common Old Testament, conspire to change it to support the views of a common enemy, the Muslims? It does not make any sense. What is more, at the supposed time of the textual changes, Jews and Christians were spread all over the world, making the supposed collaboration to corrupt the text impossible. And the number of copies of the Old Testament in circulation were too numerous for the changes to be uniform. Also, there is no mention of any such changes by former Jews or Christians of the time who became Muslims, something that they surely would have done if it were true (see McDowell, 52–53).

Contrary to the Factual Evidence. Furthermore, Muslim's rejection of the New Testament is contrary to the overwhelming manuscript evidence. All the Gospels are preserved in the Chester Beatty Papyri, copied in about 250. And the entire New Testament exists in Vaticanus Ms. (B) which dates from about 325–50. There are more than 5300 other manuscripts of the New Testament (*see* New Testament Manuscripts), dating from the second century to the fifteenth century (hundreds of which are from before Muhammad) which confirm that we have substantially the same text of the whole New Testament as existed in Muhammad's day. These manuscripts also confirm that the text is the same basic New Testament text as was written in the first century. These manuscripts provide an unbroken chain of testimony. For example, the earliest fragment of the New Testament, the John Ryland Fragment, is dated about 117–38. It preserves verses from John 18 just as they are found in today's New Testament. Likewise, the Bodmer Papyri from ca. 200 preserves whole books of Peter and Jude as we have them today. Most of the New Testament, including the Gospels, is in the Beatty Papyri, and the entire New Testament is in Vaticanus from about 325. There is absolutely no evidence that the New Testament message was destroyed or distorted, as Muslims claim it was (see Geisler and Nix, chap. 22).

Finally, Muslims use liberal critics of the New Testament to show that the New Testament was corrupted, misplaced, and outdated. However, the late liberal New Testament scholar John A. T. Robinson concluded that the Gospel record was written well within the lives of the apostles, between a.d. 40 and 60 (*see* New Testament, Historicity of; Bible Criticism). Former Bultmannian New Testament critic Eta Linnemann has more recently concluded that the position that the New Testament as preserved in the manuscripts does not accurately preserve the words and deeds of Jesus, is no longer defensible. She writes: "As time passes, I become more and more convinced that to a considerable degree New Testament criticism as practiced by those committed to historical-critical theology does not deserve to be called science" (Linnemann, 9). She adds, "The Gospels are not works of literature that creatively reshape already finished material after the manner in which Goethe reshaped the popular book about Dr. Faust" (ibid., 104). Rather, "Every Gospel presents a complete, unique testimony. It owes its existence to direct or indirect eyewitnesses" (ibid., 194).

Further, the use of these liberal critics by Muslim apologists undermines their own view of the *Qur'an.* Muslim writers are fond of quoting the conclusions of liberal critics of the Bible without serious consideration as to their presuppositions. The antisupernaturalism that led liberal critics of the Bible to deny that Moses wrote the Pentateuch, noting the different words for God used in different passages, would likewise argue that the *Qur'an* did not come from Muhammad. For the *Qur'an* also uses different names for God in different places. *Allah* is used for God in suras 4, 9, 24, 33, but *Rab* is used in suras 18, 23 and 25 (Harrison, 517). Muslims seem blissfully unaware that the views of these critics are based on an antisupernatural bias that, if applied to the *Qur'an* and the *hadith*, would destroy basic Muslim beliefs as well. In short, Muslims cannot consistently appeal to criticism of the New Testament based on the belief that miracles do not occur, unless they wish to undermine their own faith.

Conclusion. If Christians in Muhammad's day were obligated to accept the New Testament, and if abundant manuscript evidence confirms that the New Testament of today is essentially the same, then, according to the teachings of the *Qur'an* itself, Christians are obligated to accept the teachings of the New Testament. But the New Testament today affirms that Jesus is the Son of God, who died on the cross for our sins and rose again three days later. But this is contrary to the *Qur'an*. Thus, Muslim rejection of the authenticity of the New Testament is inconsistent with their own belief in the inspiration of the *Qur'an*.[221]

Communicating the Truth to Atheists

First, it should be recognized that today's atheist is not the same as the atheist of 30-50 years ago. The atheists of the 1950s to the 1980s simply did not believe in creation or a Creator and were not eager to share that belief with others. Today, the atheist movement is more involved in sharing their beliefs than Christians are. Their messages are on billboards, the radio and on television, and they have actually written many apologetic books defending their faith, i.e., secularism, humanism, relativism, and nihilism. We have now entered the era of New Atheism.

New Atheism is a social and political movement that began in the early 2000s in favor of atheism and secularism promoted by a collection of modern atheist writers who have advocated the view that "religion should

---

[221] Norman L. Geisler, "Bible, Islamic View Of," *Baker Encyclopedia of Christian Apologetics*, Baker Reference Library (Grand Rapids, MI: Baker Books, 1999), 96–99.

not simply be tolerated but should be countered, criticized, and exposed by rational argument wherever its influence arises."[222] There is uncertainty about how much influence the movement has had on religious demographics worldwide. In England and Wales, as of 2011 the increase in atheist groups, student societies, publications and public appearances coincided with the non-religious being the largest growing demographic, followed by Islam and Evangelicalism.[223] New Atheism lends itself to and often overlaps with secular humanism and antitheism, particularly in its criticism of what many New Atheists regard as the indoctrination of children and the perpetuation of ideologies.[224]

While the New Atheists authors write mainly from a scientific perspective, we should not assume that every atheist is a scientist. Many atheists have read the bestselling books by such authors as Christopher Eric Hitchens (1949–2011),[225] Richard Dawkins,[226] Sam Harris,[227] and Daniel Dennett.[228] Christopher Hitchens said that a person "could be an atheist and wish that belief in god were correct," but that "an antitheist, a term I'm trying to get into circulation, is someone who is relieved that there's no evidence for such an assertion."[229] Another thing that we should not assume about all atheists is that they are super intelligent, and there is no way that we could ever compete with them in a conversation about science.

---

[222] Hooper, Simon. "The rise of the New Atheists". CNN. Retrieved 16 March 2010.

[223] "Census 2011: religion, race and qualifications - see how England & Wales have changed". The Guardian.

[224] New Atheism - Wikipedia, the free encyclopedia, http://en.wikipedia.org/wiki/New_atheism (accessed September 15, 2015).

[225] Christopher Hitchens was the author of *God Is Not Great* and was named among the "Top 100 Public Intellectuals" by Foreign Policy and Prospect magazine. In addition, Hitchens served on the advisory board of the Secular Coalition for America.

[226] Richard Dawkins is the author of *The God Delusion*, which was preceded by a Channel 4 television documentary titled The Root of all Evil? He is also the founder of the Richard Dawkins Foundation for Reason and Science.

[227] Harris is the author of the bestselling non-fiction books, *The End of Faith, Letter to a Christian Nation, The Moral Landscape*, and *Waking Up: A Guide to Spirituality Without Religion*, as well as two shorter works initially published as e-Books, Free Will and Lying. Harris is a co-founder of the Reason Project.

[228] Daniel Dennett, author of *Darwin's Dangerous Idea, Breaking the Spell* and many others, has also been a vocal supporter of The Clergy Project, an organization that provides support for clergy in the US who no longer believe in God, and cannot fully participate in their communities any longer.

[229] Christopher Hitchens' *Religion and Political Views* | The .., http://hollowverse.com/christopher-hitchens/ (accessed September 15, 2015).

Most atheists only know what they have read from the atheist books listed in the footnotes, which are not science textbooks.

Well, it should be noted that we have some Christian apologists who have done the work for us, giving us the material so that if we choose to have a better understanding and wish to at least hold our own in such a conversation, we can. The Christian apologists highlighted below are not given extra space because they are all around the best apologists. Christian apologist can have a vast knowledge of many subject areas but they cannot be an expert on everything. While one may be an expert on textual criticism, defending the trustworthiness of Scripture, another may be a Christian philosopher and theologian, while others may be a physicist, mathematician, or scientist, studying philosophy of science, it is the latter, who are focused on here because of the subject matter.

The leading Christian apologist is **William Lane Craig**. He is a Research Professor of Philosophy at Talbot School of Theology and Professor of Philosophy at Houston Baptist University. He is an American Christian apologist, analytic Christian philosopher, and theologian. Craig's philosophical work focuses primarily on the philosophy of religion and metaphysics and philosophy of time. His theological interests are in historical Jesus studies and philosophical theology. He is known for his debates on the existence of God with public figures such as Christopher Hitchens and Lawrence Krauss. Craig established an online apologetics ministry, Reasonable Faith. His current research deals with divine aseity and the challenge posed by Platonist accounts of abstract objects. Craig is also an author of several books, including Reasonable Faith, which began as a set of lectures for his apologetics classes.[230]

John C. Lennox is an Irish mathematician, philosopher of science, Christian apologist, and Professor of Mathematics at the University of Oxford. He is a Fellow in Mathematics and Philosophy of Science at Green Templeton College, Oxford University. He is also Pastoral Advisor of Green Templeton College and Fellow of Wycliffe Hall. He is a leading

---

[230] *On Guard: Defending Your Faith with Reason and Precision* (Mar 1, 2010) by William Lane Craig and Lee Strobel; *Reasonable Faith (3rd edition): Christian Truth and Apologetics* (Jun 15, 2008) by William Lane Craig; *Contending with Christianity's Critics: Answering New Atheists and Other Objectors* (Aug 1, 2009) by William Lane Craig and Paul Copan; *Come Let Us Reason: New Essays in Christian Apologetics* (Mar 1, 2012) by William Lane Craig and Paul Copan

voice defending the notion of the relationship between science and religion. Lennox is a leading figure in the evangelical intelligentsia movement.[231]

Christian apologist **Stephen C. Meyer** received his Ph.D. from the University of Cambridge in the philosophy of science. A former geophysicist and college professor, he now directs the Center for Science and Culture at the Discovery Institute in Seattle.[232] Christian Apologist **William A. Dembski** is a mathematician and philosopher. He is a Research Professor in Philosophy at Southwestern Seminary in Ft. Worth, where he directs its Center for Cultural Engagement. He is also a senior fellow with Discovery Institute's Center for Science and Culture in Seattle. Previously he was the Carl F. H. Henry Professor of Theology and Science at The Southern Baptist Theological Seminary in Louisville, where he founded its Center for Theology and Science. Before that, he was an Associate Research Professor in the Conceptual Foundations of Science at Baylor University, where he headed the first intelligent design think-tank at a major research university: The Michael Polanyi Center.

Christian Apologist **Norman L. Geisler** (PhD, Loyola University) has taught theology, philosophy, and apologetics on the college or graduate level for over 50 years. He has served as a professor at Trinity Evangelical Seminary, Dallas Theological Seminary, and Liberty University. He was the co-founder of both Southern Evangelical Seminary and Veritas Evangelical Seminary. He currently is the Chancellor of Veritas Evangelical Seminary, the Distinguished Professor of Apologetics at Veritas Evangelical Seminary, and a Visiting Professor of Apologetics at Southern Evangelical Seminary.[233]

Overview of Atheism

Atheism. Whil. polytheism dominated much of ancient Greek thought and theism dominated medieval Christian view, atheism has had its

---

[231] *God's Undertaker* (Feb 18, 2011) by John Lennox; *Seven Days That Divide the World: The Beginning According to Genesis and Science* (Aug 23, 2011) by John Lennox; *God and Stephen Hawking* (Feb 18, 2011) by John Lennox; *Gunning for God* (Oct 21, 2011) by JOHN C. LENNOX

[232] Darwin's Doubt: The Explosive Origin of Animal Life and the Case for Intelligent Design (Jun 3, 2014) by Stephen C. Meyer; *Signature in the Cell* (Jun 23, 2009) by Stephen C. Meyer

[233] I Don't Have Enough Faith to Be an Atheist (Mar 15, 2004) by Norman L. Geisler and Frank Turek; Christian Apologetics (May 15, 2013) by Norman L. Geisler; Christian Ethics: Contemporary Issues and Options (Jan 1, 2010) by Norman L. Geisler; The Big Book of Bible Difficulties: Clear and Concise Answers from Genesis to Revelation (Jun 1, 2008) by Norman L. Geisler and Thomas Howe

day in the modern world. Of course not all who lack faith in a divine being wish to be called "atheist." Some prefer the positive ascription of "Humanist" (*see* Humanism, Secular). Others are perhaps best described as "materialists." But all are nontheists, and most are antitheistic. Some prefer the more neutral term a-theists.

In distinction from a theist, (*see* Theism) who believes God exists beyond and in the world, and a pantheist, who believes God is the world, an atheist believes there is no God either beyond or in the world. There is only a universe or cosmos and nothing more.

Since atheists share much in common with agnostics (*see* Agnosticism) and skeptics, they are often confused with them (see Russell, "What Is an Agnostic?"). Technically, a skeptic says "I *doubt* that God exists" and an agnostic declares "I *don't know* (or can't know) whether God exists." But an atheist claims to *know* (or at least believe) that God does not exist. However, since atheists are all nontheists and since most atheists share with skeptics an antitheistic stand, many of their arguments are the same. It is in this sense that modern atheism rests heavily upon the skepticism of David Hume and the agnosticism of Immanuel Kant.

Varieties of Atheism. Broadly speaking, there are differing kinds of atheism. *Traditional* (metaphysical) atheism holds that there never was, is, or will be a God. The many with this view include Ludwig Feuerbach, Karl Marx, Jean-Paul Sartre, and Antony Flew. *Mythological* atheists, such as Friedrich Nietzsche, believe the God-myth was never a Being, but was once a live *model* by which people lived. This myth has been killed by the advancement of man's understanding and culture. There was a short-lived form of *dialectical* atheism held by Thomas Altizer which proposed that the once-alive, transcendent God actually died in the incarnation and crucifixion of Christ, and this death was subsequently realized in modern times. S*emantical* atheists (*see* Verification, Empirical) claim that God-talk is dead. This view was held by Paul Van Buren and others influenced by the logical positivists who had seriously challenged the meaningfulness of language about God. Of course, those who hold this latter view need not be actual atheists at all. They can admit to the existence of God and yet believe that it is not possible to talk about him in meaningful terms. This view has been called "acognosticism," since it denies that we can speak of God in cognitive or meaningful terms. *Conceptual* atheism believes that there is a God, but he is hidden from view, obscured by our conceptual constructions (*see* Buber, Martin). Finally, *practical* atheists confess that God exists but believes that we should live *as if* he did not. The point is that we should not use God as a crutch for our failure to act in a spiritual and responsible way (some of Dietrich Bonhöffer's writings can be interpreted in this category).

There are other ways to designate the various kinds of atheists. One way would be by the philosophy by which they express their atheism. In this way one could speak of *existential* atheists (Sartre), *Marxist* atheists (Marx), *psychological* atheists (Sigmund Freud), *capitalistic* atheists (Ayn Rand), and *behavioristic* atheists (B. F. Skinner).

For apologetics purposes the most applicable way to consider atheism is in a metaphysical sense. Atheists are those who give reasons for believing that no God exists in or beyond the world. Thus we are speaking about philosophical atheism as opposed to practical atheists who simply live as though there were no God.

Arguments for Atheism. The arguments for atheism are largely negative, although some can be cast in positive terms. Negative arguments fall into two categories: (1) arguments against proofs for God's existence (*see* God, Objections to Proofs for), and (2) arguments against God's existence (*see* God, Alleged Disproofs of). On the first set of arguments most atheists draw heavily on the skepticism of Hume and the agnosticism of Kant.

Atheists offer what they consider to be good and sufficient reasons for believing no God exists. Four such arguments are often used by atheists: (1) the fact of evil (*see* Evil, Moral Problem of); (2) the apparent purposelessness of life; (3) random occurrence in the universe; and (4) the First Law of Thermodynamics—that "energy can neither be created or destroyed" as evidence that the universe is eternal and, hence, needs no Creator.

Responses to the Arguments. *The Existence of Evil.* A detailed response to the problem of evil is given elsewhere (*see* Evil, Problem of), so it will be treated here only in general terms. The atheist's reasoning is circular. Former atheist C. S. Lewis argued that, in order to know there is injustice in the world one has to have a standard of justice. So, to effectively eliminate God via evil one is to posit an ultimate moral standard by which to pronounce God evil (*Mere Christianity*). But for theists God is the ultimate moral standard, since there cannot be an ultimate moral law without an Ultimate Moral Law Giver.

Atheists argue that an absolutely good God must have a good purpose for everything, but there is no good purpose for much of the evil in the world. Hence, there cannot be an absolutely perfect God.

Theists point out that just because we do not know the purpose for evil occurrences does not mean that there is no good purpose. This argument does not necessarily disprove God; it only proves our ignorance of God's plan. Along the same reasoning, just because we do not see a purpose for all evil now, does not follow that we never will. The atheist is premature in his judgment. According to theism, a day of justice is coming. If there is a God, he must have a good purpose for evil, even if we do not know it. For a theistic God is omniscient and knows everything. He is omnibenevolent and has a good reason for everything. So, by his very nature he must have a good reason for evil.

Purposelessness. In assuming that life is without purpose, the atheist is again both a presumptuous and premature judge. How does one know there is no ultimate purpose in the universe? Simply because the atheist knows no real purpose for life does not mean God does not have one. Most people have known times that made no sense for the moment but eventually seemed to have great purpose.

The Random Universe. Apparent randomness in the universe does not disprove God. Some randomness is only apparent, not real. When DNA was first discovered it was believed that it split randomly. Now the entire scientific world knows the incredible design involved in the splitting of the double helix molecule known as DNA. Even actual randomness has an intelligent purpose (*see* Teleological Argument). Molecules of carbon dioxide are exhaled randomly with the oxygen (and nythogine in the air), but for a good purpose. If they did not, we would inhale the same poisonous gases we have exhaled. And some of what seems to be waste may be the product of a purposeful process. Horse manure makes good fertilizer. According to the atheist's time scale the universe has been absorbing and neutralizing very well all its "waste." So far as we know, little so-called waste is really wasted. Even if there is some, it may be a necessary byproduct of a good process in a finite world like ours, just like sawdust results from logging.

The Eternality of Matter (Energy). Atheists often misstate the scientific first law of thermodynamics. It should not be rendered: "Energy *can* neither be created *nor* destroyed." Science as science should not be engaged in "can" or "cannot" statements. Operation science deals with what *is* or *is not*, based on observation. And observation simply tells us, according to the first law, that "The amount of actual energy in the universe remains constant." That is, while the amount of *usable* energy is decreasing, the amount of *actual* energy is remaining constant in the universe. The first law says absolutely nothing about the *origin* or *destruction* of energy. It is merely an observation about the continuing presence of energy in the cosmos.

Unlike the second law of thermodynamics, which tells us the universe is running out of usable energy and, hence, must have had a beginning, the first law makes no statement about whether energy is eternal. Therefore, it cannot be used to eliminate a Creator of the cosmos.

Tenets of Atheism. Atheists do not have identical beliefs, any more than do all theists. However, there is a core of beliefs common to most atheists. So while not all atheists believe all of the following, all of the following are believed by some atheists. And most atheists believe most of the following:

About God. True atheists believe that only the cosmos exists. God did not create man; people created God.

About the World. The universe is eternal. If it is not eternal, then it came into existence "out of nothing and by nothing." It is self-sustaining and self-perpetuating. As astronomer Carl Sagan put it, "The Cosmos is all there is, all there was, and all there ever will be" (Sagan, *Cosmos*, 4). If asked "what caused the world?" most atheists would reply with Bertrand Russell that it was not caused; it is just there. Only the parts of the universe need a cause. They all depend on the whole, but the whole needs no cause. If we ask for a cause for the universe, then we must ask for a cause for God. And if we do not need a cause for God, then neither do we need one for the universe.

If one insists that *everything* needs a cause, the atheist simply suggests an infinite regress of causes that never arrives at a first cause (i.e., God). For if everything must have a cause, then so does this "first cause." In that case it really isn't first at all, nor is anything else (see Sagan, *Broca's Brain*, 287).

About Evil. Unlike pantheists (*see* Pantheism) who deny the reality of evil, atheists strongly affirm it. In fact, while pantheists affirm the reality of God and deny the reality of evil, atheists, on the other hand, affirm the reality of evil and deny the reality of God. They believe theists are inconsistent in trying to hold to both realities.

About Human Beings. A human being is matter in motion with no immortal soul. There is no mind apart from brain. Nor is there a soul independent of body. While not all atheists are strict materialists who identify soul and body, most do believe that the soul is dependent on the body. The soul in fact dies when the body dies. The soul (and mind) may be more than the body, the way a thought is more than words or symbols. But as the shadow of a tree ceases to exist when the tree does, so the soul does not survive the body's death.

About Ethics. No moral absolutes exist, certainly no divinely authorized absolutes. There may be some widely accepted and long enduring values. But absolutely binding laws would seem to imply an absolute Law Giver, which is not an option (*see* Morality, Absolute Nature of).

Since values are not *discovered* from some revelation of God, they must be *created*. Many atheists believe values emerge by trial and error the way traffic laws developed. Often the right action is described in terms of what will bring the greatest good in the long run (*see* Utilitarianism). Some frankly acknowledge that relative and changing situations determine what is right or wrong. Others speak about the expedient behavior (what "works"), and some work out their whole ethic in terms of self-interest. But virtually all atheists recognize that each person must determine personal values, since there is no God to reveal what is right and wrong. As the *Humanist Manifesto* put it, "Humanism asserts that the nature of the universe depicted by modern science makes unacceptable any supernatural or cosmic guarantees of human values" (Kurtz, 8).

About Human Destiny. Most atheists see no eternal destiny for individual persons, though some speak of a kind of collective immortality of the race. But the denial of individual immortality notwithstanding, many atheists are utopians. They believe in an earthly paradise to come. Skinner proposed a behaviorally controlled utopia in *Walden Two*. Marx believed an economic dialectic of history would inevitably produce a communist paradise. Others, such as Rand, believe that pure capitalism can produce a more perfect society. Still others believe human reason and science can produce a social utopia. Virtually all, however, recognize the ultimate mortality of the human race but console themselves in the belief that its destruction is millions of years away.

Evaluation. *Positive Contributions of Atheism.* Even from a theistic point of view, not all views expressed by atheists lack truth. Atheists have provided many insights into the nature of reality.

The reality of evil. Unlike pantheists, atheists do not close their eyes to the reality of evil. In fact, most atheists have a keen sensitivity to evil and injustice. They rightly point to the imperfection of this world and to the need for adjudication of injustice. In this regard they are surely right that an all-loving, all-powerful God would certainly do something about the situation.

Contradictory concepts of God. In contending that God is not caused by another, some have spoken of God as though he were a self-caused being *(causa sui).* Atheists rightly point out this contradiction, for no being can cause its own existence. To do this it would have to exist and not exist at the same time. For to cause existence is to move from nonexistence to existence. But nonexistence cannot cause existence. Nothing cannot cause something (*see* Causality, Principle of). On this point atheists are surely right.

Positive human values. Many atheists are humanists. With others they affirm the value of humanity and human culture. They earnestly pursue both the arts and the sciences and express deep concern in ethical issues. Most atheists believe that racism, hatred, and bigotry are wrong. Most atheists commend freedom and tolerance and have other positive moral values.

The Loyal Opposition. Atheists are the loyal opposition to theists. It is difficult to see the fallacies in one's own thinking. Atheists serve as a corrective to invalid theistic reasoning. Their arguments against theism should give pause to dogmatism and temper the zeal with which many believers glibly dismiss unbelief. In fact, atheists serve a significant corrective role for theistic thinking. Monologues seldom produce refined thought. Without atheists, theists would lack significant opposition with which to dialogue and clarify their concepts of God.

A Critique of Atheism. Still, the position that God does not exist lacks adequate rational support. The atheist's arguments against God are insufficient (*see* Atheism). Further, there are good arguments for the existence of God (*see* God, Evidence for). For many things, atheism provides no satisfactory answer.

Why is there something rather than nothing? Atheism does not provide an adequate answer as to why anything exists when it is not necessary for anything at all to exist. Nonexistence of everything in the world is possible, yet the world does exist. Why? If there is no cause for its existence, there is no reason why the world exists (*see* Cosmological Argument).

What is the basis for morality? Atheists can believe in morality, but they cannot *justify* this belief. Why should anyone be good unless there is a Definer of goodness who holds people accountable? It is one thing to say that hate, racism, genocide, and rape are wrong. But if there is no ultimate standard of morality (i.e., God), then how can these things be wrong? A moral prescription implies a Moral Prescriber (*see* Moral Argument for God).

What is the basis for meaning? Most atheists believe life is meaningful and worth living. But how can it be if there is no purpose for life, nor destiny after this life? Purpose implies a Purposer. But if there is no God, there is no objective or ultimate meaning. Yet most atheists live as if there were.

What is the basis for truth? Most atheists believe that atheism is true and theism is false. But to state that atheism is true implies that there is such a thing as objective truth. Most atheists do not believe that atheism is true only for them. But if atheism is true, there must be a basis for objective truth (*see* Truth, Nature of). Truth is a characteristic of a mind, and objective truth implies an objective Mind beyond our finite minds.

What is the basis for reason? Most atheists pride themselves on being rational. But why be rational if the universe is the result of irrational chance? There is no reason to be reasonable in a random universe. Hence, the very thing in which atheists most pride themselves is not possible apart from God.

What is the basis for beauty? Atheists also marvel at a beautiful sunset and are awestruck by the starry heavens. They enjoy the beauty of nature as though it were meaningful. Yet if atheism is true, it is all accidental, not purposeful. Atheists enjoy natural beauty as though it were meant for them, and yet they believe no Designer exists to mean it for them.[234]

Reasons for Disbelief

Not all atheists were born to atheist parents. Many were a part of some religion or another, believing in God, but over time abandoned their faith. Their faith was weakened by severe health problems in the family, a death of a loved one, or some great injustice that befell them. For others, it was

---

[234] Norman L. Geisler, "Atheism," *Baker Encyclopedia of Christian Apologetics*, Baker Reference Library (Grand Rapids, MI: Baker Books, 1999), 55–58.

one agnostic or atheist professor after another once they reached schools of higher learning, which eroded their belief in the Bible or God.

A man was born with a debilitating illness. As an infant, he had been baptized into Catholicism; he had long felt there was no God. The end came one day when he asked the priest, "Why did God make give me this illness?" The priest replied, "Because he loves you." The answer was so insane, so he walked out, never looking back. Consider a young woman diagnosed with cancer at the age of thirteen, who spent most of her youth in and out of hospitals. The mother of this child was so desperate; she brought a Pentecostal into the hospital to pray for the young girl because the word was he could heal the sick. Sadly, though, there was no cure; there was no miraculous healing. After her daughter's death, the most swore that she would never believe in some God, becoming an atheist.

- "I have seen many friends that I went to high school with just completely abandon their faith, and I was in danger of doing the same when I first went to college." – Chad, college junior

- "No matter what background you come from, the transition from high school to college will try your faith." – Vanessa, college sophomore[235]

- A pastor's kid tells his father, "I'm not a Christian anymore. I don't know what happened. I just left it."[236]

Again, we turn to William Lane Craig's words, as he offers the following exhortation to parents, which would also apply to pastors and elders as well,

> I think the church is really failing these kids. Rather than provide them training in the defense of Christianity's truth, we focus on emotional worship experiences, felt needs, and entertainment. It's no wonder they become sitting ducks for that teacher or professor who rationally takes aim at their faith. In high school and college, students are intellectually assaulted with every manner of non-Christian philosophy conjoined with an

---

[235] Top 10 Challenges Christian Students Face in College | eNews .., http://www.cedarville.edu/eNews/ParentPrep/2012/Challenges-Christian-Students-Fa (accessed September 15, 2015).

[236] The Leavers: Young Doubters Exit the Church | Christianity Today, http://www.christianitytoday.com/ct/2010/november/27.40.html (accessed September 15, 2015).

overwhelming relativism and skepticism. We've got to train our kids for war. How dare we send them unarmed into an intellectual war zone? Parents must do more than take their children to church and read them Bible stories. Moms and dads need to be trained in apologetics themselves and so be able to explain to their children simply from an early age and then with increasing depth why we believe as we do. Honestly, I find it hard to understand how Christian couples in our day and age can risk bringing children into the world without being trained in apologetics as part of the art of parenting.[237]

Reaching the Heart of an Atheist

Many are like the above example or have other reasons as to why they abandoned the faith. The key ingredient is their reason, which they have dwelled on to the point they have hardened their hearts. If we repeatedly violate the Christian conscience trained to distinguish between good and bad, it will become calloused and unfeeling. To violate the conscience is to ignore it, when it is tugging at you to do the right thing. While this applies largely to sinning and ignoring the Christian conscience, it can just as easily apply to irrational thinking as well. If we have an issue with God, with his Word, with the faith, with someone in the faith, with injustices of the world and we ignore these, failing to find an answer, we will eventually fall away from the faith. Paul called this a spiritual shipwreck. Paul told young Timothy "some have rejected and suffered shipwreck in regard to their faith." (1 Tim 1:19) If we entertain our false reasons, our confidence in God and his Word of truth, the Bible, can grow weak, and our faith can die. Just as we have reasons for the hope that dwells in us, we can also have reasons if they go unanswered or at least addressed; they can kill the hope that dwells in us.

Many of these ones, not all, simply need a solution to their reason for abandoning the faith. 'Why does evil exist?' 'Why does an all-powerful God of love allow evil to exist?'[238] 'Why do bad things happen to good people?' 'Why is life so unfair?'[239] 'What is the meaning of life?' 'Why is there so much religious hypocrisy?' If we lack understanding of an issue that is

---

[237] Craig, William Lane (2010-03-01). On Guard: Defending Your Faith with Reason and Precision (Kindle Locations 267-274). David C. Cook. Kindle Edition.

[238] http://www.christianpublishers.org/suffering-evil-why-god

[239] http://www.christianpublishers.org/why-is-life-so-unfair

eating at us, we begin to drift away, become sluggish, become hardened by the not knowing, so that we shrink back to destruction. Just as we entered the path of life, we can also reenter the path of death.

When someone says, 'I am an atheist,' our first goal is to ask why. If he is open to talking further, we need to try to find out what led his reason and his falling away. As we listen to his story, we need to do so with empathy because this could be us, or it could be a loved one, and we would want an empathetic ear if that were the case. After we have what we need to make a spiritual diagnosis, we can look for a solution. We can start by saying, it has been our experience that there is a reasonable and logical answer to every Bible difficulty that we have encountered. We can show even more empathy if we have struggled with something that made us pause for a moment. After this rapport, ask something like, "What if I can find you a reasonable, logical answer to this issue that has plagued you for so long. Even if you still choose to remain an atheist, would it not be a relief to have that answer?" If he answers yes, we now have a serious job ahead of ourselves. Undoubtedly, there is much information on the issue. We must find it and the answer that we promised. Undeniably, not all atheists are going to accept the truth. However, there are many who are willing to find a response to the issue that tore them from their faith. Use reason, logic, persuasion, and, above all, the power of God's Word, to lead them into the truth or back to the truth.[240] – Acts 28:23-24; Heb. 4:12.

EXCURSION Certainty/Certitude

Certainty is the confidence that something is true. Sometimes certainty is distinguished from *certitude*. Certainty is objective, but certitude is subjective. A first principle or self-evident statement is objectively certain, whether a person is sure about it or not. Certitude involves a knower's assent to that which is certain; it is a subjective acceptance of what is objectively so. In common usage the terms are employed interchangeably. The difference is that certainty exists where there is objective reasons or evidence that are commensurate to the degree of certainty claimed. With certitude, however, there need not be a commensurate degree of objective reasons or evidence for the degree one possesses.

---

[240] This author has accomplished this several times with ones who have left the faith. They bought out the time and over an extended period, they finally saw their way out of the long years of darkness, and the light of God's Word was eventually a welcome sight.

Kinds of Certainty. Certainty falls into categories of logical, moral, practical, and spiritual.

Logical Certainty. Logical certainty is found largely in mathematics and pure logic. This kind of certainty is involved where the opposite would be a contradiction. Something is certain in this sense when there is no logical possibility it could be false. Since mathematics is reducible to logic it fits into this category. It is found in statements such as $5 + 4 = 9$. It is also found in tautologies or statements that are true by definition: All circles are round, and no triangle is a square.

Metaphysical Certainty. There are, however, some other things of which we can be absolutely certain that are not statements empty of content. For example, I know for certain that I exist. This is undeniably so, since I cannot deny my existence without existing to make the denial. First principles can also be known for certain, since the subject and predicate say the same thing: "Being exists"; "Nonbeing is not Being." "Nonbeing cannot produce Being" is also certain, since *produce* implies an existing producer.

Moral Certainty. Moral certainty exists where the evidence is so great that the mind lacks any reason to veto the will to believe it is so. One rests in a moral certainty with complete confidence. Of course, there is a logical possibility that things of which we are morally certain are false. However, the evidence is so great there is no reason to believe it is false. In legal terms this is what is meant by "beyond all reasonable doubt."

Practical Certainty (High Probability). Practical certainty is not as strong as moral certainty. Persons claim to be "certain" about things they believe have a high probability of truth. One may be certain she had breakfast today, without being able to prove it mathematically or metaphysically. It is true unless something changed her perception, so that she was deluded into thinking she ate breakfast. It is possible to be wrong about these matters.

Spiritual (Supernatural) Certainty. If we grant the theist God's existence, he could give supernatural assurance that something is true. Likewise, if God speaks directly to a person (for example, Abraham in Genesis 22), then that person could have a spiritual certainty that transcends other kinds of certainty, because it comes directly from God. Those *who have direct mystical experiences* of God (*see* Mysticism), such as Paul describes in 2 Corinthians 12, have this kind of certainty. It would be greater than any other kind of certainty, since an omniscient being is its guarantor and omniscience cannot be wrong. As to how or whether such assurance

267

actually exists apart from a supernatural act is a moot point among theologians, although many classical apologists and others argue that it does (*see* Holy Spirit, Role in Apologetics).

Certainty and Assent. Certainty is always accompanied by assent. That is, the mind always assents to propositions that are certain, *if it properly understands them.* However, not all assent is accompanied by certitude. In everyday life, one frequently assents to something as being only probable and not necessary. In business affairs there is usually no absolute certainty; one must assent based on varying degrees of probability. This is virtually always the case in inductive reasoning, since the reasoner is moving from particular to general and is not sure about all the particulars. A complete induction would be an exception, since every particular is known. For instance, "There are three and only three marbles in my right hand" can be known with moral certainty. Though it is possible the person has not seen or counted correctly, the probability of correctness is high enough for the proposition to be morally certain (*see* Inductive Method).

A person can possess intellectual certainty about a proposition, yet lack subjective or emotional certitude. That is the common experience with doubt. There is emotional fear, despite rational verification. A person might have moral certainty that God exists and still feel his absence.

Subjective certitude often works in the opposite direction as well. A feeling of conviction so overpowers rational analysis as to move the will to assent with little or no evidence.

Certainty and Error. Subjective certitude is one way in which it is possible to have moral certainty and/or certitude about the truth of something that is objectively false. The will to believe may overpower the lack of evidence, so that one has tenacity of belief without the veracity of it. Reasons for error include defective senses or mental processes, incomplete consciousness, the drive of the will, and the need to act in the absence of compelling evidence.

One cannot be wrong about first principles or self-evident propositions. Once the mind understands them it is compelled to assent to them. There is no freedom not to assent to a self-evident truth. While this natural inclination to the truth is an unconscious drive, it would seem that, properly speaking, the assent to certitude is conscious. One can only be certain who understands that the truth is a first principle or reducible to it. This degree of analysis requires awareness. Only when one understands the principle and the truth becomes unmistakably clear is assent necessary and certitude guaranteed.

Certitude Involves a Repose. Since certitude involves a conscious assent to the certainty of the truth for which a human being has an unconscious appetite, the possession of this truth by the intellect is the reward of certitude. In the presence of such truths, nothing in the world could deprive the intellect of this possession. The reward of the hunger for truth is certitude which one consciously enjoys who perceives the certainty and necessity of the truth he or she has possessed.[241]

EXCURSION Faith and Reason

Faith and Reason. The relation of faith to reason is of utmost importance for the thinking believer. The problem of how to combine these aspects of personhood has existed from the earliest apologists. Justin Martyr, Clement of Alexandria, and Tertullian all struggled. Augustine made the first serious attempt to relate the two, but the most comprehensive treatment came at the end of the medieval period when Christian intellectualism flowered in the work of Thomas Aquinas.

Relation of Faith to Reason. Aquinas held that faith and reason intertwine. Faith uses reason, and reason cannot succeed in finding truth without faith.

Reason Cannot Produce Faith. Reason accompanies, but does not cause, faith. Faith is *consent without inquiry* in that faith's assent is not caused by investigation. Rather, it is produced by God. Commenting on Ephesians 2:8–9, Aquinas contended that "free will is inadequate for the act of faith since the contents of faith are above reason.... That a man should believe, therefore, cannot occur from himself unless God gives it" (Aquinas, *Ephesians*, 96; unless noted, all citations in this article are from works by Thomas Aquinas). Faith is a gift of God, and no one can believe without it.

Nonetheless, "this does not prevent the understanding of one who believes from having some discursive thought of comparison about those things which he believes" (*On Truth*, 14.A1.2). Such discursive thought, or reasoning from premises to conclusions, is not the *cause* of the assent of faith, but it can and should accompany it (ibid., 14.A1.6). Faith and reason

---

[241] Norman L. Geisler, "Certainty/Certitude," *Baker Encyclopedia of Christian Apologetics*, Baker Reference Library (Grand Rapids, MI: Baker Books, 1999), 124–125.

are parallel. One does not cause the other because "faith involves *will* (freedom) and reason doesn't coerce the will" (ibid.). A person is free to dissent, even though there may be convincing reasons to believe.

As a matter of tactical approach in apologetics, if the authority of Scripture is accepted (faith), appeal can be made to it (reason). "Thus, against the Jews we are able to argue by means of the Old Testament, while against heretics we are able to argue by means of the New Testament. But Mohammedans [*see* Islam] and the pagans accept neither the one nor the other.... We must, therefore, have recourse to the natural reason, to which all men are forced to give their assent" (*Summa Theologica*, 1a.2.2).

However, some Christian truths are attainable by human reason, for example, that God exists and is one. "Such truths about God have been proved demonstratively by the philosophers, guided by the light of the natural reason" (ibid., 1a.3.2)

Three Uses of Reason. Reason or philosophy can be used in three ways, Aquinas says:

1.   It demonstrates the "preambles of faith" (that God exists, that we are his creatures ...; *see* Cosmological Argument; God, Evidence for).

2.   It analyzes teachings of philosophers in order to reveal corresponding concepts in Christian faith. Aquinas gives the example of Augustine's *On the Trinity*, which draws on philosophy to help explain the Trinity.

3.   It opposes attacks against faith from logic (*Gentiles*, 1.9).

Reason can be used to prove natural theology, which studies the existence and nature of one God. It can be used to *illustrate* supernatural theological concepts, such as the Trinity and the Incarnation (*see* Christ, Deity of). And it can be used to refute false theologies (*De Trinitate*, 2.3). The apologist directs the person to accept two kinds of truth about divine things and to destroy what is contrary to truth. The person is directed to the truths of natural theology by the investigation of the reason and to the truths of supernatural theology by faith.

So to make the first kind of divine truth known, we must proceed through demonstrative arguments. However,

since such arguments are not available for the second kind of divine truth, our intention should not be to convince our adversary by arguments:

It should be to answer his arguments against the truth; for, as we have shown, the natural reason cannot be contrary to the truth of faith. The sole way to overcome an adversary of divine truth is from the authority of Scripture—an authority divinely confirmed by miracles. For that which is above the human reason we believe only because God has revealed it. Nevertheless, there are certainly likely [probable] arguments that should be brought forth in order to make divine truth known. [*Gentiles*, 1.9; *see* Miracles, Apologetic Value of]

God's existence is self-evident absolutely (in itself) but not relatively (to us) (ibid., 1.10–11; *see* First Principles). Hence, in the final analysis, one must receive *by faith* those things that can be known by reason, as well as those things that lie above reason. Intellectual assent that lacks faith cannot have certitude, for human reason is notoriously suspect when it comes to spiritual matters. Consequently, "it was necessary for divine truth to be delivered by way of faith, being told to them as it were, by God Himself Who cannot lie" (*Summa Theologica*, 2a2ae.1, 5.4).

Divine Authority. Aquinas did not believe that reason provides the basis for believing in God. It can prove *that* God exists, but it cannot convince an unbeliever to believe *in* God.

Reason Prior to Faith. We may believe (assent without reservation) in something that is neither self-evident nor deduced from it by a movement of the will. However, this does not mean that reason plays no prior role to belief. We judge a revelation to be worthy of belief "on the basis of evident signs or something of the sort" (ibid., 2a2ae.1, 4. ad 2).

Reason inquires about what is to be believed before it believes in it. "Faith does not involve a search by natural reason to prove what is believed. But it does involve a form of inquiry unto things by which a person is led to belief, e.g. whether they are spoken by God and confirmed by miracles" (ibid., 2a2ae.2, 1, reply). Demons are not willingly convinced by the evidence that God exists but are intellectually forced by confirming signs to the fact that what the faithful believe is true. Yet they cannot truly be said to *believe* (*On Truth*, 14.9. ad 4).

The Testimony of the Spirit. In order to believe in God one must have the inner testimony of the Holy Spirit (*see* Holy Spirit, Role in Apologetics). For "one who believes does have a sufficient motive for believing, namely the authority of God's teaching, confirmed by miracles, and—what is greater—the inner inspiration [*instinctus*] of God inviting him to believe" (*Summa Theologica*, 2a2ae.6.1). The Holy Spirit uses two causes to stimulate voluntary faith. The persuasion may be from without, for example, a miracle that is witnessed. Or persuasion may be from within. The first cause is never enough for one inwardly to assent to the things of faith. The assent of faith is caused by God as he moves the believer inwardly through grace. Belief is a matter of the will, but the will needs to be prepared by God "to be lifted up to what surpasses nature" (ibid., 2a2ae.2, 9. ad 3).

Reason in Support of Faith. Commenting on the use of *reason* in 1 Peter 3:15, Aquinas argued that "human reasoning in support of what we believe may stand in a two-fold relation to the will of the believer." First, the unbeliever may not have the will to believe unless moved by human reason. Second, the person with a will ready to believe loves the truth, thinks it out, and takes to heart its evidence. The first, unbelieving will may come to a faith of sorts, but there will be no merit in it, because belief does not extend far beyond sight. The second person also studies the human reasoning, but it is a meritorious work of faith (ibid., 2a2ae.2, 10).

Positive Evidence. Faith is supported by, though not based on, probable evidence. "Those who place their faith in this truth, however, 'for which the human reason offers no experimental evidence,' do not believe foolishly, as though 'following artificial fables'" (2 Peter 1:16). Rather, "It reveals its own presence, as well as the truth of its teaching and inspiration, by fitting arguments; and in order to confirm those truths that exceed natural knowledge, it gives visible manifestations to works that surpass the ability of all nature." The kind of positive evidence that Aquinas used included such things as raising the dead, miracles, and the conversion of the pagan world to Christianity (*On Truth*, 14.A1).

Negative Evidence. The negative evidence encompasses arguments against false religions, including things like their fleshly appeal to carnal pleasures, their teachings that contradict their promises, their many fables and falsities, the lack of miracles to witness to divine inspiration of their holy book (like the *Qur'an*), use of warfare (arms) to spread their message, the fact that wise men did not believe Muhammad, only ignorant, desert wanderers, the fact that there were no prophets to witness to him, and Muslim perversions of Old and New Testament stories (*Gentiles*, 1.6).

Faith and Fallible Testimony. How can we be sure when the support of our faith rests on many intermediary (fallible) testimonies? Aquinas responds that the intermediaries are above suspicion if they were confirmed by miracles (for example, Mark 16:20). "We believe the successors of the apostles and prophets only in so far as they tell us those things which the apostles and prophets have left in their writings" (*On Truth*, 14.10, ad 11). The Bible alone is the final and infallible authority for our faith (*see* Bible, Evidence for).

Faith and Demonstrative Arguments. Aquinas distinguished between two kinds of rational arguments: demonstrative and persuasive. "Demonstrative, cogent, and intellectually convincing argument cannot lay hold of the truths of faith, though it may neutralize destructive criticism that would render faith untenable." On the other hand, "persuasive reasoning drawn from probabilities … does not weaken the merit of faith, for it implies no attempt to convert faith into sight by resolving what is believed into evident first principles" (*De Trinitate*, 2.1, ad 5).

Distinguishing Faith and Reason. Though faith is not separated from reason, Aquinas does formally distinguish between them. He believed they are related, but the relationship does not coerce a person to believe.

Faith in Relation to Reason. Human reason does not force faith. If it did, then faith would not be a free act. What happens is that "the mind of the one believing settles upon the one side of a question not in virtue of his reason but in virtue of his will. Therefore assent is understood in the definition [of faith] as an act of the mind in so far as the mind is brought to its decision by the will" (ibid., 2a2ae. 2, 1, ad 3).

Faith is not unreasonable. Faith is reason with assent. For "to ponder with assent is, then, distinctive of the believer: this is how his act of belief is set off from all other acts of the mind concerned with the true and the false" (*Summa Theologica*, 2a2ae.2, 1, reply). Faith, then, is defined as *"that habit of mind whereby eternal life begins in us and which brings the mind to assent to things that appear not."* Faith differs from science in that the object of faith is unseen. It also differs from doubt, suspicion and opinion in that there is evidence to support faith.

Faith is a free act. Aquinas quotes Augustine with approval that "Faith is a virtue by which things not seen are believed" (ibid., 2a2ae.4, 1, reply). He declares that

to believe is an act of mind assenting to the divine truth by virtue of the command of the will as this is moved by God through grace; in this the act stands under control of free will and is directed toward God. The act of faith is, therefore, meritorious. That is, one is rewarded for believing in what he does not see. There is no merit (reward) in believing what can be seen, since there is no faith involved; it can be seen. The scientist [i.e., philosopher] is impelled to assent by force of a conclusive proof. Thus the assent is not meritorious. [ibid., 2a2ae. 2, 9]

Faith is an act of mind and will. Since belief is an act of the intellect under the impetus of the will, it issues from both mind and will, and both are perfectible by action. "If an act of faith is to be completely good, then, habits must necessarily be present in both mind and will" (ibid., 2a2ae. 4, 2, reply). That is, one cannot be saved without a willingness to do something with faith. Saving faith will produce good works.

Meritorious Nature of Faith. Faith is meritorious, not because one has to work for it, but because it involves the will to believe. It "depends on the will according to its very nature (ibid., ad 5). "For in science and opinion [probable arguments] there is no inclination because of the will, but only because of reason" (ibid., 14.3, reply). But "no act can be meritorious unless it is voluntary, as has been said" (ibid., 14.5, reply).

Aquinas believed that Hebrews 11:1 is a good definition of faith, for it describes not merely what faith *does* but what it *is*. He saw in it the three essentials:

1. It mentions the will and the object that moves the will as principles on which the nature of faith is based.

2. In it we can distinguish faith from those things which appear not, as opposed to science and understanding.

3. The whole definition reduces to the essential phrase, "the substance of things hoped for." (ibid., 14.2)

The formal difference between faith and reason is that one cannot both know and believe the same thing at the same time. For "Whatever things we know with scientific knowledge properly so called we know by reducing them to first principles which are naturally present to the understanding."

Faith and Knowledge about the Same Object. Scientific knowledge culminates in sight of the thing believed, so there is no room for faith. One cannot have faith and scientific knowledge about the same thing (ibid., 14.9, reply). The object of true faith is above senses and understanding. "Consequently, the object of faith is that which is absent from our understanding." As Augustine said, "we believe that which is absent, but we see that which is present" (ibid., 14.9, reply).

This does not mean, of course, that everyone will necessarily believe what I can see without faith (*Summa Theologica*, 2a2ae.1, 5). It does mean that the same person cannot have both faith and proof of the same object. One who sees it, does not believe it by faith on the testimony of others. One who believes it on the testimony of another does not see (know) it personally.

Probable Knowledge and Faith. Likewise, one cannot have "opinion" (probable knowledge) and "science" (certain knowledge) about the same object. As Aquinas notes, "opinion includes a fear that the other part [of the contradiction] is true, and scientific knowledge excludes such fear. However, this fear that the opposite may be true does not apply to matters of faith. For faith brings with it a greater certitude than what can be known by reason" (*On Truth*, 14.9, ad 6).

Creedal Knowledge and Faith. If the existence of God can be proved by reason, and if what is known by reason cannot also be a matter of faith, then why is belief in God proposed in the Creed? Aquinas responds that not all are capable of demonstrating God's existence. "We do not say that the proposition, God is one, in so far as it is proved by demonstration, is an article of faith, but something presupposed before the articles. For the knowledge of faith presupposes natural knowledge, just as grace presupposes nature" (ibid., 14.9, ad 8).

Perfected by Love, Produced by Grace. Reason can go only so far. Faith goes beyond reason and completes it. "Faith does not destroy reason, but goes beyond it and perfects it" (ibid., 14.10, reply, ad 7). "Love is the perfection of faith. Since charity is a perfection of the will, faith is formed by charity" (ibid., ad 1). "It is called form in so far as faith acquires some perfection from charity" (ibid., ad 7). But "the act of faith which precedes charity is an imperfect act awaiting completion from charity" (ibid., 14.A5, reply). So love perfects faith. Since believing depends on the understanding and the will, "such an act cannot be perfect unless the will is made perfect by charity and the understanding by faith. Thus formless faith cannot be a virtue" (ibid., ad 1).

However, "that which faith receives from charity is accidental to faith in its natural constitution, but essential to it with reference to its morality" (ibid., 14.6, reply).

Not only is love necessary to perfect faith, but grace is necessary to produce it. "Now, grace is the first [that is, remote] perfection of the virtues, but charity is their proximate perfection" (ibid., 14.A5, ad 6).

The Limitations of Reason. Aquinas did not believe that human reason was without limitations. In fact he offered many arguments as to why reason is insufficient and revelation is needed.

Five Reasons for Revelation. Following Jewish philosopher Moses Maimonides, Aquinas set forth five reasons why we must first believe what we may later be able to provide good evidence for (Maimonides, 1.34):

1.   The object of spiritual understanding is deep and subtle, far removed from sense perception.

2.   Human understanding is weak as it fights through these issues.

3.   A number of things are needed for conclusive spiritual proof. It takes time to discern them.

4.   Some people are disinclined to rigorous philosophical investigation.

5.   It is necessary to engage in other occupations besides philosophy and science to provide the necessities of life (*On Truth*, 14.10, reply).

Aquinas said it is clear that, "if it were necessary to use a strict demonstration as the only way to reach a knowledge of the things which we must know about God, very few could ever construct such a demonstration and even these could do it only after a long time." Elsewhere, Aquinas lists only three basic reasons divine revelation is needed.

1.   Few possess the knowledge of God, some do not have the disposition for philosophical study, and others do not have the time or are indolent.

2.   Time is required to find the truth. This truth is very profound, and there are many things that must be presupposed. During youth the soul is distracted by "the various movements of the passions."

3.   It is difficult to sort out what is false in the intellect. Our judgment is weak in sorting true from false concepts. Even in demonstrated propositions there is a mingling of false.

"That is why it was necessary that the unshakable certitude and pure truth concerning divine things should be presented to men by way of faith" (*Gentiles*, 1.4, 2–5).

The Noetic Effects of Sin. Clearly, the mind falls far short when it comes to the things of God. As examples of weakness Aquinas looked at the philosophers and their errors and contradictions. "To the end, therefore, that a knowledge of God, undoubted and secure, might be present among men, it was necessary that divine things be taught by way of faith, spoken as it were by the Word of God who cannot lie" (ibid., 2a2ae. 2, 4). For "the searching of natural reason does not fill mankind's need to know even those divine realities which reason could prove" (ibid., 2a2ae.2, 4, reply).

As a result of the noetic effects of sin, grace is needed. Aquinas concluded that "If for something to be in our power means that we can do it without the help of grace, then we are bound to many things that are not within our power without healing grace—for example to love God or neighbor." The same is true of belief. But with the help of grace we do have this power (ibid., 2a2ae.2, 6, ad 1).

However, Aquinas did not believe that sin destroyed human rational ability. "Sin cannot destroy man's rationality altogether, for then he would no longer be capable of sin" (ibid., 1a2ae.85, 2).

Things above Reason. Not only is faith necessary because of human depravity, but also because some things simply go beyond the power of reason. That does not mean they are contrary to reason, but that they are not fully comprehensible. "Faith, however, is said to surpass reason, not because there is no act of reason in faith, but because reasoning about faith cannot lead to the sight of those things which are matters of faith" (ibid., 14.A2, ad 9). If one could base faith fully on reason, faith would not be a free act; it would be consent caused by the mind.

At two levels a matter of faith may be "above reason." At its highest level it can be above reason absolutely—if it exceeds the intellectual capacity of the human mind (e.g., the Trinity). It is impossible to have scientific knowledge of this. Believers assent to it only on the testimony of God." Or, it may not absolutely exceed the intellect capacity of all, but is exceedingly difficult to comprehend, and is above the intellectual capacity of some (for example, that God exists without body). "These we may have scientific proofs of and, if not, we may believe them" (*On Truth*, 14.9, reply).

We must have faith when the light of grace is stronger than the light of nature. For "although the divinely infused light is more powerful than natural light, in our present state we do not share it perfectly, but imperfectly." Therefore, "because of this defective participation, through that infused light itself we are not brought to the vision of those things for the knowledge of which it was given us. But we will have it in heaven when we share that light perfectly and in the light of God we will see light" (*Gentiles*, 14.8, ad 2).

Faith, then, surpasses reason. For "some truths about God exceed all the ability of the human reason. Such is the truth that God is triune" (ibid., 1.3). The ineffable essence of God cannot be known by human reason. The reason for this is that the mind depends on the senses. "Now, sensible things cannot lead the human intellect to the point of seeing in them the nature of the divine substance; for sensible things are effects that fall short of the power of their cause" (ibid., 1.3, 3).

Just because we have no reasons for things that go beyond reason does not mean they are not rational. Every belief that is not self-evident can be defended as necessary. We may not know the argument, but it exists. It at least is known to God "and to the blessed who have vision and not faith about these things" (*De Trinitate*, 1.1.4; *On Truth*, 14.9, ad 1). While human reason cannot attain to the things of faith, it is the preface to them. While "philosophical truths cannot be opposed to truths of faith, they fall short indeed, yet they also admit common analogies; and some moreover are foreshadowing, for nature is the preface of grace" (*De Trinitate*, 2.3).

"Although the truth of the Christian faith which we have discussed surpasses the capacity of the reason, nevertheless that truth that the human reason is naturally endowed to know cannot be opposed to the truth of the Christian faith" (*Gentiles*, 1.7, [1]).

Summary. Aquinas's view of the relation of faith and reason blends positive elements of presuppositionalism and evidentialism, of rationalism (*see* Descartes, Rene; Leibniz, Gottfried) and fideism. Aquinas stresses the need for reason before, during, and after beliefs are acquired. Even the mysteries of faith are not irrational.

On the other hand, Aquinas does not believe that reason alone can bring anyone to faith. Salvation is accomplished only by the grace of God. Faith can never be *based on* reason. At best it can only be *supported by* reason. Thus, reason and evidence never coerce faith. There is always room for unbelievers not to believe *in* God, even though a believer can construct a valid proof *that* God exists. Reason can be used to demonstrate that God exists, but it can never in itself persuade someone to believe in God. Only God can do this, working in and through their free choice.

These distinctions of Aquinas are eminently relevant to the discussion between rationalists and fideists or between evidentialists and presuppositionalists. With regard to belief that God exists, Aquinas sides with the rationalists and evidentialists. But with respect to belief in God, he agrees with fideists (*see* Fideism) and presuppositionalists (*see* Apologetics, Presuppositional).[242]

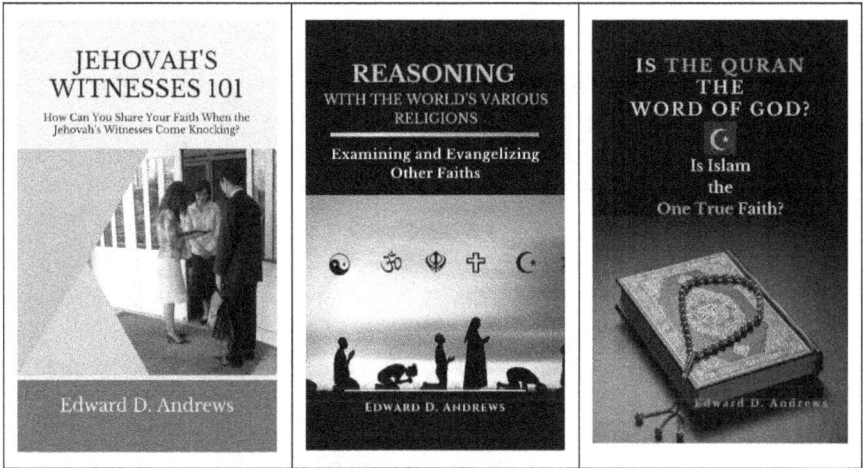

Each year, the Jehovah's Witnesses spend about 2 billion hours evangelizing their communities around the world in 357 languages. Many think that they know the Jehovah's Witnesses, but the sources are usually twofold: **(1)** They are misinformed Bible scholars who have read books and websites by disgruntled ex-Jehovah's Witnesses. **(2)** They have read books or comments by disgruntled ex-Jehovah's Witnesses. Herein you will learn a lot that you may have not known and learn some things about how to better evangelize them, or if you are even up to evangelize them. Moreover, we will use some arguments often raised about Jehovah's Witnesses as our text case from such persons as J. Warner Wallace, a leading Evangelical Christian apologist today. Here is what you will need to know in order to effectively share your faith with JWs when they come knocking.

Review Questions

(1) How can we effectively communicate the truth to Muslims?

(2) How can we effectively communicate the truth to Atheists?

---

[242] Norman L. Geisler, "Faith and Reason," *Baker Encyclopedia of Christian Apologetics*, Baker Reference Library (Grand Rapids, MI: Baker Books, 1999), 239–243.

CHAPTER 18 Bible Difficulties Explained

IT SEEMS THAT the charge that the Bible contradicts itself has been made more and more in the last 20 years. Generally, those making such claims are merely repeating what they have heard because most have not even read the Bible, let alone done an in-depth study of it. I do not wish, however, to set aside all concerns as though they have no merit. There are many who raise legitimate questions that seem, on the surface anyway, to be about well-founded contradiction. Sadly, these issues have caused many to lose their faith in God's Word, the Bible. The purpose of this books is, to help its readers to be able to defend the Bible against Bible critics (1 Pet. 3:15), to contend for the faith (Jude 1:3), and help those, who have begun to doubt. – Jude 1:22-23.

Before we begin explaining things, let us jump right in, getting our feet wet, and deal with two major Bible difficulties, so we can see that there are reasonable, logical answers. After that, we will delve deeper into explaining Bible difficulties.

Is God permitting Human Sacrifice?

Judges 11:29-34, 37-40? Updated American Standard Version (UASV)

²⁹ Then the Spirit of the Lord was upon Jephthah, and he passed through Gilead and Manasseh; and passed on to Mizpah of Gilead, and from Mizpah of Gilead he passed on to the sons of Ammon. ³⁰ And Jephthah **made a vow** to Jehovah and said, "If You will indeed give the sons of Ammon into my hand, ³¹ then it shall be that **whatever** comes out of the doors of my house to meet me when I return in peace from the sons of Ammon, it shall be Jehovah's, and I will offer it up as a burnt offering." ³² So Jephthah crossed over to the sons of Ammon to fight against them; and Jehovah gave them into his hand. ³³ He struck them with a very great slaughter from Aroer as far as Minnith, twenty cities, and as far as Abel-keramim. So the sons of Ammon were subdued before the sons of Israel.

³⁴ When Jephthah came to his house at Mizpah, behold, **his daughter was coming out to meet him** with tambourines and with dancing. Now she was his one and only child; besides her he had no son or daughter.

³⁷ And she said to her father, "Let this thing be done for me: leave me alone two months, that I may go up and down on the mountains and weep because of my virginity, I and my companions." ³⁸ And he said, "Go." So he sent her away for two months; and **she left with her companions, and wept on the mountains because of her virginity**. ³⁹ At the end of two months she returned to her father, who **did to her according to the vow that he had made**; and she never known a man.²⁴³ Thus it became a custom in Israel, ⁴⁰ that the daughters of Israel went year by year **to commemorate²⁴⁴ the daughter** of Jephthah the Gileadite four days in the year.

It is true; to infer that having the idea of an animal sacrifice would really have not been an impressive vow, which the context requires. Human sacrifice will be repugnant if we are talking about taking a life. Jephthah had no sons, so he likely knew it was the daughter, who would come to greet him.

First, the text does not say he killed his daughter. The idea of some that he did kill her is concluded only by inference. While it is not good policy to interpret backward, using Paul on Judges, he does say humans are to be **"as a living sacrifice."** Therefore, Jephthah could have offered his daughter at the temple, "as a living sacrifice" in service, like Samuel.

This is not to be taken dismissively, because, under Jewish backgrounds, it is no small thing to offer a **perpetual virginity** as a sacrifice. This would mean Jephthah's lineage would not be carried on, the family name, was no more.

Second, the context says she went out to weep for two months, not mourn her death. It says, "she left with her companions, and **wept on the mountains because of her virginity."**

If she was facing imminent death, she could have married, and spent that last two months as a married woman. There would be absolutely no reason for her to mourn her virginity if she were not facing perpetual virginity. – Exodus 38:8; 1 Samuel 2:22

Third, it was completely forbidden to offer a human sacrifice. – Leviticus 18:21; 20:2-5; Deuteronomy 12:31; 18:10

---

²⁴³ I.e., *never had relations with a man*

²⁴⁴ Or *lament*

Imagine an Israelite believing that he could please God with a human sacrifice that was intended to offer up a human life. To do so would have been a rejection of Jehovah's Sovereignty (the very person you are asking for help), and a rejection of the Law that made them a special people. Worse still, this interpretation would have us believe that Jehovah knew this was coming, allowed the vow, and then aided this type of man to succeed over his enemies.

The last point is simple enough. If such a man as one who would make such a vow, in gross violation of the law, and then carry it out; there is no way he would be mentioned by Paul in Hebrews chapter 11 among the most faithful men and women in Israelite history.

In review, there is no way God would have granted and helped in Jephthah's initial success knowing the vow that was coming because both Jehovah and Jephthah would be as bad as the Canaanites. There is no way that God would accept such a vow and then go on to help Jephthah with his enemies yet again. Then, to allow such a vow to be carried out, to then put Jephthah on the wall of star witnesses for God in Hebrews chapter 11.

Does Isaiah 45:7 mean that God Is the Author of Evil?

Isaiah 45:7 King James Version (KJV)	**Isaiah 45:7** English Standard Version (ESV)
7 I form the light, and create darkness: I make peace, and **create evil**: I the Lord do all these things.	7 I form light and create darkness, I make well-being and **create calamity**, I am the Lord, who does all these things.[245]

Encarta Dictionary: (Evil) (1) morally bad: profoundly immoral or wrong (2) deliberately causing great harm, pain, or upset

QUESTION: Is this view of evil always the case? No, as you will see below.

Some apologetic authors try to say, 'we do not understand Isaiah 45:7 correctly, because there are other verses that say God is not evil (1 John 1:5), cannot look approvingly on evil (Hab. 1:13), and cannot be tempted by

---

[245] See Jeremiah 18:11, Lamentations 3:18, and Amos 3:6

evil. (James 1:13)' Well, while all of these things are Scripturally true, the question at hand is not: Is God evil, can God approvingly look on evil, or can God be tempted with evil? Those questions are not relevant to the one at hand, as God cannot be those things, and at the same time, he can be the yes to our question. The question is, is God the author, the creator of evil?

We would hardly argue that God was **not** **just** in his bringing "calamity" or "evil" down on Adam and Eve. Thus, we have Isaiah 45:7 saying that God is the creator of "calamity" or "evil."

Let us begin simple, without trying to be philosophical. When God removed Adam and Eve from the Garden of Eden, he sentenced them and humanity to sickness, old age, and death. (Rom. 5:8; i.e., enforce penalty for sin), which was to bring "calamity" or "evil" upon humankind. Therefore, as we can see "evil" does not always mean wrongdoing. Other examples of God bringing "calamity" or "evil" are Noah and the flood, the Ten Plagues of Egypt, and the destruction of the Canaanites. These acts of evil were not acts of wrongdoing. Rather, they were righteous and just, because God, the Creator of all things, was administering justice to wrongdoers, to sinners. He warned the perfect first couple what the penalty was for sin. He warned the people for a hundred years by Noah's preaching. He warned the Canaanites centuries before.

Nevertheless, there are times, when God extends mercy, refraining from the execution of his righteous judgment to one worthy of calamity. For example, he warned Nineveh, the city of blood, and they repented, so he pardoned them. (Jonah 3:10) God has made it a practice to warn persons of the results of sin, giving them undeservedly many opportunities to change their ways. – Ezekiel 33:11.

God cannot sin; it is impossible for him to do so. So, when did he create evil? Without getting into the eternity of his knowing what he was going to do, and when, let us just say, evil did not exist when he was the only person in existence. We might say the idea of evil existed because he knew what he was going to do. However, the moment he created creatures (spirit and human), the potential for evil came into existence because both have free will to sin (fall short of perfection). Evil became a reality the moment Satan entertained the idea of causing Adam to sin, to get humanity for himself, and then acted on it.

God has the right and is just to bring the *calamity of* or *evil* down on anyone that is an unrepentant sinner. God did not even have to give us the underserved kindness of offering us his Son. God is the author or agent of evil regardless of the source books that claim otherwise. If he had never created free will beings, evil would have never gone from the idea of evil to the potential of evil, to the existence of evil. However, God felt that it was better to get the sinful state out of angel and human existence, recover, and then any who would sin thereafter; he would be justified in handing out evil or calamity to only that person or angel alone.

Who among us would argue that he should have created humans and angels like robots, automatons with no free will? The moment he chose the free will, he moved evil from an idea to a potential, and Satan moved it to reality. God has a moral nature that does not bring about evil and sin when he is the only person in existence. However, the moment he created beings in his image, which had the potential to sin, he brought about evil. The moment we have a moral code of good and evil that is placed upon one's with free will; then, we have evil as a potential.

In English, the very comprehensive Hebrew word ra' is variously translated as "bad," "downcast (sad, NASB)," "ugly," "evil," "grievous (distressing, NASB)," "sore," "selfish (stingy, HCSB)," and "envious," depending upon the context. (Gen 2:9; 40:7; 41:3; Ex 33:4; Deut. 6:22; 28:35; Pro 23:6; 28:22)

Evil as an adjective **describes** the **quality of** a class of people, places, or things, or of a specific person, place, or thing

Evil as a noun, **defines** the **nature** of a class of people, places, or things, or of a specific person, place, or thing (e.g., the evil one, evil eye).

We can agree that "evil" is a thing. Create means to bring something into existence, be it people, places, or things, as well something abstract, for lack of a better word at the moment. We would agree that when God was alone evil was not a reality; it did not exist? We would agree that the moment that God created free will creatures (angels and humans), creating humans in his image, with his moral nature, he also brought the potential for evil into existence, and it was realized by Satan?

Inerrancy: Can the Bible Be trusted?

If the Bible is the Word of God, it should be in complete agreement throughout; there should be no contradictions. Yet, the rational mind must ask, why is it that some passages appear to be contradictions when compared with others? For example, Numbers 25:9 tells us that 24,000 died from the scourge, whereas at 1 Corinthians 10:8, the apostle Paul says it was

23,000. This would seem to be a clear error. Before addressing such matters, let us first look at some background information.

Full inerrancy in this book means that the original writings are fully without error in all that they state, as are the words. The words were not dictated (automaton), but the intended meaning is inspired, as are the words that convey that meaning. The Author allowed the writer to use his style of writing, yet controlled the meaning to the extent of not allowing the writer to choose a wrong word, which would not convey the intended meaning. Other more liberal-minded persons hold with *partial inerrancy*, which claims that as far as faith is concerned, this portion of God's Word is without error, but that there are historical, geographical, and scientific errors.

There are several different levels of inerrancy. *Absolute Inerrancy* is the belief that the Bible is fully true and exact in every way; including not only relationships and doctrine, but also science and history. In other words, all information is completely exact. *Full Inerrancy* is the belief that the Bible was not written as a science or historical textbook, but is phenomenological, in that it is written from the human perspective. In other words, speaking of such things as the sun rising, the four corners of the earth or the rounding off of number approximations are all from a human perspective. *Limited Inerrancy* is the belief that the Bible is meant only as a reflection of God's purposes and will, so the science and history is the understanding of the author's day, and is limited. Thus, the Bible is susceptible to errors in these areas. *Inerrancy of Purpose* is the belief that it is only inerrant in the purpose of bringing its readers to a saving faith. The Bible is not about facts, but about persons and relationships, thus, it is subject to error. *Inspired: Not Inerrant* is the belief that its authors are human and thus subject to human error. It should be noted that this author holds the position of full inerrancy.

For many today, the Bible is nothing more than a book written by men. The Bible critic believes the Bible to be full of myths and legends, contradictions, and geographical, historical, and scientific errors. University professor Gerald A. Larue had this to say, "The views of the writers as expressed in the Bible reflect the ideas, beliefs, and concepts current in their own times and are limited by the extent of knowledge in those times."[246] On the other hand, the Bible's authors claim that their writings were inspired of God, as Holy Spirit moved them along. We will discover shortly that the Bible critics have much to say, but it is inflated or empty.

---

[246] Gerald Larue, "The Bible as a Political Weapon," *Free Inquiry* (Summer 1983): 39.

2 Timothy 3:16-17 Updated American Standard Version (UASV)

16 All Scripture is inspired by God and profitable for teaching, for reproof, for correction, for training in righteousness; 17 so that the man of God may be fully competent, equipped for every good work.

2 Peter 1:21 Updated American Standard Version (UASV)

21 for no prophecy was ever produced by the will of man, but men carried along by the Holy Spirit spoke from God.

The question remains as to whether the Bible is a book written by imperfect men and full of errors, or is written by imperfect men, but inspired by God. If the Bible is just another book by imperfect man, there is no hope for humankind. If it is inspired by God and without error, although penned by imperfect men, we have the hope of everything that it offers: a rich, happy life now by applying counsel that lies within and the real life that is to come, everlasting life. This author contends that the Bible is inspired of God and free of human error, although written by imperfect humans.

Before we take on the critics who seem to sift the Scriptures looking for problematic verses, let us take a moment to reflect on how we should approach these alleged problem texts. The critic's argument goes something like this: 'If God does not err and the Bible is the Word of God, then the Bible should not have one single error or contradiction, yet it is full of errors and contradictions.' If the Bible is riddled with nothing but contradictions and errors as the critics would have us believe, why, out of 31,173 verses in the Bible, should there be only 2-3 thousand Bible difficulties that are called into question, this being less than ten percent of the whole?

First, let it be said that it is every Christian's obligation to get a deeper understanding of God's Word, just as the apostle Paul told Timothy:

1 Timothy 4:15-16 Updated American Standard Version (UASV)

15 Practice these things, be absorbed in them, so that your progress will be evident to all. 16 Pay close attention to yourself and to your teaching; persevere in these things, for as you do this you will ensure salvation both for yourself and for those who hear you.

Paul also told the Corinthians:

2 Corinthians 10:4-5 Updated American Standard Version (UASV)

⁴ For the weapons of our warfare are not of the flesh[247] but powerful to God for destroying strongholds.[248] ⁵ We are destroying speculations and every lofty thing raised up against the knowledge of God, and we are taking every thought captive to the obedience of Christ,

Paul also told the Philippians:

Philippians 1:7 Updated American Standard Version (UASV)

⁷ It is right for me to feel thus about you all, because I hold you in my heart, for you are all partakers with me of grace, both in my imprisonment and in the defense and confirmation of the gospel.

In being able to defend against the modern-day critic, one has to be able to reason from the Scriptures and overturn the critic's argument(s) with mildness. If someone were to approach us about an alleged error or contradiction, what should we do? We should be frank and honest. If we do not have an answer, we should admit such. If the text in question gives the appearance of difficulty, we should admit this as well. If we are unsure as to how we should answer, we can simply say that we will look into it and get back to them, returning with a reasonable answer.

However, we do not want to express disbelief and doubt to our critics, because they will be emboldened in their disbelief. It will put them on the offense and us on the defense. With great confidence, we can express that there is an answer. The Bible has withstood the test of 2,000 years of persecution and interrogation and yet it is the most printed book of all time, currently being translated into 2,287 languages. If these critical questions were so threatening, the Bible would not be the book that it is.

When we are pursuing the text in question, be unwavering in purpose, or resolved to find an answer. In some cases, it may take hours of digging to find the solution. Consider this: as we resolve these difficulties, we are also building our faith that God's Word is inerrant. Moreover, we will want to do preventative maintenance in our personal study. As we are doing our Bible reading, take note of these surface discrepancies and resolve them as we work our way through the Bible. We need to make this part of our prayers as well. I recommend the following program. Below are several books that deal with difficult passages. As we daily read and study our Bible from Genesis to Revelation, do not attempt it in one year; make it a four-

---

[247] That is *merely human*

[248] That is *tearing down false arguments*

year program. Use a good exegetical commentary like *The Holman Old/New Testament Commentary* (HOTC/HNTC) or *The New American Commentary* set, and *The Big Book of Bible Difficulties* by Norman L. Geisler, as well as *The Encyclopedia of Bible Difficulties* by Gleason Archer.

We should be aware that men under inspiration penned the originally written books. In fact, we do not have those originals, what textual scholars call autographs, but we do have thousands of copies. The copyists, however, were not inspired; therefore, as one might expect, throughout the first 1,400 years of copying, thousands of errors were transmitted into the texts that were being copied by imperfect hands that were not under inspiration when copying. Yet, the next 450 years saw a restoration of the text by textual scholars from around the world. Therefore, while many of our best literal translations today may not be inspired, they are a mirror-like reflection of the autographs by way of textual criticism.[249] Therefore, the fallacy could be with the copyist error that has simply not been weeded out. In addition, we must keep in mind that God's Word is without error, but our interpretation and understanding of that Word is not.

It should be noted that the Bible is made up of 66 smaller books that were hand-written over a period of 1,600 years, having some 40 writers of various trades such as shepherd, king, priest, tax collector, governor, physician, copyist, fisherman, and a tentmaker. Therefore, it should not surprise us that some difficulties are encountered as we casually read the Bible. Yet, if one were to take a deeper look, one would find that these difficulties are easily explained. Let us take a few pages to examine some passages that have been under attack.

This chapter's objective is not to be exhaustive, not even close. What we are looking to do is cover a few alleged contradictions and a couple of alleged mistakes. This is to give us a small sampling of the reasonable answers that we will find in the above recommended books. Remember, our Bible is a sword that we must use both offensively and defensively. One must wonder how long a warrior of ancient times would last who was not expertly trained in the use of his weapon. Let us look at a few scriptures that support our need to learn our Bible well so will be able to defend what we believe to be true.

---

[249] Textual criticism is the study of copies of any written work of which the autograph (original) is unknown, with the purpose of ascertaining the original text. Harold J. Green, Introduction to New Testament Textual Criticism (Peabody, MA: Hendrickson, 1995), 1.

When "false apostles, deceitful workmen, disguising themselves as apostles of Christ" were causing trouble in the congregation in Corinth, the apostle Paul wrote that under such circumstances, we are to *tear down their arguments* and *take every thought captive*. (2 Corinthians 10:4, 5; 11:13–15) All who present critical arguments against God's Word, or contrary to it, can have their arguments overturned by the Christian, who is able and ready to defend that Word in mildness. – 2 Timothy 2:24–26.

1 Peter 3:15 Updated American Standard Version (UASV)

[15] but sanctify Christ as Lord in your hearts, always being prepared to make a defense[250] to anyone who asks you for a reason for the hope that is in you; yet do it with gentleness and respect;

Peter says that we need to be prepared to make a *defense*. The Greek word behind the English 'defense' is *apologia*, which is actually a legal term that refers to the defense of a defendant in court. Our English apologetics is just what Peter spoke of, having the ability to give a reason to any who may challenge us, or to answer those who are not challenging us but who have honest questions that deserve to be answered.

2 Timothy 2:24-25 Updated American Standard Version (UASV)

[24] For a slave of the Lord does not need to fight, but needs to be kind to all, qualified to teach, showing restraint when wronged [25] with gentleness correcting those who are in opposition, if perhaps God may grant them repentance leading to accurate knowledge[251] of the truth,

Look at the Greek word (*epignosis*) behind the English "knowledge" in the above. "It is more intensive than *gnosis* (1108), knowledge because it expresses a more thorough participation in the acquiring of knowledge on the part of the learner."[252] The requirement of all of the Lord's servants is that they be able to teach, but not in a quarrelsome way, and in a way to correct his opponents with mildness. Why? Because the purpose of it all is that by God, and through the Christian teacher, one may come to repentance and begin taking in an accurate knowledge of the truth.

---

[250] Or *argument*, or *explanation*

[251] *Epignosis* is a strengthened or intensified form of *gnosis* (*epi*, meaning "additional"), meaning, "true," "real," "full," "complete" or "accurate," depending upon the context. Paul and Peter alone use *epignosis*.

[252] Spiros Zodhiates, *The Complete Word Study Dictionary: New Testament*, Electronic ed. (Chattanooga, TN: AMG Publishers, 2000, c1992, c1993), S. G1922.

Inerrancy: Practical Principles to Overcoming Bible Difficulties

Below are several ways of looking at the Bible that enable the reader to see he is not dealing with an error or contradiction, but rather a Bible difficulty.

Different Points of View

At times, you may have two different writers who are writing from two different points of view.

Numbers 35:14 Updated American Standard Version (UASV)

¹⁴ You shall give three cities across the Jordan and three cities you shall give in the land of Canaan; they will be cities of refuge.

Joshua 22:4 Updated American Standard Version (UASV)

⁴ And now Jehovah your God has given rest to your brothers, as he spoke to them; therefore turn now and go to your tents, to the land of your possession, which Moses the servant of Jehovah gave you beyond the Jordan. [on the other side of the Jordan, ESV]

Here we see that Moses is speaking about the east side of the Jordan when he says, "on this side of the Jordan." Joshua, on the other hand, is also speaking about the east side of the Jordan when he says "on the other side of the Jordan." So, who is correct? Both are. When Moses was penning Numbers the Israelites had not yet crossed the Jordan River, so the east side was "this side," the side he was on. On the other hand, when Joshua penned his book, the Israelites had crossed the Jordan, so the east side was just as he had said, "on the other side of the Jordan." Thus, we should not assume that two different writers are writing from the same perspective.

A Careful Reading

At times, it may simply be a case of needing to slow down and carefully read the account, considering exactly what is being said.

Joshua 18:28 Updated American Standard Version (UASV)

²⁸ and Zelah, Haeleph and the Jebusite (that is, Jerusalem), Gibeah, Kiriath; fourteen cities with their villages. This is the inheritance of the sons of Benjamin according to their families.

Judges 1:21 Updated American Standard Version (UASV)

²¹ But the sons of Benjamin did not drive out the Jebusites who lived in Jerusalem; so the Jebusites have lived with the sons of Benjamin in Jerusalem to this day.

Joshua 15:63 Updated American Standard Version (UASV)

⁶³ But as for the Jebusites, the inhabitants of Jerusalem, the sons of Judah could not drive them out; so the Jebusites live with the sons of Judah at Jerusalem until this day.

Judges 1:8-9 Updated American Standard Version (UASV)

⁸ And then the sons of Judah fought against Jerusalem and captured it and struck it with the edge of the sword and set the city on fire. ⁹ And afterward the sons of Judah went down to fight against the Canaanites living in the hill country and in the Negev²⁵³ and in the Shephelah.²⁵⁴

2 Samuel 5:5-9 Updated American Standard Version (UASV)

⁵ At Hebron he reigned over Judah seven years and six months, and in Jerusalem he reigned thirty-three years over all Israel and Judah.

⁶ And the king and his men went to Jerusalem against the Jebusites, the inhabitants of the land, and they said to David, "You shall not come in here, but the blind and lame will turn you away"; thinking, "David cannot come in here." ⁷ Nevertheless, David captured the stronghold of Zion, that is the city of David. ⁸ And David said on that day, "Whoever would strike the Jebusites, let him get up the water shaft to attack 'the lame and the blind,' who are hated by David's soul." Therefore it is said, "The blind and the lame shall not come into the house." ⁹ And David lived in the stronghold and called it the city of David. And David built all around from the Millo and inward.

There is no doubt that even the advanced Bible reader of many years can come away confused because the above accounts seem to be contradictory. In Joshua 18:28 and Judges 1:21, we see that Jerusalem was an inheritance of the tribe of Benjamin, yet the Benjamites were unable to conquer Jerusalem. However, in Joshua 15:63 we see that the tribe of Judah could not conquer them either, with the reading giving the impression that it was a part of their inheritance. In Judges 1:8, however, Judah was

---

²⁵³ I.e. *South*

²⁵⁴ I.e., lowland

eventually able to conquer Jerusalem and burn it with fire. Yet, to add even more to the confusion, we find at 2 Samuel 5:5–8 that David is said to have conquered Jerusalem hundreds of years later.

Now that we have the particulars let us look at it more clearly. The boundary between Benjamin's inheritances ran right through the middle of Jerusalem. Joshua 8:28 is correct, in that what would later be called the "city of David" was in the territory of Benjamin, but it also in part crossed over the line into the territory of Judah, causing both tribes to go to war against this Jebusite city. It is also true that the tribe of Benjamin was unable to conquer the city and that the tribe of Judah eventually did. However, if you look at Judges 1:9 again, you will see that Judah did not finish the job entirely and moved on to conquer other areas. This allowed the remaining ones to regroup and form a resistance that neither Benjamin nor Judah could overcome, so these Jebusites remained until the time of David, hundreds of years later.

Intended Meaning of Writer

First, the Bible student needs to understand the level that the Bible intends to be exact in what is written. If Jim told a friend that 650 graduated with him from high school in 1984, it is not challenged, because it is all too clear that he is using rounded numbers and is not meaning to be exactly precise. This is how God's Word operates as well. Sometimes it means to be exact, at other times, it is simply rounding numbers, in other cases, the intention of the writer is a general reference, to give readers of that time and succeeding generations some perspective. Did Samuel, the author of judges, intend to pen a book on the chronology of Judges, or was his focus on the falling away, oppression, and the rescue by a judge, repeatedly. Now, it would seem that Jeremiah, the author of 1 Kings was more interested in giving his readers an exact number of years.

Acts 2:41 Updated American Standard Version (UASV)

[41] So those who received his word were baptized, and there were added that day about three thousand souls.

As you can see here, numbers within the Bible are often used with approximations. This is a frequent practice even today, in both written works and verbal conversation.

Acts 7:2-3 Updated American Standard Version (UASV)

²And Stephen said:

"Brothers and fathers, hear me. The God of glory appeared to our father Abraham when he was in Mesopotamia, before he lived in Haran, ³and said to him, 'Go out from your land and from your kindred and go into the land that I will show you.'

If you were to check the Hebrew Scriptures at Genesis 12:1, you would find that what is claimed to have been said by God to Abraham is not quoted word-for-word; it is simply a paraphrase. This is a normal practice within Scripture and in writing in general.

Numbers 34:15 Updated American Standard Version (UASV)

¹⁵The two and a half tribes have received their inheritance beyond the Jordan opposite Jericho, eastward toward the sunrising."

Just as you would read in today's local newspaper, the Bible writer has written from the human standpoint, how it appeared to him. The Bible also speaks of "to the end of the earth" (Psalm 46:9), "from the four corners of the earth" (Isa 11:12), and "the four winds of the earth" (Revelation 7:1). These phrases are still used today.

Unexplained Does Not mean Unexplainable

Considering that there are 31,173 verses in the Bible, encompassing 66 books written by about 40 writers, ranging from shepherds to kings, an army general, fishermen, tax collector, a physician and on and on, and being penned over a 1,600 year period, one does find a few hundred Bible difficulties (about one percent). However, 99 percent of those are explainable. Yet no one wants to be so arrogant to say that he can explain them all. It has nothing to do with the inadequacy of God's Word but is based on human understanding. In many cases, science or archaeology and the field of custom and culture of ancient peoples has helped explain difficulties in hundreds of passages. Therefore, there may be less than one percent left to be answered, yet our knowledge of God's Word continues to grow.

Guilty Until Proven Innocent

This is exactly the perception that the critic has of God's Word. The legal principle of being "innocent until proven guilty" afforded mankind in courts of justice is withheld from the very Word of God. What is ironic here is that this policy has contributed to these Bible critics looking foolish over and over again when something comes to light that vindicates the portion of Scripture they are challenging.

Daniel 5:1 Updated American Standard Version (UASV)

[1] Belshazzar the king made[255] a great feast for a thousand of his nobles, and he was drinking wine in the presence of the thousand.

Bible critics had long claimed that Belshazzar was not known outside of the book Daniel; therefore, they argue that Daniel was mistaken. Yet it hardly seems prudent to argue error from absence of outside evidence. Just because archaeology had not discovered such a person did not mean that Daniel was wrong, or that such a person did not exist. In 1854, some small clay cylinders were discovered in modern-day southern Iraq, which would have been the city of Ur in ancient Babylonia. The cuneiform documents were a prayer of King Nabonidus for "Bel-sar-ussur, my eldest son." These tablets also showed that this "Bel-sar-ussur" had secretaries as well as a household staff. Other tablets were discovered a short time later that showed that the kingship was entrusted to this eldest son as a coregent while his father was away.

He entrusted the 'Camp' to his oldest (son), the firstborn [Belshazzar], the troops everywhere in the country he ordered under his (command). He let (everything) go, entrusted the kingship to him and, himself, he [Nabonidus] started out for a long journey, the (military) forces of Akkad marching with him; he turned towards Tema (deep) in the west."[256]

Ignoring Literary Styles

The Bible is a diverse book when it comes to literary styles: narrative, poetic, prophetic, and apocalyptic; also containing parables, metaphors, similes, hyperbole, and other figures of speech. Too often, these alleged errors are the result of a reader taking a figure of speech as literal, or reading a parable as though it is a narrative.

Matthew 24:35 Updated American Standard Version (UASV)

[35] Heaven and earth will pass away, but my words will not pass away.

---

[255] I.e., held

[256] J. Pritchard, ed., *Ancient Near Eastern Texts* (1974), 313.

If some do not recognize that they are dealing with a figure of speech, they are bound to come away with the wrong meaning. Some have concluded from Matthew 24:35 that Jesus was speaking of an eventual destruction of the earth. This is hardly the case, as his listeners would not have understood it that way based on their understanding of the Old Testament. They would have understood that he was simply being emphatic about the words he spoke, using hyperbole. What he was conveying is that his words are more enduring than heaven and earth, and with heaven and earth being understood as eternal, this merely conveyed even more so that Jesus' words could be trusted.

Two Accounts of the Same Incident

If you were to speak to officers that take accident reports for their police department, you would find that there is cohesion in the accounts, but each person has merely witnessed aspects that have stood out to them. We will see that this is the case as well with the examples below, which is the same account in two different gospels:

Matthew 8:5 Updated American Standard Version (UASV)

[5] When he[257] had entered Capernaum, a centurion came forward to him, imploring him,

Luke 7:2-3 Updated American Standard Version (UASV)

[2] And a centurion's[258] slave, who was highly regarded[259] by him, was sick and about to die. [3] When he heard about Jesus, he sent some older men of the Jews[260] asking him to come and bring his slave safely through.[261]

Immediately we see the problem of whether the centurion or the elders of the Jews spoke with Jesus. The solution is not really hidden from us. Which of the two accounts is the most detailed account? You are correct if you said, Luke. The centurion sent the elders of the Jews to represent him to Jesus, so; that whatever response Jesus might give, it would be as though he were addressing the centurion; therefore, Matthew

---

[257] That is *Jesus*

[258] I.e., army officer over a hundred solderiers

[259] Lit *to whom he was honorable*

[260] Or *Jewish elders*

[261] I.e., *save the life of his slave*

gave his readers the basic thought, not seeing the need of mentioning the elders of the Jews aspect. This is how a representative was viewed in the first century, just as some countries see ambassadors today as being the very person they represent. Therefore, both Matthew and Luke are correct.

Man's Fallible Interpretations

Inspiration by God is infallible, without error. Imperfect man and his interpretations over the centuries, as bad as many of them have been, should not cast a shadow over God's inspired Word. The entire Word of God has one meaning and one meaning only for every penned word, which is what God willed to be conveyed by the human writer he chose to use.

The Autograph Alone Is Inspired and Inerrant

It has been argued by conservative scholars that only the autograph manuscripts were inspired and inerrant, not the copying of those manuscripts over the next 3,000 years for the Old Testament and 1,500 years for the New Testament. While I would agree with this position as well, it should be noted that we do not possess the autographs, so to argue that they are inerrant is to speak of nonexistent documents. However, it should be further understood that through the science of textual criticism, we can establish a mirror reflection of the autograph manuscripts. B. F. Westcott, F. J. A. Hort, F. F. Bruce, and many other textual scholars would agree with Norman L Geisler's assessment: "The New Testament, then, has not only survived in more manuscripts than any other book from antiquity, but it has survived in a purer form than any other great book—*a form that is 99.5 percent pure.*"[262]

An example of a copyist error can be found in Luke's genealogy of Jesus at Luke 3:35–37. In verse 37 you will find a Cainan, and in verse 36 you will find a second Cainan between Arphaxad (Arpachshad) and Shelah. As one can see from most footnotes in different study Bibles, the Cainan in verse 36 is seen as a scribal error, and is not found in the Hebrew Old Testament, the Samaritan Pentateuch, or the Aramaic Targums, but is found in the Greek Septuagint. (Genesis 10:24; 11:12, 13; 1 Chronicles 1:18, but not 1 Chronicles 1:24) It seems quite unlikely that it was in the earlier copies of the Septuagint, because the first-century Jewish historian Josephus

---

[262] Norman L. Geisler and William E. Nix: *A General Introduction to the Bible* (Chicago, Moody Press, 1980), 367. (Emphasis is mine.)

lists Shelah next as the son of Arphaxad, and Josephus normally followed the Septuagint.[263] So one might ask why this second Cainan is found in the translations at all if this is the case? The manuscripts that do contain this second Cainan are some of the best manuscripts that are used in establishing the original text: 01 B L A¹ 33 (Kainam); A 038 044 0102 A¹³ (Kainan).

The Bible Was Miraculously Restored, not Miraculously Preserved

The Hebrew text was like the Greek NT; it had accumulated copyist errors, a few intentional, a good number accidental, between the Malachi days of 440 BCE and Rabbi Judah ha-Nasi (135 to 217 CE). The same thing happened to the Greek New Testament from about 400 CE to 1550 CE, a period of copyist errors. The good news is for the NT is fourfold: (1) the 144 NT papyri discovered in the early part of the 20th century, (2) a number of them dated within decades of the originals, and the great Codex Vaticanus (300-330 CE) and Codex Sinaiticus (330-360 CE), (3) that we have 5,898 Greek NT MSS; (4) then, there was the era of many dozens of textual scholars, from 1550 to the present who restored the text to its original words.

So, the Hebrew OT corruption ran in earnest between 440 BCE to 220 CE. At that time, the Greek Septuagint, a translation of the Hebrew Scriptures, was produced between 280 – 150 BCE, which became favored by the Jews to the point that they claimed it was inspired. However, the fact that the lingua franca of the Roman Empire ran from 330 BCE to 330 CE, the Christians in the first century CE wisely used the Greek Septuagint to evangelize, to show that Jesus Christ was the long-awaited Messiah. Then, Jerusalem was destroyed by General Titus and the Roman army in 70 CE, killing one million one hundred thousand Jews and carrying another seventy thousand back to Rome as slaves. No temple led to the creation of the Mishnah, an authoritative collection of exegetical material embodying the oral tradition of Jewish law and forming the first part of the Talmud. During the 150 years in the wake of the temple's destruction in Jerusalem in 70 CE, rabbinic sages throughout Israel at once were quick to seek out a new source for preserving Jewish practice. They debated and combined various traditions of their oral law. Growing this foundation, they set new

---

[263] *Jewish Antiquities,* I, 146 [vi, 4].

constraints, boundaries, and requirements for Judaism. This gave the Jewish people direction for their day-to-day life of holiness, even though they lacked a temple. This new spiritual structure was summarized in the Mishnah, which Judah ha-Nasi compiled by about 200-217 CE.

In addition, the Jewish scholars set about creating a corrected text of the Hebrew Old Testament because they realized it had some textual variants from the sopherim (scribes). But it was the greatest textual scholars who have ever lived, the Masoretes, who made corrected copies from 500 to 900 CE. Below is an article about them. The beauty is that they did not erase the manuscripts with the errors; they kept them, then simply put the corrections in the margin, called the Masorah. So, the Hebrew text was corrected just as the Greek text was. And then, in 1947, we found the Dead Sea Scrolls, which dated as early as the 3rd century BCE and validated the Masoretic text. And ironically at this same time, many of the **best** NT papyri were coming to light that validated the work of Johann Jakob Wettstein [1693-1754 A.D.], Karl Lachmann [1793-1851], Samuel Prideaux Tregelles [1813-1875], Friedrich Constantin von Tischendorf [1815-1874], and especially Westcott and Hort of 1881.

MIRACULOUS RESTORATION, NOT MIRACULOUS PRESERVATION

OLD TESTAMENT
Transmission: 1500 BCE – 440 BCE
Corruption: 440 BCE – 220 CE
Restoration: 500 – 900 CE – Present
Corroboration MSS (Dead Sea Scrolls): 1947

NEW TESTAMENT
Transmission: 45 CE – 98 CE
Corruption: 440 CE -1550 CE
Restoration: 1550 CE – Present
Corroboration MSS (NT Papyri): 1900s-1960s-Present

A Lack of <u>Preservation</u> Does Not Mean a Lack of <u>Inspiration</u>

- The Bible **was miraculously inspired** as men were moved along by the Holy Spirit (*Absolute Inerrancy*)

- The Bible **was not miraculously preserved** as men's human imperfection gave us corruption (*Limited Inerrancy*)

- The Bible **was restored** through tens of millions of hours by many hundreds of (men) textual scholars from the 16th to the 21st centuries. (*Absolute Inerrancy Restored*)

The **men who restored the text** are no more perfect than the **men who** intentionally and unintentionally **corrupted the text**. However, even hundreds of **imperfect men**, through dozens of lifetimes of sweat and toil, arrived at **a perfect text** that was lost but now is found. With the copyists, you have tens of thousands of men **focusing on their work as an individual** in reproducing a copy; with the textual scholars, it is teams of hundreds of men focusing on all of the manuscripts to ascertain the original words of the original texts.

Many of the above scholars gave their entire lives to God and the Hebrew and Greek text.[264] Each of these could have an entire book devoted to them and their work alone. The amount of work they accomplished before the era of computers is nothing short of astonishing. Rightly, the preceding history should serve to strengthen our faith in the authenticity and general integrity of the Hebrew Scriptures and the Greek New Testament. Unlike Bart D. Ehrman, men like Sir Frederic Kenyon have been moved to say that the books of the Greek New Testament have "come down to us substantially as they were written." And all this is especially true of the critical scholarship of the almost two hundred years since the days of Karl Lachmann. All today can feel confident that what they hold in their hands is a mirror reflection of the Word of God that was penned in twenty-seven books, some two thousand years ago.

It is true that the Jewish copyists and the later Christian copyists were not led along by the Holy Spirit, and therefore their manuscripts were not inerrant, infallible. Errors (textual variants) crept into the manuscripts unintentionally and intentionally. However, the vast majority of the Hebrew Old Testament and Greek New Testament has not been infected with textual errors. For the portions impacted with textual errors, it is the many tens of thousands of copies that we have to help us to weed out the errors. How? Well, not every copyist made the same textual errors. Hence, by comparing the work of different copyists and different manuscripts, textual scholars can identify the textual variants (errors) and remove those, leaving us with the original content.

---

[264] **The Climax of the Restored Text**

Yes, it would be the greatest discovery of all time if we found the actual original five books that were penned by Moses himself, Genesis through Deuteronomy. However, there would be no way of establishing that they were the originals. The fact is, we do not need the originals. We do not need those original documents. What is so important about the documents? The documents are not important; it is the content on the original documents that we are after. And truly, miraculously, we have more copies than needed to do just that. We do not need miraculous preservation because we have miraculous restoration. We now know beyond a reasonable doubt that the Hebrew Old Testament and the Greek New Testament critical texts are a 99.99% reflection of the content that was in those ancient original manuscripts. Some textual scholars might say that I am exaggerating with the 99.99%. An example of how that is not so can be found in the 1881 Westcott and Hort critical Greek NT, which is 99.5% the same as the 2012 28th edition of the critical Greek NT. The discovery of the NT papyri from the 1900s to the 1960s and up to the present has validated Westcott and Hort's Greek NT and let us know that the 2012 Nestle-Aland Greek NT is a mirror-like reflection of the original. To be frank, there are about 100+ textual variants where Westcott and Hort were correct, and the Nestle-Aland text is likely not correct. This is because they took the textual eclecticism method of determining the original, which was to focus on both external and internal evidence. Still, they leaned heavily on internal evidence, which is a bit more subjective. Regardless, we have the apparatus in the 28th edition of the Nestle-Aland that gives the translator the variants, allowing him to make an objective determination. Therefore, the 100+ textual variants can be decided on a case-by-case basis. So, yes, what we have is 99.99% reflective of the original.

The critical text of Westcott and Hort of 1881 [(FENTON JOHN ANTHONY HORT (1828 – 1892) and BROOKE FOSS WESTCOTT (1825 – 1901)] has been commended by leading textual scholars over the last one hundred and forty years, and still stands as the standard. Numerous additional critical editions of the Greek text came after Westcott and Hort: Richard F. Weymouth (1886), Bernhard Weiss (1894–1900); the British and Foreign Bible Society (1904, 1958), Alexander Souter (1910), Hermann von Soden (1911–1913); and Eberhard Nestle's Greek text, *Novum Testamentum Graece*, published in 1898 by the Württemberg Bible Society, Stuttgart, Germany. The Nestle in twelve editions (1898–1923) to subsequently be taken over by his son, Erwin Nestle (13th–20th editions, 1927–1950), followed by Kurt Aland (21st–25th editions, 1952–1963), and lastly, it was coedited by Kurt Aland and Barbara Aland (26th–28th editions, 1979, 1993, 2012).

Look at the Context

Many alleged inconsistencies disappear by simply looking at the context. Taking words out of context can distort their meaning. *Merriam-Webster's Collegiate Dictionary* defines context as "the parts of a discourse that surround a word or passage and can throw light on its meaning."[265] Context can also be "the circumstances or events that form the environment within which something exists or takes place." If we were to look in a thesaurus for a synonym, we would find "background" for this second meaning. At 2 Timothy 2:15, the apostle Paul brings home the point of why context is so important: "Do your best to present yourself to God as one approved, a worker who has no need to be ashamed, rightly handling the word of truth."

Ephesians 2:8-9 Updated American Standard Version (UASV)

[8] For by grace you have been saved through faith; and that not of yourselves, it is the gift of God; [9] not from works, so that no man may boast.

James 2:26 Updated American Standard Version (UASV)

[26] For as the body apart from the spirit[266] is dead, so also faith apart from works is dead.

So, which is it? Is salvation possible by faith alone as Paul wrote to the Ephesians, or is faith dead without works as James wrote to his readers? As our subtitle brings out, let us look at the context. In the letter to the Ephesians, the apostle Paul is speaking to the Jewish Christians who were looking to the works of the Mosaic Law as a means to salvation, a righteous standing before God. Paul was telling these legalistic Jewish Christians that this is not so. In fact, this would invalidate Christ's ransom because there would have been no need for it if one could achieve salvation by meticulously keeping the Mosaic Law. (Rom. 5:18) But James was writing to those in a congregation who were concerned with their status before other men, who were looking for prominent positions within the congregation,

---

[265] Merriam-Webster, Inc: *Merriam-Webster's Collegiate Dictionary.* Eleventh ed. (Springfield, Mass.: Merriam-Webster, Inc. 2003).

[266] Or *breath*

and not taking care of those that were in need. (Jam. 2:14–17) So, James is merely addressing those who call themselves Christian, but in name only. No person could truly be a Christian and not possess some good works, such as feeding the poor, helping the elderly. This type of work was an evident demonstration of one's Christian personality. Paul was in perfect harmony with James on this. – Romans 10:10; 1 Corinthians 15:58; Ephesians 5:15, 21–33; 6:15; 1 Timothy 4:16; 2 Timothy 4:5; Hebrews 10:23-25.

Inerrancy: Are There Contradictions?

Below I will follow this pattern. I will list the critic's argument first, followed by the text of difficulty, and conclude with an answer to the critic. What should be kept at the forefront of our mind is this: one is simply looking for the best answer, not absoluteness. If there is a reasonable answer to a Bible difficulty, why are the critics able to set them aside with ease? Because they start with the premise that this is not the Word of God, but only a book by imperfect men and full of contradictions; thus, the bias toward errors has blinded their judgment.

Critic: The critic would argue that there was an Adam and Eve, and an Abel who was now dead, so, where did Cain get his wife? This is one of the most common questions by Bible critics.

Genesis 4:17 Updated American Standard Version (UASV)

[17] Cain had sexual relations[267] with his wife and she conceived, and gave birth to Enoch; and he built a city, and called the name of the city Enoch, after the name of his son, Enoch.

Answer: If one were to read a little further along, they would come to the realization that Adam had a son named Seth; it further adds that Adam "became father to sons *and daughters*." (Genesis 5:4) Adam lived for a total of 800 years after fathering Seth, giving him ample opportunity to father many more sons and daughters. So it could be that Cain married one of his sisters. If he waited until one of his brothers and sisters had a daughter, he could have married one of his nieces once she was old enough. In the beginning, humans were closer to perfection; this explains why they lived longer and why at that time there was little health risk of genetic defects in the case of children born to closely related parents, in contrast to how it is

---

[267] Lit *knew*

today. As time passed, genetic defects increased and life spans decreased. Adam lived to see 930 years. Yet Shem, who lived after the Flood, died at 600 years, while Shem's son Arpachshad only lived 438 years, dying before his father died. Abraham saw an even greater decrease in that he only lived 175 years while his grandson Jacob was 147 years when he died. Thus, due to increasing imperfection, God prohibited the marriage of closely related people under the Mosaic Law because of the likelihood of genetic defects.—Leviticus 18:9.

Critic: If God is here hardening Pharaoh's heart, what exactly makes Pharaoh responsible for the decisions he makes?

Exodus 4:21 Updated American Standard Version (UASV)

²¹ Jehovah said to Moses, "When you go and return to Egypt see that you perform before Pharaoh all the wonders which I have put in your hand; but I will harden his heart so that he will not let the people go.

Answer: This is actually a prophecy. God knew that what he was about to do would contribute to a stubborn and obstinate Pharaoh, who was going to be unwilling to change or give up the Israelites so they could go off to worship their God. Therefore, this is not stating what God is going to do; it is prophesying that Pharaoh's heart will harden because of the actions of God. The fact is, Pharaoh allowed his own heart to harden because he was determined not to agree with Moses' wishes or accept Jehovah's request to let the people go. Moses tells us at Exodus 7:13 (ESV) that "Pharaoh's heart was hardened, and he would not listen to them, as the Lord had said." Again, at 8:15 we read, "When Pharaoh saw that there was a respite, he hardened his heart and would not listen to them, as the Lord had said."

Critic: The Israelites had just received the Ten Commandments, with one commandment being: "You shall not make for yourself a carved image or any likeness of anything that is in heaven above, or that is in the earth beneath, or that is in the water under the earth." Therefore, how is the bronze serpent not a violation of this commandment?

Numbers 21:9 Updated American Standard Version (UASV)

⁹ And Moses made a bronze serpent and set it on the standard;²⁶⁸ and it came about, that if a serpent bit any man, when he looked to the bronze serpent, he lived.

Answer: First, an idol is "a representation or symbol of an object of worship; *broadly*: a false god."²⁶⁹ Second, it should be noted that not all images are idols. The bronze serpent was not made for the purpose of worship, or for some passionate devotion or veneration. There were times, however, when images were created with absolutely no intention of it receiving devotion, veneration, or worship, yet were later made into objects of veneration. That is exactly what happened with the copper serpent that Moses had formed in the wilderness. Many centuries later, "in the third year of Hoshea son of Elah, king of Israel, Hezekiah the son of Ahaz, king of Judah, began to reign. He removed the high places and broke the pillars and cut down the Asherah. And he broke in pieces the bronze serpent that Moses had made; for until those days the people of Israel had made offerings to it (it was called Nehushtan)."—2 Kings 18:1, 4.

Critic: Deuteronomy 15:11 (NET) says: "*There will never cease to be some poor people in the land;* therefore, I am commanding you to make sure you open your hand to your fellow Israelites who are needy and poor in your land." Is this not a contradiction of Deuteronomy 15:4? Will there be no poor among the Israelites, or will there be poor among them? Which is it?

Deuteronomy 15:4 Updated American Standard Version (UASV)

⁴ However, there will be no poor among you, since Jehovah will surely bless you in the land which Jehovah your God is giving you as an inheritance to possess,

Answer: If you look at the context, Deuteronomy 15:4 is stating that if the Israelites obey Jehovah's command to take care of the poor, "there should not be any poor among" them. Thus, for every poor person, there will be one to take care of that need. If an Israelite fell on hard times, there was to be a fellow Israelite ready to step in to help him through those hard times. Verse 11 stresses the truth of the imperfect world since the rebellion of Adam and inherited sin: there will always be poor among mankind, the Israelites being no different. However, the difference with God's people is that those who were well off financially were to offset conditions for those

---

²⁶⁸ I.e., *pole*

²⁶⁹ Merriam-Webster, Inc: *Merriam-Webster's Collegiate Dictionary*. Eleventh ed. (Springfield, Mass.: Merriam-Webster, Inc., 2003).

who fell on difficult times. This is not to be confused with the socialistic welfare systems in the world today. Those Jews were hard-working men, who labored from sunup to sundown to take care of their families. But if disease overtook their herd or unseasonal weather brought about failed crops, an Israelite could sell himself into the service of a fellow Israelite for a period of time; thereafter, he would be back on his feet. And many years down the road, he may very well do the same for another Israelite, who fell on difficult times.

Critic: Joshua 11:23 says that Joshua took the land according to what God had spoken to Moses and handed it on to the nation of Israel as planned. However, in Joshua 13:1, God is telling Joshua that he has grown old and much of the Promised Land has yet to be taken possession of. How can both be true? Is this not a contradiction?

Joshua 11:23 Updated American Standard Version (UASV)

²³ So Joshua took the whole land, according to all that Jehovah had spoken to Moses, and Joshua gave it for an inheritance to Israel according to their divisions by their tribes, and the land had rest from war.

Joshua 13:1 Updated American Standard Version (UASV)

13 Now Joshua was old and advanced in years, and Jehovah said to him, "You are old and advanced in years, and there remains yet very much land to possess.

Answer: No, it is not a contradiction. When the Israelites were to take the land, it was to take place in two different stages: the nation as a whole was to go to war and defeat the 31 kings of this land; thereafter, each Israelite tribe was to take their part of the land based on their individual actions. (Joshua 17:14–18; 18:3) Joshua fulfilled his role, which is expressed in 11:23 while the individual tribes did not complete their campaigns, which is expressed in 13:1. Even though the individual tribes failed to live up to taking their portion, the remaining Canaanites posed no real threat. Joshua 21:44, *ASV,* reads: "Jehovah gave them rest round about."

Critic: The critic would point out that John 1:18 clearly says that "*no one has ever seen God,*" while Exodus 24:10 explicitly states that Moses and Aaron, Nadab and Abihu, and seventy of the elders of Israel "*saw the God of Israel.*" Worse still, God informs them in Exodus 33:20: "You cannot see my face, for man shall not see me and live." The critic with his knowing smile says, 'This is a blatant contradiction.'

John 1:18 Updated American Standard Version (UASV)

¹⁸ No one has seen God at any time; the only begotten god²⁷⁰ who is in the bosom of the Father,²⁷¹ that one has made him fully known.

Exodus 24:10 Updated American Standard Version (UASV)

¹⁰ and they saw the God of Israel; and under his feet was what seemed like a sapphire pavement, as clear as the sky itself.

Exodus 33:20 Updated American Standard Version (UASV)

²⁰ But he [God] said, "You cannot see my face, for no man can see me and live!"

Answer: Exodus 33:20 is one-hundred percent correct: No human could see Jehovah God and live. The apostle Paul at Colossians 1:15 tell us that Christ is the image of the invisible God, and the writer informs us at Hebrews 1:3 that Jesus is the "exact representation of His nature." Yet if you were to read the account of Saul of Tarsus (the apostle Paul), you would see that a mere partial manifestation of Christ's glory blinded Saul – Acts 9:1–18.

When the Bible says that Moses and others have seen God, it is not speaking of *literally* seeing him, because first of all He is an invisible spirit person. It is a *manifestation* of his glory, which is an act of showing or demonstrating his presence, making himself perceptible to the human mind. In fact, it is generally an angelic representative that stands in his place and not him personally. Exodus 24:16 informs us that "the glory of the Lord dwelt on Mount Sinai," not the Lord himself personally. When texts such as Exodus 24:10 explicitly state that Moses and Aaron, Nadab and Abihu, and seventy of the elders of Israel "*saw the God of Israel*," it is this "glory of the Lord," an angelic representative. This is shown to be the case at Luke 2:9, which reads: "And *an angel of the Lord* appeared to them, and *the glory of the Lord shone around them* [the shepherds], and they were filled with fear."

Many Bible difficulties are cleared up elsewhere in Scripture; for example, in the New Testament, you will find a text clarifying a difficulty from the Old Testament, such as Acts 7:53, which refers to those "who received the law *as delivered by angels* and did not keep it." Support comes

---

²⁷⁰ Jn 1:18: "only-begotten god", P⁶⁶ℵ*BC*Lsyrʰᵐᵍ·ᵖ; **[V1]** "the only-begotten god," P⁷⁵¹33ℵcopᵇᵒ; **[V2]** "the only-begotten Son." AC³(Wˢ)QΨf1,¹³ MajVgSyrᶜ

²⁷¹ Or *at the Father's side*

306

from Paul at Galatians 3:19: "Why then the law? It was added because of transgressions until the offspring should come to whom the promise had been made, and it was put in place through angels by an intermediary." The writer of Hebrews chimes in at 2:2 with "For since the message *declared by angels* proved to be reliable, and every transgression or disobedience received a just retribution. . . ." As we travel back to Exodus again, to 19:19 specifically, we find support that it was not God's own voice, which Moses heard; no, it was an angelic representative, for it reads: "Moses was speaking, and God was answering him with a voice." Exodus 33:22–23 also helps us to appreciate that it was the back of these angelic representatives of Jehovah that Moses saw: "While my glory passes by . . . Then I will take away my hand, and you shall see my back, but my face shall not be seen."

Exodus 3:4 states: "God called to him out of the bush, 'Moses, Moses!' And he said, 'Here I am.'" Verse 6 informs us: "I am the God of your father, the God of Abraham, the God of Isaac, and the God of Jacob." Yet, in verse 2 we read: "And the angel of the Lord appeared to him in a flame of fire out of the midst of a bush." Here is another example of using God's Word to clear up what seems to be unclear or difficult to understand at first glance. Thus, while it speaks of the Lord making a direct appearance, it is really an angelic representative. Even today, we hear such comments, as 'the president of the United States is to visit the Middle East later this week.' However, later in the article it is made clear that he is not going personally, but it is one of his high-ranking representatives. Let us close with two examples, starting with,

Genesis 32:24-30 Updated American Standard Version (UASV)

[24] And Jacob was left alone, and a man wrestled with him until daybreak. [25] When he saw that he had not prevailed against him, he touched the socket of his thigh; so the socket of Jacob's thigh was dislocated as he wrestled with him. [26] Then he said, "Let me go, for the dawn is breaking." But he said, "I will not let you go unless you bless me." [27] And he said to him, "What is your name?" And he said, "Jacob." [28] And he said, "Your name shall no longer be called Jacob, but Israel,[272] for you have struggled with God and with men and have prevailed." [29] Then Jacob asked him and said, "Please tell me your name." But he said, "Why is it that you ask my

---

[272] Meaning *he contends with God*

name?" And he blessed him there. ³⁰ So Jacob named the place Peniel,²⁷³ for he said, "I have seen God face to face, yet my soul has been preserved."

It is all too obvious here that this man is simply a materialized angel in the form of a man, another angelic representative of Jehovah God. Moreover, the reader of this book should have taken in that the Israelites as a whole saw these angelic representatives and spoke of them as though they were dealing directly with Jehovah God himself.

This proved to be the case in the second example found in the book of Judges where an angelic representative visited Manoah and his wife. Like the above mentioned account, Manoah and his wife treated this angelic representative as if he were Jehovah God himself: "And Manoah said to the angel of the Lord, 'What is your name, so that, when your words come true, we may honor you?' And the angel of the Lord said to him, 'Why do you ask my name, seeing it is wonderful?' Then Manoah knew that he was the angel of the Lord. And Manoah said to his wife, "We shall surely die, *for we have seen God*." – Judges 13:3–22.

Inerrancy: Are There Mistakes?

I have addressed the alleged contradictions, so it would seem that our job is done here, right? Not hardly. Yes, there are just as many who claim that the Bible is full of mistakes.

Critic: Matthew 27:5 states that Judas hanged himself, whereas Acts 1:18 says, "Falling headlong, he burst open in the middle and all his intestines gushed out."

Matthew 27:5 Updated American Standard Version (UASV)

⁵ And he threw the pieces of silver into the temple and departed; and he went away and hanged himself.

Acts 1:18 Updated American Standard Version (UASV)

¹⁸ (Now this man acquired a field with the price of his wickedness, and falling headlong, he burst open in the middle and all his intestines gushed out.

Answer: Neither Matthew nor Luke made a mistake. What you have is Matthew giving the reader the manner in which Judas committed suicide.

---

²⁷³ Meaning *face of God*

On the other hand, Luke is giving the reader of Acts, the result of that suicide. Therefore, instead of a mistake, we have two texts that complement each other, really giving the reader the full picture. Judas came to a tree alongside a cliff that had rocks below. He tied the rope to a branch and the other end around his neck and jumped over the edge of the cliff in an attempt at hanging himself. One of two things could have happened: (1) the limb broke plunging him to the rocks below, or (2) the rope broke with the same result, and he burst open onto the rocks below.

Critic: The apostle Paul made a mistake when he quotes how many people died.

Numbers 25:9 Updated American Standard Version (UASV)

⁹ The ones who died in the plague were twenty-four thousand.

1 Corinthians 10:8 Updated American Standard Version (UASV)

⁸ Neither let us commit sexual immorality, as some of them committed sexual immorality, only to fall, twenty-three thousand of them in one day.

Answer: We must keep in mind the above principle that we spoke of, the *Intended Meaning of the Writer*. We live in a far more precise age today, where specificity is highly important. However, we round large numbers off (even estimate) all the time: "there were 237,000 people in Time Square last night." The simplest answer is that the number of people slain was in between 23,000 and 24,000, and both writers rounded the number off. However, there is even another possibility, because the book of Numbers specifically speaks of "all the chiefs of the people" (25:4-5), which could account for the extra 1,000, which is mentioned in Numbers 24,000. Thus, you have the people killing the chiefs of the people and the plague killing the people. Therefore, both books are correct.

Critic: After 215 years in Egypt, the descendants of Jacob arrived at the Promised Land. As you recall they sinned against God and were sentenced to forty years in the wilderness. But once they entered the Promised Land, they buried Joseph's bones "at Shechem, in the piece of land that *Jacob bought* from the sons of Hamor the father of Shechem," as stated at Joshua 24:32. Yet, when Stephen had to defend himself before the Jewish religious leaders, he said that Joseph was buried "in the tomb that *Abraham had bought* for a sum of silver from the sons of Hamor." Therefore, at once it appears that we have a mistake on the part of Stephen.

Acts 7:15-16 Updated American Standard Version (UASV)

¹⁵ And Jacob went down to Egypt and died, he and our fathers. ¹⁶ And they were brought back to Shechem and buried in the tomb that Abraham had bought for a sum of silver from the sons of Hamor in Shechem.

Genesis 23:17-18 Updated American Standard Version (UASV)

¹⁷ So Ephron's field, which was in Machpelah, which faced Mamre, the field and cave which was in it, and all the trees which were in the field, that were in all its border around, were made over ¹⁸ to Abraham for a possession in the presence of the sons of Heth, before all who went in at the gate of his city.

Genesis 33:19 Updated American Standard Version (UASV)

¹⁹ And he bought the piece of land where he had pitched his tent from the hand of the sons of Hamor, Shechem's father, for one hundred qesitahs.[274]

Joshua 24:32 Updated American Standard Version (UASV)

³² As for the bones of Joseph, which the sons of Israel brought up from Egypt, they buried them at Shechem, in the piece of land that Jacob bought from the sons of Hamor the father of Shechem for one hundred qesitahs.[275] It became an inheritance of the sons of Joseph.

Answer: If we look back to Genesis 12:6-7, we will find that Abraham's first stop after entering Canaan from Haran was Shechem. It is here that Jehovah told Abraham: "To your offspring I will give this land." At this point Abraham built an altar to Jehovah. It seems reasonable that Abraham would need to purchase this land that had not yet been given to his offspring. While it is true that the Old Testament does not mention this purchase, it is likely that Stephen would be aware of such by way of oral tradition. As Acts chapter seven demonstrates, Stephen had a wide-ranging knowledge of Old Testament history.

Later, Jacob would have had difficulty laying claim to the tract of land that his grandfather Abraham had purchased, because there would have been a new generation of inhabitants of Shechem. This would have been many years after Abraham moved further south and Isaac moved to Beersheba, and including Jacob's twenty years in Paddan-aram (Gen 28:6, 7). The simplest answer is that this land was not in use for about 120

---

[274] Or *pieces of money*; money of unknown value

[275] Or *pieces of money*; money of unknown value

310

years because of Abraham's extensive travels and Isaac's having moved away, leaving it unused; likely it was put to use by others. So, Jacob simply repurchased what Abraham had bought over a hundred years earlier. This is very similar to the time Isaac had to repurchase the well at Beersheba that Abraham had already purchased earlier. – Genesis 21:27–30; 26:26–32.

Genesis 33:18–20 tells us that 'Jacob bought this land for a hundred pieces of money, from the sons of Hamor.' This same transaction is also mentioned at Joshua 24:32, in reference to transporting Joseph's bones from Egypt, to be buried in Shechem.

We should also address the cave of Machpelah that Abraham had purchased in Hebron from Ephron the Hittite. The word "tomb" is not mentioned until Joshua 24:32, and is in reference to the tract of land in Shechem. Nowhere in the Old Testament does it say that Abraham bought a "tomb." The cave of Machpelah obtained by Abraham would eventually become a family tomb, receiving Sarah's body and, eventually, his own, and those of Isaac, Rebekah, Jacob, and Leah. (Genesis 23:14–19; 25:9; 49:30, 31; 50:13) Gleason L. Archer, Jr., concludes this Bible difficulty, saying:

> The reference to a *mnema* ("tomb") in connection with Shechem must either have been proleptic [to anticipate] for the later use of that shechemite tract for Joseph's tomb (i.e., 'the tomb that Abraham bought' was intended to imply 'the tomb location that Abraham bought'); or else conceivably the dative relative pronoun *ho* was intended elliptically [omission] for *en to topo ho onesato Abraam* ("in the place that Abraham bought") as describing the location of the *mnema* near the Oak of Moreh right outside Shechem. Normally Greek would have used the relative-locative adverb *hou* to express 'in which' or 'where'; but this would have left *onesato* ("bought") without an object in its own clause, and so *ho* was much more suitable in this context. (Archer 1982, 379–81)

Another solution could be that Jacob is being viewed as a representative of Abraham, for he is the grandson of Abraham. This was quite appropriate in Biblical times, to attribute the purchase to Abraham as the Patriarchal family head.

Critic: 2 Samuel 24:1 says that God moved David to count the Israelites, while 1 Chronicles 21:1 Satan, or a resister did. This would seem to be a clear mistake on the part of one of these authors.

2 Samuel 24:1 Updated American Standard Version (UASV)

¹ Now again the anger of Jehovah burned against Israel, and it incited David against them to say, "Go, number Israel and Judah."

1 Chronicles 21:1 Updated American Standard Version (UASV)

¹ Then Satan stood up against Israel and moved David to number Israel.

Answer: In this period of David's reign, Jehovah was very displeased with Israel, and therefore he did not prevent Satan from bringing this sin on them. Often in Scripture, it is spoken of as though God did something when he allowed an event to take place. For example, it is said that God 'hardened Pharaoh's heart' (Exodus 4:21), when he actually allowed the Pharaoh's heart to harden.

Inerrancy: Are There Scientific Errors?

Many truths about God are beyond the scope of science. Science and the Bible are not at odds. In fact, we can thank modern day science as it has helped us to better under the creation of God, from our solar system to the universes, to the human body and mind. What we find is a level of order, precision, design, and sophistication, which points to a Designer, the eyes of many Christians, to an Almighty God, with infinite intelligence and power. The apostle Paul makes this all too clear, when he writes, "For his invisible attributes, namely, his eternal power and divine nature, have been clearly perceived, ever since the creation of the world, in the things that have been made. So they are without excuse." – Romans 1:20.

Back in the seventeenth century, the world-renowned scientist Galileo proved beyond any doubt that the earth was not the center of the universe, nor did the sun orbit the earth. In fact, he proved it to be the other way around (no pun intended), with the earth revolving around the sun. However, he was brought up on charges of heresy by the Catholic Church and ordered to recant his position. Why? From the viewpoint of the Catholic Church, Galileo was contradicting God's Word, the Bible. As it turned out, Galileo and science were correct, and the Church was wrong, for which it issued a formal apology in 1992. However, the point we wish to make here is that in all the controversy, the Bible was never in the wrong. It was a misinterpretation on the part of the Catholic Church and not a fault with the Bible. One will find no place in the Bible that claims the sun orbits the earth. So where would the Church get such an idea? The Church got such an idea from Ptolemy (b. about 85 C.E.), an ancient astronomer, who argued for such an idea.

As it usually turns out, the so-called contradiction between science and God's Word lies at the feet of those who are interpreting Scripture incorrectly. To repeat the sentiments of Galileo when writing to a pupil–Galileo expressed the same sentiments: "Even though Scripture cannot err, its interpreters and expositors can, in various ways. One of these, very serious and very frequent, would be when they always want to stop at the purely literal sense."[276] I believe that today's scholars, in hindsight, would have no problem agreeing.

While the Bible is not a science textbook, it is scientifically accurate when it touches on matters of science.

The Circle of the Earth Hangs on Nothing

Isaiah 40:22 Updated American Standard Version (UASV)

[22] It is he who sits above **the circle of the earth,**
   and its inhabitants are like grasshoppers;
who stretches out the heavens like a curtain,
   and spreads them like a tent to dwell in.

More than 2,500 years ago, the prophet Isaiah wrote that the earth is a circle or sphere. First, how would it be possible for Isaiah to know the earth is a circle or sphere, if not from inspiration? Scientific America writes, "As countless photos from space can attest, Earth is round–the "Blue Marble," as astronauts have affectionately dubbed it. Appearances, however, can be deceiving. Planet Earth is not, in fact, perfectly round."[277] Scientifically speaking, the sun is not perfectly, absolutely 100 percent round but in everyday speech, this verse is both acceptable and accurate, when we keep in mind it is written from a human perspective, not from a scientific perspective. Moreover, Isaiah was not discussing astronomy; he was simply making an inspired observation that man came to realize once he was in space, looking back at the earth, it is round. See the section about title, "Intended Meaning of Writer."

---

[276] Letter from Galileo to Benedetto Castelli, December 21, 1613.

[277] Charles Q. Choi (April 12, 2007). Scientific America. Strange but True: Earth Is Not Round. Retrieved Monday, August 03, 2015.

http://www.scientificamerican.com/article/earth-is-not-round/

Job 26:7 Updated American Standard Version (UASV)

⁷ "He stretches out the north over empty space
and hangs the earth on nothing.

Here the author describes the earth as hanging upon nothing. Many have never heard of the Greek mathematician and astronomer Eratosthenes. He was born in about 276 B.C.E. and received some of his education in Athens, Greece. In 240 B.C., the "Greek astronomer, geographer, mathematician and librarian Eratosthenes calculates the Earth's circumference. His data was rough, but he wasn't far off."[278] While man very early on used their God given intelligence to arrive at some outstanding conclusion that was actually very accurate, we learn two points here. Eratosthenes was a very astute scientist, while Isaiah, who wrote some 500 years earlier, was no scientist at all. Moreover, Moses, who wrote the book of Job over 1,230 years before Eratosthenes, knew that the earth hung upon nothing.

How Is the Sun Standing Still Possible?

Joshua 10:13 Updated American Standard Version (UASV)

¹³ And the sun stood still, and the moon stopped,
until the nation avenged themselves of their enemies.

Is this not written in the Book of Jashar? The sun stopped in the midst of heaven and did not hurry to set for about a whole day.

The Canaanites had besieged the Gibeonites, a group of people that gained Jehovah God's backing because they had faith in Him. In this battle, Jehovah helped the Israelites continue their attack by causing "the sun [to stand] still, and the moon stopped, until the nation took vengeance on their enemies." (Jos 10:1-14) Those who accept God as the creator of the universe and life can accept that he would know a way of stopping the earth from rotating. However, there are other ways of understanding this account. We must keep in mind that the Bible speaks from an earthly observer point of view, so it need not be that he stopped the rotation. It could have been a refraction of solar and lunar light rays, which would have produced the same effect.

Psalm 136:6 Updated American Standard Version (UASV)

⁶ to him who spread out the earth above the waters,

---

[278] Alfred, Randy (June 19, 2008). "June 19, 240 B.C.E: The Earth Is Round, and It's This Big". Wired. Retrieved Monday, August 03, 2015.

314

for his lovingkindness is everlasting;

Hebrews 3:4 Updated American Standard Version (UASV)

⁴ For every house is built by someone, but the builder of all things is God.

2 Kings 20:8-11 Updated American Standard Version (UASV)

⁸ And Hezekiah said to Isaiah, "What shall be the sign that Jehovah will heal me, and that I shall go up to the house of Jehovah on the third day?" ⁹ And Isaiah said, "This shall be the sign to you from Jehovah, that Jehovah will do the thing that he has spoken: shall the shadow go forward ten steps or go back ten steps?" ¹⁰ And Hezekiah answered, "It is an easy thing for the shadow to decline ten steps; no, but let the shadow turn backward ten steps." ¹¹ And Isaiah the prophet cried to Jehovah, and he brought the shadow on the steps back ten steps, by which it had gone down on the steps of Ahaz.

How is it that the stars fought on behalf of Barak?

Judges 5:20 Updated American Standard Version (UASV)

²⁰ From heaven the stars fought, from their courses they fought against Sisera.

Judges 4:15 Updated American Standard Version (UASV)

¹⁵ And Jehovah routed Sisera and all his chariots and all his army with the edge of the sword before Barak; and Sisera alighted from his chariot and fled away on foot.

In the Bible, you have Biblical prose, and Biblical poetry.

Prose: language that is not poetry: (1) writing or speech in its normal continuous form, without the rhythmic or visual line structure of poetry **(2)** ordinary style of expression: writing or speech that is ordinary or matter-of-fact, without embellishment.

Poetry: literature in verse: (1) literary works written in verse, in particular verse writing of high quality, great beauty, emotional sincerity or intensity, or profound insight **(2) beauty or grace:** something that resembles poetry in its beauty, rhythmic grace, or imaginative, elevated, or decorative style.

We have a beautiful example of both of these forms of writing communication in chapters four and five of the book of Judges. Judges, Chapter 4 is a prose account of Deborah and Barak, while Judges Chapter 5 is a poetic account. As we have learned from the above, poetry is less concerned with accuracy than evoking emotions. Poetry has a license to say things like what we find in of 5:20, which is in the poetry chapter: "from heaven the stars fought." This can be said, and the reader is expected not to take the language literally. What we can surmise from it though, is that God was acting against Sisera in some way, there was divine intervention.

Procedures for Handling Biblical Difficulties

1. You need to be completely convinced a reason or understanding exists.

2. You need to have total trust and conviction in the inerrancy of the Scripture as originally written down.

3. You need to study the context and framework of the verse carefully, to establish what the author meant by the words he used. In other words, find the beginning and the end of the context that your passage falls within.

4. You need to understand exegesis: find the historical setting, determine author intent, study key words, and note parallel passages. You need to slow down and carefully read the account, considering exactly what is being said

5. You need to find a reasonable harmonization of parallel passages.

6. You need to consider a variety of trusted Bible commentaries, dictionaries, lexical sources, encyclopedias, as well as books on Bible difficulties.

7. You should investigate as to whether the difficulty is a transmission error in the original text.

8. You must always keep in mind that the historical accuracy of the biblical text is unmatched; that thousands of extant manuscripts some of which date back to the second century B.C. support the transmitted text of Scripture.

9. We must keep in mind that the Bible is a diverse book when it comes to literary styles: narrative, poetic, prophetic, and apocalyptic; also containing parables, metaphors, similes, hyperbole, and other figures of

speech. Too often, these alleged errors are the result of a reader taking a figure of speech as literal, or reading a parable as though it is a narrative.

10. The Bible student needs to understand what level that the Bible intends to be exact in what is written. If Jim told a friend that 650 graduated with him from high school in 1984, it is not challenged, because it is all too clear that he is using rounded numbers and is not meaning to be precise.

Review Question

(1) What is inerrancy, and why can the Bible be trusted?

(2) What are the practical principles for overcoming Bible difficulties? (offer examples)

(3) Are There Contradictions? Explain

(4) Are There Mistakes? Explain

(5) Are There Scientific Errors? Explain

(6) Offer some evidence that points to the creative days being time periods, not literal 24-hour days.

(7) What procedures for handling Bible difficulties does this chapter end with?

Bibliography

Akin, Daniel L. *The New American Commentary: 1, 2, 3 John*. Nashville, TN: Broadman & Holman , 2001.

Akin, Daniel L., David P. Nelson, and Jr. Peter R. Schemm. *A Theology for the Church*. Nashville: B & H Publishing, 2007.

Aland, Kurt and Barbara. *The Text of the New Testament*. Grand Rapids: Eerdmans, 1987.

Alden, Robert L. *Job, The New American Commentary, vol. 11* . Nashville: Broadman & Holman Publishers, 2001.

Aldrich, C Joseph. *Lifestyle Evangelism*. Portland, OR: Multnoma Press, 1981.

Alleman, H. C., and E. E. Flack. *Old Testament Commentary*. Philadelphia: Fortress Press, 1954.

Anders, Max. *Holman New Testament Commentary: vol. 8, Galatians-Colossians* . Nashville, TN: Broadman & Holman Publishers, 1999.

—. *Holman New Testament Commentary: vol. 8, Galatians, Ephesians, Philippians, Colossians*. Nashville, TN: Broadman & Holman Publishers, 1999.

—. *Holman Old Testament Commentary - Proverbs* . Nashville: B&H Publishing, 2005.

Anders, Max, and Doug McIntosh. *Holman Old Testament Commentary - Deuteronomy (pp. 359-360)*. . Nashville: B&H Publishing, 2009.

—. *Holman Old Testament Commentary - Deuteronomy*. Nashville: B&H Publishing, 2009.

Anders, Max, and Steven Lawson. *Holman Old Testament Commentary - Psalms: 11*. Grand Rapids: B&H Publishing, 2004.

Anders, Max, and Trent Butler. *Holman Old Testament Commentary: Isaiah*. Nashiville, TN: B&H Publishing, 2002.

Anderson, Neil T. *Discipleship Counseling: The Complete Guide to Helping Others: Walk in Freedon and Gow in Christ*. Ventura: Regal Books, 2003.

Andrews, Edward D. *OVERCOMING BIBLE DIFFICULTIES: Answers to the So-Called Errors and Contradictions*. Cambridge: Christian Publishing House, 2015.

—. *THE COMPLETE GUIDE TO BIBLE TRANSLATION: Bible Translation Choices and Principles.* Cambridge: Christian Publishing House, 2012.

—. *THE EVANGELISM HANDBOOK: How All Christians Can Effectively Share God's Word in Their Community.* Cambridge: Christian Publishing House, 2013.

Andrews, Edward D. *AN INTRODUCTION TO BIBLE DIFFICULTIES So-Called Errors and Contradictions.* Cambridge: Christian Publishing House, 2011.

—. *An Introduction to Bible Difficulties: So-called Errors and Contradictions.* Cambridge, OH: Christian Publlishing House, 2012.

—. *BIBLE DIFFICULTIES: Debunking the Documentary Hypothesis.* Cambridge: Christian Publishing House, 2011.

—. *BOOKS OF 2 JOHN 3 JOHN and JUDE CPH New Testament Commentary.* Cambridge: Christian Publishing House, 2013.

—. *CHRISTIAN THEOLOGY: The Evangelism Study Tool.* Cambridge, OH: Christian Publishing House, 2016.

—. *CONVERSATIONAL EVANGELISM: Defending the Faith, Reasoning from the Scriptures, Explaining and Proving, Instructing in Sound Doctrine, and Overturning False Reasoning.* Cambridge, OH: Christian Publishing House, 2015.

—. *CRISIS OF FAITH: Saving Those Who Doubt .* Cambridge, OH: Christian Publishing House, 2015.

—. *EVIDENCE THAT YOU ARE TRULY CHRISTIAN: Keep Testing Yourselves to See If You Are In the Faith - Keep Examining Yourselves.* Cambridge, OH: Christian Publishing House, 2015.

—. *PUT OFF THE OLD PERSON WITH ITS PRACTICES And Put On the New Person.* Cambridge: Christian Publishing House, 2014.

—. *THE CHRISTIAN APOLOGIST: Always Being Prepared to Make a Defense .* Cambridge: Christian Publishing House, 2014.

—. *The Text of the New Testament: A Beginner's Guide to New Testament Textual Criticism.* Cambridge, OH: Bible-Translation.Net Books, 2012.

Andrews, Edward. *Misrepresenting Jesus: Debunking Bart D. Ehrman's Misquoting Jesus [Second Edition].* Cambridge: Christian Publishing House, 2016.

319

Andrews, Stephen J, and Robert D Bergen. *Holman Old Testament Commentary: 1-2 Samuel.* Nashville: Broadman & Holman, 2009.

Archer, Gleason L. *A Survey of Old Testament Introduction.* Chicago: Moody, 1994.

—. *Encyclopedia of Bible Difficulties.* Grand Rapids: Zondervan, 1982.

Arndt, William, Frederick W. Danker, and Walter Bauer. *A Greek-English Lexicon of the New Testament and Other Early Christian Literature. 3rd ed.* . Chicago: University of Chicago Press, 2000.

Arnold, Clinton E. *Zondervan Illustrated Bible Backgrounds Commentary Volume 2: John, Acts.* . Grand Rapids, MI: Zondervan, 2002.

—. *Zondervan Illustrated Bible Backgrounds Commentary Volume 3: Romans to Philemon.* Grand Rapids: Zondervan, 2002.

—. *Zondervan Illustrated Bible Backgrounds Commentary Volume 4: Hebrews to Revelation.* Grand Rapids, MI: Zondervan, 2002.

—. *Zondervan Illustrated Bible Backgrounds Commentary: Matthew, Mark, Luke, vol. 1.* Grand Rapids, MI: Zondervan, 2002.

Backus, William. *The Healing Power of A Christian Mind: How Biblical Truth Can Keep You Healthy.* Minneapolis: Bethany House, 1996.

—. *The Hidden Rift With God.* Minneapolis: Bethany House, 1990.

—. *What Your Counselor Never Told You.* Bloomington: Bethany House, 2000.

—. *Why Do I Do What I Don't Want To Do?* Minneapolis: Bethany House, 1984.

Backus, William, and Marie Chapian. *Telling Yourself the Truth: Find Your Way Out of Depression, Anxiety, Fear, Anger, and Other Common Problems by Applying the Principles of Misbelief* . Bloomington: Bethany House Publishers, 2000.

Baer, Daniel. *The Unquenchable Fire.* Maitland, FL: Xulon Press, 2007.

Bahnsen, Greg, and Van Til. *Apologetic* . (Phillipsburg, NJ: Presbyterian and Reformed, 1998.

Balz, Horst, and Gerhard Schneider. *Exegetical Dictionary of the New Testament.* Edinburgh: T & T Clark Ltd, 1978.

Barclay, William. *The Letter to the Hebrews (New Daily Study Bible)*. Louisville, KY: Westminster John Knox Press, 2002.

Barker, Kenneth L., and Waylon Bailey. *The New American Commentary: vol. 20, Micah, Nahum, Habakkuk, Zephaniah*. Nashville, TN: Broadman & Holman Publishers, 2001.

Barnett, Paul. *Jesus & the rise of early Christianity: a history of New Testament times*. Downer Groves: InterVarsity Press, 1999.

—. *The Birth of Christianity: The First Twenty Years (After Jesus, Vol. 1)* . Grand Rapids, MI: Wm. B. Eerdmans , 2005.

Beck, Aaron T. *LOVE IS NEVER ENOUGH: How Couples Can Overcome Misunderstandings, Resolve Conflicts, and Solve Relationship Problems Through Cognitive Therapy*. New York: Harper Perennial, 1989.

Benner, David G., and Peter C Hill. *Baker Encyclopedia of Psychology and Counseling (Second Edition)*. Grand Rapids: Baker Books, 1985, 1999.

Bercot, David W. *A Dictionary of Early Christian Beliefs*. Peabody: Hendrickson, 1998.

Black, Allen, and Mark C Black. *THE COLLEGE PRESS NIV COMMENTARY 1 & 2 PETER*. Joplin: College Press Publishing Company, 1998.

Bland, Dave. *The College Press NIV Commentary: Proverbs, Ecclesiastes & Song of Songs, .* Joplin: College Press Pub. Co., 2002.

Blenkinsopp, Joseph. *Isaiah 56-66: A New Translation with Introduction and Commentary*. New York: Anchor Bible, 2003.

Blomberg, Craig. *The New American Commentary: Matthew* . Nashville, TN : Broadman & Holman Publishers, 2001.

—. *The New American Commentary: Matthew*. Nashville, TN: Broadman & Holman Publishers, 1992.

Boa, Kenneth, and Kruidenier. *Holman New Testament Commentary: Romans*. Nashville: Broadman & Holman, 2000.

Boa, Kenneth, and William Kruidenier. *Holman New Testament Commentary: Romans*. Nashville: Broadman & Holman, 2000.

Bock, Darrell L. *Baker Exegetical Commentary on the New Testament: Luke Volume 1: 1:1-9:50*. Grand Rapids, Mich: Baker Books, 1994.

Boles, Kenneth L. *The College Press NIV commentary: Galatians & Ephesians.* Joplin, MO: College Press, 1993.

Borchert, Gerald L. *The New American Commentary: John 1-11 .* Nashville, TN: Broadman & Holman Publishers, 2001.

Borchert, Gerald L. *The New American Commentary vol. 25B, John 12–21.* Nashville: Broadman & Holman Publishers, 2002.

Boyd, Gregory A, and Paul R Eddy. *Across the Spectrum [Secon Edition].* Grand Rapids: Baker Academic, 2002, 2009.

Brand, Chad, Charles Draper, and England Archie. *Holman Illustrated Bible Dictionary: Revised, Updated and Expanded.* Nashville, TN: Holman, 2003.

Bratcher, Robert. "Inerrancy: Clearing Away Confusion." *Christianity Today,* May 29, 1981: 12.

Bratcher, Robert G., and Howard Hatton. *A Handbook on the Revelation to John.* New York: United Bible Societies, 1993.

Bridges, Jerry. *The Practice of Godliness .* Colorado Springs, CO: : NavPress, 1983.

Briley, Terry R. *The College Press NIV Commentary: Isaiah.* Joplin, MO: ollege Press Pub, 2000.

Bromiley, Geoffrey W. *The International Standard Bible Encyclopedia (Vol. 1-4).* Grand Rapids, MI: William B. Eerdmans Publishing Co., 1986.

—. *The International Standard Bible Encyclopedia.* Grand Rapids, MI: William B. Eerdmans Publishing Co., 1986.

Bromiley, Geoffry W., and Gerhard Friedrich. *Theological Dictionary of the New Testament, ed. Gerhard Kittel, vol. 4.* Grand Rapids, MI: Eerdmans, 1964-.

Brooks, James A. *The New American Commentary: Mark (Volume 23).* Nashville: Broadman & Holman Publishers, 1992.

Brotzman, Ellis R. *Old Testament Textual Criticism.* Grand Rapids: Baker Academic, 1994.

Bruce, F. F. *The New International Commentary on the New Testament: The Epistle to the Hebrews (Revised).* Grand Rapids, MI: William B. Eermans Publishing Company, 1990.

Bullinger, Ethelbert William. *Figures of Speech Used in the Bible*. London; New York: E. & J. B. Young & Co., 1898.

Burns, David D. *Feeling Good: The New Mood Therapy*. New York, NY: Avon Books, 199.

Buter, Trent C. *Holman New Testament Commentary: Luke*. Nashville, TN: Broadman & Holman Publishers, 2000.

Butler, Trent C. *Holman New Testament Commentary: Luke*. Nashville, TN: Broadman & Holman Publishers, 2000.

Butler, Trent C. *Holman Old Testament Commentary - Hosea, Joel, Amos, Obadiah, Jonah, Micah* . Nashville: Broadman & Holman Publishers, 2005.

Caba, Tedl et al.,. *The Apologetics Study Bible: Real Questions, Straight Answers, Stronger Faith*. Nashville: Holman Bible Publishers, 2007.

Cairns, Earle E. *Christianity through the Centuries*. Grand Rapids, MI: Zondervan, 1996.

Calloway, Brent A. *THE BOOK OF JAMES: CPH CHRISTIAN LIVING COMMENTARY*. Cambridge: Chriwstian Publishing House, 2015.

Cameron, Kirk, and Ray Comfort. *The School of Biblical Evangelism: 101 Lessons: How to Share Your Faith Simply, Effectively, Biblically—the Way Jesus Did*. Gainesville, FL: Bridge-Logos Publishers, 2004.

Campbell, Alexander. *The Christian System (6th ed.;*. Cincinnati: Standard, 1850.

Carson, D. A. *The Gospel According to John*. Grand Rapids, MI: William B. Eerdmans Publishing Company, 1991.

Carson, D. A, and Douglas J Moo. *An Introduction to the New Testament*. Grand Rapids, MI: Zondervan, 2005.

Carson, D. A. *New Bible Commentary: 21st Century Edition. 4th ed.* Downers Grove: Inter-Varisity Press, 1994.

Clinton, Tim, and George Ohlschlager. *Complete Christian Counseling: Foundations & Practice of Compassionate Soul Care*. Colorado Springs: WaterBrook Press, 2008.

Clinton, Tim, Archibald Hart, and George Ohlschlager. *Caring For People God's Way: Personal and Emotional Issues, Addictions, Grief and Trauma.* Nashville: Thomas Nelson, Inc., 2005.

Coleman, E. Robert. *The Master Plan of Evangelism.* Westwood, NJ: Fleming H. Revell Company, 1964.

Collins, John. *Genesis 1-4: A Linguistic, Literary, and Theological Commentary.* Philipsburg: P&R, 2006.

Comfort, Philip. *Encountering the Manuscripts: An Introduction to New Testament Paleography and Textual Criticism.* Nashville: Broadman & Holman, 2005.

—. *Encounterring the Manuscripts: An Introduction to New Testament Paleography and Textual Criticism.* Nashville: Broadman & Holman, 2005.

Comfort, Philip W. *New Testament Text and Translation Commentary.* Carol Stream: Tyndale House Publishers, 2008.

Comfort, Philip, and David Barret. *The Text of the Earliest New Testament Greek Manuscripts.* Wheaton: Tyndale House Publishers, 2001.

Cooper, Lamar Eugene. *The New American Commentary, Ezekiel, vol. 17.* Nashville, TN: Broadman & Holman Publishers, 1994.

Cooper, Rodney. *Holman New Testament Commentary: Mark.* Nashville: Broadman & Holman Publishers, 2000.

Cornwall, Judson, and Stelman Smith. *The Exhaustive Dictionary of Bible Names.* Gainsville: Bridge-Logos, 1998.

Cottrell, Peter, and Maxwell Turner. *Linguistics and Biblical Interpretation.* Downers Grove: InterVarsity Press, 1989.

Cruse, C. F. *Eusebius' Eccliatical History.* Peabody, MA: Hendrickson, 1998.

Davis, John J. *Paradise to Prison: Studies in Genesis.* Salem: Sheffield, 1975.

Dockery, David S. *HOLMAN CONCISE BIBLE COMMENTARY Simple, straightforward commentary on every book of the Bible.* Nashville: Broadman & Holman, 1998.

Easley, Kendell H. *Holman New Testament Commentary, vol. 12, Revelation.* (Nashville, TN: Broadman & Holman Publishers, 1998.

Easton, M. G. *Easton's Bible Dictionary.* Oak Harbor, WA: Logos Research Systems, 1996, c1897.

Ehrman, Bart D. *Misquoting Jesus: The Story Behind Who Changed the Bible and Why.* New York: Harper One, 2005.

Eims, LeRoy. *One to One Evangelism.* Wheaton, IL: Victor Books, 1974, 1990.

Ellingworth, Paul. *The Epistle to the Hebrews: A Commentary on the Greek Text.* Grand Rapids, MI: W.B. Eerdmans, 1993.

Elliott, Charles. *Delineation Of Roman Catholicism: Drawn From The Authentic And Acknowledged Standards Of the Church Of Rome, Volume II.* New York: George Lane, 1941.

Elwell, Walter A. *Baker Encyclopedia of the Bible.* Grand Rapids: Baker Book House, 1988.

—. *Evangelical Dictionary of Theology (Second Edition).* Grand Rapids: Baker Academic, 2001.

Elwell, Walter A, and Philip Wesley Comfort. *Tyndale Bible Dictionary.* Wheaton, Ill: Tyndale House Publishers, 2001.

Enns, Paul P. *The Moody Handbook of Theology.* Chicago: Moody Press, 1997.

Erickson, Millard J. *The Concise Dictionary of Christian Theology.* Wheaton: Crossway Books, 2001.

Erickson, Milliard J. *Christian Theology (Third Edition).* Grand Rapids, MI: Baker Academic, 2013.

—. *Christian Theology.* Grand Rapids, MI: Baker Academic, 1998.

Ferguson, Everett. *Backgrounds of Early Christianity.* Grand Rapids, MI: Wm. B. Eerdmans, 2003.

—. *Baptism in the Early Church: History, Theology, and Liturgy in the First Five Centuries.* Grand Rapids, MI: Eerdmans, 2009.

Fields, Lee M. *Hebrew For The Rest of Us: Using Hebrew Tools Without Mastering Biblical Hebrew.* Grand Rapids, MI: Zondervan, 2008.

Finney, Paul Corby. *Art, Archaeology, and Architecture of Early Christianity.* New York: Garland, 1993.

Frame, John M. *Apologetics to the Glory of God.* Phillipsburg: P&R Publishing, 1994.

Friberg, Timothy, Barbara Friberg, and Neva F. Miller. *Analytical Lexicon of the Greek New Testament.* Grand Rapids: Baker Books, 2000.

—. *Analytical Lexicon of the Greek New Testament, Baker's Greek New Testament Library.* Grand Rapids, MI: Baker Books, 2000.

Friedman, Richard Elliot. *Who Wrote The Bible.* San Francisco: Harper Collins, 1997.

Friedman, Richard Elliott. *The Bible With Sources Revealed.* Northampton: Harper Collins, 2005.

Gamble, Henry Y. *Books and Readers in the Early Church: A History of Early Christian Texts.* New Haven: New Haven University Press, 1995.

Gangel, Kenneth O. *Holman New Testament Commentary: Acts.* Nashville, TN: Broadman & Holman Publishers, 1998.

Gangel, Kenneth O. *Holman New Testament Commentary, vol. 4, John .* Nashville, TN: Broadman & Holman Publishers, 2000.

—. *Holman Old Testament Commentary: Daniel.* Nashville: Broadman & Holman Publishers, 2001.

Garland, David E. *1 Corinthians, Baker Exegetical Commentary on the New Testament.* Grand Rapids, MI: : Baker Academic, 2003.

Garrett, Duane A. *Proverbs, Ecclesiastes, Song of Songs, The New American Commentary, vol. 14.* Nashville: Broadman & Holman Publishers, 1993.

Garrett, Duane. *Rethinking Genesis: The Sources and Authorship of the First Book of the Pentateuch .* Grand Rapids: Baker Books, 1991.

Geisler, Norman L. *Systematic Theology in One Volume.* Minneapolis, MN: Bethany House, 2011.

—. *SYSTEMATIC THEOLOGY: God and Creation (Vol. 2).* Minneapolis: Baker Publishing Group, 2003.

Geisler, Norman L, and William E Nix. *A General Introduction to the Bible.* Chicago: Moody Press, 1996.

Geisler, Norman L., and Thomas Howe. *The Big Book of Bible Difficulties.* Grand Rapids: Baker Books, 1992.

Geisler, Norman, and David Geisler. *CONVERSATION EVANGELISM: How to Listen and Speak So You Can Be Heard.* Eugene: Harvest House Publishers, 2009.

——. *CONVERSATION EVANGELISM: How to Listen and Speak So You Can Be Heard.* Eugene: Harvest House Publishers, 2014.

Geisler, Norman, and Ron Brooks. *When Skeptics Ask* . Grand Rapids, MI: Baker Books, 1996.

George, Timothy. *The New American Commentary: Galatians* . Nashville, TN: Broadman & Holman Publishers, 2001.

Green, Joel B, Scot McKnight, and Howard Marshall. *Dictionary of Jesus and the Gospels.* Downers Grove, IL: InterVarsity Press, 1992.

Greenlee, J Harold. *Introduction to New Testament Textual Criticism.* Peabody: Hendrickson, 1995.

Grudem, Wayne. *Making Sense of the Bible: One of Seven Parts from Grudem's Systematic Theology (Making Sense of Series).* Grand Rapids: Zondervan, 2011.

Grudem, Wayne, Leland Ryken, John C Collins, Vern S Poythress, and Bruce Winter. *Translating Truth: The Case for Essentially Literal Bible Translation.* Wheaton: Crossway Books, 2005.

Gruden, Wayne. *Are Miraculous Gifts for Today?: 4 Views (Counterpoints: Bible and Theology).* Grand Rapids: Zondervan, 2011.

Gunkel, Hermann. *The Stories of Genesis. Translated by John J. Scullion. Edited by William R. Scott.* Berkeley: BIBAL, 1994.

Guthrie, Donald. *Introduction to the New Testament (Revised and Expanded).* Downers Grove, IL: InterVarsity Press, 1990.

Guthrie, George H. *The NIV Application Commentary: Hebrews.* Grand Rapids, MI: Zondervan, 1998.

Hall, Donald P. *Breaking Through Depression: A Biblical and Medical Approach to Emotional Wholeness* . Eugene: Harvest House Publishers, 2009.

Harley, Willard F. Jr. *His Needs, Her Needs: Building an Affair-Proof Marriage.* Grand Rapids, MI: Revell, 2011.

Harris, Robert Laird, Gleason Leonard Archer, and Bruce K Waltke. *Theological Wordbook of the Old Testament.* Chicago: Moody Press, 1999, c1980.

Harrison, R. K. *Introduction to the Old Testament.* Massachusetts: Hendrickson, 2004.

Hastings, James, John A Selbie, and John C Lambert. *A Dictionary of Christ and the Gospels.* New York, NY: Charles Scribner's Sons, 1907.

Hill, Charles E., and Michael J. Kruger. *The Early Text of the New Testament.* Oxford: Oxford University Press, 2012.

Hill, Jonathan. *Zondervan Handbook to the History of Christianity.* Oxford: Lion, 2006.

Hindson, Ed, and Ergun Caner. *The Popular Encyclopedia of Apologetics: Surveying the Evidence for the Truth of Christianity.* Eugene: Harvest House, 2008.

Hoerth, Alfred. *Archaeology and the Old Testament.* Grand Rapids: Baker, 1998.

House, Paul R. *The New American Commentary: 2 Kings .* Nashville: Broadman & Holman Publishers, 2001.

House, Paul R., and Eric Mitchell. *Old Testament Survey (2nd Edition).* Nashville, TN: B&H Publishing Group, 2007.

Kaiser Jr., Walter C. *The Old Testament Documents: Are They Reliable & Relevant?* Downer Groves: InterVarsity Press, 2001.

Kass, Leon R. *The Beginning of Wisdom: Reading Genesis.* New York: Free Press, 2003.

Keener, Craig S. *The IVP Bible Background Commentary: New Testament.* Downer Groves, IL: InterVarsity Press, 1993.

Keil, Carl Friedrich, and Franz Delitzsch. *Commentary on the Old Testament.* Peabody, MA: Hendrickson, 2002.

—. *Commentary on the Old Testament.* Peabody, MA: Hendrickson, 1996.

Kennedy, D. James. *Evangelism Explosion.* Wheaton, IL: Tyndale House Publishers, 1977.

Kenneth, Boa., and Kruidenier. *Holman New Testament Commentary: Romans, Vol. 6.* Nashville, TN: Broadman & Holman, 2000.

—. *Romans: Holman New Testament Commentary.* Nashville: Broadman & Holman, 2000.

Killen, W. D. *The Ancient Church: Its History, Doctrine, Worship, and Constitution, Traced for the First Three Hundred Years (Reprint).* London: Forgotten Books, 1883, 2012.

Kissling, Paul J. *The College Press NIV commentary: Genesis*. Joplin, MO: College Press Pub. Co., 2004.

Kistemaker, Simon J, and William Hendriksen. *New Testament Commentary: Exposition of the Acts of the Apostles*. Grand Rapids, MI: Baker Book House, 1953-2001.

—. *New Testament Commentary: vol. 15, Exposition of Hebrews*. Grand Rapids: Baker Book House, 1953-2001.

Kitchen, K A. *On the Reliability of the Old Testament*. Grand Rapids: Eerdmans, 2003.

—. *The Ancient Orient and the Old Testament*. Chicago: Tyndale Press, 1966.

Kitchen, K. A. *Ancient Orient and Old Testament*. Downers Grove, IL: InterVarsity Press, 1975.

Kittel, Gerhard, Gerhard Friedrich, and Geoffrey William Bromiley. *Theological Dictionary of the New Testament*. Grand Rapids: Eerdmans, 1995, c1985.

Knight, George W. *The Pastoral Epistles: A Commentary on the Greek Text, New International Greek Testament Commentary*. Grand Rapids, MI; Carlisle, England: W.B. Eerdmans; Paternoster Press, 1992.

Koehler, Ludwig. "Problem in the Study in the Language of the Old Testament." *Journal of Semitic Studies*, 1956: 3-24.

Koehler, Ludwig, Walter Baumgartner, M E J Richardson, and Johann Jakob Stamm. *The Hebrew and Aramaic Lexicon of the Old Testament*. Leiden; New York: E. J. Brill, 1999.

Kollar, Charles Allen. *Solution-Focused Pastoral Counseling: An Effective Short-Term Approach for Getting People Back on Track*. Grand Rapids: Zondervan, 1997.

Language, John Peter. *A Commentary on the Holy Scriptures: Genesis*. Bellingham: Logos Research Systems, 1939, 2008.

Larsen, L. David. *The Evangelism Mandate*. Wheaton: Crossway Books, 1992.

Larson, Knute. *Holman New Testament Commentary, vol. 9, I & II Thessalonians, I & II Timothy, Titus, Philemon*. Nashville, TN: Broadman & Holman Publishers, 2000.

Lasor, William Sanford, David Allan Hubbard, and Frederic Williams Bush. *The Message, Form, and Background of the Old Testament: Old Testament Survey (2nd ed.).* Grand Rapids: Wm. B. Eerdmans, 1996.

Lea, Thomas D. *Holman New Testament Commentary: Hebrews, James.* Nashville, TN: Broadman & Holman Publishers, 1999.

—. *Holman New Testament Commentary: Vol. 10, Hebrews, James.* Nashville, TN: Broadman & Holman Publishers, 1999.

Lea, Thomas D., and Hayne P. Griffin. *The New American Commentary, vol. 34, 1, 2 Timothy, Titus.* Nashville: Broadman & Holman Publishers, 1992.

Lenski, R. C. H. *The Interpretation of St. John's Gospel.* Minneapolis: Augsburg Fortress, 1942, 2008.

Lenski, R. C. H. *Interpretation of the I & II Epistles of Peter the Three Epistles of John, and the Epistle of Jude.* Minneapolis: Augsburg Fortress, 1945, 2008.

—. *The Interpretation of The Acts of the Apostles.* Minneapolis, MN: Ediciones Sigueme, 1961.

Lightfoot, Neil R. *How We Got the Bible.* Grand Rapids, MI: Baker Books, 1963, 1988, 2003.

Little, Paul E. *Know What You Believe .* Downers Grove. ILL: InterVarsity Press, 2008.

Longman III, Tremper. *How to Read Genesis.* Downers Groves, IL: Intervarsity Press, 2005.

Longman, Tremper III. *Reading the Bible: With Heart & Mind.* Colorado Springs: NavPress, 1997.

Longman, Tremper III, and Raymond B Dillard. *An Introduction to the Old Testament.* Grand Rapids: Zondervan, 2006.

Louw, Johannes P, Eugene A Nida, Smith. Rondal B, and Karen A Munson. *GREEK-ENGLISH NEW TESTAMENT Based on Semantic Domains (Vol. 1, Second Edition).* New York: United Bible Societies, 1988, 1989.

MacArthur, John. *The MacArthur Bible Commentary.* Nashville: Thomas Nelson, 2005.

Machen, J. Gresham. "Christianity and Culture." *Princeton Theological Review*, 1913: 7.

Marshall, Thomas. *BOOK OF PHILIPPIANS (CPH New Testament Commentary 11)*. Cambridge: Christian Publishing House, 2014.

Martin, D Michael. *The New American Commentary 33 1, 2 Thessalonians*. Nashville, TN: Broadman & Holman, 2001, c1995.

Martin, Glen S. *Holman Old Testament Commentary: Numbers*. Nashville: Broadman & Holman Publishers, 2002.

Mathews, K. A. *The New American Commentary vol. 1A, Genesis 1-11:26*. Nashville: Broadman & Holman Publishers, 2001.

Matthews, K. A. *The New American Commentary Vol. 1B, Genesis 11:27-50:26*. Nashville: Broadman and Holman Publishers, 2001.

Mayers, Mark K. *Christianity Confronts Culture: A Strategy for Crosscultural Evangelism*. Grand Rapids : Zondervan, 1987.

McCue, Rolland. *Promises Unfulfilled: The Failed Strategy of Modern Evangelism*. Greenville, SC: Ambassador Group, 2004.

Mcgrath, Alister E. *Christian Theology: An Introduction*. Malden, MA: Blackwell, 2001.

McGrath, Alister. "Why Evangelicalism is the Future of Protestantism." *Christianity Today*, June 19, 1995: 18-23.

McMinn, Mark R. *Psychology, Theology, and Spirituality in Christian Counseling (AACC Library)*. Carol Stream, IL: Tyndale House Publishers, 2010.

McRaney, William. *The Art of Personal Evangelism*. Nashville: Broadman & Holman, 2003.

McReynolds, Paul R. *Word Study: Greek-English*. Carol Stream: Tyndale House Publishers, 1999.

Melick, Richard R. *The New American Commentary: Philippians, Colossians, Philemon, electronic ed., Logos Library System*. Nashville: Broadman & Holman Publishers, 2001.

—. *The New American Commentary: vol. 32, Philippians, Colissians, Philemon*. Nashville, TN : Broadman & Holman Publishers, 2001.

Metzger, Bruce M. *The Text of the New Testament: Its Transmission, Corruption, and Transmission*. New York: Oxford University Press, 1964, 1968, 1992.

Metzger, Bruce M. *A Textual Commentary on the Greek New Testament*. New York: United Bible Society, 1994.

Microsoft. *Encarta ® World English Dictionary*. Redmond: Microsoft Corporation, 1998-2010.

Miller, Stephen R. *The New American Commentary: Volume 18 Daniel*. Nashville: Broadman & Holman Publishers, 1994.

Mirriam-Webster, Inc. *Mirriam-Webster's Collegiate Dictionary. Eleventh Edition*. Springfield: Mirriam-Webster, Inc., 2003.

Morgenthaler, Sally. *Worship Evangelism*. Grand Rapids: Zondervan Publishing House, 1995.

Morris, Henry M. *The Genesis Record: A Scientific and Devotional Commentary on the Book of the Beginnings*. Grand Rapids: Baker Books, 2007, 1976.

Morris, Leon. *The Gospel According to Matthew*. Grand Rapids, MI: Inter-Varsity Press, 1992.

Mounce, Robert H. *Romans: The New American Commentary 27*. Nashville: Broadman & Holman, 2001, c1995.

Mounce, Robert H. *The New American Commentary: Vol. 27 Romans*. Nashville, TN: Broadman & Holman Publishers, 2001.

Mounce, William D. *Mounce's Complete Expository Dictionary of Old & New Testament Words*. Grand Rapids, MI: Zondervan, 2006.

Mounce, William D. *Basics of Biblical Greek Grammar*. Grand Rapids: Zonervan, 2009.

Myers, Allen C. *The Eerdmans Bible Dictionary* . Grand Rapids, Mich: Eerdmans, 1987.

Niessen, Richard. "The virginity of the `almah in Isaiah 7:14." *Bibliotheca Sacra 137* , 1980: 133-50.

Oden, Thomas C. *Ministry Through Word and Sacrament, Classic Pastoral Care*. New York: Crossroad, 1989.

Ortberg, John. *The Life You've Always Wanted: Spiritual Disciplines for Ordinary People*. Grand Rapids, MI: Zondervan, 2002.

Oswalt, John N. *The NIV Application Commentary: Isaiah.* Grand Rapids, MI: Zondervan, 2003.

Outlaw, W. Stanley. *The Book of Hebrews* . Nashville, TN: Randall House, 2005.

Packer, J. I. *Evangelism and Sovereignty of God.* Downers Grove, Il: InterVarsity Press, 1961.

Packer, J. I. *Evangelism and the Sovereignty of God.* Downers Grove, IL: InterVarsity Press, 1979.

Pink, Arthur Walkington. *An Exposition of Hebrews.* Swengel, PA: Bible Truth Depot, 1954.

Polhill, John B. *The New American Commentary 26: Acts.* Nashville: Broadman & Holman Publishers, 2001.

Posterski, C. Donald. *Reinventing Evangelism.* Downers Grove, IL: InterVarsity Press, 1989.

Powell, Doug. *Holman QuickSource Guide to Christian Apologetics.* Nashville, TN: Holman Reference, 2006.

Pratt Jr, Richard L. *Holman New Testament Commentary: I & II Corinthians, vol. 7.* Nashville: Broadman & Holman Publishers, 2000.

Pratt Jr, Richard L. *I & II Corinthians, vol. 7, Holman New Testament Commentary* . Nashville, TN: , 2000: Broadman & Holman Publishers, 2000.

Rainer, S. Thomas. *Evangelism in the Twenty-First Century.* Wheaton, IL: Harold Shaw Publishers, 1989.

Rainer, Thom S. *Surprising Insights From the Unchurched and Proven Ways to Reach Them.* Grand Rapids, MI: Zondervan, 2001.

Ramsey, Boniface (Editor). *Manichean Debate (Works of Saint Augustine).* New City Press: Hyde Park, 2006.

Reid, Alvin. *Introduction to Evangelism.* Nashville: Boardman & Holmes , 1998.

Reid, Alvin L. *Radically Unchurched: Who They are and How to Reach Them.* Grand Rapids: Kregel, 2002.

Reyburn, William David, and Euan Mc G. Fry. *A Handbook on Genesis (UBS Handbook Series).* New York: United Bible Societies, 1997.

Richards, E. Randolph. *Paul And First-Century Letter Writing: Secretaries, Composition and Collection.* Downers Grove: InterVarsity Press, 2004.

Richardson, Kurt. *The New American Commentary Vol. 36 James.* Nashville: Broadman & Holman Publishers, 1997.

Roberts, Alexander, James Donaldson, and Cleveland Coxe. *The Ante-Nicene Fathers Vol.I: Translations of the Writings of the Fathers Down to A.D. 325.* Oak Harbor: Logos, 1997.

Robertson, A. T. *An Introduction to the Textual Criticism of the New Testament.* London: Hodder & Stoughton, 1925.

Robertson, A.T. *Word Pictures in the New Testament.* Oak Harbor, MI: Logos Research Systems, 1933, 1997.

Robertson, Paul E. "Theology of the Healthy Church." *The Theological Educator: A Journal of Theology and Ministry,* Spring 1998: 45-52.

Rooker, Mark F. *Leviticus: The New American Commentary.* Nashville: Broadman & Holman, 2001.

Rooker, Mark F. *Holman Old Testament Commentary: Ezekiel.* Nashville: Broadman & Holman Publishers, 2005.

Ryken, Leland. *Choosing a Bible: Understanding Bible Translation Differences.* Wheaton: Crossway Books, 2005.

—. *The Word of God in English.* Wheaton: Crossway Books, 2002.

—. *Understanding English Bible Translation: The Case for an Essentially Literal Approach.* Wheaton, IL: Crossway Books, 2009.

Ryrie, Charles C. *Basic Theology.* Chicago, IL: Moody Press, 1999.

Schaeffer, Francis A. *Genesis in Space and Time: The Flow of Biblical History.* Downers Groves: Intervarsity Press, 1972.

Schreiner, Thomas R. *The New American Commentary: 1, 2 Peter, Jude.* Nashville: Broadman & Holman, 2003.

Sisson, Dick. *Evangelism Encounter.* Chicago, IL: Victor Books, 1988.

Smith, Gary. *The New American Commentary: Isaiah 1-39, Vol. 15a.* Nashville, TN: B & H Publishing Group, 2007.

—. *The New American Commentary: Isaiah 40-66, Vol. 15b.* Nashville, TN: B&H Publishing, 2009.

Smyth, Herbert. *Greek Grammar for Colleges* . New York: American Book Company, 1916.

Souter, Alexander. *The Text and Canon of the New Testament.* New York: Charles Scribner's Sons, 1913.

Speiser, E. A. *Genesis Anchor Bible 1.* Garden City: Doubleday, 1964.

Sproul, R.C. *Knowing Scripture.* . Downers Grove, IL: Intervarsity Press, 1978.

Stein, Robert H. *A Basic Guide to Interpreting the Bible: Playing by the Rules.* Grand Rapids: Baker Books, 1994.

—. *The New American Commentary: Luke.* Nashville, TN: Broadman & Holman , 2001, c1992.

Stuart, Douglas K. *The New American Commentary: An Exegetical Theological Exposition of Holy Scripture EXODUS.* Nashville: Broadman & Holman, 2006.

Swanson, James. *A Dictionary of Biblical Languages - Greek.* Washington: Logos Research Systems, 1997.

Sweeney, Z. T. *The Spirit and the Word (: , n.d.), 121–26.* Nashville: Gospel Advocate, 2005.

Swenson, Richard A. *Margin: Restoring Emotional, Physical, Financial, and Time Reserves to Overloaded Lives.* Colorado Springs: Nav Press, 2004.

Swindoll, Charles R, and Roy B. Zuck. *Understanding Christian Theology.* Nashville, TN: Thomas Nelson Publishers, 2003.

Terry, Milton S. *Biblical Hermeneutics: A Treatise on the Interpretation of the Old and New Testaments.* Grand Rapids: Zondervan, 1883.

Thomas, Robert L. *New American Standard Hebrew-Aramaic and Greek Dictionaries: Updated Edition.* Anaheim: Foundation Publications, Inc., 1998, 1981.

—. *Revelation 1-7: An Exegetical Commentary* . Chicago, IL: Moody Publishers, 1992.

—. *Revelation 8-22: An Exegetical Commentary* . Chicago, IL: Moody Publishers, 1995.

Thomas, Robert L., and F. David Farnell. *THE JESUS CRISIS: The Inroads of Historical Criticism in Evagelical Scholarship.* Grand Rapids, MI: Kregel Publications, 1998.

Torrey, Reuben A., and Edward D. Andrews. *DIFFICULTIES IN THE BIBLE Alleged Errors and Contradictions: Updated and Expanded Edition.* Cambridge: Christian Publishing House, 2012.

Towns, Elmer L. *Concise Bible Dictrines: Clear, Simple, and Easy-to-Understand Explanations of Bible Doctrines.* Chattanooga: AMG Publishers, 2006.

—. *Theology for Today.* Belmont: Wadsworth Group, 2002.

Tozer, A.W. *The Pursuit of God: The Human Thirst for the Divine.* Camp Hill, PA: Christian Publications, Inc., 1993.

Vine, W E. *Vine's Expository Dictionary of Old and New Testament Words.* Nashville: Thomas Nelson, 1996.

Wallace, Daniel. *Greek Grammar Beyond the Basics.* Grad Rapids: Zondervan, 1996.

Walls, David, and Max Anders. *Holan New Testament Commentary I & II Peter, I, II & III John, Jude.* Nashville: Broadman & Holman Publishers, 1999.

—. *Holman New Testament Commentary: I & II Peter, I, II & III John, Jude.* Nashville: Broadman & Holman Publishers, 1996.

Walton, John H. *Zondervan Illustrated Bible Backgrounds Commentary (Old Testament) Volume 1: Genesis, Exodus, Leviticus, Numbers, Deuteronomy.* Grand Rapids, MI: Zondervan, 2009.

—. *Ancient Near Eastern Thought and the Old Testament.* Grand Rapids: Baker Academic, 2006.

Walton, John H. "Isaiah 7:14: what's in a name?" *Journal of the Evangelical Theological Society 30*, 1987: 289-306.

—. *Zondervan Illustrated Bible Backgrounds Commentary (Old Testament) Volume 3: 1 & 2 Kings, 1 & 2 Chronicles, Ezra, Nehemiah, Esthe.* Grand Rapids, MI: Zondervan, 2009.

—. *Zondervan Illustrated Bible Backgrounds Commentary (Old Testament) Volume 5: The Minor Prophets, Job, Psalms, Proverbs, Ecclesiastes, Song of Songs.* Grand Rapids, M: Zondervan, 2009.

Walton, John H. *THE NIV APPLICATION COMMENTARY Genesis.* Grand Rapids: Zondervan, 2001.

Walton, John H., Victor H. Matthews, and Mark W Chavalas. *The IVP Bible Background Commentary: Old Testament.* Downers Grove: IVP Academic, 2000.

Watson, Richard. *A Biblical and Theological Dictionary: Explanatory of the History, Manners and Customs of the Jews.* New York: Waugh and T. Mason, 1832.

Weatherly, Jon A. *THE COLLEGE PRESS NIV COMMENTARY: 1 & 2 Thessalonians.* Joplin: College Press Publishing Company, 1996.

Weber, Stuart K. *Holman New Testament Commentary, vol. 1, Matthew.* Nashville, TN: Broadman & Holman Publishers, 2000.

Wegner, Paul D. *A Student's Guide to Textual Criticism of the Bible: Its History Methods & Results.* Downers Grove: InterVarsity Press, 2006.

Westcott, B. F., and Hort F. J. A. *The New Testament in the Original Greek, Vol. 2: Introduction, Appendix.* London: Macmillan and Co., 1882.

Whiston, William. *The Works of Josephus.* Peabody, MA: Hendrickson, 1987.

Whitney, Donald S. *Spiritual Disciplines for the Christian Life with Bonus Content (Pilgrimage Growth Guide).* Colorado Springs, CO: Navpress, 1991.

Wolf, Herbert M. "Solution to the Immanuel Prophecy in Isaiah 7:14-8:22." *Journal of Biblical Literature 91* , 1972: 449-56.

Wood, D R W. *New Bible Dictionary (Third Edition).* Downers Grove: InterVarsity Press, 1996.

Wright, N. T. *Hebrews for Everyone.* London: Westminster John Knox Press, 2003.

Wuest, Kenneth S. *Wuest's Word Studies from the Greek New Testament: For the English Reader.* Grand Rapids: Eerdmans, 1997, c1984.

Zodhiates, Spiros. *The Complete Word Study Dictionary: New Testament.* Chattanooga: AMG Publishers, 2000, c1992, c1993.

Zuck, Roy B. *Basic Bible Interpretation: A Prafctical Guide to Discovering Biblical Truth.* Colorado Springs: David C. Cook, 1991.